THE
DRIFT
TO WAR
1922–1939

THE
DRIFT
TO WAR
1922–1939

Richard Lamb

St. Martin's Press
New York

Library of Congress Cataloging-in-Publication Data

Lamb, Richard.
    The drift to war, 1922-1939 / Richard Lamb.
      p.   cm.
    Originally published: London : W.H. Allen, 1989.
    Includes index.
    ISBN 0-312-05858-6
    1. World War, 1939-1945—Causes. 2. Europe—Politics and
government—1918-1945. 3. Great Britain—Foreign
relations—1910-1936. 4. Great Britain—Foreign
relations—1936-1945. I. Title.
D741.L29   1991
909.82′2—dc20   90-28087
                                                      CIP

First published in Great Britain by W. H. Allen & Co. Plc.

First U.S. Edition: May 1991
10 9 8 7 6 5 4 3 2 1

CONTENTS

INTRODUCTION

THE BOOK divides itself into two parts – the first until January 1933 while Germany was ruled by democratic governments; the second when Britain and France faced the Nazi dictatorship. Astonishingly Britain took a hard line with the reasonable German leaders Stresemann, Müller and Brüning, and a soft one with Hitler. Harold Nicolson told the Commons on 26 March 1936 that 'pro-Germanism' was only apparent in England when Germany was not weak, and whereas Britain had not helped Stresemann's and Brüning's struggles to save an insecure liberal Germany, now that Germany was totalitarian and strong we were saying 'Heil Hitler.' His words were abundantly justified.

Lloyd George opposed the policy of making defeated Germany pay large sums in reparations. If he had prevailed, reparations would have been cancelled at the Genoa Conference in 1922, but by a stroke of ill fortune Briand, the French Premier, who was co-operative, was replaced by Poincaré, who had a hatred of Germany. Bonar Law, as Prime Minister, wanted to continue Lloyd George's policy, but by January 1923 he was a sick man and he did not have the strength to coerce Curzon, his Foreign Secretary, and his Cabinet into forbidding the occupation of the Ruhr by the French and Belgians and the forced recovery of reparations.

The occupation of the Ruhr was a deadly blow to liberal German politicians; it not only created the climate in which Communism and Nazism thrived, but it fostered a spirit of revenge in the German people because not only were they humiliated, but they also suffered economic distress and starvation, while the German mark completely lost its value. As a result the savings of all German people became valueless and the middle class was ruined, with accompanying bitterness and destruction of morale.

However, out of the abyss Gustav Stresemann and Hjalmar Schacht, Governor of the Reichsbank, created an economic miracle, and a golden era of international co-operation was inaugurated with Austen Chamberlain as British Foreign Secretary and Aristide Briand and Gustav Stresemann in charge of French and German foreign policy. Thus in 1925 the Treaty of Locarno was signed with Germany treated as an equal, not as a vanquished enemy. The high point of German post-war relations with Britain and France was reached at Thoiry in 1926 when Briand, with Austen Chamberlain's approval, agreed with Stresemann far-sighted plans for German recovery.

When 1929 dawned the prospects of long-lasting peace in Europe were bright. Germany was able to pay the reduced reparations of the Dawes Plan without ruining her economy, although her prosperity had a brittle base. Then Briand produced his plan for a Federal Europe without customs barriers which if put into execution would have produced the same favourable climate for European co-operation as the Common Market in 1957. A strange unfair clause in the Treaty of Versailles forbade customs unions between the defeated powers, although the post-war frontier revisions and reparations clauses made an overwhelming case for a free trade area. Stresemann and Willy Graham, Labour President of the Board of Trade, welcomed Briand's plan, but the British Cabinet and the anti-German elements in France vetoed it, while a later sensible German plan for an Austrian–German customs union was also turned down. Instead Britain aggravated German economic problems by devaluing the pound and putting tariff duties on imports from Germany.

By the beginning of 1932 Germany was in a shocking economic position from which she could only be rescued by acts of generosity by the victorious powers. Although Hoover engineered a twelve-months moratorium on war debts, little generosity was shown by the British although the writing was on the wall with the rising popularity and electoral gains of the Nazis. In the General Election of 1932 the Nazis doubled the vote they obtained in September 1930, with almost 14 million voting for Hitler. The last good democratic Chancellor of Germany, Brüning, was forced to resign in the spring of 1932 because he had to deflate the economy and reduce unemployment pay and social benefits to prevent Germany becoming bankrupt.

Even in the summer of 1932 the Nazis might have been kept out of power if von Papen's Government had been given diplomatic successes at the Disarmament Conference at Geneva and the Reparations Conference at Lausanne. Instead, although the Cabinet had decided to cancel German reparations, at Lausanne Neville Chamberlain sided with the French and bullied the Germans into offering a final reparations settlement, while at Geneva the principle of equality of arms was denied to a democratic Germany. This played into the hands of Hitler, who promised to rearm Germany and not pay a penny in reparations, which was excellent election propaganda. Only when von Papen had been toppled and replaced by a pro-Nazi Chancellor was the principle of equality of arms conceded, and once Hitler was in power Germany paid no more reparations.

The British Embassy in Berlin left the Cabinet in no doubt about the nature of the Nazi regime and made it crystal-clear that in addition to its pogrom against the Jews, and its imprisonment and murder of political opponents, Nazi Germany was rearming as fast as possible with a view to a war of aggression. Despite these warnings the same Ministers, Chamberlain and Simon, who had taken a tough stand against democratic German Governments over rearmament and reparations, together with Baldwin and MacDonald, leant over backwards to appease Hitler. They acquiesced in non-payment of reparations by Nazi Germany, and made concessions to her at the Disarmament Conference. However, when Hitler was told by his generals that no system of German arms-inspection was practical without disclosing the enormity of their breaches of the Versailles Treaty, Germany walked out of the Disarmament Conference.

Germany announced not only the reintroduction of conscription but the existence of an illegal air force. The French were horrified, and wanted to arraign Germany before the League of Nations for breaking the Versailles Treaty. Britain would not support France, and Simon even negotiated the Anglo-German Naval Agreement which drove a coach and horses through the Versailles restrictions on the German navy.

Nor would Britain give France a guarantee of military aid if she was attacked by Germany. Telling the French they would have to stand on their own feet would have been the decent, honest thing to do, but the British wanted to be the senior partner and negotiate a 'general' European settlement which would satisfy Hitler. Britain thought Versailles was outdated, and that it would be unthinkable to send an army to the Continent to fight to enforce it. They desperately tried to legalize German rearmament, hoping Hitler was still ready to pay something for it. What sort of 'general' settlement the Cabinet thought would satisfy Hitler has never been defined.

In 1935 Mussolini was ready to take a tough line against Hitler. When Hitler threatened Austria the Duce invited France and Britain to a Conference at Stresa in Northern Italy. Here the three victorious powers of the First World War met in agreement for the last time, and issued a warning to Hitler not to threaten Austrian independence. But at Stresa the British were lukewarm in their opposition to Hitler compared with France and Italy.

The Foreign Secretary, John Simon (much influenced by his wife), looked on Abyssinia as a sink of iniquity because slavery was rampant there, and on the Emperor as a devil. At Stresa he made the monstrous error of tipping the wink to Mussolini to go ahead with the invasion of Abyssinia.

Britain was in a passionate pacifist mood, and the Covenant of the League of Nations was idealized by many. Enthusiasts for the League were horrified at the prospect of Italy invading the territory of a sovereign member of the League of Nations, ignoring the fact that Abyssinia should never have been admitted to the League and that Britain had opposed her admission. The Peace Ballot in 1935 showed an enormous majority in favour of economic sanctions against any aggressor who breached the Covenant, and the Baldwin Government was forced to change course and take sanctions against Italy after the Abyssinian war started.

Desperately the Government sought a solution which would both satisfy the League and appease Mussolini. A reasonable diplomatic solution known as the Hoare–Laval Plan was produced, but before it could be implemented there was such an outcry from public opinion in Britain that it had to be abandoned, causing Baldwin and his Cabinet acute embarrassment. It is a myth that Eden opposed Hoare–Laval; he approved it in Cabinet and in his Foreign Office minutes beforehand. Hoare was sacked and Eden appointed in his place. Britain and France continued sanctions against Italy and Eden threatened an oil sanction, with the result that Mussolini changed course and went into Hitler's camp, although from 1922 until 1935 he had aligned Italian foreign policy with Britain's.

In 1937 the new Prime Minister, Neville Chamberlain, was horrified by the prospect of Hitler annexing Austria because he knew Eastern Europe would then be defenceless. Eden did not object to the Anschluss, and the Prime Minister and Foreign Secretary in 1937 differed fundamentally. Eden, in spite of the danger to Austria from Germany, refused to try to appease Mussolini – ostensibly because of the part Italy was taking in the Spanish Civil War, but in fact because of deep enmity to the Duce and Italy.

Too late Chamberlain sacked Eden – not because the latter disapproved of Chamberlain's appeasement of Hitler, but because he refused to make overtures to Mussolini to persuade him to prevent the Anschluss. Within weeks of Eden's resignation the Anschluss became a *fait accompli*, and Hitler was menacing Czechoslovakia. Chamberlain believed that now the Czech fortifications had been turned by the German army in Austria the Sudetenland must be ceded to Hitler in an effort to appease him. The French and Russians were prepared to fight to save Czechoslovakia, and the British Cabinet refused to agree to the demands for the immediate cession of the Sudetenland and the Czech fortifications framed in Hitler's ultimatum at Godesberg. Chamberlain hated the idea of fighting in alliance with Russia, and behind his Cabinet's back sent friendly messages to Hitler and Mussolini which resulted in the Munich Conference in September 1938. Here Chamberlain acquiesced in the Hitler demands which his Cabinet had refused to accept.

Hitler was bluffing at Munich because his armies were too weak to fight in the east and west simultaneously, but Chamberlain hoped that appeasing him would turn him into a peaceful animal. Such hopes were misplaced, and when in March Hitler seized Prague and the rump of Czechoslovakia Chamberlain immediately gave Poland a military guarantee which could only be implemented with Russian co-operation. Although negotiations with Stalin began, Chamberlain could not bring himself seriously to contemplate a military alliance with Russia. He looked on Hitler as a buffer against the spread of Communism, so in the summer of 1939 he made secret overtures to Hitler while military talks with the Russians were in progress. Stalin found out, and as a consequence made the fatal deal with Hitler to partition Poland.

Even after Germany had invaded Poland and bombed Warsaw and other Polish cities Chamberlain still wanted to give Hitler Danzig and the Polish Corridor. His Cabinet colleagues and the Commons would not support him, and reluctantly he was forced to declare war, but gave no orders to British forces to help Poland by attacking Germany.

This is in part the story of my own times. I voted in the Oxford Union for the motion that in no circumstances would we fight for King and Country; I was enthusiastic for the Peace Ballot and hostile to the Hoare–Laval Pact which I now consider sound diplomacy. I am a lover of Italy, and was appalled how unpopular Britain became with Italians and at the way British policy drove Mussolini into Hitler's arms. I witnessed how the MacDonald, Baldwin and Chamberlain Governments tried to appease Nazi Germany by condoning her rearmament and acquiescing in the remilitarization of the Rhineland, the Anschluss, the rape of Czechoslovakia and the final humiliation of offering Hitler Danzig and the Polish Corridor, until the Poles forced Britain to go to war. The archives reveal clearly the cowardice and hesitations of most British politicians in the 1930s, apart from Winston Churchill, Leo Amery, Viscount Hailsham, Alfred Duff Cooper (Viscount Norwich), and Austen Chamberlain. It is a sad tale, from which few in high places in Britain emerge with credit.

ACKNOWLEDGEMENTS

I am most grateful to the following for help with this book:

Sir Richard Acland Bt.
Julian Amery
David Astor
Christabel Bielenberg
Charles H. Bogart
Andrea Bosco
The late Roger Bullen
H. James Burgwyn
Axel van der Bussche
The late Sir John Colville
Sir William Deakin
Professor David Dilks
Elizabeth Evans
Lord Gladwyn
The late Sir Hugh Carleton Greene
Lord Hailsham
Archduke Charles Habsburg
Archduke Otto Habsburg
Hans von Herwath
Professor Peter Hoffman

Lord Home of the Hirsel
Deborah Lavin
Judith, Countess of Listowel
Brian MacDermot
The late Sir Ivo and Lady Mallet
T. B. Martin
Patricia Meehan
Professor Karl Müller
Sir Godfrey Nicholson
George Peden
Sir Frank Roberts
Anthony Seldon
Enrico Serra
Lord Sherfield
Sir Maurice Shock
Viscount and Viscountess Simon
Gordon Etherington Smith
Professor Denis Mack Smith
Antonio Varsori
Gervaise Vaz

I am most indebted to the following for reading parts of the manuscript:

Professor Anthony Adamthwaite
Dr Martin Alexander
Denys Blakeway
Professor Brian Bond

Tom Braun
Dr David Carlton
Christopher Seton-Watson

I am deeply grateful to Dr Benediks, Curator of the Chamberlain Archives at Birmingham University; and to the staff of the Public Record Office, Kew; the London Library; the Library of the Royal Institute of International Affairs (Chatham House); the Library of the United Services Institute; the Wiltshire County Library; and the Librarian of the United Oxford and Cambridge Club for their help and unfailing courtesy.

Derek Johns (formerly at Harrap) gave me great encouragement, and I am most grateful to Susanne McDadd and Roy Minton for their care over the editing.

Finally, I give warmest thanks to Joan Moore and John Mark for secretarial assistance, and to my wife for reading parts of the manuscript under the umbrella pines.

Transcripts of the copyright material in the Public Records Office appear by kind permission of the Controller of Her Majesty's Stationery Office.

Richard Lamb

PART ONE
THE WEIMAR REPUBLIC

CHAPTER ONE

VERSAILLES AND THE REPARATIONS CRISIS

'Recent researchers take a different view from that of most contemporary researchers about how far the Treaty of Versailles contributed to the rise of Nazism.' (Kolb, *The Weimar Republic (1988)*, page 169.)

AFTER THE First World War was over the victorious powers (France, Belgium, Britain, USA and Italy) were able to dictate peace terms to the defeated countries (Germany, Austria, Hungary and Bulgaria). The seeds of the Second World War lay in the terms of Treaties of Versailles, St Germain and Trianon signed in 1919 and 1920. The settlement of Europe at the Congress of Vienna lasted in broad outline for over a hundred years. The 1919 settlement was relatively short-lived.

At Vienna in 1814 and 1815 the victorious powers were lenient to France, and even after Napoleon's Hundred Days in 1815 the terms imposed were only slightly more onerous. Similar generosity (for whatever reason) was not shown to Germany, Austria, Hungary and Bulgaria in 1919.

On 3 October 1918 the German Government had asked Wilson, the American President, to negotiate an armistice based on the fourteen points which he had issued on 4 January 1918. The Allied Governments accepted the fourteen points, some of which were capable of a variety of interpretations. Unfortunately, an amplification known as the Cobb–Lippman document, interpreting many of the points emphatically in the Allies' favour, was not shown to the Germans. This verged on deception. Also, there were secret Treaties made by the Allies without the knowledge of the

USA: the Allies made strong reservations about reparations for damage to civilian life and property.

In Paris the principal delegates were Lloyd George, Clemenceau, Wilson and Orlando. Wilson insisted that priority must be given to the Covenant on the League of Nations, for which he had called in his fourteen points, and this was agreed on 28 April 1919. This covenant was an integral part of the peace treaty, and was to come into effect simultaneously in January 1920.

There were serious clashes over the proposed German frontiers. The French demanded that their frontier should be on the Rhine which was strongly opposed by Wilson and Lloyd George. They gave way, but secured the permanent demilitarization of a zone west of the Rhine after an Allied occupation of fifteen years and the promise of a tripartite agreement in which Great Britain and America guaranteed France against a German attack. Alas, Congress refused to ratify the Tripartite Guarantee.

Poland was to be recreated as a state after a lapse of more than a century. Wilson and Clemenceau supported extreme Polish territorial claims at the expense of Germany. Lloyd George opposed them, and even threatened to withdraw British military co-operation until they were reduced. As a result Danzig was made a free city instead of being ceded to Poland, and the Polish Corridor was formed between East Prussia and the bulk of Germany, while the future of industrial Upper Silesia was to be settled by a plebiscite. Poland was fighting the Bolsheviks in the east; Russia was not present at the Peace Conference, and in Paris the delegates had no expectation that in 1920 the Polish army would have a military triumph, driving the Russians back to the Niemen and obtaining in 1921 at the Treaty of Riga an unexpectedly large tract of former Tsarist territory. Danzig and the enlarged Polish eastern frontier were to be for Poland accessions which in the long run were to threaten her existence.

By the Treaties of Saint-Germain (1919) and Trianon (1920) the Austro-Hungarian Empire of the Habsburgs was dismantled, with Austria losing her connections with Hungary, Bohemia and Moravia, Austrian Poland (Galicia), the Serbo-Croat states. Instead of being the heart of an empire she became a small state of 6½ million people with over 2 million in Vienna and the rest in the Alpine provinces, and almost exclusively German-speaking. Her economic position was appalling, and her only salvation seemed to lie either in union with Germany or in a confederation of the Danubian states. Even a Customs Union with Germany was prohibited, while Hungary lost 58 per cent of her former population, mainly to Czechoslovakia and Romania.

In June 1918 the Czech deputies in the Austrian Parliament had formed themselves into a national committee and, rejecting the Emperor Karl's

Europe after Versailles

offer of autonomy within a federal Habsburg state, declared Czechoslovakia independent. Under the Treaties a new state was created in 1919, and 3¼ million Germans in the Sudetenland, former Habsburg subjects, were incorporated in it. Out of the total population of 15 million only two-thirds were Czech by speech, while in addition to the Germans there were ½ million Ukrainians, and almost ¾ million Magyars. It was an artificial state, always coveted by Germany.

Few major frontier adjustments were made at Germany's expense in the Treaty of Versailles, but she lost around 13 per cent of her territory and 80 per cent of her iron-production in Lorraine. She was left with full sovereignty, but she had to acknowledge her war guilt, give up her colonies, disarm and pay reparations; while some parts of her territory to the west of the Rhine (and a few bridgeheads to the east) were to be occupied for five years, yet others for ten, and others still for fifteen.

The Treaty of Versailles imposed intolerable reparations on Germany because she was forced to accept responsibility for all the loss and damage caused 'to the Allied and associated Governments and their nationals by German aggression'. In Paris Lloyd George in particular recognized that the amount Germany could pay must be determined by German resources, and in their deliberations the Peace Conference found it impossible to fix an arbitrary sum. Instead it was referred to the Reparations Commission. Germany was forced to make a first payment of 20,000 million gold marks (£1 billion), and after that the Reparations Commission demanded reparations on a scale which Germany could not possibly pay without bankrupting herself. Another pernicious clause of the Versailles Treaty forbade Customs Unions among the defeated powers, although it should have been crystal clear that European Free Trade was the key to economic recovery. Keynes, in his *The Economic Consequences of the Peace*, proved that the peacemakers knew that the reparation clauses and the inhibitions on free trade would prevent Germany (and Europe) achieving prosperity.

If Germany could not achieve commercial prosperity within a few years it was obvious that the Treaty could only be enforced by the threat of military measures. As it was, the savage reparations ground Germany to her knees economically, and reparations were a key factor in initiating Europe's drift towards the Second World War.

In February 1921 the Reparations Commission presented Germany with a bill for £1⅓ billion. This figure was beyond her capacity to pay, and although it was nearly halved in May, she fell into arrears. Inflation, economic distress and hunger were accelerating alarmingly, and so she applied formally for a moratorium – as she was entitled to do under the Treaty – on the grounds that she could not afford to pay. Unfortunately, the Reparations Commission was now without an American delegate. When the

United States refused to ratify the treaty they withdrew their delegate from the Reparations Commission – a disaster, because only Britain and America were dispassionate about the issue. The French and Belgian delegates were controlled by their Governments which, backed by public opinion, were determined to extract the maximum sums from Germany, while the British and American delegates behaved like impartial bankers.

Unlike the French, Lloyd George recognized that if Germany in her impoverished condition transferred large sums across her frontiers it would be disastrous not only for herself but for the rest of Europe. It would create trade imbalances which must threaten the mark. Accordingly, when the Reparations Commission failed to come to an agreement in December 1921 about a moratorium he decided to call a giant international conference in 1922 to consider not only reparations but the rehabilitation of the whole European economy. The Russians as well as the Germans were invited.

A preliminary conference was held at Cannes in January 1922, attended by the French Prime Minister, Briand. He was genial, tolerant, broad-minded, and in favour of meeting Germany's request if he could swing French public opinion behind him. He got on very well with the Welsh Lloyd George. Rathenau, a fine German statesman, also attended and discussed reparations with Lloyd George and Briand. All went well at first, and it seemed likely that an agreement would be reached to limit total reparations to £7½ billion and to grant Germany a moratorium.

Lloyd George held out hopes to Briand that despite the American defection, Britain might guarantee the defence of French soil against German aggression 'on the distinct condition that France would cooperate with Britain in the reconstruction of Central Europe and Russia'. Briand responded warmly and agreed to a full European Economic Conference beginning in Genoa on 1 March, with the participation of Russia, Germany, Japan, Belgium, Italy and the smaller European powers.[1]

Briand's acceptance in principle of Lloyd George's ideas aroused criticism in France that he was subservient to the British, and this was intensified when photographs were published of Lloyd George giving the French Premier a golf lesson. Briand's position at home became shaky at a crucial moment in Europe's affairs.[2]

When Rathenau reached Cannes there was optimism that an agreement was in sight; he was explaining why Germany had been unable to comply with the terms of payment, when news arrived from Paris that Briand's Government had fallen unexpectedly. He was succeeded as Prime Minister by Poincaré.

Poincaré was violently anti-German. A Lorrainer, he had twice seen his home village ravaged by German troops, and after the 1870 war a large part of his beloved province grabbed by Germany. He was cold, reserved, rigid and without any sense of humour, and in conference was dour and morose – more Flemish than French. The appointment of the Poincaré Government in Lloyd George's words 'made it quite impossible for any more business to be done at Cannes with regard to reparations', although the British Prime Minister viewed the plan for the Genoa Conference as 'a completed matter'. However, before Poincaré had time to give contrary orders to the French delegate the Reparations Commission granted a temporary moratorium to Germany which greatly improved the climate.[3]

Lloyd George's ambitious plan was that the Genoa Conference should result in Russia and Germany being no longer the outcast nations of Europe. Possibly if Briand had remained Prime Minister of France, this might have happened, but with the Poincaré Government installed, Lloyd George's far-sighted and statesmanlike design was blocked.

Poincaré agreed that France would take part in the Genoa Conference, but insisted that it should be postponed until 10 April. He met Lloyd George at Boulogne on 25 February and was adamant that the reparations issue must not be discussed at Genoa. Lloyd George argued hard that it was 'impossible' to discuss the economic situation of Europe without referring to the subject, but Poincaré replied brusquely that unless there were 'absolute guarantees' that reparations would not be raised the French would not go to Genoa. Rather than see the Genoa Conference aborted, Lloyd George reluctantly agreed, although he knew full well that without help for Germany on reparations the economic rehabilitation of Europe would be impossible. His verdict was: 'the gathering was doomed to partial impotency.'[4]

The Russians accepted the invitation to Genoa with alacrity. They were glad to have a chance of renewing diplomatic contacts with the West, but they had no intention of honouring the Tsarist external debts, or of meeting the claims of foreign property-owners. On 15 and 21 April they appeared momentarily willing to make concessions, but by 11 May it was clear there was no chance of a compromise.[5]

Neither the Americans nor Poincaré himself would come to Genoa. From Paris the French Prime Minister kept up a long-range bombardment of his Foreign Minister, Barthou, with telegrams designed to thwart any efforts at European appeasement. Even while the conference was sitting he made a speech at Bar-le-Duc threatening that if Germany failed to meet her reparation instalment (due at the end of May) France would invade the Ruhr regardless of whether her allies co-operated. Lord Hardinge, British Ambassador in Paris, reported that Poincaré's speech was received by the entire Paris Press (except the Socialists) with 'most rapturous applause' and that Poincaré was biased by personal animosity to Lloyd George.

The only concrete result of Genoa was the Treaty of Rapallo (renouncing war reparations) between Germany and Russia, whose groundwork had previously been laid in Berlin. This was badly received by the Allies, but as the purpose of the conference was to promote European friendship and co-operation no real objection could be raised. The Treaty of Rapallo had sinister undertones. The Germans exploited it to obtain Soviet help in building up a new army in defiance of Versailles; Germans were trained in flying and the use of tanks in Russia, while German technical military advice was made available to Russia. The military and commercial contacts created between the Soviet Union and Germany continued into the days of Hitler.[6]

Genoa accomplished nothing. It accentuated Franco-British differences, and in face of Poincaré's attitude no other outcome was possible. Curzon, the Foreign Secretary, was on bad terms with Lloyd George, being so anti-Russian that he opposed not only *de jure* recognition of them but even their presence at Genoa. The Foreign Office looked on Genoa as 'ill conceived and ill conducted', believing that instead we should have continued the negotiations for financial assistance to Russia which were in progress in November 1921 when Lloyd George abruptly took matters out of Curzon's hands. Curzon refused to come to Genoa on spurious grounds of ill health. In a Cabinet memorandum circulated after Lloyd George had fallen from power he wrote:

> . . . better results would have been obtained . . . if negotiations had been left in the hands of the Foreign Office. Deprived of the prestige which the invitation to Genoa accorded, and of the hopes of further undeserved success uncourted and isolated in Moscow, the Russian Government might have been induced gradually to commit itself to a further step on the road to a saner policy . . . The situation was singularly ill adapted for the Prime Minister's special gifts.[7]

Other members of Lloyd George's coalition Government, especially Churchill, shared Curzon's views about the inadvisability of negotiating at Genoa with Russia; this division in the Cabinet became well known, and weakened the Prime Minister's position. Genoa was a lost opportunity for a new European accord with benefits for all countries including Russia. The Genoa Conference achieved nothing, but it was in principle a fine constructive effort to revise the peace treaties and produce a new European order. Its failure was no fault of Lloyd George; it was due to the unfortunate coincidence of the fall of Briand and his replacement by the implacable Poincaré.

After the Paris negotiations in 1919 the USA had agreed that interest and 'amortization' of the Allied debts to her incurred during and just after the war should remain in abeyance for three years after 1919; Britain also abstained from asking for interest (or amortization) on the debts due from her Allies. Lloyd George had suggested to Wilson in 1919 that all war debts should be wiped out; a 1919 Treasury memorandum by Sir Otto Niemeyer argued that 'debt repayments lay like a dead weight upon the credit of Continental Europe and made reconstruction even slower and more painful than it needed to be', and concluded that 'the statesmanlike thing for the United Kingdom and the United States of America would be to make a *beau geste* by offering to wipe out the whole of such indebtedness by the stroke of a pen – the problem being the United States Treasury who would have none of it'. Niemeyer's attitude appealed strongly to Lloyd George, who from then on argued continuously and cogently that war debts and indeed the bulk of reparations should be wiped out completely.[8]

The US Government rejected Lloyd George's arguments, and in 1922 passed the Refunding Act and set up the Debt Commission. Soon a request for payment was sent to Britain, and Lloyd George's Government decided to begin making payments while the Chancellor of the Exchequer, Horne, was detailed to go to Washington to negotiate a settlement. However, before Horne could go the government fell, and Baldwin replaced Horne as Chancellor of the Exchequer.

Meanwhile in August the Lloyd George government produced the famous Balfour Note (with Balfour deputizing for Curzon), expressing its wish for all war debts to be cancelled, offering to forgo Britain's share of reparations and stating that whatever the result of the negotiations Britain would in no circumstances ask for more by way of interest and payments from its debtors than it needed to pay to the USA.*

Lloyd George himself drafted the Balfour Note. Its reception was strangely cold; Lloyd George's broad-minded view aroused no positive response from the Allies. In a letter to Lloyd George on 1 September 1922 Poincaré maintained that there was no connection between reparations and inter-Allied war debts, and that even if the USA insisted on claiming her war debts there could be no question of a settlement until reparations had been paid in full. It was an ungracious reply to the generous offer by Britain to cancel all debts due to her from France.

Lloyd George's hopes that the Balfour Note would swing America round to cancellation or part-remission of the European debts due to her were misplaced. Baldwin commented cynically that the note meant 'We will pay if we must, but you will be cads if you ask us to do so.' In America its reception was icy.[9]

---

*(At the Spa Conference in 1920 the percentage of reparations was fixed as France 52 per cent; Britain 22 per cent; Italy 10 per cent; Belgium 8 per cent; other participants 8 per cent.)

Now the value of the mark began to fall drastically. It stood at 1,200 to the pound at the beginning of June 1922, but by mid-July it had fallen to 2,400. With her currency in disarray, there was no chance of Germany raising a foreign loan to meet her reparation obligations. In August 1922 Poincaré came to England for the London Conference of the Allies. The Frenchman's wild proposals shocked Lloyd George: Poincaré urged that the Allies should occupy the Ruhr and take over the German customs, state coal-mines and forests.

Lloyd George replied that nothing would be forthcoming except 'paper marks' which no one would exchange, and which would cause a further shattering fall in the value of the mark the moment they were placed on the market. The British Prime Minister also argued that the Allies could only manage the forests and mines with the goodwill of German workmen; the employment of forced labour was unthinkable, and a profitable undertaking could quickly become bankrupt,[10] while it would do nothing to solve the whole problem of reparations.

Lloyd George's view was shared by the more responsible French statesmen. Tardieu considered that in order to control public utilities an 'enormous personnel would be necessary', and would lead inevitably to 'total and prolonged occupation' of German territory with military police everywhere, to which none of the Allies would consent, and which would be out of the question because the necessary forces were not available. 'No-one would have risked such an adventure without the prospect of real advantage. But what advantage would there have been?'

The London Conference broke up with Poincaré deaf to the arguments that occupation would destroy Germany economically and result in any marks recovered being valueless. The Italian Schanzer and the Belgian Prime Minister Theunis agreed with Lloyd George, and Poincaré was warned that he might destroy not only the Entente but the Treaty of Versailles.*[11]

In October 1922 the Lloyd George coalition fell and Bonar Law became Prime Minister. He continued with Lloyd George's sensible policy over German reparations, but did not take anything like so firm a line with Poincaré over preventing a French invasion of the Ruhr. Bonar Law consulted with Keynes about Germany's ability to pay reparations, and said, 'I may have to choose between two evils – between a breach with France which would mean chaos in Europe, or concessions to France which would also involve great misfortunes.' On 9 December Poincaré came again to London for consultations, but without result.[12]

---

*Lloyd George's view was that Poincaré really had the design of wrecking German unity and encouraging the creation of separatist states in Germany.

With little hope of French agreement, the British Cabinet concocted a plan for Bonar Law to take to Paris at the end of December under which Germany would pay no reparations for four years; thereafter £100 million per annum for four years; then £125 million for two years; and after ten years an amount to be fixed by an impartial tribunal, but not less than £125 million. This was a reasonable solution. On 29 December the Cabinet approved the Prime Minister's request that if the French threatened to take strong action against Germany and refused to discuss any reasonable proposals, he should be authorized to state that this would 'raise large questions such as the future participation of the British Government in the Conference of Ambassadors and in the Reparations Commission and on the retention of a British garrison on the Rhine. In those circumstances Bonar Law would insist on consulting the Cabinet.'[13]

Armed with this support from his colleagues, Bonar Law arrived on 1 January 1923 in Paris where he had summoned Curzon from Lausanne for a one-night conference. Curzon was being supported by the French at Lausanne in long, complicated negotiations over a settlement in the Middle East and avoidance of a war with Turkey, and the Foreign Secretary told the Prime Minister that in return for their co-operation at Lausanne the French expected cooperation in Paris over demands on Germany for reparations. This was not what Bonar Law wanted to hear. Curzon felt that the Prime Minister in Paris was excessively gloomy – telling Harold Nicolson when he got back to Lausanne, 'The feet of the Prime Minister were glacial, positively glacial.' Bonar Law's biographer writes that the Prime Minister was beginning to 'hold doubts about Curzon's character', and Curzon's relations with Bonar Law were little better than they had been with Lloyd George.* It is not surprising the Prime Minister was gloomy when his Foreign Secretary was un-cooperative in face of the worst crisis with France since the end of the war.[14]

The Bonar Law plan released in Paris on 2 January was badly received by Poincaré and the French press. *Le Temps* wrote, 'The ties which existed during the war between the two countries have disappeared.' However, *The Times* leader commented, 'The policy outlined by the Prime Minister was to treat our Continental debtors with a generosity unparalleled in history', and the gift would be chiefly to France as the amount Germany could pay in reparations could only be guessed by the Committee on Reparations. Now

---

*On 6 January Curzon wrote to the Prime Minister 'I wonder whether it was altogether wise to publish our scheme in advance and expose it to the ruthless fangs of the Paris press'; to which Bonar Law replied correctly that Curzon had not understood the situation because 'our' scheme was handed to the Conference simultaneously with the French scheme and both were published together.

there was the same gap between Bonar Law and Poincaré as there had been between Lloyd George and the French leader, and Bonar Law remarked 'it was a ditch no bridge could span'. The British plan was summarily rejected by the French, with Poincaré refusing to accept it even as a basis of discussion.

Bonar Law said publicly in Paris that Poincaré aimed 'to get a little more now by any means and destroy the chances of something much greater later'. Poincaré now insisted that France must take unilateral action as Germany was in default, and must occupy the Ruhr. The French rejection of the British plan was followed by another catastrophic fall in the value of the mark. Poincaré told the French Chamber, 'The British plan not only reduced the sum due to France, but replaced the Reparations Commission by a Committee in which Germany had a place. I could not bring myself to accept a group of international bankers as the arbiter of my country's destiny.'

During the talks Poincaré argued that German default existed, and that therefore France must take action. Bonar Law contradicted him, saying 'Britain needed reparations as much as anyone else; [he] would like to get every penny Germany could pay,' but large sums could not be paid by Germany without a moratorium. Stabilization of the mark was essential because of German inflation, and they must re-establish German credit. Poincaré replied that Bonar Law was redrawing the Treaty of Versailles. A German offer was similarly rejected out of hand by the French, although D'Abernon, the British Ambassador, had reported from Berlin that the Germans would 'go to the utmost limit of concessions to prevent France occupying the Ruhr'.[15]

On 9 January Poincaré acted and French troop-trains poured over the German frontier to occupy the Ruhr. Belgian troops followed. Crewe (the Ambassador in Paris) reported, 'The tone of Paris is hysterical in its Anglophobia', and Cadogan minuted: 'The French Press at the moment are in such a hysterical state that it would be kinder to pay no attention to what they say or write.' However, the right-wing press in Britain demonstrated the divisions in Conservative circles, with the *Daily Mail* writing 'Less than six weeks after the polls Bonar Law has imperilled the Entente, played into the hands of Germans and created general consternation among the Allies. Why did he publish a plan which they were well aware would be rejected by the French? We disapprove of four years' grace.' But the *Manchester Guardian* wrote, 'The French plan would lose the German Treasury so much money that it could only be made good by printing Marks.' In fact the rejection of the British plan was followed by a catastrophic fall in the value of the mark, so that it stood at 41,000 to the pound. Bonar Law rejected the option of removing the British garrisons from the Rhineland. Although

13

Lloyd George had restrained Poincaré in August, Bonar Law was weaker and feared he could not count on the support of his colleagues.

On 11 January the Cabinet agreed that there should be no breach with the French because of the illegal occupation of the Ruhr. This was condoning the folly of France's aggression. Curzon's influence was largely responsible for this weakness. The Foreign Secretary was preoccupied with the need to soothe the French so that they would continue to support him in his tortuous negotiations over Turkey in Lausanne. When the Americans asked through their London Embassy whether Britain would withdraw her troops from the Rhine in consequence of the French action, Curzon minuted, 'We would endeavour to avoid all friction with France consequent upon her independent action . . . French delegates were acting as harmoniously as ever in Lausanne.' The USA withdrew all her troops from the Rhineland on 10 January as a gesture of severe disapproval. However, Mussolini refused a French request to send Italian troops to the Ruhr.[16]

Almost immediately another squall blew up over war debts and reparations which almost brought the Bonar Law government down. This was the settlement of the American debt. Bonar Law's policy was the same as Lloyd George's, and he had enthusiastically endorsed the Balfour Note, believing that the only sensible solution was either complete cancellation or payment all round. He was horrified at the prospect of Britain being faced with a huge burden of debt to the USA: this would force her to extract massive reparations from Germany so that she could recover her payments to the USA from the other Allies.

On 27 December 1922 Stanley Baldwin, Chancellor of the Exchequer, sailed for New York accompanied by Montagu Norman, head of the Bank of England, on the mission which Horne would have undertaken in October if Lloyd George had stayed in power. Harvey, the US Ambassador in London, had told Bonar Law that Congress might accept reduction of the total debt. This was over-optimistic. Norman was a high priest of banking with little diplomatic or political talent. Baldwin was inexperienced. Lloyd George commented unkindly 'No worse team could have been found,' and Norman was a dangerous counsellor for Baldwin.[17]

While Baldwin was on the high seas, the breakdown of the Paris negotiations on reparations and the occupation of the Ruhr made it even more imperative that Britain did not agree to over-stringent terms. Baldwin failed to realize this, but Bonar Law was acutely conscious, telegraphing to Baldwin:

> I am most unwilling to differ from you, but since you left the reasons against making a settlement at a higher rate have been strengthened. The action of the French may

destroy hopes of reparations and with it any chance of our being paid debts owed to us. It may also damage the chance of recovery of trade as to make action here worse and there is always the chance that with this big annual payment of dollars, a real danger that the exchange may go seriously against us and greatly add to the annual burden.

Horne was in New York, and had advised Baldwin that if he did not accept the terms offered only worse ones would follow. The Prime Minister telegraphed to Horne:

Since Baldwin left, what is happening in the Ruhr has made the prospect of obtaining anything from Germany, and consequently from our debtors, much smaller and in my opinion at a time when the future is so dark and uncertain the American Government should not ask us to sign bonds on such terms and my feeling at present is that no British Government would be justified in doing it.

Britain owed America around £900 million. Bonar Law was unwilling to concede more than 2½ per cent interest, giving an annual payment of around £25 million. Contrary to his instructions, Baldwin agreed annual payments of £34 million over ten years, and thereafter £40 million. On Horne's advice Baldwin decided that this was the best offer which could be obtained, and he accepted it without consulting the Cabinet. Bonar Law's view was that in the long run the onerous Baldwin settlement must have a long-term damaging effect on Anglo-American relations, and he much preferred no settlement at all, although this carried the risk of temporary estrangement. Both Keynes and MacKenna (the former Chancellor of the Exchequer) advised the Prime Minister to repudiate the Baldwin settlement.[18]

At the Cabinet meeting on 15 January the seven Ministers present agreed with the Prime Minister that they should not accept the *fait accompli*, and Bonar Law telegraphed to Baldwin: 'You must say to the American Government you are not empowered to accept these terms which are far above anything contemplated when you left, and you must return to discuss the matter in person with the British Government.' The telegram was agreed by all the members of the Cabinet.

Baldwin had to comply with these peremptory instructions, and he told the Americans it was an 'adjournment', not a 'breakdown' of negotiations; he landed at Southampton on 27 January, and immediately made the crisis worse by attacking the USA's mid-West states, saying that their senators did not understand problems of international finance. These remarks, distorted in transmission, caused a furore in America. The Foreign Office comment was that it would be a great relief if 'we' could say Mr Baldwin had been misreported at Southampton but they could not; he had made a gigantic gaffe.[19]

On 30 January the Cabinet with Stanley Baldwin present reconsidered its decision about the Baldwin settlement. Bonar Law said he would not agree to interest at a higher rate than 3½ per cent, and that if the settlement was approved his name would be cursed in two or three years' time. Bonar Law quickly found he was in a minority on this issue, and so if the Cabinet decided to accept 'it would have to be without him'. He added that he felt so strongly because it was tying us hand and foot when we did not know if we could get anything out of Europe to offset it. The Cabinet was adjourned without a decision. The next morning all the Ministers met in the House of Lords without the Prime Minister and considered the grave situation for the Conservative Party if their leader resigned. The Conservatives had been out of office for seventeen years. They had lost their image of being the party of government, and a general election could have been disastrous. This point was relayed to the Prime Minister, and in the afternoon Bonar Law agreed to accept the settlement. If Bonar Law had stuck to his resignation threat the other Ministers would almost certainly have climbed down, so fearful were they of the political consequences of his resignation.[20]

Instead of threatening to remove British occupying forces from the Rhine in retaliation as envisaged by Lloyd George and Bonar Law the British Government was content merely to disclaim all responsibility for measures taken by the French and Belgians in the Ruhr on the grounds of illegality. In spite of gross contraventions of the Treaty by the French, the British Government made few protests. France and Belgium made working arrangements to run the German railways, collect customs and secure deliveries of coal and timber, while the British Government showed little sympathy with German complaints, and refused to act as advisers to the German Government.

One vicious feature of the French occupation of the Ruhr was their encouragement of a movement for a separatist state in the Rhineland. This was strongly condemned by the British but resulted in much disorder. Undoubtedly Poincaré, in common with many other Frenchmen would have welcomed a separatist Rhineland state on their frontier.

The Germans retaliated by passive resistance, and refused all co-operation with the occupying powers. As a result it cost the French and Belgians disproportionate sums to collect either cash or deliveries in kind. The French franc fell sharply. The invasion of the Ruhr naturally brought to an end for the time being any German reparations to France. Instead Germany became virtually bankrupt, with ruinous inflation. The occupation of the Ruhr amounted to a state of war, with the German Government under Cuno encouraging strikes, passive resistance, sabotage and guerrilla warfare, while the French indulged in arrests, deportations and an economic blockade.

The mark fell to 160,000 to the dollar by 1 July 1923; by 1 August to 1 million; by 1 November to 133,000 million. This produced not only widespread bankruptcies but food shortages and unprecedented unemployment. The morale of the middle classes and the working classes alike was shattered as their savings were wiped out at a stroke, while a few industrialists and property-owners prospered. The inflation destroyed German morale and produced the climate in which revolutionary organizations flourished.

In spite of the violence of the crisis and the rapidity of the fall of the mark (its value against gold fell to one millionth of a millionth of its face value), in spite of the utter failure of Germany to try to stabilize the currency, neither Baldwin nor Curzon felt a strong lead by Britain was necessary.[21]

The crisis reached its peak in August 1923 when the Cuno Government fell and Stresemann became Chancellor. On 26 September the new Chancellor Stresemann called off the official campaign of passive resistance and lifted the ban on reparation deliveries to France and Belgium. Negotiations began for an agreed settlement. Although Stresemann only stayed as Chancellor until November, he remained Foreign Minister, and retained the post until his death in 1929. He was able to inaugurate a better relationship between Germany and France.

According to his friend and admirer D'Abernon (British Ambassador in Berlin), Stresemann might have been Winston Churchill's brother –

> the same silhouette, almost identical colouring; and in temperament and mental characteristics a close analogy. Both brilliant, daring and bold. In both more than a dash of recklessness – and a pronounced predilection for the unorthodox.[22]

Other British observers have recorded that Stresemann was too Prussian. Perhaps he was a German Winston. Originally he had been a strong monarchist and nationalist, but his essential policy in his six years in office as Foreign Minister was to allay the hostility between Germany and France and bring about European pacification. Over the Rhineland he consistently argued that Germany was ready to stop using the area as a base for military preparations provided France did the same. He was never reconciled to Germany's loss of territory in the east to Poland, but waived any idea of using force to recover it.

Thanks to American participation in the Reparations Advisory Committee, a plan was agreed for two committees of experts to report – one to inquire into how to stabilize the German currency and balance her budget, and the other to investigate German balances abroad. In December the United States Government formally agreed to participate in the work of the two committees, and General Charles Dawes became chairman of the first committee.[23]

A sinister development was the attempted Hitler – Ludendorff coup in Munich on 8 and 9 November 1923. The British Consul General in Munich (Clive) reported that at a mass political meeting the political agitator Hitler had suddenly produced a revolver and threatened to shoot von Kahr, the right-wing head of the Bavarian government, unless he agreed to head a new Bavarian government which was to supersede Ebert's existing government in Berlin, after a march on the city. Instead of the Ebert government Germany was to be ruled by Hitler with General Ludendorff in charge of the army. The next day the German army restored order and Hitler and Ludendorff were arrested. But Hitler had made it clear that if he ruled he would confiscate the fortunes of the Jews. Clive reported: 'If Hitler had stayed in complete power for even one day I do not believe there would have been a French officer alive in Munich.' By that time the distress and starvation in German towns was such that a Hitler revolution might well have succeeded.

The Foreign Office reaction to the Hitler coup was muted. Cadogan minuted: 'Poincaré in his mad policy of encouraging dismemberment of Germany is playing with fire.' Curzon instructed Crewe to tell Poincaré that the failure of the Munich coup obviated any need to discuss it, and Poincaré said disingenuously that he had 'never favoured a separate Rhineland State although French opinion was vocal for it', while D'Abernon reported from Berlin, 'Food supplies in towns and industrial districts are very short and they are in danger of famine; the conditions and prospects of the middle class are appalling.'

The British and French Governments ignored the lesson that should have been learnt – which was that the German Government had permitted the Hitlerites to parade as a normal political party when their open and avowed aim was the overthrow of the state by revolution. In his show trial Hitler was allowed to make political speeches by the judge, and made himself very popular by attacking the Republic and declaring that there was 'no such thing as high treason against the traitors of 1918'. This speech became front-page news all over Germany, and he made a telling bid for the co-operation of the army in a future bid for power.[24] In the outcome he received a five-year prison sentence, but served only a scarcely rigorous year.

Bonar Law – who had already been feeling the effects of an ultimately fatal illness in January – became so ill that he was forced to resign on 20 May 1923, to be succeeded as Prime Minister by Baldwin. Baldwin had less sympathy than Bonar Law or even Curzon with Germany's plight. While

Curzon was ill Poincaré and Baldwin met in Paris on 20 September 1923, and afterwards issued a communiqué to the effect that there was no divergence of views. The false interpretation was put on their words that Britain was condoning all aspects of French policy in the Ruhr. When Curzon read it on his sick-bed he is said to have considered it a repudiation of his French policy, in which he had expressed his strong disapproval of French occupation of the Ruhr.[25]

In January 1924 Ramsay MacDonald became the first Labour Prime Minister, and was his own Foreign Secretary. A conscientious objector in the war, he believed earnestly that an equitable solution of the reparations problem was the key to a prosperous Europe. Far more than Baldwin and Curzon, he held the Keynes theory – which was endorsed by Lloyd George and Bonar Law – that the victors could not prosper while the vanquished starved.

According to D'Abernon, it was

> remarkable to note the change in the tone of Poincaré since the Labour Government has come into office in England. Is this because Paris considers that Labour will be less amenable than its predecessors? I have always held the view that Poincaré's obstinacy and apparent strength was based on nothing so much as the weakness and hesitation of English policy.

D'Abernon went on that the false interpretation put on the Baldwin – Poincaré communiqué of 20 September in Paris had resulted in Britain losing influence 'in determining Anglo-French policy' and becoming 'subordinate to our ally'.[26]

MacDonald quickly re-established the lead over France which Lloyd George had previously held in German relations and in April the Dawes Committee produced a new schedule of reparation payments conditional upon the abandonment of the Belgian-French occupation of the Ruhr. The new assessment under the Dawes Plan was 2½ billion gold marks, which was 500 million less than the Reparations Commission claim of 1921. The MacDonald Government welcomed the proposal, but Poincaré turned it down; fortunately, the Poincaré Government fell in July and Herriot became French Prime Minister. The scholarly Herriot had been mayor of Lyons; he was less unyielding with regard to Germany. MacDonald invited him to Chequers, and after tense discussion he agreed that the Dawes Plan could be the basis of discussion at an Allied Conference to be held in London. There in July, despite difficulties from Philip Snowden, his own Chancellor of the Exchequer, MacDonald succeeded in obtaining agreement on the Dawes figure for reparations and the evacuation of the Rhineland. This was the high point of MacDonald's career.

It was the end of the tragic episode of the French occupation of the Ruhr whose greatest evil consequence was galloping inflation which destroyed the base of the German middle classes, but an almost equal loss was the renewed enmity between France and Germany and the alienation of world sympathy from the former.

In October the MacDonald Government fell and Baldwin became Prime Minister. He sensibly chose Austen Chamberlain as Foreign Secretary instead of Curzon, allegedly because he felt that Curzon had made an enemy of Mussolini and too many others in Europe.

Austen knew the Continent well and was determined to build on the foundations laid by MacDonald. He was helped by the personalities of Briand and Stresemann who became close personal friends, and Chamberlain shared in their friendship. Thanks to Chamberlain, Stresemann and Briand, the period of storm and stress for Germany came to an end with the withdrawal of the French from the Ruhr in 1925. Then Hjalmar Schacht, President of the Reichsbank, with great astuteness managed to stabilize the mark and end inflation at the same time, although nothing could remedy the harm done by the ruin of the middle classes.

In this happier climate in 1925 Stresemann put forward proposals to the British and French for a Rhineland Treaty which would result in the removal of British and French troops from the region, and after a thorough preparation of the ground facilitated by the warm relations between Briand and Chamberlain (in marked contrast with the antipathy between Curzon and Poincaré two years before) a Conference was held at Locarno from 5–16 October 1925. Stresemann was ready to abandon German claims to Alsace-Lorraine, and even to accept the demilitarized zone. Germany was treated as an equal, not as a defeated power, in the Locarno negotiations, and the result was the initialling of the Locarno Pact, which was signed as a Treaty six weeks later. The agreement guaranteed Germany's western frontiers in return for a pledge to keep the Rhineland demilitarized, and Germany was to become a member of the League of Nations.

Locarno was a Treaty of Mutual Guarantee with the obligations of France to Germany the same as the obligations of Germany to France; the same was true of Belgium and Germany, while the obligations of the guaranteeing powers, Italy and Great Britain, were the same to Germany as to France and Belgium. The great weakness of Locarno was that it left unguaranteed the frontiers of Poland, Czechoslovakia and Austria against Germany, and herein lay the seeds of the Second World War. Still, the Locarno Pact was the greatest achievement of British diplomacy between the two wars and prospects of a prolonged period of peace were better then than they were to be later.

It was generally believed that Germany had turned over a new leaf, although Hitler and the Nationalist Party made clear their detestation of the League, claiming it stood for maintaining for ever the German frontiers laid down by Versailles.

Locarno ended the system of one-sided alliances because Great Britain and Italy in the event of any future Franco-German conflict undertook to throw all their weight, both moral and material, on whichever side was deemed to be the innocent one. Locarno was also designed to reassure France and Belgium against the danger of an attack from Germany. Similarly, it reassured a disarmed Germany against any abuse of strength by a fully armed France and her many allies. In effect it restored the balance of power, and was acclaimed as doing so throughout Europe at the time although its reception in Germany was surprisingly cold.

The high point of Franco-German post-war co-operation and friendship was reached at Thoiry in the French Jura near Geneva on 17 September 1926. Briand (now Foreign Secretary) and Stresemann met in secrecy at a small hotel and, cheered by good food and wine, arrived at far-reaching agreements. Austen Chamberlain had given Briand *carte blanche* to find the best possible solution of the outstanding problems.

Briand and Stresemann agreed that Germany's war guilt should be wiped out; Germany should have colonial mandates; the Saar should be returned to Germany without a plebiscite; and the Rhineland evacuated within a year. In return France would receive annuities in advance under the Dawes Plan, Germany would repurchase the Saar mines for around 300 million gold marks, and buy back the industrial districts of Eupen and Malmédy from Belgium. At that time Belgium and France were in economic difficulties with their currencies under pressure, and it looked as if Germany with her basically stronger economy could afford large payments which would strengthen the Belgian and French economies.

Poincaré, who had succeeded Briand as French Premier on 23 July, had agreed in principle with Briand that it was in France's interest to have advance reparation payments to bolster the franc in return for the evacuation of the Rhineland.

At a press conference in Geneva after the meeting Stresemann in ebullient form recited the Thoiry achievements. This received worldwide publicity, and was held to herald a new dawn for Europe. Stresemann told the journalists that the natural consequences of the Locarno Pact would be that Germany would receive a colonial mandate, and that the occupation of the Rhineland would be terminated (*balayé*).

A French Government-inspired article in *Le Temps* stated that if Germany wished the Rhineland to be evacuated 'she would have to make heavy financial sacrifices'. The Foreign Office described French press reaction as 'one of not hostile reserve', and that while the German press had received it 'nowhere rhapsodically, the comment in general is entirely favourable save on the extreme right and left wings'.[27]

Stresemann was criticized in France and Britain for overstating the concessions to Germany, and he made an indiscreet speech the day after Thoiry to German residents in Geneva. According to D'Abernon, 'in a bout of convivial cordiality Briand and Stresemann promised one another a good deal which it may be difficult to perform', and reported to Chamberlain that Stresemann had returned to Berlin in exuberant spirits; D'Abernon stressed the danger of

> an undue extension of these lovers' meetings if the subject of finance is involved. Neither statesman is equipped with a technical knowledge of financial detail nor endowed with a temperament which facilitates its acquisition. There is consequently a risk that they will get on to a romantic basis from which it will be difficult to retrieve the discussion . . . we should participate at the earliest stage in the ventilation of any proposal which involves finance.

D'Abernon was right. Thoiry foundered on the financial implications. Buying France out of the Rhineland and the Saar would depend on the USA lending Germany money, and it soon became clear France would be better off borrowing direct from the USA than getting money indirectly from Germany by important political concessions. D'Abernon later reported that Stresemann was meeting considerable opposition from the German Treasury, and that the British Treasury under Winston Churchill poured cold water on the financial provisions.[28]

Stresemann informed the head of the Reparations Commission that Briand was prepared to conclude a bargain by which the Rhineland was evacuated in return for a payment of 250 million gold marks, plus a further cash payment to Belgium for the return of Eupen and Malmédy. Stresemann proposed that the German payments should be financed by bonds sold to private investors and secured on the German railways. The British Treasury objected strongly because they feared this would endanger recovery of Belgian and French war debts if Germany had another financial crisis and defaulted on the interest payments, while the Wilhelmstrasse felt it would prejudice a favourable resettlement of the whole reparations question. Meanwhile the French franc was unexpectedly stabilized and France no longer needed financial assistance. As a result Thoiry was aborted, and the German dream of buying their freedom from Versailles came to nothing. When reparations and evacuation were reconsidered in 1929 France was in an immeasurably stronger economic position.*

---

*Stresemann and Schacht also hoped that parts of Poland might be returned to Germany in return for financial assistance to Warsaw. Schacht believed that Germany should use the stable mark and her strong financial position for adroit political manoeuvres. These came to nothing.

Overcoming the inflation period of the early 1920s, Germany was reasonably prosperous by the end of the decade, although this prosperity was based on her being able to undersell foreign competitors. Production costs were lower, through inflation wiping out all loan charges on manufacturers, while international loans financed the reparations payments.

Germany was able not only to make her reparation payments but also to finance new factories and machinery for industry, together with great increases in social services and a steady rise in the standard of living. In 1928 unemployment dropped to 650,000. This meant more food, more jobs and a return of the feeling of security which had disappeared during the period of galloping inflation. Not surprisingly, Hitler's propaganda made little headway, and in the Reichstag elections in May 1928 the Social Democrat vote rose to over 9 million, while the right-wing Nationalist and Nazi vote dropped sharply. After the 1928 general election the Social Democrat Hermann Müller became Chancellor and he and Stresemann co-operated well over foreign policy. Stresemann and Müller considered that in order to stifle Nationalist and Nazi propaganda an early date must be fixed for the evacuation of the Allied military forces from the Rhineland. Chamberlain, Stresemann and Briand came to an informal agreement that in return for a more permanent settlement than the Dawes Plan regarding Germany's reparations liability, the military occupation of the Rhineland should be ended.

Austen Chamberlain, elated by the Social Democrats' success in the May 1928 general election, urged the French and Belgian governments that the former allies should

> do all we can to make it possible for Republican Germany to achieve without further delay that state of complete normality in her international relations which has always been her aim, and which the Nationalists [the Nazis and Hugenberg's party] have hitherto always declared to be impossible by means of the policy of Locarno.

In order to put this policy into practice Chamberlain wanted the opening of negotiations for the 'early evacuation of occupied Rhineland'.

This was the heyday of the Briand–Stresemann–Chamberlain co-operation, and there was reason to believe that the Locarno policy would bring a lasting solution of the German problem.

In December America agreed to participate in the work of a Committee of Experts, and the Young Committee under an American chairman was set up. Reparations were fixed at £120 billion, to be paid over 59 years. Proposals were also made that Britain should renounce £200 million of war debts payments (which she had already made to the United States) and not claim this from the amount paid by Germany. This proposal was strongly

23

resisted by Winston Churchill, Chancellor of the Exchequer. The Commercial Secretary in Berlin, F. Thelwall, had reported that Germany had made 'immense strides' since 1924 and any 'substantial reduction of her annual reparations payments . . . would give her a most unfair advantage over a heavily burdened country like Great Britain'. On the other hand, Lindsay, Ambassador in Berlin, and the Treasury knight Sir Ernest Rowe Dutton 'feared a severe depression (in Germany) during the winter 1928–29 when payments under the Dawes Plan reached their maximum'.[29]

The Foreign Office became concerned that over-spending and over-borrowing by Germany might bring about an economic crisis which would jeopardize the position of the Government and give the Nazis victory in a general election. Tyrell stressed to the Treasury that failure to make concessions to Germany could 'be very far reaching indeed'. The Treasury archives show little sympathy with this Foreign Office view. Meanwhile Snowden, shadow Chancellor of the Exchequer, was making effective political propaganda by castigating the Conservative Government for being ready to give away war debts due to them under the Balfour Note. On 24 April 1929, shortly before the general election which was to bring the second Labour Government to power, Winston Churchill told the Cabinet he expected the Young Committee would ask Britain to surrender around £2 million of her dues under the Balfour Note, and reminded his colleagues that he had always thought the summoning of this Conference of Experts was 'premature', but reasonably he agreed the 'Experts' should be allowed to come to their conclusions without interference from the Government.[30]

Owen Young, who was the leading American expert on reparations, conducted the negotiations of the Experts skilfully, and early in June 1929 their report was ready. The Baldwin Government had fallen and been replaced by MacDonald's second Labour government on 3 June. The early evacuation of the Rhineland had been prominent in Labour's election programme, and the French were agreeable both to evacuation and to the debt agreement. It was clear that the governments chiefly concerned were all in favour of the Young Report. An inter-governmental conference assembled at The Hague in August. Here Philip Snowden, Chancellor of the Exchequer, insisted on financial concessions to Britain, much to the annoyance of Arthur Henderson, the new Foreign Secretary, and the Prime Minister, but the Hague Conference finally reached agreement on reparations and reduced the German payments under the Dawes Plan; it also decided that evacuation of the Rhineland should be carried out five years in advance of the date fixed in the Treaty of Versailles. The result was a triumph for six years of diplomacy by Gustav Stresemann as Minister of Foreign Affairs. All seemed set to liberate Germany from the restraints of

Versailles so that she could re-establish herself in the international community.[31]

When Stresemann failed to obtain concessions from Poincaré in 1923 he insisted on Britain being a party to all future negotiations. This policy paid off, especially when Austen Chamberlain became Foreign Secretary and his friend. Stresemann's great achievements were ending the occupation of the Ruhr, the Dawes Plan, the Locarno Treaty, and the Young Plan, with its promise of an early end to the military occupation of the Rhineland. He raised Germany from the position of a crippled and disarmed enemy to that of a diplomatic equal with international guarantees for her frontiers. When he died in 1929 Germany was far stronger and Europe far more peaceful than in 1923. It was no fault of his that the great depression destroyed all his fine work.

Unfortunately Germany was still left with too heavy a burden of reparations payments, and although this had proved sustainable during the prosperous years 1924–29 it became intolerable again as the depression hit Germany soon after The Hague Conference.

Alfred Hugenberg, an industrialist and newspaper proprietor who had profited from the 1923 inflation, now came together with Hitler and organized a campaign to overthrow the Social Democrat Government because it had agreed to pay more reparations. They failed to secure a plebiscite to prevent the Reichstag authorizing the Young Plan, and on 13 March 1930 the Plan became law. Nevertheless, during the campaign against it the Nazis received massive donations from Thyssen and other industrialists and made themselves into a potent and persuasive political force.

The world depression began with the crash on Wall Street in October 1929. The German economy was particularly susceptible to it; German prosperity was artificial, being based on a succession of new short-term loans from abroad, and insufficient provision had been made for the repayment of these loans in the event of the supply of borrowed money drying up. This occurred in 1930, when contraction in world trade extinguished German exports, and no country thought Germany credit-worthy. Unemployment rose from 1,320,000 in September 1929 to 3 million in September 1930, to peak at over 6 million in 1933. This mass unemployment produced the same starvation and distress that had occurred during the galloping inflation of 1923, and it again made millions of Germans feel as if the solid framework of their society and their state alike were cracking.

Stresemann, worn out by his toils, died in October 1929, leaving Müller to continue the Locarno policy in an economic climate which was deteriorating fearfully.

Stresemann was one of the few German statesmen of this period who can be described as entirely honest and a good European. True, he was a Nationalist and hoped to recover Germany's lost lands, and he connived at secret rearmament contrary to Versailles. However, he looked on this rearmament as a means of gaining strength for Germany at the negotiating table; he had no intention of attacking in the east. His memory was loathed by the Nazis.

Tragically, the great depression ended the high hopes brought about by Stresemann, Briand and Chamberlain's dedicated work for peace. Britain stood aside as the Nazis climbed to power through electoral successes and the German voters saw the accomplishments of the Weimar Republic turn to ashes.

CHAPTER TWO

ITALY, ABYSSINIA AND THE LEAGUE OF NATIONS 1922–4

'Abyssinia is quite unfit to be admitted, and her admission will neither redound to (the) future credit of League nor promote the interests of Britain.' (Lord Curzon, September 1923.)

Lord Cecil 'had received the instructions [to oppose the admission of Abyssinia], and then put them in an envelope containing other material of a less important nature.' (Foreign Office Minute.)

THE ADMISSION of Abyssinia (later Ethiopia)* to the League of Nations in 1923 was an important contributory factor in the outbreak of the Second World War, for in 1935 Mussolini attacked a League member.

Admission to the League was accomplished against the wishes of the British Foreign Secretary, Lord Curzon, because of an almost farcical misunderstanding between himself and Lord Robert Cecil, head of the British delegation to the League of Nations at Geneva.

Abyssinia applied for admission to the League on 12 August 1923. According to the Foreign Office, the French may well have prompted her to make the application in an effort to damage Britain and Italy in Africa, and to further their own interests. An attempted explanation of the French motivation comes in a letter dated 23 September 1923 to the Foreign Office. This emanated from the War Office, and stated that the Army

---

*Modern historians refer to Abyssinia as Ethiopia.

Council considered 'the following military objects' might underly the efforts of France to obtain the entry of Abyssinia into the League of Nations:

(a) The unrestricted sale of arms and ammunition to Abyssinia by France.
(b) An increase of French influence over North African nations and tribes generally by supporting them in this application.
(c) An attempt to damage our influence in Abyssinia.

The letter went on:

> The Army Council consider that (a) would be an inevitable sequel to Abyssinian entry into the League; that (b) is a logical deduction from the established French policy *vis-à-vis* the North African race; and that as regards (c) the French would welcome, in accordance with this policy, this or any other chance of weakening our position in North Africa by the establishment of a preponderating French influence on the borders of the Sudan and Kenya Colony.[1]

There is other evidence that in 1923 the French wanted to clip not only British but Italian wings in Africa.

On 3 September Curzon instructed Cecil, in Geneva, to oppose Abyssinian entry and informed him that the Italian representative on the League had been ordered by Mussolini not to oppose the admission of Abyssinia openly, but to keep in close touch with his British colleague with a view to exacting such conditions from Abyssinia as to make such admission practically impossible. Paradoxically, if the British representative raised no opposition, the Italian representative was to go to 'even greater lengths in supporting admission'. (Hedging his bets with a vengeance!) Lord Robert Cecil's views were invited in a Foreign Office telegram.

Relations between Italy and Britain were clouded in September 1923 by the Corfu affair, which must have made co-operation between Cecil and the Italian representative on the League difficult. The author has not been able to trace why Curzon was able to tell Cecil categorically on 3 September that the Italian representative at Geneva had been ordered to oppose Abyssinia's entry if Britain co-operated. Judging by Curzon's meticulous attention to detail, it is likely that this statement originated with Mussolini himself.

On 8 September Cecil telegraphed to the Foreign Office that he had had 'some conversation' with the Italian representative, and that he (Lord Cecil) would personally regret the exclusion of Abyssinia from the League. This ignores the fact that Curzon and the Foreign Office were bitterly opposed to entry, both because of the slavery existing within the Abyssinian empire and on account of their arms traffic. Mr Warner's minute, endorsed by Curzon, said:

> Conditions in the country are so bad that Abyssinia ought not to be admitted . . . the prestige of the League will suffer. What will be said in America and the anti-League press there? . . . We have a strong case for *resistance à l'outrance*, and [that]

the Italians will back us up when they see we are firm. We know them to be secretly opposed to admission.

Francis Russell, the head of the British Legation in Abyssinia, was even more emphatic:

> I trust the League of Nations realise the admission of Abyssinia here will be a blow to the cause of progress here. Success of application will be regarded by its promoters as a compliment to their abstention from culture. I hope . . . British delegate will urge rejection of application.

In another despatch Russell quoted not only slavery and the arms traffic, but 'the defective administration of justice in respect of foreigners'.

Meanwhile the Foreign Office were worried by Cecil's message, and began to wonder if he had received their instructions of 3 September, because although he gave his own view that Abyssinia should be admitted, he did not refer to communicating with the Italian delegate to ensure Abyssinia was excluded. In fact, reports make it clear that the Abyssinian application was making rapid progress through the committees. Accordingly a telegram was sent to Cecil on 8 September asking if he had received the instruction of 3 September. He replied that he had not, and duplicates were sent on 10 September. On 11 September Cecil found the original instructions, together with a further memorandum instructing him to raise a recent case of bad faith by the French Government in allowing an unauthorized consignment of rifles to pass through Jibuti.

Cecil had received the instructions and then put them in an envelope containing other material of 'a less urgent nature'. Cecil was unconventional and an idealist, believing that the League of Nations could preserve the peace of the world. He was confident that once Abyssinia joined the evils of slavery could be stamped out because of the automatic beneficial influence of the League. Curzon, in contrast, was a pragmatist.

However, the Duke of Portland believes that Cecil's Secretary, Philip Noel-Baker, a fanatical believer in the League of Nations, deliberately put the telegram to one side because he was so anxious for Abyssinia to become a member.

By the time the British delegation tried to act on Curzon's instructions of 3 September it was too late, in the words of the Foreign Office, 'to chill the misplaced sentimentality' which had been generated in the sub-committees. On 19 September Edward Wood MP (later Lord Halifax), spoke at length, but the sub-committee had already decided to recommend the application provided declarations about slavery and the arms traffic were signed. Wood explained how the British Government had suffered through the uncontrolled importation of arms into Abyssinia, but the Foreign Office commented: 'Unfortunately he did not take the opportunity of referring to the recent irregular consignment from Jibuti in regard to which instructions had been given on 11 September.'

In the sub-committees the Abyssinian delegation stated that their government intended to suppress the slave trade in so far as it still existed, and said the so-called slaves of Abyssinia were merely serfs of a comparatively enviable type who could appeal to a court if they were maltreated. Nothing could have been more tendentious.

Tufton, a diplomat, reported from Geneva that 'the whole brunt of showing that Abyssinia is not fit has been thrown upon us'. This was due to Cecil disobeying his orders to co-operate with the Italians. The Foreign Office minuted in vain that should Abyssinia be admitted 'We should be liable with the whole League in respect of her territorial integrity.' This was prophetic.

By 15 September all was lost. Cecil telegraphed:

> Admission of Abyssinia is, I think, unlikely to be turned down, and it is unlikely whether postponement for another year can be achieved . . . I presume you would not wish British vote to be cast against admission in a minority without Italy and France . . . no support for British views has been forthcoming from Italian delegate, and it is quite evident that he has had instructions not to go against his French colleague.

Curzon replied on 17 September:

> I personally entertain no doubt that Abyssinia is quite unfit to be admitted and that her admission will neither redound to future credit of League nor promote the interests of Britain. Only in last week fresh official evidence has reached us as to rampant slave raiding in southern and south-western parts of country and to complete anarchy in those depopulated areas. No such conditions exist in Iraq [Cecil had argued that by refusing admission to Abyssinia Britain might damage the case for admission of Iraq, which Britain wanted to be included], and to throw shelter of League over them would, in my opinion, be contrary to principles for which League exists. If the answer be made that admission will bring about a curtailment of these shocking abuses the reply is obvious that this can only be done at the cost of an interference which would be calamitous . . . you are in a better position to judge the temper of Assembly than I am, . . . and if no-one agrees with me, I would not carry my opposition to the point of standing out alone; . . . If, on the other hand, Italy will side with us I should be inclined to maintain our opposition . . . if Abyssinia is admitted there will, be no future ground for excluding anybody.

Sir Joseph Cook, the Australian delegate, made a telling point when he emphasized the anomaly that would result if a slave-owning state were placed in a position (as a League member) to cross-question countries like Australia as to whether they had been sufficiently zealous in suppressing slavery in mandated territories committed to their charge. Unfortunately, the members of the Sixth Committee (also the Slavery Committee) who besides Britain comprised France, Italy, Romania, Finland, Latvia and Persia, gave no support to the British delegation's eleventh-hour change of front, and on 20 September recommended Abyssinia's admission to the Assembly.

On 18 September the Regent of Abyssinia, Ras Tafari (later Emperor Haile Selassie) complained of Britain's attitude in a personal letter to Baldwin, the Prime Minister. The Foreign Office soon found out the letter had been composed in the French Legation in Addis Ababa. Baldwin did not reply.

On 13 October 1923 the League Assembly voted unanimously for Abyssinia to be admitted after an enthusiastic speech in support by the Italian delegate; Britain voted for admission. Cadogan minuted: 'Unless more effective control over the proceedings of the British delegation by the Foreign Office can be established, it is to be feared that similar incidents may occur in the future. A. C.' This was strong criticism of Cecil's behaviour.

In the middle of December Russell reported a raid by Abyssinian tribesmen into Kenya which resulted in the carrying off of 19,000 cattle and 50,000 sheep and goats. On this Curzon minuted: 'A deplorable situation; these are the people whom our representative, contrary to clear instructions, admitted to the League of Nations – Curzon.'[2]

If only Cecil had carried out Curzon's wishes, Mussolini would have authorized co-operation in committee with Britain, and Abyssinia would have been excluded. Cecil was an autocratic aristocrat, son of a prime minister, and he burned with zeal for the League, and despised Curzon for not sharing his romantic enthusiasm.

It seems likely that the French had been successful in a cynical manoeuvre, and that the Italian Foreign Office foolishly fell into the French trap. In his early days of power Mussolini was not sufficiently aware of the complexity of the Abyssinian problem.

The Abyssinians were xenophobic, and opposed to development or progress as understood in the Western world. Their only motive for reform was fear of invasion by a foreign power. In the event they interpreted membership as meaning that there was no longer any reason why they should introduce reforms because they were no longer in danger of coercion. If there was coercion they could appeal to the League, which under the Covenant must support them.

In 1923 Britain could have produced an unanswerable case against Abyssinia being admitted to the League if Cecil had not bungled. Much of the so-called Abyssinian Empire was not legally a state. In 1891 Anglo-Italian protocols had assigned almost all of this part of north-east Africa to

Italy, apart from French Somaliland. In 1906 after the battle of Adowa the Italian Government was not enthusiastic for acquiring colonies, and the disputed area was given to Abyssinia by a French-Italian-British agreement, apart from the coastal strips of Italian Eritrea and Somaliland. The ruler of Abyssinia then conquered and occupied all the tribal territories up to the coastal strip, but the frontiers were never properly drawn. The ruling Amharas were settled on the land at the expense of the existing inhabitants, and each Amharic family was allocated one or more families of the conquered tribes in servitude. If the serfs escaped they were subject to barbarous penalties.

The total population of the so-called Abyssinian Empire was between 5 and 10 million, but the ruling Amharas under Menelik occupied less than one-third of the territory – in the central nucleus surrounding the capital Addis Ababa – and were less than one-third of the total population. In 1935 around two-thirds of the population consisted of the conquered tribes, who differed from the Amharas in almost every respect. The Amharas were Christian, and they all spoke a common language. The conquered tribes were pagan or Muslim and spoke seventy different languages. The whole economic social system depended on slavery, which was supported and practised even by the Church. Abyssinia was not only a source of slaves for the Arab market but also a slave-trade route connecting the Sudan with the Red Sea.

Abyssinia continually attacked her neighbours over the ill-defined frontiers – not only Kenya and the Sudan, but also Eritrea and Kenya. To protect these colonies both Britain and Italy needed troops.

The Abyssinian Government was impotent to deal with slavery. Lady Simon and the Anti-Slavery League claimed that nothing short of a crusade would ever free Abyssinia from the disgrace of the slave trade. Not only were the peasant agricultural labourers bound to the land as serfs, but a flourishing export trade in slaves from Africa to Arabia and Iraq continued unabated.

The better course would have been to create a mandate for Abyssinia and either to have divided it out between Great Britain, France and Italy on the basis of the 1906 Agreement, or to have given all the mandate to Italy as part of the spoils due to her as a victor of the First World War under the Treaty of London. Such a mandate would have been in the true interests of the inhabitants. No one at the time foresaw the enormous importance that this seemingly petty international problem was destined to assume. Mussolini probably calculated that Abyssinia was about to crumple, and that it was merely a matter of time before she was handed over to Italy.

In his reminiscences Cecil recorded how dificult he found it to get on with Curzon, and this personality clash may have been largely responsible for the disaster of Abyssinia being admitted to the League of Nations. When Cecil joined the Baldwin Government in May 1923 as Lord Privy Seal with responsibility for League of Nations affairs he was promised by Baldwin a room in the Foreign Office. Curzon 'peremptorily' refused, saying there could not be two Cabinet ministers in the Foreign Office in spite of Lords Grey and Balfour having managed it perfectly well. According to Cecil the result was 'continual friction and difficulty'. Curzon had little faith in the League and never went to Geneva; he and Cecil were poles apart over its role.[3]

At the end of August General Tellini and other Italian officers under international auspices were on a mission to Greece to mark out the border with Albania, when they were all murdered on the frontier. Immediately Mussolini bombarded the Greek island of Corfu and occupied it with Italian troops. Polities, the Greek delegate at Geneva, was ordered by his government to bring the matter before the League and also to the Council of Ambassadors which was meeting in Paris to deal with subsidiary questions arising under the peace treaties, including the boundary between Greece and Albania, and which was responsible for the Tellini mission.

Cecil's reaction was that the dispute and the Italian aggression must be handled by the League, which would insist on Mussolini withdrawing from Corfu under pain of sanctions. After forty-eight hours Curzon's more pragmatic view prevailed.

Cecil's telegram to Curzon from Geneva on 1 September showed that he felt the League must bring Mussolini to heel.

> Action of Italy in occupying Greek islands appears to be clear breach of article 15 of Covenant, and exposes them to action provided for in article 16. In absence of instructions, presume His Majesty's Government will desire me to do everything possible to uphold Covenant. Greek Government have formally asked for intervention of League of Nations.

The Foreign Office replied to Cecil that Curzon would need to know 'exactly where pressing for discussion of the dispute by the League would lead him'. This produced from Cecil:

> Italian evidently hopes that you and France (will) declare matter is not within the competence of League but must be dealt with by Conference of Ambassadors. There is, I feel sure, no danger of such a deplorable decision as far as His Majesty's Government are concerned, as any failure of League in this grave crisis would do irreparable harm and perhaps lead to disintegration of the League itself.

Unfortunately for Cecil's hopes, Curzon stood firm behind the Covenant only briefly, and then sought a solution outside the League, to Cecil's grief.

Kennard was in charge of the Rome embassy in Graham's absence on leave. On 2 September he telegraphed that Italian foreign policy was 'in the hands of a man [Mussolini] who has no experience of diplomacy or statesmanship', who since he came to power 'has sought every opportunity of displaying to the world that Italy intends to play the rôle of a great power, and any direct intervention might induce Mussolini to take some rash and impulsive step which might greatly react on the people of Europe'. He argued that the matter be dealt with by the Council of Ambassadors (in permanent session in Paris to deal with Treaty problems) and not by the League.

Kennard's advice contradicted Cecil, who informed Curzon simultaneously that the view of the great majority of Council members in Geneva was that an act of war had been committed, and the Greek representative had said they did not propose to resist but preferred to appeal to the League, and that 'the important point to bear in mind' was that the effect of the failure of the League 'to settle this crisis would be almost certainly be followed by a general exodus from the League of Nations of smaller States.' Later on the same day another message from Kennard stated that he had seen Mussolini, who told him he was strongly opposed to the League dealing with the dispute, and that he [Mussolini] had added he had always been strongly prejudiced against the League, but he would accept 'action' by the Conference of Ambassadors.

Curzon was on the horns of a dilemma, and at first he inclined to the Cecil view, telling the Italian Ambassador in London that Cecil 'had already received instructions to uphold the Covenant'. Curzon had obviously been influenced by a further telegram from Cecil reporting that opinion at Geneva was hardening 'in favour of a League solution' and that

> I have had a private message from French that if Italian Prime Minister goes on he will have to face the rest of the world under the leadership of England, without any support from France.

Baldwin, holidaying at Aix-les-Bains, at first agreed with Cecil, telling Curzon by cable:

> I approve entirely language held by you to Italian Ambassador. I regard attitude of Italian Government towards League of Nations as test case of their sincerity to respect rights of small countries. Agree that Ambassadors' Conference is not suitable body to conduct enquiry in circumstances so clearly envisaged by Covenant.'[4]

Thus briefly it looked as if Cecil's passionate desire for the Covenant to be upheld would be realized, and that Mussolini might go down to history as a ruler whose aggression had been prevented by the League of Nations, which would have raised its prestige to a great height. This was not to be.

On 3 September 1923 Mussolini declared that he refused to accept the competence of the League, *inter alia* because the Greek Government had not been officially recognized, and because the delimitation commission of the Ambassadors' Conference was well qualified to investigate the 'crime'. The next day Mussolini announced that if the League of Nations were to act, Italy would leave the League, and the Italian Ambassador told the Foreign Office this officially. Kennard reported to Curzon that Mussolini had already 'gone so far in opposing submission to League that if he now acquiesced his prestige here, which is always his main consideration, will be greatly affected'.

During the afternoon of 4 September Kennard saw Mussolini and, off his own bat, made a suggestion to him which was to alter Curzon's attitude. He put it to the Duce that although the League might decide that the dispute was fully within its competence, it could well leave action to the Conference of Ambassadors. Mussolini, in an amiable mood, replied that 'this formula might prove acceptable'. The Foreign Office reaction was anger with Kennard, and Tyrrell was on the brink of sending him a cautionary telegram to cease exceeding his instructions. However, Curzon, after receiving advice from Graham who was in London, and minuting that British Ambassadors 'always seem to be shooting or holidaying' when there is a crisis, decided to follow Kennard's lead.

From Geneva Cecil reported that he was constantly hampered because as soon as he got members of the Council to agree what was to be said, Paris phoned instructions to Hanotaux, the French representative, 'not to take any action against vote of Italian'. France was out to foment trouble between Italy and Britain.[5]

Curzon was keen on the Entente, and it was the French attitude which led him to turn his back on Cecil. He feared that without help from France to solve the crisis there would be a wide rift in mutual relations, so he plumped for a solution by the Conference of Ambassadors on the lines Kennard had proposed to Mussolini. The French Government was agreeable. Cecil, much to his unhappiness, had to climb down, and the Council of the League requested the Conference of Ambassadors to appoint neutral representatives to a Committee of Enquiry, and to separate the issue of reparations to Italy for the murder of Tellini and his colleagues from the occupation of Corfu, now nominally in the hands of the League. Curzon put the onus of getting Mussolini out of Corfu on to Poincaré, the French Prime Minister, whom the British Foreign Secretary threatened by saying if the issue of Corfu came before the League Assembly Britain would support sanctions under the Covenant. The League, cleverly manipulated by Curzon and the French, in the end played no part in the settlement of the dispute. The upshot was that the Conference of Ambassadors persuaded

Greece to pay Italy an indemnity of 50 million lire, and Mussolini promised to evacuate Corfu by 27 September.

Cecil, with strong support from the smaller nations at Geneva, still hankered after a Declaration of the League's competence to adjudicate over the Italian aggression at Corfu in order to uphold the League's credibility. This infuriated Mussolini, who threatened that he would not evacuate Corfu if the issue was pressed, and expressed much anger against both Cecil and Curzon.

Curzon was incensed when Mussolini threatened to go back on his promise to evacuate Corfu, minuting on 16 September: 'I really am not at all disposed to yield to the threats of this man who having agreed to evacuate announces his intention on the flimsiest of pleas to break his word and re-occupy.' Harold Nicolson minuted:

> Although we must discount the exuberant petulance of Mussolini's language, yet it is evident that he is determined in the end to secure the triumph of 'Might against right'. To him this phrase is no vapid or ecstatic formula, but a firm political conviction. We must cope with it as such. We were able, by diverting the dispute from Geneva to Paris, to evade the embarrassing question 'Will HMG uphold the Covenant or will they not? . . . we must face the fact that Mussolini will defy everything except force . . . unless we are prepared to go the whole length, it would be better to retreat at once and to allow M. Mussolini to secure a triumph, which may well be galling but can hardly be permanent . . . if we are not prepared to defy M. Mussolini, we should instruct Lord R. Cecil to use every endeavour to prevent this matter being raised at the Assembly in any form, and endeavour in the last resort to pacify M. Mussolini by confining the League's action to a mere reference without debate to the Hague Tribunal.

Cadogan minuted: 'Mussolini . . . refuses to contemplate the possibility of the League desiring to censure him for the violation of the Covenant.'[6]

Britain climbed down. Eventually a Committee of Jurists was set up by the Council of the League to report whether incidents like Corfu came within the competence of the League. Their report was ambivalent, and thus approved by Italy. It created what Robert Dell called a bad precedent which left 'a dangerous latitude' for members of the League to evade the terms of the Covenant. Mussolini had done grave damage to the League and secured a notable diplomatic victory. This was unfortunate for his future behaviour.[7]

★   ★   ★

Smarting under their defeat by Mussolini over Corfu, Curzon and the Foreign Office were in no mood to give in to Italy over the other controversial items on the Agenda in 1923 – the Dodecanese islands in the

36

Aegean and Jubaland, which was British territory adjoining Italian Somaliland.

In October Mussolini antagonized the Foreign Office by making a speech
attacking the League. Cecil wrote from Geneva:

> It really amounts to a declaration by the Prime Minister [sic the Duce] who is also
> the dictator of a great power that he was quite ready to tear up the Covenant and go
> to war without notice ... I really think that this Government must lose no
> opportunity of upholding the sanctity of treaties or not only the League, but Europe
> will be lost.

Francesco Coppola, one of the Italian delegates to Geneva, had early in
October written articles highly critical of the League. Graham commented:
'Italy, deprived of the fruits of her great victory, regarded the League as an
international instrument for her own repression,' but Cecil's reaction was:
'It is a little short of an outrage that one of the delegates should publicly
advocate the destruction of the League from within by Italian efforts.' Sir
Eyre Crowe cooled Cecil down, saying it was inadvisable to raise these
matters in Rome as the Duce was having friendly talks with Graham.[8]

Mussolini was anxious to separate the issue of Jubaland from that of the
Dodecanese. He wanted to claim that as a result of his exertions the Allies
had given Jubaland to Italy as a reward for the latter's part in the victory over
Germany. Curzon insisted that Jubaland would only be ceded as part of a
general settlement with Italy in which Mussolini made large concessions
over the Dodecanese.

Under the secret Treaty of London in 1915 Italy had been promised the
Dodecanese and additional territory in Africa as a reward for joining the
Allied side. The Dodecanese issue became most complicated when Turkey
emerged, according to Curzon, as 'a quasi-victorious power' instead of a
defeated one after the war was over, and the abortive Treaty of Sèvres left
the problem in the air, with Italy committed to make some withdrawals.

On 10 October Curzon saw Torretta, the Italian Ambassador in London,
and they agreed that bygones should be bygones over Corfu, but Curzon
recorded that he had insisted as he had done 'a score of times' that Jubaland
could only be ceded by Britain to Italy as part of general settlement
including the Dodecanese.[9]

A Foreign Office memorandum by Harold Nicolson stated that Italy had
complete rights on paper both to compensation in Africa and to the
Dodecanese.

> 'We thus designed to use the question of Jubaland as a lever to force the Italians to
> an agreement over the Dodecanese refusing to cede the territory promised until the
> Dodecanese could be settled. The result of this policy was a deadlock and relations
> between Great Britain and Italy were unquestionably affected.[10]

The Baldwin Government was defeated in the general election on 10 December 1923. Ramsay MacDonald became the first Labour Prime Minister on 18 January 1924. After 10 December it was virtually certain that the Conservatives would have to leave office, but Curzon continued to work as hard as ever at the Foreign Office. He saw Torretta again on 16 December, and reiterated that Juba would not be conceded unless there was agreement over the Dodecanese, and christened Torretta 'Grabski' because of his request for extra territory adjoining Italian Somaliland.[11]

On 12 January Graham reported that Contarini, Italian Secretary General for Foreign Affairs, had explained to him that from the point of view of internal politics, Mussolini felt it was 'absolutely necessary . . . to show that he had obtained . . . something more than had been considered insufficient by preceding Italian Governments'. This had no effect on Curzon, who saw Torretta again on 21 January, and left a note for his successor of the Italian Ambassador's proposals:

> As to Jubaland we were to surrender the maximum of what we had ever offered, for no return at all, . . . Had I continued in office I could not have concluded an agreement on any such terms . . . Signor Mussolini's passionate desire to represent every situation as a triumph for his own diplomacy over other Powers makes me more than doubtful. . . . We must not act unfairly to the Greeks . . . and we must on no account allow Signor Mussolini first to dupe us and then to bully or squeeze them. The one effective card that Italy can play is of course the annexation of the whole of the islands. But if she proceeds to that extreme, I hope we shall recede from the Jubaland offer except for the minimum.

Ramsay MacDonald decided to be his own Foreign Secretary, and was more conciliatory to Mussolini than Curzon had been over Jubaland. At first MacDonald continued Curzon's policy of insisting on linking the settlement of Jubaland with satisfactory negotiations between Italy and Greece over the Dodecanese. However, Graham reported in a private telegram on 6 March to the Prime Minister that Mussolini was inclined to give up all hopes of an enlarged Jubaland and to annex all the Dodecanese, and suggested a private letter from the Prime Minister to Mussolini offering to hand over Jubaland to Italy on terms which would give great pleasure to the Duce, if it emphasized also that there was no connection between Jubaland and the Dodecanese.

Graham's suggestion was ill received in the Foreign Office, but MacDonald recorded that while he could not pretend his predecessors had been completely wrong in connecting Jubaland with the Dodecanese, he had no desire to score a diplomatic triumph over Mussolini, and was ready to agree a formula which would save his face. Accordingly he wrote a personal letter on 1 April to the Duce saying that he would like to settle Jubaland and the Dodecanese concurrently, but without making the settlement of the one depend on that the other, and that he was 'anxious immediately to execute the promises which we have made to you in regard to Jubaland'.[12]

This resulted in the Jubaland Treaty being concluded in June, although Mussolini showed no haste over his negotiations with the Greeks. The discussions were amicable, and conducted by Guariglia for the Italians, and Nicolson for the British. Instead of the minimum wanted by Curzon, Mussolini secured the maximum, and made much of his second diplomatic triumph in the Italian press.

Ramsay MacDonald's Labour Government fell in October 1924, and Baldwin became Prime Minister again.

Now, with the change of government, Austen Chamberlain became Foreign Secretary. Much to Mussolini's impatience, the Jubaland Treaty still had to be ratified by Parliament, but Chamberlain told Torretta on 14 November: 'There is no difference between us and our predecessors over Jubaland,' and sent a message to Mussolini that he wanted to visit him in Italy where he had spent 'many happy holidays'.[13]

CHAPTER THREE

REPARATIONS AND THE FALL OF BRÜNING

'At the conclusion of the Lausanne Conference [1932] I told MacDonald and Herriot "You must provide me with a foreign political success for my Government is the last bourgeois Government in Germany. After me there will be only extremists of the right and left." But they did not believe me' (Papen in evidence at Nuremberg.)

'Bruning's first priority was the cancelling of reparations . . . [this] is amply confirmed by the latest research based on all relevant sources.' (Kolb, *The Weimar Republic*, page 184.)

HERMANN MÜLLER, the last Social Democrat Chancellor, resigned in March 1930 after an inter-party dispute over the unemployment insurance fund. He had been in power for a year and nine months. Another coalition of democratic parties was formed with Heinrich Brüning of the Catholic Centre Party as Chancellor. Brüning had the backing of the sinister and unreliable political manipulator Schleicher, who was a friend of Hindenburg.

Brüning was intelligent, moderate, honest and dedicated to rescuing Germany from the slump and her chaotic financial position. Unwisely, he called a general election for 14 September 1930 after the final withdrawal of occupation troops from the Rhineland. The result was disastrous. In a whirlwind campaign Hitler became amazingly popular by calling for repudiation of both reparations and the Versailles Treaty, and promising jobs and food for everyone in the rapidly mounting queue of the unemployed.

During the campaign the Nazis disgusted many sensible Germans by their excesses – smashing windows and calling for the confiscation of Jewish money and the suppression of Jewish-owned newspapers – but although the Nazis had only polled 810,000 votes and returned 12 members in the general election two years before, this time their vote rose to 8½ million. This gave them 107 seats in the Reichstag, where they became the second largest party. The Communists, also campaigning for abolition of reparations, increased their votes from 3¼ million to 4½ million, while the centre parties lost heavily. Brüning's coalition was now in a minority of 159 instead of a majority of 15, but in order to keep the Hitlerites out of government Müller and the SDP (still the largest party) supported the Brüning government loyally. (See Table, p. 341).

During the election campaign some of Brüning's ministers demanded that the the demilitarization of the Rhineland be rescinded, and Treviranus, a right-wing minister and a headstrong former naval officer, spoke in favour of a revision of Germany's eastern frontiers, although he declared that he did not contemplate accomplishing this by force. These speeches were poorly received in France, and Vansittart minuted: 'The evacuation of the Rhineland and the reparation settlement reached at The Hague' did not mark the end of the German Government's foreign policy objectives. However, such speeches were made for internal consumption as a riposte to Nazi and Communist propaganda, and Brüning himself was more interested in putting the financial affairs of the Reich in order than in seeking to adjust the eastern frontiers.[1]

Horace Rumbold, who had succeeded D'Abernon as Ambassador in Berlin, described Brüning as 'one of the few responsible statesmen in Germany,' but warned that as a result of the Nazi success at the polls 'any Government would have to pursue a forward foreign policy, including probably a demand for the revision of the Young Plan'. Indeed, on 27 October 1930 Curtius, the Finance Minister, told Rumbold that because of the slump Germany would probably have to ask for a two-year moratorium as provided for in the Young Plan. The Foreign Secretary, Arthur Henderson, told Rumbold to convey the British Government's stern disapproval.

Here Henderson was ignoring not only Germany's unprecedented economic distress but also the successful Nazi propaganda and agitation which made a political crisis likely. The Foreign Office pointed out that there was only 'a small group of responsible and able statesmen powerful enough to hold the country's existing structure together', and Rumbold reported 'It is difficult to think of anybody in the Germany of to-day more capable of directing the affairs of the Reich than the present Chancellor, and it would be a misfortune for the country if he had to go.'[2]

As 1931 opened Brüning was in grave difficulties; the depression had put 5 million wage-earners out of work; many businesses faced ruin, and the farmers were unable to meet their mortgage payments, while Parliament was paralysed, with the 84-year-old President Hindenburg sinking into senility.

Brüning had resorted to government by decree, and his regime was unpopular. He was known as the 'Hunger Chancellor', because to deal with the dire economic situation he had decreed lower wages and lower prices, had clamped down on business and had reduced unemployment benefit. His hopes for the survival of his Government depended on negotiating with the Allies cancellation of the reparations payments, or at the very least a massive reduction in them. Hitler and his lieutenants were attributing the slump to reparations, and loudly proclaiming on every possible occasion that once the Nazis formed the Government of Germany they would not pay a penny more in what they described as 'unjust tribute'.

Unfortunately, the omens for Brüning's success over cancellation of reparations were poor. The French were opposed to further concessions, and the British Labour Government was unforthcoming, although Vansittart had told it on 29 January 1931, 'We are all agreed that Bruning's Government is the best we can hope for; its disappearance would be followed by a Nazi avalanche; it will hardly hold without something to put in the shop window,' and that the Hitler Movement and the economic depression were 'a very formidable combination'.[3]

Hugh Dalton, Under-Secretary at the Foreign Office, was more understanding of the need to help Brüning than was the Foreign Secretary, Arthur Henderson. On 22 April Dalton forwarded a letter to Vansittart from a Labour MP (almost certainly Rennie Smith) who much admired Brüning, stating it was a 'faithful record'.

> Brüning had been back less than a month from his tour of the eastern frontiers where he had been met by hostile crowds everywhere, even in his own constituency which strecches from Breslau to Glatz. This hostility had been fostered by the Nazis and by the Hugenberg faction and by the Communists, all of whom parrot the cries 'Down with Chancellor Brüning! Down with the Hunger Chancellor!' This reception, and the critical state of his country, appear to have changed the man. He has become grim. He is certainly tired, not the least indication of this being the lack of his former fluency in the English language. He is not satisfied with his Cabinet. He gives me the impression that he regards no member of it as sufficiently big for the grave responsibilities entrusted to him. Treviranus, without whose support he would not have become Chancellor on the fall of the Mueller Cabinet, and with whom he is on terms of the friendliest intimacy, he treats as a well intentioned boy whose burden of office has got to be borne for him.
> Curtius, his Foreign Minister, he appears to dislike personally and is not impressed by his ability. He seems to think that we are so obsessed with our own

internal problems that we have no time for worrying about those of Germany.[4]

On 13 March Rumbold suggested that Brüning's position might be strengthened if he was invited by the Prime Minister to Chequers. MacDonald approved, and an invitation was sent for German ministers to come on 1 May. The German newspapers applauded, but the French were critical, saying that the visit was designed to embarrass Briand. Tyrrell commented: 'Such people are suspicious of any gesture which might be interpreted as an encouragement to Germany.'[5]

In 1929 and 1931 two important international initiatives (much overlooked by historians of the period) might have made a considerable contribution to easing Germany's economic problems and thus helping a German democratic Government to withstand Nazi propaganda. They were Briand's proposal for a Federal Europe and the suggested Austro-German Customs Union. Neither materialized.

It was a tragedy that the Briand Plan of 1929 for a Federal and Free Trade Europe did not come to fruition. If it had, rising German prosperity and friendly co-operation with other nations would have stifled the Nazi appeal in the same way as the Schuman Plan and the Common Market in the 1950s took West Germany out of the Stalin orbit. Unfortunately, Briand's aims were aborted by British intransigence.

Briand launched his Federal Plan at the League of Nations on 5 September 1929, and afterwards invited all the European nations represented at Geneva to a Conference.* Here Willie Graham, President of the Board of Trade in the second Labour Government, welcomed the plan on behalf of Britain as a move towards freer trade in a speech made without notes which created a great impression. A leader in *The Times* welcomed Graham's speech and was favourable to Briand. Gustav Stresemann, then a sick man but still German Foreign Minister, in his last speech at Geneva was enthusiastic. Largely because of Graham's endorsement, the International Economic Conference was convened in March 1930. This accomplished nothing, and not until May 1930 were Briand's detailed proposals for a Federal Europe available in a Memorandum which proposed a permanent European Conference with a secretariat in Geneva, and emphasized that the main aim was the reduction and removal of all import tariffs on trade between European countries.

The architect of the Briand Plan was Count R. H. Coudenhove Kalurgi, the son of a former Austrian diplomat and married to a Japanese. In 1923 he had founded the Pan Europa movement and had written several books

---

*At that time Briand was Prime Minister and Foreign Minister. In November 1929 he was defeated and succeeded by Tardieu as Prime Minister, although Briand remained Foreign Minister.

suggesting a Federal Europe. According to the British Foreign Office, 'his eloquent energy and sincerity' had won many adherents to Pan Europa, and he was on friendly terms with Briand, whose proposals for a European Union were based on 'Dr. Coudenhove's conception'.

Kalurgi lived in Vienna, and was a supporter of a Habsburg restoration; he had many friends in right-wing political circles in Britain, including Leopold Amery who had joined Pan Europa and supported it enthusiastically-provided Britain was left out. Kalurgi and Briand prearranged that a large Pan Europa Conference should be held in Berlin to coincide with the publication of the Briand Memorandum in 17–19 May. Amery in a much-publicized speech with Baldwin's approval blessed the Briand Plan, but stated categorically that Britain could not be a member of a united Europe because 'Britain's heart lies outside Europe'. That encapsulated the views of the majority of the Conservative and Labour front bench in 1930; the Schuman Plan and the Messina proposals provoked an identical reaction in the 1950s.

Apart from Graham, the Labour Cabinet were hostile to the Briand Memorandum. Hugh Dalton, Under-Secretary at the Foreign Office, was cynical, minuting in February 1930: 'I am pretty sure Briand has not got a scheme . . . I shall be surprised if anything concrete appears.'

Robert Cecil (a Conservative, but Labour's delegate to the League of Nations) and Philip Noel-Baker (PPS to the Foreign Secretary, Arthur Henderson) were enthusiasts for the League of Nations. They both wanted Britain to give the Federal Plan the fullest support, although they warned it must be accomplished without injury to the League. Cecil commented: 'People like Mr. Amery have a dream of a British Empire independent of the world,' and in his autobiography wrote: '. . . if the Briand Plan had been accepted it might have changed the history of the world.'[6]

In 1930 Britain was a free-trade country, although many were in favour of tariff preferences for food from the Colonies and Dominions in return for conceding favourable tariff treatment for British exports. European countries in return for the British open door operated 'most favoured nation' treatment for British imports by customs concessions on British exports to them as a reciprocal gesture for Britain's free trade. The Briand Plan aroused fears in Whitehall that Britain's 'most favoured nation' concessions might be threatened.

This view dominated the Cabinet, and Graham's far-sighted enthusiasm for Federalism and European Free Trade was not shared by his colleagues. Graham was probably the most able Minister in Ramsay MacDonald's second Government; his speeches were always a model of clarity and reason, and at the second Young Committee meetings in January 1930 he had taken a more reasonable line than Philip Snowden, Chancellor of the

Exchequer, and created a favourable impression on European statesmen. Unfortunately, he had little personal following in the Labour Party as he had no trade union background and had been a Glasgow lecturer in Adult Education until he was elected to Parliament. He died in 1932 and has since become a forgotten figure, although if he had lived he must have had high office in Winston Churchill's wartime coalition Government.

The Foreign Secretary, Arthur Henderson, soon made his view clear. On 3 July he circulated to the Cabinet a Memorandum stating that Briand's proposals were 'unacceptable' and if adopted would be detrimental to the League of Nations; they contained a 'tendency' towards Continental organizations which might be 'fraught with danger' to the British Commonwealth and the world, although they proceeded from conceptions with which His Majesty's Government had considerable sympathy. He insisted that the proposals required careful consideration with the governments of the Dominions, and he wanted them placed on the agenda for the next Assembly of the League of Nations.

Willie Graham disagreed strongly with Henderson, and in order to avoid a Cabinet split the Prime Minister decided there should be no discussion in full Cabinet. Instead he appointed a special Committee (Cabinet Committee on Proposed Federal Union) to meet in private with no civil servants present. They met only once, on 14 July, and there is no record of the discussion. Clearly Graham was overruled by Henderson and MacDonald, and he accepted the decision without protest, although there can be no doubt that he argued strongly in private in favour of an enthusiastic response to Briand. Jim Thomas, recently promoted Dominions Secretary, was also against the Briand Plan, mainly because he was hoping for a personal success at the forthcoming Imperial Conference with a plan for tariff preference on Dominion food.

The British reply sent to Briand on 15 July expressed doubts about the 'desirability' of new and independent international institutions which would create 'confusion and rivalry' within the existing organizations of the League, while they feared an 'exclusive and independent European Union of the kind proposed might create inter-continental rivalries and hostilities'. It was insularity, and the suggestion of inter-continental rivalry was deceitful because the USA had made it plain she approved the Briand idea. Any inter-continental rivalry would come from the Dominions, and it would have been more honest to have made this clear.[7]

Mussolini was hostile; his attitude was that France would establish a Federation not of free sovereign states but of 'satellites of France under French predominance'. Mussolini was anti-French, but would have followed a strong lead by Britain. The Austrian press made clear that Austria was Pan Europa minded, although it was stressed that the main

45

attraction was the economic side, which they claimed Briand subordinated to the political. The Dutch and Belgian newspapers welcomed the move, as did Poland and the Little Entente. Widespread admiration of Briand's move was expressed by French newspapers, which claimed it was an attempt to secure lasting peace.

Sir Horace Rumbold, British Ambassador in Berlin, reported that the German Government's attitude would depend on Britain. Henderson ignored this. Brüning was now Chancellor of Germany, having succeeded Müller in April 1930; Curtius had become Foreign Minister when Stresemann died in October 1929. With the death of Stresemann the ties aligning France and Germany were broken because they depended on the close friendship between Stresemann and Briand. In Germany right-wing newspapers opposed the Briand Plan on the grounds that it would make permanent the frontiers imposed on Germany by the Versailles Treaty. However, the Centre Party newspapers said it was 'a great thought' that the European states should come together within the League to 'bury the past', but argued that the German Government could support it only if Germany received satisfaction for her 'justifiable and inalienable claims' in the east and on the Danube. For this reason Brüning felt unable to take up an enthusiastic stand for a Federal Europe. His parliamentary position was shaky and his political opponents (and Hitler especially) would have attacked him for supporting a plan which perpetuated the Versailles frontiers. Instead he argued, as did the other defeated powers Hungary and Bulgaria, that neither lasting peace nor Federal Union could be achieved in Europe without frontier readjustments. Nevertheless, according to Rumbold the Bruning Government would have fallen into line if Britain had supported Briand.[8]

Henderson gave the final British verdict to the French that 'mature examination will show that the establishment of new and independent international institutions was not desirable or necessary'. Instead Britain favoured 'Regionalism within the League' to achieve lower tariffs. This killed the plan, much to Briand's disappointment. At the September General Assembly of the League of Nations Briand was on the brink of abandoning it, but instead he successfully moved a Resolution for the establishment of a Committee of Enquiry into European Union (CEEU). The plan was already a lost cause, and it was in the words of the historian David Carlton 'a face saving device'.[9]

★   ★   ★

As no tariff reductions resulted from the proceedings of the CEEU Germany decided to take the initiative herself towards 'regionalising within the League' as favoured by Henderson. The world depression was hitting

46

both Austria and Germany hard with rising unemployment and poverty, and a Customs Union between the two countries would be a godsend for both. Accordingly Curtius went to Vienna on 3 March 1931 with a plan for abolishing import duties between the two countries. Johannes Schober, the Austrian Chancellor, agreed enthusiastically, and on 21 March without previous consultation with France and Britain the plan was made public. Both Austria and Germany emphasized that other countries would be welcome within the Customs Union, and they considered it a natural extension of Briand's European Free Trade initiative. The French described the sudden announcement as tactless, and alleged that it disguised a *fait accompli*. This was incorrect; a protocol had been signed but no Treaty, and in any case there had been little previous discussion when Briand announced his Federal Plan in September 1929. The French implausibly alleged it would lead to two blocs in Europe and they would have to lead an anti-German bloc!

Public opinion in French reacted strongly against the Customs Union, arguing that it was a first step towards an Anschluss which would make Germany much stronger militarily. For internal political reasons Briand was forced to oppose the plan. However, there is reason to believe that he himself saw merit in it. Kalurgi went to see Briand and apparently convinced him that the Customs Union was 'quite in harmony' with Briand's own plan but (according to the tale told to Phipps, British Ambassador in Vienna, by the French Ambassador, Clauzel) Berthelot, the permanent Under-Secretary, undid the good work. Blum told Lord Tyrrell that Briand was not against the Union but had been forced to oppose it by the weight of public opinion and his political opponents.

The French and Czech governments denounced the plan as a first move towards Anschluss in breach of the Protocol of October 1922, which gave financial assistance to Austria in return for a promise that she would do nothing which put her economic independence at risk without the consent of the Council of the League. Although Vansittart advised that the proposal was not a breach of the 1922 Protocol, Henderson went to Paris and after talking to Briand instructed Rumbold and Phipps to tell the German and Austrian governments of his serious misgivings about breaches of treaty obligations aroused by their action, and of the danger that Briand might no longer be able to control his more extreme fellow-countrymen. Henderson asked for the Council of the League of Nations to be allowed to decide whether or not the 1922 Protocol had been breached by Austria. On 6 May he told the Cabinet 'means must be found for removing this proposal from the domain of international politics', and he would like to replace the dangerous Austro-German Customs Union by some progressive scheme for the economic union of Europe.

Brüning refused to agree that Germany's right to enter into the Customs Union should be examined by the Council of the League from a political point of view because the agreement was purely economic, and argued the French ought to be interested in the stability of his government, while he did not agree Briand's political position was prejudiced. However, Schober was willing for the legal aspects of the agreement to be considered by the League, whereupon Henderson climbed down and said he would be content if the International Court of Justice examined the legality of the agreement. Curtius insisted that the German plan should be incorporated in a wider plan, arguing that European Union could best be achieved by starting 'from a kernel of two or three states' which would gradually attract others, and that this could be a quick process whereas the Briand Plan required the agreement of twenty-seven European states at the same time.

Meanwhile Dr Beneš on behalf of Czechoslovakia was expressing all-out opposition to the plan on the grounds that it would create a German hegemony in Central Europe; he even published a pamphlet in English condemning the plan in extravagant terms, arguing that it would lead to another war.[10]

In Whitehall civil servants were not as opposed to the plan as their masters. Owen O'Malley minuted 'the Austro-German proposal has brought the idea of economic co-operation strikingly before public opinion in all European countries and has given it such a shock that now if ever there is a chance to get something done'; and later wrote after consultation with Sir Henry Fountain of the Board of Trade that there was no serious breach of any Treaty engagement

> and we should receive with great caution any French remonstrances. I do not think either Germany or Austria have any intention in the near future of even raising the question of political union . . . the question of whether or not a political union between Germany and Austria is dangerous to the peace of Europe is one of those wide questions which do not lend themselves to precise argument.

An inter-departmental memorandum said 'only tenuous grounds exist on which it could be argued that the proposed treaty prejudices the economic independence of Austria'.

However, Henderson would not change his view that the French and Czechs were justified in regarding the Customs Union as a move towards Anschluss and thus a threat to the peace of Europe and the Disarmament Conference in session at Geneva. In deference to Henderson the Foreign Office did not persist with their argument that it was purely an economic, not a political move. Philip Noel-Baker (still PPS to Henderson) saw the move as constructive, minuting on 16 April:

I believe that an opportunity may be forming itself . . . to bring off a tariff reduction agreement on a general European basis on the lines for which we have hoped for 18 months, but perhaps involving some apparent sacrifice of our rigid views about most favoured nations treatment . . . IF THERE IS ANY CHANCE OF SUCH A NEGOTIATION BEING STARTED WE SHOULD KEEP EVERY CARD IN OUR HANDS UNTIL THE RIGHT MOMENT COMES IN ORDER THAT WE MAY BE ABLE TO EXERT THE MAXIMUM PRESSURE ON BOTH SIDES TO MAKES CONCESSIONS.[11]

(Authors's capitals)

The Attorney General, Sir William Jowett, was asked to give his opinion on the legal aspect. It was futile. Jowett wrote it was for economists to decide whether Austrian independence would be threatened. 'If they say "yes" the Treaty would be a breach of the 1922 Protocol.' Everyone knew this already. Such hedging was typical of Jowett. He had been elected in 1929 as a Liberal MP, but when MacDonald offered him the post of Attorney General he fought a by-election and won as a Labour candidate.

However, as usual Willie Graham was forthright in favour of any move which led to greater free trade in Europe. He wrote a letter to Henderson stating that the effect of the Customs Union on British trade with Austria had been greatly exaggerated by Phipps and would be negligible, while it would have little effect on our trade with Germany, so that Phipps was far too pessimistic. Graham added:

It would be very short sighted to oppose such a union from an economic standpoint because if all customs were abolished Europe would be much wealthier and buy more British goods. . . . The Union is a step in the right direction which we should certainly not discourage.

This was not what Henderson wanted to hear and he did not forward Graham's statesmanlike view to the British Ambassadors overseas, neither did they appear in Foreign Office memorandum circulated to the Cabinet.[12]

Although the Austrians wanted to propitiate the French, the German Government was adamant that it would refuse to give any guarantee not to produce a *fait accompli* during the League deliberations. Nevertheless, Schober forced Curtius to agree to suspend the Customs Union deliberations until the League Council met in late May.[13]

On 11 May it was announced the Kredit-Anstalt Bank in Vienna was on the brink of failure. It was rumoured that France had triggered off a run on this bank to put political pressure of Austria, but this has not been substantiated. The Kredit-Anstalt's problems triggered off a world-wide loss of confidence and withdrawal of foreign holdings from Germany and Austria. Sensibly the Austrian Government took emergency measures and accepted responsibility for Kredit-Anstalt's deficit, but this was not enough to remedy the position and the Austrian Government had to make urgent appeals for loans in London, Paris and Switzerland. Thus when the League Council met to discuss the German Customs Union on 18 May the Austrian financial crisis overshadowed the proceedings.

Before leaving for Geneva Henderson told the Cabinet that he wanted to act as 'honest broker between France and Germany . . . to advance the cause of economic co-operation between nations and endeavour at Geneva to arrange for Customs Union to be dealt with primarily as an economic, rather than a judicial or political problem and advocate one or two special technical Committees.' This was hypocrisy, as referring it to technical League of Nations Committees was just bogging the proposal down. Later he revealed his petulant, hostile attitude by telling the Cabinet on 1 July after Hoover had announced his plan for a year's moratorium on War Debts and Reparations that he had spoken 'very strongly' to the German Ambassador and told him that if the German Government wanted the present negotiations for the Hoover moratorium brought to a successful conclusion the best thing would be to 'bury or cremate' the proposal for an Austro-German Customs Union. Of course, there was no connection between a Customs Union and the moratorium, but this was the way in which Henderson jumped to illusory conclusions.

Henderson went to Geneva determined to kill the Austro-German Customs Union. However, he persuaded Schober to state that there would be no *fait accompli* before the Hague Court had adjudicated on the legality of the plan. According to Wheeler-Bennett, Henderson humiliated Schober. Briand and Curtius were at daggers drawn because Briand insisted France would resist the Customs Union whatever the verdict of the Hague Court (much to the annoyance of Curtius), but Henderson showed tact in heading off a German-French clash in public.[14]

On 18 May Henderson at the Council of the League moved a resolution asking the Permament Court of International Justice to rule on the legality of the proposed agreement between Austria and Germany. The resolution was adopted unanimously. The Court ruled by eight votes to seven on 3 September that the proposal was illegal, with the British judge voting in the minority. This decision was much criticized in Foreign Office minutes; the standing of the Hague Court was low because too many judges looked on themselves as delegates for their governments and not as impartial judges.

However, by September the proposal was dead. The financial problems of Austria were too acute, and her need for foreign loans too urgent. On 16 June the French issued what was really an ultimatum offering a loan in return for renunciation of the proposed Customs Union. Fortunately, Britain stepped in and offered a loan without such strings. But the strain of the financial crisis was too much for the Austrian Chancellor. As early as 17 June he told Phipps unofficially that there could be no question of putting the Customs Union into execution, even if the verdict of the Hague Court was favourable. The Germans refused to capitulate, but given the Austrian attitude they had no alternative, and on 3 September (two days before the Hague Verdict was given) Austria and Germany made a joint announcement that because of the economic difficulties which had arisen in Europe they had decided not to pursue the plan. Curtius said he expected fruitful results from the CEEU. Unfortunately, it accomplished nothing. Britain ought to have looked on Austrian-German Customs Union as a natural by-product of the Briand Plan, especially in view of Henderson's enthusiasms for 'rationalising within the League'.[15]

By 1931 it was clear that Nazi popularity was increasing fast, and there was no alternative to the Brüning Government except a Hitler-Hugenberg coalition. Winston Churchill had hit the nail on the head when in April 1931 he wrote in the *New York American* 'Brüning's move would rob Hitler of his mainspring.' Yet Henderson showed no appreciation of the vital need to bolster Brüning's popularity, although he was frequently warned of the rising electoral popularity of the Nazis by Rumbold and Vansittart.

The hostility of Briand and Beneš to the Customs Union was irrational because both the Austrians and Germans were genuine in their offer to include any other countries who wished to join. Nor was it looked on by either Germany or Austria as a prelude to the Anschluss. (One Foreign Office minute pointed out that the union of Germany and Austria would add 6 million Catholic voters and be an antidote to Nazidom.) Briand himself was in two minds whether the Customs Union was or was not in conformity with his Federal Plan. However, the violent hostility of French public opinion forced him into opposing it against his better judgement. The British Cabinet, apart from Willie Graham, saw it as a threat to food exports by the Dominions to Europe and to Britain's 'most favoured nation' tariff concessions. Henderson unreasonably felt the proposal was a threat to the Disarmament Conference, of which he was proud of being President. Had Henderson taken the more reasonable attitude urged by his Foreign Office advisers and Noel-Baker, Briand would probably have seen reason. As it was the Customs Union like the Briand Federal Plan belongs to the scrapheap of history, but historians should wring their hands that these early attempts to unite Europe before the Nazi menace emerged and the iron curtain descended came to nothing.

Much to Brüning's disappointment, the British, in deference to the French, treated his visit to Chequers (see p. 43) purely as one of courtesy – not a concrete step to help the Brüning Government to end reparations. Henderson even informed Briand on 22 May that he had made it clear to

51

the Germans that 'the visit was of a purely courteous character and we had no programme for discussions'.

Despite Foreign Office memoranda giving strong warnings both about the Nazi menace and about the precarious position of the Brüning Government, at Chequers, Henderson and MacDonald refused to hold out an olive branch.

On 3 June 1931 the Chief Treasury Adviser, Sir Frederick Leith-Ross, wrote to Nichols:

> In present conditions any hopes held out to the Germans must be liable to create disappointment. There are no definite signs of any improvement in the general economic situation and the Germans are as well qualified as we are to make forecasts as to the course which the world crisis will take.
>
> As regards reparations, we are obviously not in a position to do anything until France and America are willing to reduce their claims and we have every reason to believe there is no prospect of concessions from these countries.
>
> In the circumstances it seems to us that our only course is to work on the common fears rather than to hold out hopes to them. Although things in Germany may seem bad, they will be made infinitely worse if Germany throws up the sponge and does not carry through the Young Plan as long as she possibly can. We can, of course, at the same time urge the Germans to collaborate with us in Geneva [at the Disarmament Conference] for what it is worth.

On receiving this at the Foreign Office Nichols minuted:

> The Treasury is bankrupt of constructive proposals to Germany and merely suggest that we should work on their fears, i.e. restate the arguments of last December and tell them their last state will be worse than their first if they repudiate the Young Plan . . . It will not help the Germans much *vis-à-vis* their own public opinion which after all is the one reason we have to invite them to Chequers. . . . Could we not say we will support their efforts to obtain long term credits and for any idea of a world wide economic conference.

Sargent minuted: 'Treasury would say we are NOT in a position to give German Government any promises of support either as regards long term credits or an economic conference.' Vansittart answered: 'Some non-committal arrangement on this line will at least make Chequers not feel quite barren to the visitors. The suggestion may quite probably come to nothing; that will not be our fault or responsibility.'

Henderson and Dalton read these minutes without comment, although Dalton had been impressed by a letter from Rennie Smith written on 5 June, saying 'If the preservation of the present [German] Government or the discouragement of the Nazi one or a serious internal disorder is a British interest the Government should develop an effective initiative.' This was patently obvious.[16]

52

Three weeks before Brüning arrived in England the Austrian Bank Kredit Anstalt bankruptcy undermined Germany's credit, and there had been panic withdrawal of funds from Germany by other nations. In an attempt to lever the British into action over reparations, Brüning with considerable political skill timed his arrival in London to coincide with a presidential decree that owing to the German financial crisis taxes had to be raised, the budget cut, and pay in the State sector and relief for unemployment reduced. Hindenburg signed the decree on 5 June; Brüning and Curtius arrived in London on 6 June, when at a press conference Brüning said that after the reductions in payment by Germany made by the Young Plan 'We find instead of reducing taxes we have been forced to raise taxes and cut spending.' He argued that the emergency decree of the day before was entirely due to the burden of reparations on Germany. In Germany Otto Dietrich, the Finance Minister, said, 'We can, and will, pay our debts, but we shall have a hard time doing it.' On the same day Hugenberg the Nationalist leader – now intriguing with the Nazis against Brüning – said he was one hundred per cent against raising taxes.

A press statement by the German Government summarizing the Hindenburg decree maintained that the 'tributary payments' made by Germany 'as the vanquished side in the Great War entailed very heavy burdens'. The limit of sacrifice had been reached, and Germany had the right 'to claim relief from intolerable reparation obligations'. Reparations could no longer be paid out of foreign loans; the benefits expected from the Young Plan had failed to materialize.

The British press was hostile.* On 6 June *The Times* leader commented:

> Has Germany really accepted the post-war argument [sic] among European countries even in its main lines, or is she hoping all the time to upset the arrangement . . . if modifications are to be introduced without disaster it is absolutely necessary they should be made on the general basis of existing treaties and by consent.

Although on the foreign news page of *The Times* the paper's Berlin correspondent gave a lurid account of the economic crisis, and spoke of 'the desperate state of the national finance', *The Times* leader concluded: 'Reparations were a perfectly just form of restitution of damage done. . . . Falsehoods about a plunder system of tribute come from Hitlerites and Communists.'

In 1924 during his previous Premiership MacDonald had shown real statesmanship in whittling down Germany's liabilities under the reparations

---

*The construction of a second pocket battleship in deference to Hindenburg against Brüning's wishes was causing unpopularity.

clauses of Versailles in the belief that they were ruinous to Germany and the rest of Europe. At Chequers on 7 June 1931 he displayed none of this statesmanship. Then Curtius pooh-poohed a suggestion by Vansittart that Germany's financial problems might be solved by long-term loans, saying that the country was long past this point, and Brüning said the German people were in despair; it was very difficult for him to keep control, and the growing power of the Nazis and Communists was a menace. If elections had taken place in December instead of September 'the situation would have been hopeless'. This aroused no response from MacDonald. Leith-Ross told the Germans that 'there was no hope of any revision of the Young Plan', and deprecated the insistence of the German ministers that an autumn financial crisis in Germany was a 'certainty'. Not a word was said at Chequers about disarmament.[17]

A non-committal communiqué was agreed, and the German people were left with the impression that their Chancellor had been rebuffed, while the economic crisis continued to rage. Ominously, in Munich Goering said that Germany must repudiate reparations, and declaimed, 'Borrow as much as you like. We shall pay nothing back. Foreign countries had better turn over in their minds who will govern Germany next year. Brüning or us.' Here was the writing on the wall. The speech was prominently reported in *The Times*, but it had no effect on those in power in Britain, while in Paris Briand said that the Young Plan could not be modified. When Brüning landed at Bremerhaven there was a Nazi demonstration against him.[18]

MacDonald sent a personal letter to Stimson, the American Secretary of State, about the Chequers meeting. In it he drew attention to the 'ominous prospect' of the German Government surrendering 'to the forces of revolution either of the Left or the Right . . . the Hitlerites are still increasing . . . the root cause of their trouble they consider to be the payment of reparations . . . and they could not see how they could avoid asking for a moratorium in November.' MacDonald admitted that the Germans had asked for a British declaration of willingness to assist and that this had been refused, and he advised Stimson on his forthcoming visit to Europe to concentrate on disarmament and not to give any sort of expectation that 'you are coming prepared to discuss economic and financial things'. On this last point MacDonald was hopelessly unrealistic. Disarmament was a pipe-dream; the German economic crisis a potential disaster which only the creditor nation America could avert.[19]

Immediately after the Chequers meeting on 7 June Henderson wrote:

> I have just emerged from a busy weekend entertaining the Germans. I think they have gone away satisfied with their visit notwithstanding that it has been made clear to them that we could not undertake to discuss solutions of their difficulties unless other Governments interested were present.

54

The British Foreign Secretary had even less understanding of the troubles brewing for the German Government than had the Prime Minister. The German crisis deepened, and on 12 June Brüning threatened to resign. Bank rate was raised on 15 June from 5 per cent to 7 per cent.[20]

Then rumours spread across the world that Hoover was about to take dramatic action to help Germany, so that two days later *The Times* was able to report that although the German Government had said the country was nearly bankrupt last weekend, 'the financial crisis had ended'. Sackett, the American Ambassador in Berlin, had been instructed by Stimson to keep in the closest touch with Brüning, and he warned Washington that the Berlin stock market was falling alarmingly and that a complete financial collapse in Germany was inevitable within a few days; if a declaration of a moratorium was to save the situation it should be made before 1 July.

Hoover returned to Washington on 18 June, profoundly shocked at the poverty and distress he had witnessed when touring the Midwest. He found awaiting him reports from Andrew Mellon, Secretary of the Treasury, based on talks in London with Montagu Norman, Governor of the Bank of England, and the latest dispatches from the US Paris Embassy. These convinced Hoover that Germany was on the brink of a collapse, and that this rot would spread to other markets essential to American prosperity. The depression in the Midwest – which was uppermost in the President's mind – would thereby be greatly worsened.

After twenty-four hours of negotiations with the opposition political leaders Hoover asked the German President to send to him an urgent appeal for financial help, and on the evening of 20 June announced a twelve-month moratorium on all inter-governmental debts and reparations, both capital and interest, provided there was a similar postponement by the other creditor powers of inter-governmental debts owing to them.

On 20 June Leith-Ross had sent an urgent memorandum to the Prime Minister stating that the Berlin Embassy had advised that the situation had become so serious that the German Government was considering unilaterally announcing an immediate moratorium. Simultaneously the Governor of the Bank of England had warned the Treasury that the Reichsbank had had a very bad day, and had lost some 70 million marks of foreign currency. This had brought its reserves practically to the legal minimum, 'thus facing the risk of having to issue excess currency which would probably have accentuated the flight of currency'.

After consulting Montagu Norman the Prime Minister telephoned to Stimson and urged him to act at once. Stimson was not available until late at night, but when they talked he replied that the President had already decided to take action, and was in the process of issuing an announcement to the Press of a moratorium. The British Government was in no way responsible; it was a spontaneous gesture by Hoover on his own initiative.[21]

Great Britain, Italy and Germany greeted Hoover's offer with enthusiasm, and the President's stock in the world rose enormously. His move showed great courage, because it came at a moment when he had lost popularity at home and was facing a serious budgetary deficit shortly before the primaries were due. For Germany and the Brüning Government the Hoover proposal came 'like a reprieve to a condemned man on the gallows', and it appeared as if a new era was opening for Germany.

However, unlike Italy, France hesitated. She felt that there should be no tampering with the Young Plan, and the French press and politicians emphasized that when the Plan was drafted the large sums spent by France on restoring devastated areas and compensating war victims had been an important consideration. On 27 June Mellon arrived in Paris and warned Laval, the French Prime Minister, that if the Hoover Plan was rejected Germany would unquestionably declare her own moratorium – as she was entitled to do under the Young Plan – which would result in a much greater financial loss to France. Finally on 5 July, after Hoover made a dramatic personal appeal by telephone, Laval accepted with qualifications his proposal. The long-drawn-out quibbles of the French robbed the Hoover Plan of much of its immediate psychological value. However, they showed a certain perception in prophesying that Germany would be forced to ask for another moratorium at the end of the Hoover year, and the Hoover moratorium turned out to be a false dawn.

The French delaying tactics caused further German financial troubles. Bank rate was raised from 7 per cent to 10 per cent and the Lombard rate from 8 per cent to 15 per cent; while several emergency decrees had to be issued to restrict bank lending. In spite of this there were numerous bankruptcies, including the Danat Bank, and there were rumours that the Dresden Bank was in grave trouble. Alarmed by the news from Germany, the British Government called a Conference of Ministers to meet in London on 20 July. Stimson came from America. The results were meagre and made clear that France had not modified her policy to Germany. However, central and private banks agreed to provide Germany with more credit and gradually confidence in the mark returned. MacDonald and Henderson made a return visit to Berlin on 27–29 July; here MacDonald promised that the British Government would try and help Germany by reducing import tariffs – a promise on which he was to renege twelve months later. However, a constructive step was taken by the appointment of a Committee of Experts who began meeting at Basle on 8 August. The members included the Englishman Walter Layton and the American Albery

Wiggin, Governor of the Federal Reserve Bank of New York; these two were mainly responsible for the report of the experts.[22]

In late summer of 1931 a financial crisis hit Britain. Because of a Budgetary deficit which could have been remedied by a policy of retrenchment, the pound came under pressure. The Labour Government fell, to be replaced by a Conservative-dominated coalition in which MacDonald and Snowden retained their posts as Prime Minister and Chancellor of the Exchequer, but Henderson resigned with the majority of the Cabinet on 24 August, six days after the Layton–Wiggin Report was published. On 19 September the pound was devalued; Britain left the gold standard. Germany and France were adversely affected because the cheaper pound made British exports much cheaper, and German and French imports to Britain became more expensive. Devaluation was equivalent to imposing a swingeing all-round import tariff. For example, British coal became 2s. 6d. a ton cheaper than German coal, and the devaluation of the pound was a factor in the massive increase in unemployment in Germany which had risen to almost 6 million by the end of 1931.

Meanwhile, significantly, Rumbold reported from Berlin that the Hitlerites regarded opposition to the Young Plan and reparation or 'tribute' payments as their best political card.

On 7 October Lord Reading, the new Foreign Secretary, and Leith-Ross saw Laval, Flandin and Briand in Paris. Leith-Ross argued that reparations should be cancelled altogether; Laval replied it was 'politically impossible to wipe the slate completely', and that France must be assured of some reparations. He felt that any French Prime Minister who cancelled German reparations would lose votes, but that reparations were against the long-term interests of France.[23]

Meanwhile in Berlin Brüning was reconstructing his Cabinet without Curtius. On 11 October there was a sinister political move: at Bad Harzburg in the Harz mountains a large joint Nazi–Nationalist rally was held, at which both Hitler and Hugenberg spoke. Although the unity was only skin deep, the German press forecast that it signalled the fall of Brüning. Robin Hankey wrote a minute clearly expressing the Foreign Office attitude to the German political problem on 9 October: 'Brüning's loss of prestige is unfortunate but only too comprehensible after the Customs Union incident [the proposal for a German-Austrian Customs Union]. It remains to be seen whether the ship will ride the storm any better without Curtius.'[24]

In the autumn of 1931 the Nazis' popularity increased fast. In the local elections in Hesse on 16 November they doubled their vote although they did not get an overall majority. On 27 November the Berlin Embassy reported that a revolutionary document drafted by the Hessian Nazis had come to light, showing that Hitler would violate the Constitution if he came to power. Hitler repudiated the document, but it was genuine.[25]

In early December Hitler conceived the idea of visiting the important European capitals to meet foreign statesmen in order to correct 'misunderstandings' about the Nazi programme. With commendable loyalty to Britain and France, Mussolini sent a message that he would refuse to receive him if he came to Rome, and the British Ambassador in Rome was ordered in no circumstances to meet Hitler. Hitler was told his presence in London would be unwelcome, but he sent Rosenberg, his trusted lieutenant, on an exploratory visit. Rosenberg managed a chance meeting with Lord Hailsham at the Carlton Club, when the German said that a Nazi Government would pay their commercial debts, but no reparations. This was useful, as it gave one of the most anti-German and outspoken members of the Cabinet first-hand news that Hitler, if elected, would repudiate further reparations. Hailsham wrote accordingly to Simon (who had succeeded Reading as Foreign Secretary). Although it was a chance encounter, Rosenberg issued a press statement through the German Embassy that he had been 'received by Lord Hailsham'.[26]

Laval was in Washington from 22 to 25 October 1931. Following talks between him and the President it was agreed that after the end of the Hoover year the Young Plan must come into operation again. Hoover gave in to the French Prime Minister because he was worried about the forthcoming debate in Congress on the moratorium. This was a severe setback for Brüning. On 17 November Simon met Laval in Paris and agreed to leave it to a Committee of International Experts in Basle to report how much Germany could afford to pay in reparations.* They both hoped that after the report was published in December and Congress had approved the Hoover Moratorium, a fresh International Conference to solve the reparations problem could be held in either December 1931 or January 1932.[27]

On 22 December, after a long debate and bitter controversy, Congress approved the Moratorium Bill; unfortunately, it included a clause that it was expressly against the policy of Congress that no indebtedness of foreign countries to the United States should in any manner be cancelled or reduced. The next day the Basle Report was published, and stated that Germany would be justified – in accordance with her rights under the

---

*The Second Committee of Experts had members from Italy, Belgium, U.K., Germany, Japan, France and the USA; after it opened members were added from Switzerland, the Netherlands, Yugoslavia and Sweden. It was convened under Article 127 of the Young Plan, which gave Germany the right to refer reparations to the Bank of International Settlements if her financial position made it impossible to continue payments due.

Young Plan – to claim that 'in spite of the steps she had taken to maintain the stability of her currency' she would not be able, in the year beginning July 1932, to pay the reparations due. The report also concluded that the fundamental economic basis for the Young Plan no longer existed because of the collapse in world trade, and 'In the circumstances the German problem . . . calls for concerted action which the Governments alone can take.' There was disappointment in Germany and in some circles in Britain and the USA that the Report had not recommended a further moratorium or a cancellation of reparations. However, this was impossible because then the French representative could have insisted on a minority report on which Laval would have stuck in the forthcoming negotiations.

The report was constructive in so far as it recommended a long-term loan *to* Germany and that if this was to be effective the payments *by* Germany on account of reparations must not be 'such as to imperil the maintenance of her financial stability'. It also called for a reduction in tariff barriers, which were impeding the free movement of goods. It was unanimous, and it was significant that the French financial expert Moreau after much heart-searching agreed to sign it.

With the publication of the second Basle Report and Congressional approval of the moratorium the stage was set for a new Reparations Conference. Unfortunately, it was delayed for six months, and this interval was too long for Brüning. When he read the Basle Report, MacDonald exclaimed: 'For God's sake let us meet at once!' and the British Government issued invitations for a conference at The Hague on 18 January. These were accepted in principle by the other powers, but for technical reasons the conference was postponed and the venue changed from The Hague to Lausanne.[28]

Brüning in January tried desperately to create an united German front for the Disarmament Conference at Geneva and for the Reparations Conference, conferring for several days with Hitler and Hugenberg. The Nazis hesitated, but then realizing that Brüning's difficulties over reparations would give them an opportunity for an electoral success, refused all co-operation. On 17 January 1932 Hitler sent Brüning a memorandum terminating the talks. Robert Boothby saw him on the same day. He wrote to Simon that he found the German Chancellor 'tired and despondent and emphasising the need for international economic cooperation if the collapse of Central Europe was to be avoided'; Brüning also complained of the burden of social relief and unemployment pay. Boothby told Brüning that public opinion in Britain 'was in favour of all round cancellations (of reparations) but not much hope was entertained of a satisfactory settlement at Lausanne'. Boothby saw Hitler the same evening. The Nazi leader struck Boothby as being 'rather truculent, absolutely sincere with the passion of a genuine fanatic, and not very intelligent'. Hitler's staff told Boothby that they were sure the Brüning Government would soon fall.[29]

Brüning announced on 9 January that Germany was unable to pay reparations 'either now or in the future if the economic life of the world is to be revived', and the German delegation at the Lausanne Conference must press for the total abolition of reparations. Although Brüning's statement was the natural corollary of the Basle Report, it aroused a storm of protest in France. Flandin, the French Minister of Finance, said,

> It amounts to the annulling of the Versailles Treaty and the Young Plan, and makes the holding of the Lausanne Conference useless. France cannot accept Germany's unilateral denunciation of reparations compacts freely signed which means the destruction of France's sacred rights to reparations.

Laval asked Edge, the American Ambassador in Paris, what was the American attitude. The official American reply was the same as it had been in 1922: that there was no connection between reparations and the war debts owed to America; France's attention was drawn to the hostility of Congress to cancellation, the initiative must come from Europe and the United States would view with disfavour any 'united front of debtors to whom it could not give any general undertaking', while the United States was convinced that Europe could pay her debts if she restored mutual confidence and reduced armament expenditure. A general election was due in France, and Laval was reluctant to enter into a Reparations Conference where he would be isolated in opposition to cancellation of reparations. Accordingly Laval asked the British for a postponement and on 13 February it was agreed to postpone it until 16 June.

Hitler stood against Hindenburg in the presidential election in March 1932 and although Hindenburg won, the Nazi vote everywhere showed a large and disturbing increase. Hitler polled 11 million in the first ballot and increased his vote by 2 million in the second, showing that the Nazi vote had doubled since the Reichstag elections. Local elections in Prussia, Bavaria, Württemberg and Hamburg on 24 April provided further evidence of the increasing popularity of the Nazis. Eleven days before polling in the presidential election the Brüning Government declared Hitler's storm troopers 'illegal'. This resulted in a furore; most German generals welcomed the existence of the storm-troopers as a reservoir of men trained in the use of weapons for recruitment to a new German army, and for this reason condoned their excesses and maltreatment of the Jews. General Gröner, Minister of the Interior, was forced to resign over the issue.

Brüning's position was weak. He had somehow to balance the German budget, and needed an assurance from the re-elected President of confidence in his government to carry him over the Lausanne and Geneva Conferences. With Lausanne only three weeks away, he submitted to Hindenburg a batch of emergency decrees providing for reductions in war pensions and unemployment pay. He also asked for powers to expropriate the owners of bankrupt agricultural estates in East Prussia in order to provide land on which to settle smallholders. This was too much for Hindenburg. The landowners to be expropriated were what he had come to think of as his own caste, and he turned down Brüning's proposal, hoping that the latter would then reconstruct his Cabinet with more right-wing Ministers. On 28 May the President and the Chancellor conferred while news came that in the Oldenburg local elections the Nazis had secured a majority over all other parties. Brüning resigned; the President pressed him to stay on in a new administration as Foreign Minister. Brüning refused, and quit with his whole Cabinet. This was a disaster. Had Brüning led the German delegation to Lausanne he would have insisted on cancellation of reparations and, supported by Britain and Italy must have carried the day. In that case the main propaganda weapon of the Nazi Party would have been spiked.

The Nazis, Socialists and the Catholic centre were the three main German political parties, and Hindenburg's choice as the new Chancellor fell on von Papen of the Catholic centre – also Brüning's party. Hindenburg thought that, although Papen had minimal personal political support, he would emerge as a successful leader to fight extremism and to reach an accommodation with the Nazis. General Schleicher became Minister of Defence, and he immediately lifted the ban on the SA and the SS. However, the new Foreign Minister, von Neurath, had earned a good reputation as Ambassador in Rome and Berlin and the new Finance Minister, Count Schwerin von Krosigk, was a former Rhodes scholar much respected in European financial circles.

Meanwhile Britain and Italy had moved to the 'clean slate' policy of cancelling all Germany's obligations to pay reparations; in place of a five-year moratorium.

Neville Chamberlain, Chancellor of the Exchequer, wrote to Leith-Ross on 2 January: 'We seem to have got into rather a tangle over reparations . . . I myself would prefer to stick to cancellation . . . a stopgap which lasts for 5 years appears to me to involve the danger that no-one will consider cancellation until the 5 years are up.'[30]

Tyrrell from Paris expressed hopes that many people in France realized that reparations were dead after speaking to Philippe Berthelot, permanent head of the French Foreign Office, who stated he 'had never had any doubt that once payment was suspended last July reparations were dead . . . French opinion had not yet realized the situation, but French opinion could be educated.' In February Leith-Ross wrote to Layton, 'In France . . . a good many people realize that reparations are dead . . . the only question is to find a means of giving it a decent burial.' On 30 March Leith-Ross minuted to the Chancellor of the Exchequer, 'French opinion has moved a great deal since last year and I believe we can, without great difficulty, secure agreement on a cancellation of debts and reparations.'

On 13 May Leith-Ross minuted to Chamberlain about 'them [the Foreign Office] expecting us [the Treasury] to give Dr Brüning a strong warning about the "risks of making public pronouncements which could bar the way to possible compromises', and said that when he talked to the Foreign Secretary on the next day, he proposed to take the line that Britain should eschew a compromise solution and insist instead on 'the policy of cancellation which we really favour'. He asked Chamberlain if this had his approval, and Chamberlain minuted: 'I entirely agree with these views.'[31]

On 26 May (two days before Brüning's resignation) Simon minuted that Brüning had denied the possibility of Germany resuming payment of reparations, and rejected in advance 'any suggestion that she should agree to make even a modified payment in certain contingencies at some time in the future', and 'Dr. Brüning does not intend, in any event, to be a party to any new promise which he does not see his way to perform, and he will accomplish his intention by making no new promise whatever'. According to Simon the government must accept this, and on the question whether France would agree to cancellation of reparations,

> She would certainly wish to attach the condition that there should be a cancellation of debts (e.g. by France to Britain and Britain to USA), whereas, on the above view, Germany would be asserting that reparations must be treated as finally dropped whatever may be the other consequences. [If Germany] makes this unilateral declaration, and there is no agreement regarding it, then, unquestionably, France will declare that she is unable to pay her debt to us. Our situation will then be that we are receiving neither reparations from Germany nor debt from France . . . They are accomplished facts which we have not agreed to bring about, and which we cannot prevent. Is it not a possible view that, as compared with any *practicable* alternative, this is the best position in which we can stand *vis-à-vis* the United States of America?

Thus Simon was now proposing a policy which if put into effect would have vastly strengthened the democratic parties in Germany and weakened the Nazis. Had the British stood firm on Simon's policy the French would have been isolated and forced to come into line.

On 31 May Simon, without the Prime Minister and the Chancellor of the Exchequer, held a conference with Treasury and Foreign Office officials. After the conference he wrote a memorandum for the Cabinet arguing urgently for the 'clean slate' policy.

1) We suggest that at Lausanne a resolution should be passed by the Powers there assembled to the effect that it is in the interests of the world that there should be all round cancellation of reparations.

2) This should lead to a treaty which would acknowledge the obligations of Germany to pay reparations should be treated as discharged by payments already made and that the war debts owed by European powers to one another should similarly be discharged. If default is not to occur the Treaty should be signed by 1 July.

3) USA presidential elections take place on 5 November and next instalment of war debts due to USA payable on 15 December. If Hoover wins he might take the bold line as we wish. A Democratic victory would postpone such a possibility until March at earliest. The British attitude should be an inversion of the Balfour note. We shall have to decline to pay even a reduced sum since we shall be getting nothing at all from Germany or from our European debtors. The procedure above outlined would at any rate give America the opportunity of joining in an all round cancellation; then the British taxpayer will certainly demand that we make no more payments.

It will in present circumstances be difficult enough anyhow to secure that the German spokesman at Lausanne does not blurt out Germany's resolve to repudiate in a provocative form. I should have thought that if, and only if, the British Cabinet has a scheme for Lausanne already settled and agreed with the French, it ought to be possible to make representations to Germany as to the best way in which the Germans' case should be stated.[32]

On 7 June there were two ministerial meetings with MacDonald, Baldwin, Chamberlain, Runciman and Simon. Simon's statesmanlike view prevailed and his memorandum was circulated to the other members of the Cabinet, who agreed on 8 June 'in the interests of the world recovery that there should be [at Lausanne] an all-round cancellation of reparations and war debts' which should lead up to a treaty with Germany' which would acknowledge 'that the obligations of Germany to pay reparations should be treated as discharged by payments already made, and that the war debts by European powers to one another should similarly be regarded as dis-charged'. The French decision must be made before 15 December, when the next instalment should be made.[33]

With this Cabinet decision all seemed set for a successful Lausanne Conference to herald a new dawn for Europe, with the reparations problem which had for so long bedevilled Germany's relations with the rest of Europe successfully solved. Unfortunately, Simon was to be occupied by the Disarmament Conference along the bank of Lake Geneva; and MacDonald and Chamberlain failed to stick to their guns when faced with French obstinacy. The result was tragedy.

Papen, who has been almost universally run down by historians, made a good impression when the second Lausanne Conference opened on 16 June 1932. Leith-Ross wrote that, considering he was new to diplomacy, he put his points clearly and sensibly without indulging in the exhibitionism which many Germans love.[34]

Leith-Ross also remarked that MacDonald was 'ageing, and often got very tired when he tended to give a wrong impression and I had continually to run round to see other delegates to correct misapprehensions'. As a result British responsibility fell largely on Neville Chamberlain. He much enjoyed this position, and was impressed by Papen's smooth delivery in flawless French.

Chamberlain wrote in his diary:

> Papen kicked off with an extremely good exposition of German conditions . . . Herriot followed, conciliatory to the Germans but making no sign of what he was prepared to give . . . I followed with a short but very definite pronouncement in favour of cancellation though I did not use that word . . . I am told that my speech produced a great effect and certainly my people and the Dominions reps were delighted with it.

On 19 June he wrote to his sister Hilda: 'I don't know why *The Times* suppressed my speech . . . My people are furious about it and it certainly was extremely stupid of them, if not worse, for it made a great impression and gave us the lead.' Unfortunately, Chamberlain was now falling for the charms of the French, and in the same letter commented about Herriot: 'I must say he is very attractive . . . and a capital raconteur.'

Initially MacDonald held to the 'clean slate' policy endorsed by the Cabinet on 8 June; Chamberlain wrote to Ida on 20 June that MacDonald had been encouraged by discussions with Americans: 'It helps to keep PM himself firmly on the path for cancellation which I have sometimes feared he might leave under pressure from the Yanks.'

France was isolated and MacDonald battled on as head of the British, German, Italian, Belgian 'clean-slate' brigade, but Chamberlain, on a flying visit to London at the end of June, reported to his Cabinet colleagues that the British delegation had been greatly disappointed once the conference began in real earnest because they found the French far more at variance with them than they had expected 'from the hopeful and encouraging reports they had received from the British Embassy in Paris . . . Day after day passed without any appreciable progress being made,' and while the Germans were very helpful and conciliatory, as Dr Brüning's Government had been, 'the real difficulties' were with the French.[35]

Although the French agreed Germany could pay nothing in the immediate future, they refused to abandon the principle of the Young Plan and wanted safeguards to prevent Germany gaining unfair economic advantages at the expense of France in the event of her economic recovery. The French broke down MacDonald's resistance by arguing that 'complete cancellation

. . . would be the best means of creating a spirit of hostility in the United States . . . The way to spare American feeling was to maintain a "relic" of reparation payments.'[36]

The first direct contact between Papen and Herriot went well, but both Premiers spent the weekend of 25–26 June at home. Things did not go so well afterwards. Herriot reported to MacDonald on Monday, 27 June, that before the weekend Papen had given him the impression that if France abandoned reparation payments Germany would give her economic and political compensations, and Papen had also mentioned the possibility of a military alliance between France and Germany and continuous contact between the General Staffs. Papen had ill-advisedly leaked this to the Press. Herriot went on that on his return from Berlin Papen was in quite a different mood, 'simply saying that Germany could not make any more reparation payments. As regards compensation, he had spoken only of certain help for Central Europe . . .' Herriot attributed the change to the influence brought to bear upon him in Berlin. Herriot also told MacDonald that in Paris the Cabinet had accepted his view that Franco-German reconciliation was better than 'a mere money payment'.

MacDonald saw Papen half an hour later and warned the German Chancellor off his idea of a military alliance between France and Germany because 'it would upset everything. It would completely destroy any chance of getting the United States to look favourably on such action as might be taken at Lausanne in regard to economic questions.' Papen admitted he had talked to the Press, but had been misrepresented, with the result that there had been bitter attacks on him in Berlin. Papen begged MacDonald to convince the French how close Germany was to revolution.[37]

The next day Neurath said the German condition for making any further payment would be 'a settlement of Disarmament on the basis of equality of rights'. Herriot found this German argument illogical, because Germany recognized the rights of the creditor powers to reparations although she could not pay now or in the future, but if the creditor powers would give Germany satisfaction on disarmament they could pay: this destroyed the German thesis about the impossibility of paying.[38]

Herriot's evidence that his Cabinet would have agreed to cancellation shows that MacDonald, as chairman, threw away a good chance of a settlement of the 'clean slate' terms approved by the British Cabinet.* If Brüning had led the German delegation this *would* have been achieved, but

---

*Chamberlain told the Cabinet in London on 30 June that the British delegation had ascertained from a most reliable source that when Herriot had returned to Paris he had formed the definite opinion that cancellation of reparations was inevitable and had persuaded the French Cabinet to give him a free hand, subject to one or two conditions.[40]

At this point Ramsay became ill, showing signs of acute strain with severe headaches. As a result Neville Chamberlain took charge. On this, his first important encounter with other European leaders, he failed. Instead of pursuing the agreed British policy of a 'clean slate' he now argued for a final payment by Germany, which was pandering to the French. His letter to his wife of 3 July is revealing:

> things had got in a sad tangle while I was away . . . I have the consciousness that I have done very good work since I got back. Leith-Ross was in despair over the woolliness of the talks . . . he openly rejoiced in the return to clarity. . . . I think he [MacDonald] is getting rather to depend on me.

The next day he wrote to his sister Ida:

> I get on very well with the French – the Wigrams declare that Herriot "adores" me and also with the Germans though I must say the latter, especially von Papen, are incredibly stupid. . . . The Italians I dislike very much.

Such self-congratulation was misplaced. Chamberlain had swung round to the French view that Germany should pay a lump sum regardless of the boost thios was bound to give to Nazi popularity inside Germany. On 3 July MacDonald, prompted by Chamberlain, suggested to the Germans that they should pay 4 milliard marks as a reasonable final forfeit, and in that case some removal of the war guilt clause of Versailles 'might be managed'. Papen replied 4 milliard was as much as the French had paid after the 1870 war, and offered 2 millions on the basis that such a small sum would not cause the German people to turn to Hitler.

Here Papen made a fatal error which put the future of democracy in Germany at stake. If he was to have any chance of spiking Hitler's guns his only option was, like Brüning, to insist on a 'clean slate'.

The French, by now scenting a victory which would improve their electoral position, refused the 2 millard offer. Papen then with incredible folly upped his offer to 2.6 millard provided Germany was given parity of arms and the war guilt clause of Versailles was abandoned, stating 'Only by returning with the diplomatic triumph of a 'clean slate' [e.g. over arms and war guilt] could he retain his credibility with the German people'. Papen's effort to obtain concessions over war guilt and arms during a conference convened solely to deal with reparations revealed his shortcomings and inexperience. The British and French pointed out correctly that the Disarmament Conference was the only place where equality of arms could be discussed. According to Chamberlain's diary the French now became worried that MacDonald and Papen had hatched up some secret German-British agreement, and they were in hysterics, 'Herriot even shedding tears.'

On the afternoon of 7 July draft formulas were prepared, leaving the amount to be paid by Germany blank. Chamberlain urged the Gemans to agree to a payment of 3 milliard, and suggested some sort of political formula would mitigate the German defeat and make it politically acceptable in Germany, arguing that as the French were now ready to accept 3 milliards the Germans would be taking the responsibility of wrecking the conference 'for the sake of 400 million marks'. He might equally well have said the French were wrecking it for the same sum. Chamberlain added the British would have preferred 'cancellation', but the USA and France 'rendered cancellation impossible'. Here Chamberlain was distorting the facts. After all, he had agreed with Simon in London that a 'clean slate' would put Britain into the best position *vis-à-vis* the USA.[42]

At a further meeting the next morning (8 July) Simon came from Geneva. The British failed to persuade the Germans to budge from 2.6 millards. Papen said he would consult his Cabinet in Berlin by telephone, and the British then met the French. Chamberlain said they had refused to put a German offer before the French of less than 3 milliards for which he was thanked effusively by Herriot. At 12.45 p.m. the British had a final meeting with the Germans and bullied them to agree – without any reciprocal concession over war guilt or equality of arms – to the figure of 3 milliards. Chamberlain put in his diary: 'I had warm congratulations from Runciman, Simon and our own boys (but none from the P.M!)'

Simon, who had put the case for a 'clean slate' so powerfully and cogently in London, had now eaten his own words. As Foreign Secretary it was his duty to warn his colleagues of the inevitable disastrous effects of forcing Papen to agree to Germany paying reparations. He failed utterly. MacDonald, already far past his best, was having a nervous breakdown.

Chamberlain was the driving force in abandoning the policy of the 'clean slate' and bullying Papen, into acceptance of 3 milliard.

Papen said in evidence at his Nuremberg trial that at Lausanne he warned MacDonald and Herriot that if they did not give him a diplomatic triumph his was the last democratic government they would see in Germany and his successors would be extremists of the Right or Left. This made a strong impression, and helped towards his acquittal.[43]

In his memoirs Papen wrote, 'When MacDonald made his report to the House of Commons he received an ovation . . . Herriot in his turn received a great welcome from the French Chamber. His position had been strengthened. But when I returned to Germany our delegation was received at the railway station with a shower of bad eggs and rotten apples.'[44]

The Nazi press in Germany indulged in violent abuse of Papen – even the *Deutsche Allgemeine Zeitung* was unfavourable, although it was usually the Government's chief organ. Hitler's newspaper, *Angriff,* called Lausanne strengthened. But when I returned to Germany our delegation was received at the railway station with a shower of bad eggs and rotten apples.'[44]

The Nazi press in Germany indulged in violent abuse of Papen – even the *Deutsche Allgemeine Zeitung* was unfavourable, although it was usually the Government's chief organ. Hitler's newspaper, *Angriff*, called Lausanne 'catastrophic' and said that 'before it comes into force it requires ratification by the German Parliament. The National Socialist Party will not approve of it in any form.' Other Nazi newspapers made a more sophisticated point by asking whether it was in good taste for Papen to discuss a point of honour such as the war guilt question in conjunction with the financial question. Goebbels condemned the agreement and declared the 3 milliard marks Germany had promised to pay would suffice to wipe out unemployment at one blow. The extreme Nationalist *Deutsche Zeitung* rejected the agreement on the grounds that Germany had again assumed obligations which she could not fulfil. The *Tägliche Rundschau*, the organ of the Evangelical peasants, considered the agreement disastrous and that Hindenburg should have dismissed the Chancellor, and Parliament should reject it. The staid financial daily *Börsen-Zeitung* commented: 'It is incomprehensible that the German delegation abandoned its condition that the final German payment must be the settlement of the political question'. Papen had been ham-handed. If he had stuck to Brüning's policy that no further payment of reparations was possible, and not tried to intrigue with the French, he would have had the support of the British and won the day.[45]

If the Nazis were to be kept out of power it was essential the Papen Government obtained a diplomatic triumph. Having failed at Lausanne, their last chance depended on success at the Disarmament Conference already in progress at Geneva. As will be seen in the next chapter, they were also robbed of any victory there. The Lausanne agreement was never ratified. Hitler would pay nothing, and Europe defaulted on her US debt with adverse consequences on American public opinion.

CHAPTER FOUR

THE DISARMAMENT
CONFERENCE FAILS

On the eve of the July 1932 General Election Papen said: 'It is unbearable that fourteen years after the end of the war there is no equality of rights [to arms] for us.' The election doubled the Nazi vote from 6.4 million to 13.7 million.

On 6 February 1934 when Hitler was Chancellor, John Simon told the Commons 'Germany's equality of rights could not be resisted.'

AS FAR back as 1925 the Council of the League of Nations had set up a Commission to prepare a Disarmament Conference. Germany, the United States and Russia (who were not League members) were invited, and agreed to take part. However, the preparatory commission did not report until December 1930 and the Conference finally met on 2 February 1932. Arthur Henderson, who had been Foreign Secretary until the fall of Labour in 1931, was Chairman, and in his report on the Conference published after its demise in 1935 shortly before his death he wrote:

> Little or nothing was done in the year between the convocation and the actual meeting of the Conference to obtain in advance some measure of agreement upon fundamental issues . . . suggestions differing widely from one another were therefore submitted from the outset, and these suggestions had to be discussed by the Conference before it could take any useful decision on outstanding political problems. It was soon evident the initial impetus of the Conference would spend itself in a series of fruitless decisions.[1]

The Conference was over-ambitious in that there were too many participants (sixty-two); the complete unwillingness of many governments to agree to restrictions on their national sovereignty was the rock on which it foundered. As a result no agreement could be reached on an effective international control of individual countries' armed forces. This should have been the first question discussed, and progress in other directions could never be made with this key question unsolved. Any Convention for the reduction or limitation of national armies must depend on an efficient system of permanent international control, including rights of inspection and provision of 'sanctions' against any offending power.

The Treaty of Versailles had imposed a permanent system of control on Germany; this was the Allied Military Commission of Control which had wide powers, including entry to factories without notice, and German arms manufacture was limited to specially licensed factories. Any new supernational international authority on these lines would considerably diminish national sovereignty, and at the Disarmament Conference it soon became clear that the United States, Great Britain, Germany, Italy and Japan would never consent to such restraints; of the great powers only France and the Soviet Union were agreeable.

That France accepted this loss of soverignty is proof of her deep involvement in plans to outlaw war, as a result of her appalling experiences in the Franco-Prussian war and the First World War. With Britain refusing France an automatic guarantee of armed help in the event of an attack by Germany, the French Government were prepared to grasp at any straw as it became more and more frightened by German rearmament. A reduction or limitation on national armed forces could not be discussed usefully except in the context of the necessary sacrifice of national sovereignty which makes control and supervision possible; effective international control of arms is incompatible with a totalitarian government, and it was naive to take Hitler's proposals for control of German armaments seriously. Particularly abortive was the discussion of the supervision of civil aviation to prevent governments using civil planes as bombers.

At Geneva soon after the Conference opened Brüning proposed in conversation with the British, French and American delegates that in return for an undertaking by Germany not to increase her armaments for five years, or until a second Disarmament Conference, she should be allowed to reduce her twelve-year service in the Reichswehr to five (to produce more trained men); to organize a militia and to purchase war material forbidden under the Treaty of Versailles, including offensive weapons such as tanks and aeroplanes, but he promised Germany would renounce all these if the other powers did the same. MacDonald, Stimson and Grandi (Italian Foreign Minister) considered this reasonable and an agreement came in sight which would have greatly increased Brüning's popularity in Germany and if combined with a 'clean slate' over reparations might have prevented the fall of his government. However, Tardieu the French Prime Minister, turned it down flat and refused to return to Geneva on the fictitious grounds that he had laryngitis. As a result matters were allowed to drift. Wheeler-Bennett wrote: 'The Allies were sending Dr. Brüning back to Germany with empty pockets, and were apparently unaware either that they were encompassing his defeat or of the fact that he would be succeeded by men of very different character.'[2]

British performance at the Conference was deplorable. They arrived without proposals of any kind, and during the proceedings opposed almost all those made by other delegations. The Soviet Government presented a draft convention for complete general disarmament, and an alternative plan for a reduction of 50 per cent by the heavily armed powers. The French put forward a comprehensive plan for the reduction and limitation of armaments. Neither the French nor the Soviet plan was properly discussed. In June 1932 President Hoover submitted an American proposal for a reduction of nearly one-third in the arms of the world, and the abolition of all bombing planes. Most delegations declared themselves in favour of the Hoover plan in principle, but in Henderson's words 'In certain cases such acceptance was accompanied by reservations rendering unlikely a practical or immediate application of the proposals.' Simon reduced discussion on the Hoover plan to absurdity by suggesting the appointment of expert committees to adjudicate on which arms were 'offensive' and which were not. How did he imagine any arms could be defined as solely defensive except coast defence and anti-aircraft guns? It must always depend on how they are used. When the Conference began Germany more or less could have been trusted to honour an agreement contributing to peace in Europe which they signed. The German press was campaigning for equality of rights to arms for Germany, and nothing less would satisfy German public opinion. When it was clear that the other powers would not agree to parity the German Chancellor von Papen in September 1932 withdrew from the Conference as a sop to internal German opinion. The Conference was then suspended for three months. However, on 11 December the British, French and Italian Governments declared that one of the principles which in future would guide the conference 'should be the grant to Germany, and to the other Powers disarmed by treaty, of equality of rights in a system which would provide security for all nations.'[3]

This generous gesture to the dying Weimar Republic followed ten days of secret five-power negotiations in Geneva between the USA, France, Germany, Italy and Britain, during which MacDonald, backed by Norman Davis, the USA delegate, appealed successfully to Herriot to abandon the French hard line. If only the French had conceded German parity during the first few weeks of the Conference when Brüning was German

71

Chancellor, it might have halted the rise to power of the Nazis. 'Equality' would have been a setback for the Nazis. In his memoirs Papen complains that the 11 December communiqué came a few days too late to save his government, as he had been obliged to resign the week before and had been replaced by Schleicher. Undoubtedly the 11 December statement would have saved the Papen government temporarily, but his was an unpopular administration with nothing like the hold on the nation nor the prospect of a long period in power which the Brüning government would have had if they could have produced diplomatic successes in 1932.[4]

On Germany's claim for equality of rights Leeper minuted on 4 January 1933: 'If we cannot get ahead with disarmament during the next four to five months we shall forfeit at least in Germany's eyes the moral right to prevent Germany from rearming.' This summed up both the Foreign Office view and that of most thinking people in Britain (but not in France). But when Leeper wrote this there were not four to five months left; it was less than four weeks before Hitler's assumption of power.[5]

In the German general election on 1 July 1932 the Nazis made another startling advance. With 13¾ million votes, they had 230 seats, to become the largest party in the Reichstag – although this was not a majority in a Parliament with 608 members. Hitler claimed the Chancellorship but Hindenburg refused, and the Papen government carried on. On 6 November another German general election was held. Although the Nazis lost 2 million votes and 34 seats, Papen tried to persuade Hitler to join his government but the Nazi leader would not do so, and Hindenburg made the pro-Nazi General von Schleicher Chancellor in place of von Papen. The Schleicher Government only lasted fifty-seven days, and on 30 January 1933 Hitler became Chancellor.

Under Schleicher Germany returned to the Conference, and the Hitler government also took part, but although the Nazi leader indulged in bogus conciliatory talk, he was only intent on creating as quickly as possible the most powerful German army, navy and air force he could contrive. The Disarmament Conference had been sitting for twelve months before Hitler came to power, but progress had been minimal.

At first there were only three other Nazis in Hitler's Cabinet. Papen was Vice Chancellor, and the Nationalists Hugenberg, Seldte and Blomberg remained. Fresh elections were held following the burning of the Reichstag on 5 March 1933. The Nazi vote went down, not up, but they emerged with 44 per cent of the total vote. Then 81 Communist MPs were arrested and in their absence the Nazis obtained a parliamentary majority for an Enabling Act which gave Hitler absolute power as a dictator, with only 81 Social

Democrat MPs voting against it. On 21 June Hitler arrested the opposition youth movements and outlawed the Social Democrat party. Hugenberg, who had until then zealously promoted the Nazi Party, resigned.

Horace Rumbold, the British Ambassador in Berlin, left the Foreign Office in no doubt about Hitler's intentions. On 2 March he reported that the German Government had two major dilemmas – 'how to extirpate Communism in Germany without antagonising the Soviet Government and how to extirpate parliamentary government without antagonising the rest of the world'. By 20 March he was forecasting that Hitler's action in incorporating the uniformed youth movements in the police had thereby increased 'the armed and militarised forces of Germany by many hundred thousand men', and that Goering, the new Air Minister, had announced his intention of building an air force, while Communists, Jews and intellectuals were being persecuted and fleeing the country. These exiles went mostly to Paris, so that the situation had already turned Herriot (French Prime Minister) into 'an impassioned advocate of a Franco-Soviet alliance – just as Bismarck forced Republican France to turn to Tsarist Russia'. When complaints were made that British and American subjects had been molested by Nazis, Hitler sent a message that 'if any member of his party had been implicated . . . he would have them put up against a wall and shot'. To read that a west European country was going to shoot citizens without trial must have been a severe shock to Sir John Simon.[6]

By 2 March Eden (Under-Secretary at the Foreign Office) was telling the Cabinet's Disarmament Committee that the Conference 'was tottering to failure', because the Germans were working against the French and had the support of Italy, while France was very apprehensive about Hitler's government. This induced MacDonald to state:

> We must make a really big final effort to save the Conference otherwise he would feel that he might have to go to the Cabinet and warn them that they would have to be prepared for war in two years time.

Because of the crisis in Geneva the Committee met again the next day, when Eden told them the German diplomats Nadolny and von Rheinbaben had told *him* 'quite frankly that the German Delegation (at Geneva) were working under great difficulties at present and their instructions were absolutely rigid and allowed no latitude'. Here was evidence that normal diplomacy was unsuitable with the German dictatorship. However, it was decided that Ramsay and Simon should go to Geneva to try to resolve the deadlock.

Two days later Hailsham argued strongly against putting forward a plan at Geneva, calling the idea a big blunder. He and Cunliffe-Lister told the Disarmament Committee that by any plan to do so we should be deluding

France into the belief that we were giving her security which in fact we had no intention of providing.[7]

Nazi spokesmen claimed in speeches that as a demilitarized zone existed in Germany a similar zone should be established in France; it did not bode well for the resumption of the Disarmament Conference. When Mac-Donald and Simon met Daladier, the French Prime Minister, in Paris on 10 March 1933 Daladier said correctly that Goering was organizing 'a real military air force without taking any account of the treaty clauses forbidding this'. He did not want to quote 'other facts which were very numerous', but they were running the risk of finding themselves faced by a sudden increase in the German forces and armaments in violation even of the Locarno Agreements. German troops and Hitlerite auxiliary police had marched to the middle of the Rhine bridges on the frontier and as a result of the incorporation of the paramilitary forces in the regular forces Germany had actual 'superiority over France'. Daladier added that France had a 'certain superiority in respect of material [*matériel*]'.[8] But Germany had 'increased enormously' her purchase of scrap steel from France to make weapons, so that the French Government had intervened and stopped the export.

Another ominous sign for the Disarmament Conference was a speech by Goering at Essen on 11 March in which he said the time had now come to restore Germany to her place in the air. 'All attempts at Geneva to destroy the German Air Force just as it had begun to recover would be shattered against her resistance.' On 13 March, to the British Prime Minister's annoyance, Boncour, French Foreign Minister, told him privately in Geneva that it was important Germany should be shown responsible if the Disarmament Conference failed, and that although France had given proof of her goodwill Germany had opposed every proposal, and had given proof that she 'had no intention of assisting towards a settlement'.[9]

MacDonald replied that the French point of view would 'mean war' because Germany would be released from all her obligations, and would proceed as soon as possible to rearm. Now desperate to prevent the Conference collapsing, MacDonald on 16 March submitted a British Draft Convention to the Conference. In his speech he said, 'You must all make sacrifices.' Diplomatic correspondents immediately commented that he had said 'you' not 'we' because his Convention replaced the disarmament clauses of Versailles and provided for the almost complete and immediate restoration of the armies of Germany and the other defeated powers, and argued that the convention would give Germany equality of rights for land forces – which were no threat to Britain – but not for air and sea forces (which were dangerous to Britain). It says a lot for the French desire to co-operate with the British that the French accepted MacDonald's Convention as a basis of discussion, because it implied a reduction in the size of the

French army. Cynical journalists wrote that the Convention was more a rearmament convention than a disarmament convention although it proposed 'the complete abolition of military and naval aircraft'. However, it soon became clear in discussion that the proposals for supervision of these clauses were impracticable. The weakness of the MacDonald convention lay in its inadequate powers of enforcement. A permanent disarmament commission was suggested, composed of one member from each government signing the Convention. The Commission was to investigate only when alleged infractions of the Convention were demanded by one or more governments, but there were no provisions for any action against a government violating it. The French (with every reason) insisted that there must be a preliminary period during which armaments should be limited to existing levels to prove that supervision could be made to work.

Hitler put an abrupt end to the negotiations over the MacDonald plan on 11 May, when he ordered copies of an article by Neurath to be circulated to all delegates at Geneva. Rumbold summarized it thus:

It has become clear that the highly armed States, above all France and her Allies, are not ready to agree to the demand of the disarmed States that they should disarm down to the level already imposed on the latter. Further, it is clear that in spite of their fair speeches they are wholly lacking in the will to carry out a genuine decrease in armaments.

Germany could not accept any agreement for limitation which did not give practical effect to the equality of rights accorded to Germany by the Agreement of 11 December.

The English plan is to be welcomed as an attempt to bring the Conference to practical results . . . Is it to be hoped that the air arm or even bombing planes will in future be generally forbidden and that the existing air fleets will be abolished? Certainly not. This means that Germany must establish for her own security a military and naval air force. Nor is it to be hoped that guns above 10.5 cm. will be abolished and destroyed. Therefore Germany must have guns of higher calibre . . . Similar steps must be taken as regards effectives.

Germany's demands have been used as a pretext for vilifying her before the world and for calling into question her desire for disarmament . . . That which the other States demand for their own security can no longer be refused to the security of Germany.

Eden immediately telephoned Vansittart from Geneva and asked for the Cabinet to be informed that he considered the article a notification from an authoritative quarter of the intention [by Germany] to disregard the MacDonald plan. This Plan had until then been taken as a basis of discussion by all the delegations, including the Germans. Vansittart asserted that the Germans 'simply intend to help themselves notably in regard to guns and aviation', adding that it was an unequivocal demand by Hitler for unlimited German rearmament unless France agreed to disarm.[10]

75

Hitler never wavered from this point of view, although he wrapped up his intentions in ambiguous phrases. The British Government should have taken Neurath's statement at its face value. It already possessed incontrovertible evidence of the tyrannical and warlike nature of the Hitler regime and should have considered force to restrain him as the French wanted.

They did nothing of the sort. When the Disarmament Committee met on 12 May to consider the bad news from Geneva, only Lord Hailsham sounded a note of realism by saying: 'Whatever happened Germany intended to re-arm' and that it was better for the Conference to break down now on the number of effectives than to be drawn into discussions on tanks. Vansittart told the Committee that Eden on the telephone had raised – inappropriately at this moment – details of the stipulations about tanks in the MacDonald Plan. Hailsham continued that he read Neurath's article as

> a statement that Germany intended to re-arm either with or without any agreement, and it seemed to him to be manifest that Germany was doing her best to fix on us the responsibility for the failure to reach agreement in order that she might then go ahead with her re-armament plan. He thought he must be extremely careful what we were doing.

Hitler had already decided by 11 May to withdraw from the Disarmament Conference, but he delayed announcing it for five months, hoping that world opinion would not put the blame on him. The Cabinet Disarmament Committee decided that Germany was 'manoeuvring for position' and told Eden in Geneva:

> It is essential that we should keep the discussions on the broad issues on which public opinion is united against Germany and avoid being driven into details about guns, tanks, aeroplanes, etc. on which opinion would be muddled and divided.

Eden was also asked to remain immovable on 'the large question of whether Germany accepts the principle of disarmament by stages, and nothing that could really be regarded as rearmament of Germany'.[11] It is hard to understand how the British government were able to reconcile Hitler's assurances of his peaceful intentions with the evidence of his blatant rearmament, and to ignore that as each month passed Germany became stronger militarily because on 10 May 1933 Brigadier Temperley, head of the British military delegation to the Disarmament Conference in Geneva, had sent a memorandum stating that Germany with great ingenuity had carried out a steady erosion of the (Versailles) disarmament clauses:

> Very extensive preparations have also been made to prepare German industry for industrial mobilisation. Gas, munition and optical glass factories, in which German companies have a controlling interest, have sprung up in neighbouring countries. It is also calculated that there are in the combined Nazi and Stahlhelm forces over a million young men of military age who have received some military training.

After pointing out that the incorporation of 300,000 Nazi storm-troopers in the police was a flagrant violation of the Peace Treaty, and that the British Air Ministry had identified at least 125 German military aeroplanes, and orders in Russian and German factories for more, Temperley concluded:

> No moment could be worse chosen than the present one to advocate drastic reductions in the armaments of France, the Little Entente and Poland. Moreover, the destruction of all heavy material and bombing machines belonging to the French and her Allies and to our own armed forces seems madness in the face of this direct German menace . . . There is a mad dog abroad, once more.
>
> A. G. Temperley. Brigadier.[12]

Vansittart minuted his 'entire agreement' and the memorandum was circulated to the Cabinet, who ignored this authoritative summing up of the dangerous situation.[13]

Hailsham took a strong line in the Lords on 11 May, saying that if Germany left the disarmament conference she would remain bound by the provisions of the Treaty of Versailles, and any attempt on her part to rearm in contravention of that Treaty would be a breach of it and would bring into operation the sanctions which it provided; and that Britain had acted with 'a courage almost amounting to foolhardiness in disarming itself in the hope of persuading other people to do the same'. His speech was described in the *Daily Herald* and elsewhere as 'anti-German' but it was the only sort of language which Hitler understood, although it was not echoed by Eden or any other members of the Government. Boncour said in a press statement on the same day that if owing to the intransigence of Germany the Disarmament Conference did not produce a Convention for reducing armaments, Versailles sanctions would be applied to Germany.

Eden omits Neurath's bombshell of 11 May from his memoirs. He refused to accept that the Conference would fail, and in a telephone conversation with Vansittart said he would do his best 'to rub along somehow' in talks with Nadolny of the German delegation. Such talks got nowhere and the Conference was adjourned.[14]

At a meeting of the Disarmament Committee on 25 July 1933 Baldwin offered to meet the French leaders in Paris on his way home from his holiday at Aix. Baldwin is often accused by historians of taking little interest in foreign affairs. This is incorrect. He attended all the meetings of the Disarmament Committee and was well briefed. However, this offer to go to Paris is a rare example of his taking part in negotiations outside Britain. The Committee felt it would be 'extremely difficult to insist that France would be safer after having reduced her forces and got a Convention than she would be if the situation remained as it was now'. Some members of the Committee 'were inclined to feel that the situation would, perhaps, be better if there was no Convention'. Doubts were also expressed whether with the present temper of Germany 'we' would be justified in attempting to make France reduce her armaments to the level suggested in the Mac-Donald Plan and draft Convention.[15]

Four days before Baldwin arrived in Paris Eden talked to Daladier there on 18 September 1933, shortly before the Disarmament Conference was due to reassemble in Geneva.

The French Prime Minister said that he had no doubt that Germany was determined to rearm, and although the great bulk of French opinion 'in the light of recent events' in Germany wanted France to leave the Disarmament Conference (and go ahead with maintaining their lead in armaments) he himself was reluctant to do this, preferring to seek in conjunction with Great Britain some common accord which might save the Disarmament Conference.

Daladier wanted the British to give France a guarantee of aid if France was attacked by Germany, and he asked Eden what Britain would do if there was a disarmament agreement and France disarmed while Germany rearmed 'in violation of her undertakings'. All Eden could say was that 'he was quite unable to answer the question' but he would submit it to his government. As this was the key problem worrying the French it was an unsatisfactory reply. Later in the conversation, when Daladier had emphasized the extent of German rearmament and her breaches of Locarno, Eden said he 'would emphasise' to his government that the French government sought some formula whereby Daladier could reassure French opinion on the British attitude in the event of a breach of a disarmament convention by Germany.

The crunch came four days later when Baldwin, with Simon and Eden, confronted Daladier and Boncour at the British Embassy. After some technical discussion of disarmament Daladier asked bluntly what guarantees there would be for the observance of the Convention. He produced a dossier on German rearmament and claimed that 'it appeared nothing practically was left of the Treaty of Versailles and . . . there were Nazi garrisons and arms in the Rhineland. Further, there was excessive activity in the factories throughout the Reich'. He emphasized that he could not get French public opinion to support a disarmament convention without 'some guarantees'.

Then came the statement which marked the fatal divide between France and Britain. Simon replied that HMG 'could not accept new responsibilities in the nature of sanctions . . . Public opinion in England would not support it'.

Baldwin gave the impression to the French that Britain wanted to isolate herself from the Continent by saying: 'No nation was likely to break the

Convention except Germany. In no other country was there any desire for war. Any sanction would therefore appear to be aimed against Germany, and against her alone; and it might make acceptance therefore by Germany difficult . . . if . . . it could . . . be proved that Germany was rearming, then a new situation would immediately arise, which Europe would have to face.' He could not conceive that European countries were going to

> allow one country to convert Europe once again into a butcher's shop. If that situation arose, His Majesty's Government would have to consider it very seriously, but that situation had not yet arisen. But a grave situation might have to be faced, and he could not believe that British statesmen would be behindhand in making the most sincere efforts for the maintenance of peace.

The declaration that Britain 'would not be behindhand' in 'efforts for peace' was far too weak for Daladier, who then emphasized the need for sanctions, crystallizing his remarks by saying 'they should all declare their readiness to impose acceptance (e.g. discontinuance of rearming), if necessary by force. Otherwise there would be a confused period which would only be of advantage to the violating nation'. Simon surprisingly said the 'last difficulty' (over sanctions and eventual use of force) had not thrown 'a shadow over the proceedings'.[16]

Baldwin, with the steam-roller Conservative majority in the Commons, was the real ruler of Britain. He was rigidly opposed to a plan for another British expeditionary force in France as in 1914, and expected Hitler would eventually declare war on Russia, from which contest Britain could stand aloof. The result of Baldwin's conversation in Paris was that France decided Britain would never guarantee her security, and as a result she slid into the Franco-Soviet Pact, which was abhorred by Baldwin.

At Geneva Cadogan talked to Massigli, the French delegate, who raised the same proposal for sanctions made to Baldwin on 22 September in Paris, and said that in conversation with Aloisi and Suvich he had been given to understand that Italy would be ready to give effect to the French idea (sanctions) but was embarrassed because Britain was hanging back. Massigli suggested that any violations of the Convention should be treated as a violation of Locarno, and would thus entail upon the Locarno signatories all the obligations resulting from that Treaty. Cadogan told Massigli that he expected anything like this would be 'unacceptable' to the British Government. Nevertheless, the French persisted in trying to get results from the Disarmament Conference. But the end was in sight.

The German generals made strong protests to Hitler about the Disarmament Conference and pointed out to the Führer that Germany needed to rearm openly because their rearmament was already so advanced that they could not possibly agree to any system of international control. Hitler agreed, and decided to implement the decision he had made in May to withdraw from Geneva. The Germans alleged that Sir John Simon on 4 October told Neurath, the German Foreign Secretary, in a private session that Germany would not be allowed anti-aircraft guns under the Convention. Phipps was told in Berlin that this created 'a disastrous impression' in Germany. Simon denied making any such remark. Then on 6 October the German delegate put forward 'enlarged' demands, and on 9 October complained doubts were being thrown on Germany's good faith.[17] On 14 October 1933 Simon made a speech outlining new proposals which the German government incorrectly interpreted as meaning that eight years must elapse before Germany obtained equality of arms.

On the same day Germany withdrew from the Conference. It was not due to Simon's speech; it was a deliberate preconceived decision by Hitler, although some journalists and British enthusiasts for the League at the time tried to put the blame on Simon. Germany also left the League of Nations.[18]

★   ★   ★

Eden commented in his diary 'The conference was becoming a sham so that it is perhaps just as well now. All the same I should not like Simon's conscience about the earlier part of last year when Brüning was still in power. We missed the bus then and could never overtake it.' With this judgment the author entirely agrees. Eden was more anxious for negotiation with Germany and more optimistic about the likely result than either MacDonald or Simon. After one lunch with Simon and MacDonald when they had discussed disarmament Eden wrote in his diary 'It was a depressing luncheon with the Tory [Eden himself] anxious for disarmament, the Liberal sceptic, and the Socialist vehemently reactionary.'[19]

Immediately after Hitler's withdrawal from the League there was an opportunity to nip his rearmament in the bud through a veto followed by concerted action by France, Italy and Britain and the Little Entente. Mussolini had a vested interest in the preservation of Nazism because Germany was a totalitarian state like Italy, but he was bitterly opposed to Hitler's efforts to annex Austria, and during 1934 and the early months of 1935 was co-operative with Britain and France. The opportunities were frittered away by MacDonald, Simon and Eden, who did nothing in face of the deadly danger arising from Hitler's rapid rearmament and refused to back France when the French wanted to invoke Versailles and Locarno, and if necessary resort to force. During this period while Mussolini was anti-German this would have been practical, and once Hitler was humiliated by the League the democratic forces in Germany might have overthrown him.

On 24 October 1933 the new British Ambassador to Germany, Sir Eric Phipps, saw Hitler for the first time and asked him how he 'envisaged the resumption of negotiations for disarmament'. Hitler replied that 'The highly armed states, especially France, would never be allowed by their Parliaments to proceed to real disarmament', but later he said more co-operatively that he was ready for the highly armed states to retain their armaments. These should, however, be limited to their present numbers by convention and 'France could retain her offensive weapons and her army of over 600,000 . . . He would only demand for Germany a short-time army of 300,000 men, with no *offensive* weapons such as tanks, heavy artillery or bombing aeroplanes, but complete liberty to have as many *defensive* weapons as might be necessary for this number.'

This pleased MacDonald, who then decided it was worth while wooing Germany again in the hope of achieving a disarmament convention regardless of the objections of the French, and he prevailed on his Cabinet colleagues to go along with his plan. However, the small print of Phipps's despatch should have alerted the Cabinet to the folly of treating Hitler as a normal ruler who would honour his obligations. Later in this despatch Phipps wrote that it was

> an all too bald account of a most strange interview. My several interpolations could only be made when the Führer paused for breath in the torrent of his eloquence . . . At one moment he told me with passionate emphasis that death meant nothing to him. Once or twice I felt inclined to smile at Herr Hitler's shouting crescendo, but the seriousness, not to say tragedy, of the situation prevented that inclination from developing. It was in the hands of so unbalanced a being.

Phipps also recorded that Neurath, whom MacDonald and Simon knew well and liked from private talks at Geneva, 'was present, but did nothing to disturb or enliven the proceedings, for he sat through like a wooden image without uttering a word'.

Probably Neurath was ashamed of his hysterical master. The next day Phipps called on Papen, and wrote 'I went from the fanatic, to the man of the world, and confess that I personally preferred the former.' It was a strange judgement.[20]

On 11 November Dr Brüning had sent a message to Simon via Phipps that he was 'on the run' to escape arrest, having been denied a passport, and that this was due to his refusal to allow the Nazis to include his name as a government candidate in the Rhineland where Hugenberg and Papen were on the list. On 9 November the French Permanent Foreign Secretary, Léger, sent a message that 'in no circumstances can French Government be

a party to holding out further concessions to Germany. Those offered by M. Daladier remain 'irreducible (sic) maximum' to which they are able to go'. Lord Tyrrell commented 'They are under no illusion that any offer that did not go beyond that of 14 October would fail to move Germany from her present attitude . . . and believe that no concessions, however extensive, would induce her to return to Geneva as she has cut definitely adrift from the League and is set upon destroying it.' The French view proved to be correct, but neither this cold douche nor the news about the harassment of Brüning made any difference to MacDonald.[21]

Disturbing news was received from Paris on 17 November that General Weygand (Chief of Staff), General Corap and Colonel de Lattre confirmed the tremendous rate at which the German army was expanding, which made them believe that Germany would be ready to wage war on a large scale 'by June 1935 or the beginning of 1936 at the latest', and that Weygand 'could not, and would not, agree to . . . the MacDonald plan'. Furthermore, the French thought that if Germany accepted the disarmament convention it might be 'to achieve the disorganisation of the French army, and with the intention of themselves going on with their camouflaged rearmament'. All this was abundantly justified, but ignored by MacDonald and Simon.[22]

On 4 December Colonel Heywood, the British military attaché in Paris, communicated fresh French estimates of the strength of the German army, which was that they would be able to mobilize in the spring of 1934 twenty-one infantry divisions with their complete 'allotment' of divisional artillery plus four or five cavalry divisions, one or two mechanized formations and forty to fifty *Grenzschutz* (territorial) divisions. In 1938 the French General Staff estimated Germany would be able to mobilize an additional twenty to twenty-five infantry divisions, while German factories could produce the 'artillery and other material' without having to work at 'war-time pressure'. By 1938, according to the French, the Germans would have recruited a powerful army, approximately equal to the French metropolitan army in number of its divisions, but superior in strength owing to the *Grenzschutz* divisions. It would also be superior in armament, it would be 'in fact an army far more powerful than the German army of 1914'. He concluded 'One is left with the impression that by 1938, with almost incredible speed, the German General Staff will have built up and will hold at the disposal of whatever Government is in power in Germany a practically unequalled instrument of force.'*

Here was a dire warning for the British Cabinet of the dangerous waters into which they were sailing, but they proceeded to inquire from Hitler what

---

*On 26 October Heywood had reported that steps were being taken to organize the Nazi SA units 'into a militia at least 300,000 strong capable of taking the field on the outbreak of war'.

would be his terms for an agreement on disarmament, blithely believing he would honour any commitment into which he entered.[23]

The wide divergence between the French and British governments in regard to German demands for rearmament came to a head when on 7 December Phipps was instructed to tell Hitler that HMG 'earnestly desired . . . to hammer out without delay, in co-operation with Germany and other States, a practical basis for agreement for limitation of world armaments'. Phipps was told that he must also say that the increase in the German army from 200,000 to 300,000 would be considered excessive, and that the SS and SA must be absorbed into the new army and not continue to exist as supplementary organizations.

When Phipps saw Hitler the Führer stated categorically that he insisted on an army of 300,000 and that the SS and SA 'were in no sense military'. François-Poncet, the French Ambassador in Berlin, also saw Hitler and Neurath; he found them 'in a bad temper and inclined to be obstructive', but managed to make it clear that France would accept no further German rearmament. Hitler replied that he would await proposals for French disarmament, but would not accept anything in the nature of a trial period. Tyrrell commented that Hitler was intending to spin matters out in the hope of a change in government in France more favourable to conversations. On 31 December the French Government sent a formal note to Germany to the efect that it could agree to neither the immediate substantial rearmament asked for by Germany nor the maintenance in their present forms of parallel military associations 'which would constitute a vast reservoir of highly trained reserves'. This firm French statement was applauded warmly in the French press.

On 3 January 1934 Simon saw Mussolini in Rome. Mussolini stated that he attached great importance to the condition that as part of the projected arrangement Germany should return to Geneva and the League of Nations. He added that he had no desire to see Germany become unduly strong and that it was a mistake to suppose that Italian and German policy followed a common line; in Austria, Italy was 'wholly opposed to Germany'. Mussolini appeared to agree, however, that Germany should be allowed an army of 300,000 men.

When the French Government had pressed Britain to examine the evidence of illicit German rearmament with a view to arraigning Germany before the League under Article 213 of the Treaty of Versailles, on 27 November 1933 Simon replied that 'such an examination (which could conceivably become a matter of public knowledge) might . . . seriously prejudice the impending conversations between Governments on disarmament', and refused the request. Lord Tyrrell, after being taken to task for this reply by Léger, the French Foreign Minister, wrote to Simon in

December that the British War Office concurred 90 per cent with the French evidence, and that the refusal would have a bad effect on French confidence. Simon ignored this and sent a message on 5 December that Hitler's (disarmament) proposals 'were engaging our close attention'.[24]

At the same time as France was proposing to arraign Germany before the League of Nations for illegal rearmament Austria wanted to do the same on account of German interference in her internal affairs. Mussolini was ready to back both applications at the end of 1933. His own extra-territorial ambitions for Italy were enormous, but the outlook for peace in 1933 and 1934 with Mussolini supporting Britain and France was infinitely better than when Italy became aligned with Germany.

Germany replied uncompromisingly to both the British and French Notes on 19 January 1934, insisting that she must be allowed to rearm to achieve parity with other powers.

The Cabinet decided on further concessions to Hitler, and on 29 January these were formulated in a note to Germany (the Simon Memorandum) which was less harsh than the MacDonald plan of the previous year. Germany would be allowed as before only 200,000 troops, but she would be permitted tanks of up to 6 tons, and if no world-wide agreement on abolition of military aviation ws reached within two years she could build fighting aircraft until she reached parity with her neighbours after ten years.[25] In the Commons on 6 February 1934 Simon said, 'Germany's equality of rights could not be resisted.' Austen Chamberlain interjected 'This is a dangerous phrase' and asked for disavowal of equality with Germany at sea, adding that the maintenance of the demilitarized zone was a cardinal feature of British policy not affected by any phrase used in relation to equality status. Simon qualified his earlier remarks by saying he had used the word equality erroneously; 'equality of rights could not and ought not to be resisted ... British Government would view with repugnance any settlement which provided for equality of rights without any reduction of armaments.' Simon added that if the plan set out in his latest memorandum failed Britain would increase her armaments.

The *New York Times* commented that as the MacDonald Government had little expectation that the plan would be accepted by France and Germany this hint from the Foreign Secretary had more importance as a prediction of what is going to happen than as an added inducement to persuade France and Germany to agree, and Simon had added 'nothing new to the British memorandum published last week'.[26]

In the debate Attlee said that the Simon memorandum was a most lamentable production and the Labour Party 'had no use for the latest memorandum nor the British draft convention of last March'. Simon had not realized the gravity of the crisis into which Europe had been plunged by Hitler's assumption of absolute power, and had nothing constructive to say.

Simon admitted that his new scheme was not ideal, and excused its provisions for allowing Germany some rearmament on the grounds that a great nation could not be held in a perpetual state of inferiority. 'We were not offering the French any guarantee, only provision for consultation . . . it is not an Anglo Saxon habit to make a definite engagement for undefined circumstances.' The *New York Times* commented that Simon's immediate programme was to press the British plan upon France and Germany 'as a broker'.

Negotiations with Hitler on the memorandum were left to Eden. He had been made Lord Privy Seal with responsibility for League affairs, but without a seat in the Cabinet. He was ready to go far to find common ground with the German dictator. Accompanied by Strang and Robin Hankey, son of Lord Hankey (and now Eden's private secretary) he left London en route for Berlin and arrived in Paris on 16 February. There he found the French Government in disarray under a new Prime Minister (Doumergue) because of the Stavisky financial scandal. Eden talked to Doumergue, Barthou and Herriot. They were all hostile to the British Note, and indignant at Hitler causing trouble and unrest in Austria. On 2 February the outgoing Prime Minister, Daladier, had condemned the British Note, and the new Prime Minister was equally dismissive.

This was the first important diplomatic mission undertaken by Eden overseas, and he botched it. Naively in Berlin he took Hitler's words at their face value, ignoring the warning a few days before which said Nazi Germany believed in 'neither the League nor negotiation' and intended to fuse with Austria, rectify her eastern frontiers, and recover her colonies.[27]

From Berlin on 21 February Eden wrote in his diary and in letters to Baldwin and his wife about Hitler '. . . he seemed to me more sincere than I had expected'; 'without doubt the man has charm'; 'Dare I confess it? I rather liked him.'

Eden in his memoirs recorded that he thought at the time Hitler might be genuine when he said he would honour Locarno but not Versailles.

After talking to Hitler Eden cabled to Simon that he had received confidential important proposals which if accepted would enable Hitler to agree to the United Kingdom memorandum. This was stretching the likelihood of agreement to its limits. In fact Hitler had said that Germany must from the beginning of the Convention have the right to 50 per cent of France's air force, and if Germany was granted 300,000 men he would reduce his police force by 50,000 men and would undertake to disarm the SS and SA. An army of 300,000 was a far cry from accepting the UK note.

In an effort to drive a wedge between France and Britain Hitler suggested to Eden his proposals should be put forward NOT by Germany, but by Britain. Instead of rejecting this monstrous suggestion out of hand, Eden cabled Simon that

> the Ambassador and I take the view that in being thus frank the Chancellor has taken us into his confidence. The publication of these proposals in respect of SA and police as coming from the Chancellor might make serious difficulties for him here despite his strong position.

Even when Neurath made another clumsy suggestion that Eden should bypass Paris on his way home (to further the subterfuge that Hitler's revised proposals came from Britain, not Germany), Eden showed no indignation, although he told Hitler 'it might be said the United Kingdom memorandum had been torn up and a new memorandum proposed'.

On the night of 21 February Eden wrote to MacDonald that the Chancellor's proposals were much better than 'we expected'. MacDonald disagreed, and minuted on Eden's telegram 'We should not allow Germany to dump its confidences upon us in order to use us for its own policy. Hitler should know at once that his proposals in substance and in method of handling are unacceptable.' Vansittart was appalled, and he persuaded Simon to send this response to Eden:

> *Foreign Office,*
> *February 23, 1934, 1.20 p.m.*

> . . . Your telegram . . . puts us in a position of great embarrassment. The proposals contained in it are such as we could not possibly ourselves put forward and sponsor. We do not indeed desire at all ourselves to undertake the revision of our own proposals (which, as you are aware, have already been criticised in many quarters here as going too far in the German direction) . . . it would manifestly be not only unwise but hopeless for His Majesty's Government to put forward a suggestion that Germany should begin at once with a fleet of 1,000 aeroplanes. Such a suggestion would raise the loudest outcry in France and lead immediately to a vast increase in our own strength. His Majesty's Government themselves could not moreover consider a proposal which would destroy the whole character of their draft, entailing a rearmament race rather than disarmament and a rejection of our proposal by our own people . . . the initiative and responsibility in the matter of new proposals must necessarily and rightly come from and rest upon those who make them. And since the Chancellor has made these proposals, and they can neither be concealed nor denied for long in any case, we feel most strongly that the Chancellor should either himself make his proposals openly and officially, or that His Majesty's Government should be free to communicate them to the Italian and French Governments as coming not from His Majesty's Government but from the German Government.

This was an exceptional snub, and shows lack of confidence in the 36-year old Minister entrusted with an important task.

To MacDonald Eden wrote: 'I think we can trust the Chancellor not to go back on his word.' Thus Eden believed that an agreement with Hitler on limitation of armaments could not only be made, but would be honoured.

Leeper minuted on receipt of Eden's telegram:

> Once Germany has an authorised airforce and air staff – 1) She will with her civil aviation uncontrolled become a great, and soon the greatest, air power. 2) Proper investigation of the future of aviation will be doomed from the start. 3) The convention would cease to be in any sense a disarmament convention, and acceptance is impossible.

Three days later Leeper wrote: 'If we start altering our memo in Germany's favour e.g. granting her airforce, we forfeit French co-operation,' and on 1 March: 'I am afraid that a convention which grants Germany what she wants in the air will be of little use to world peace or to our own security.' Vansittart minuted: 'I agree,' but Eden wrote: 'I do not agree. A. E. March 5.' Eden was out of line with his advisers, having been disowned by the Foreign Office, and pique over this may have been a factor in his insistence later that a disarmament pact and a general settlement with Hitler was the right policy.

An article appeared in the *Observer* criticizing Eden on 25 February. Eden's official biographer claims that it was 'clearly inspired' by Vansittart. He is probably correct. The article was headed 'Berlin disappoints Mr. Eden – no possible basis of agreement' and it declared: 'He is not competent either to negotiate or to prepare for negotiation.'

Leeper minuted: 'I should have thought it may prove quite a good thing that the impression that the Germans and we were in full agreement should have been cancelled.' Eden was furious, and wrote after Leeper's minute:

> The publication in the *Observer* made my task in Paris infinitely more difficult. It was grossly inaccurate and gave the impression, eagerly taken up by the *Temps*, that HMG were displeased with Berlin and perhaps also with myself. Therefore no need for the French Government to bestir themselves in any way, and they did not. A. E.

In his diary Eden wrote that these events were 'profoundly irritating . . . showing Simon and Van manifest mistrust in all I am doing. It is really hopeless to work for such a man. He is not only a national, but an international calamity. A wretched business.' In his autobiography Eden wrote: 'My authority was slender enough without being undermined.'[28]

Eden's stay in Berlin gave Hitler the impression Britain was prepared to condone Germany's rapid rearmament in spite of it being a gross breach of Versailles. As this was not Simon's view, Simon or Eden should have resigned when this clash occurred. Unfortunately, Eden, whose faith in Hitler's peaceful intentions outstripped that of his colleagues, was to have more and more influence on Britain's foreign policy in the following four years.

Another revealing piece of evidence of Eden's pro-German attitude comes in a minute by him dated 24 March. On a despatch from the British Ambassador in Moscow (Lord Chilston) which stated 'We shall need Germany to be shown in the light she deserves [if disarmament talks broke down] and probably Russia also . . . it will not suit our book that France should foolishly elbow her way into the dock.' Vansittart and Simon agreed; but Eden wrote 'But if France does not want a convention and Germany does?'[29]

Hitler obligingly informed Italy and France of his proposed modifications to the British Convention, so that the furore over Eden's telegram of 23 February became a storm in a teacup. Eden had proceeded from Berlin to Rome. Mussolini and he got on well. In his memoirs Eden described Mussolini then as being 'lively, friendly and entertaining', and the discussions as 'crisp and easy'. At that time Mussolini wanted to bring Germany back into the League, believing this was the only way to keep her rearmament within bounds. Unlike Eden, he was sceptical about France ever accepting the alterations Hitler wanted in the British memorandum.

Mussolini thought that by agreeing to a German air force he might obtain a quid pro quo from Hitler in Austria. Although the Italian dictator shared Eden's willingness to legalize the German air force, the Foreign Office thought otherwise. On a report of the Mussolini–Eden conversation Leeper minuted:

> I find it hard to understand what particular advantage this country or France would gain . . . Is it a *British* interest to authorize Germany to have a regular military air force which backed by the most effivient civil aviation in Europe would soon dominate the air . . Now that Herr Hitler has completely rejected all the main proposals of our memorandum ought we not to wind up the Disarmament Conference as soon as possible . . .?

Sargent found some value in Hitler's proposal, but Vansittart thought we must stick by the French. 'For whatever the figure claimed by Germany be it 750 or 1000, we should be simpletons indeed if we thought she would not find means of exceeding her own figure seeing that she already has 300–500 more than she should have.'

Lord Stanhope, Foreign Under-Secretary in the House of Lords, minuted his entire agreement with Vansittart. Unfortunately, Vansittart and Stanhope were not in charge, and their masters Eden and Simon continued to pursue the will o' the wisp of control over a legalized German air force, regardless of the risk of a split with France.[30]

On his journey back to London Eden stopped in Paris. His talks with the French should have made it crystal clear to him once again that the French would never agree to the scale of rearmament demanded by Hitler. Eden refused to accept this, and on his return persuaded the British Government to continue overtures to both Germany and France until on 17 April France finally rejected further negotiations.

The official French reasons for this grave step were that any convention would legalize German rearmament and that the recent sharp increases in German military estimates 'denoted' Germany's intention to rearm without waiting for legislation. In addition, the French said they had no faith that Germany could be made to honour any obligations undertaken by her unless she returned to the League.

The British Government were profoundly disappointed, but how could they expect France to agree to reduce her armed forces and at the same time legalize Hitler's rearmament? They were asking for the moon as far as France was concerned. Domergue explained to Campbell 'the underlying inspiration' of the French note was 'fear', and they had left Eden in no doubt about this, while he also hoped that French firmness might undermine Hitler's regime.

Phipps reported the next day that 'The German man in the street is distinctly nervous regarding German military estimates and fears French action; he knows that if the roles were reversed Germany would act with energy.' They would not have 'feared' if they had known that the British Cabinet's Disarmament Committee had recorded on 6 December that 'force' to stop German rearmament was 'unthinkable', and it was also 'unthinkable' that France should use force on her own.[31]

On 30 May 1934 the final meeting of the Disarmament Conference took place at Geneva. A speech by Barthou giving the formal final French position made it clear further discussion was useless. Barthou in an emotional attack on Germany was amusingly critical of Simon, asking why he, who had opposed German rearmament in his speech of 14 October (which was the excuse for Germany leaving the League), had now weakened in favour of Germany after the latter had left the League.[32]

It was tragic that Britain only came out in favour of concessions to Germany after Hitler came to power, and refused them to democratic German governments before January 1933, when they could have been a potent factor in keeping the Nazis out of power.

In their enthusiasm for world disarmament Britain had for years been chasing a mirage. Now they had to face the stark reality that nothing except war could stop Germany becoming the strongest power in Europe, while Britain had reduced her own armed forces to a dangerously weak level.

PART TWO

HITLER
IN POWER

CHAPTER FIVE

MUSSOLINI SAVES AUSTRIA

In 1933 Winston Churchill praised Mussolini as the 'Roman genius' who was 'the greatest lawgiver amongst living men'.

AUSTRIA WAS target number one in Hitler's expansionist policies; on the first page of *Mein Kampf* he had called for its annexation by Germany. Within four months of seizing power Hitler started a cold war against Austria; he stopped German tourists going there by imposing a 1,000-mark fine, and he applied other hostile economic measures which crippled the Austrian economy, while the Nazi propaganda machine tried to undermine the Austrian State. In May 1933 Hitler explained to the Cabinet of the Third Reich that the Austrians were becoming less pan-German and wanted 'Switzerlandization', while the Vatican, the Habsburgs and the Jews were becoming increasingly influential there. A determined fight against all this must be started at once, declared Hitler. He ordered Austrian Nazis to start terror campaigns with bomb attacks on institutions and vicious propaganda against political opponents like Dollfuss, Fey, Starhemberg and Steidle. It was crystal-clear that Hitler's aim was annexation.

In 1933 Austria hit back and was the first state to organize resistance to Hitler. The Chancellor, Engelbert Dollfuss, was strongly supported by Mussolini, who openly encouraged Austrian resistance to Hitler, but Britain and France were apathetic. Mussolini was also exasperated by Germany secretly supplying arms to Abyssinia, and there was acute tension between Mussolini and Hitler over Austria.

At Geneva in March 1933 Ramsay MacDonald was downcast at the adverse French reception of his Disarmament Plan, but when Mussolini invited him for a visit to Rome he was much cheered. Mussolini's relations with the Baldwin Government of 1924–29 had been extremely good. Fascism was disliked by the Labour Movement, and especially by trade unionists who had been on friendly terms with Italian colleagues such as Pietro Nenni who were put in prison by Mussolini. Matteotti, murdered by the Fascists in Mussolini's early days of power, had been a Socialist MP with strong links with the British Labour Party. His case aroused emotion on the Left. However the Conservative Party on the whole applauded Mussolini's regime.

Winston Churchill, Baldwin's Chancellor of the Exchequer, and Austen Chamberlain, Foreign Secretary, were particularly enthusiastic for Mussolini in the late 1920s. Churchill negotiated a generous settlement of Italy's war debts to Britain in January 1925, and when he signed the settlement he spoke warmly of Italy possessing a government 'under the commanding leadership of Signor Mussolini which does not shrink from the logical consequences of economic facts'. During a trip to Genoa in 1927 Churchill was much struck by the atmosphere of the Fascist state, writing to his wife: 'This country gives the impression of discipline, order, goodwill and smiling faces.' He went on to Rome to see Mussolini, and told journalists that he could not help being charmed by the Italian dictator:

> 'Anyone could see that he thought of nothing but the lasting good . . . of the Italian people . . . it was quite absurd to suggest that the Italian Government does not stand upon a popular basis or that it is not upheld by the active and practical assent of the great masses . . . if I had been an Italian I am sure I would have been wholeheartedly with you from the start . . . your movement has rendered service to the whole world.

Such praise from the Chancellor of the Exchequer aroused a furore in Labour circles. Again, in 1933 Churchill praised Mussolini as the 'Roman genius' whom he described as 'the greatest lawgiver amongst living men'. (When Mussolini was executed in 1945 he was carrying letters from Churchill for use at his trial as a war criminal; they have not survived.)

Although when Curzon was Foreign Secretary he had abominated Mussolini, Austen Chamberlain as Foreign Secretary became a firm friend, staying on Mussolini's yacht, and describing him as 'a strong man of singular charm . . . and of not a little tenderness and loneliness of heart . . . I am confident that he is a patriot and sincere man; I trust his word when given, and I think we might easily go far before finding an Italian with whom it would be so easy for the British Government to work.'

The friendly relations between Austen and Mussolini made Mussolini co-operative over the Locarno Treaty, evacuation of the Rhineland, the Briand-Stresemann accord and the Dawes Plan. In fact, Mussolini aligned Italian foreign policy with British. MacDonald had delighted Mussolini by being co-operative about the Jubaland Treaty and the Dodecanese when he was his own Foreign Secretary in 1924. Thus MacDonald and Simon had every reason to believe their reception in Rome would be warm, and they were not to be disappointed.

The Italian Government sent two luxurious wagon-lits to Geneva, and Simon and MacDonald travelled in them to Genoa. Ishbel MacDonald accompanied her father. At Genoa Mussolini had provided them with a large seaplane which was piloted by General Balbo (the young and enthusiastic Minister for Air). The usually undemonstrative Genoese gave the British Prime Minister and Foreign Secretary an enthusiastic welcome. Mussolini and other high officials went to Ostia airport to welcome the British, and in the evening the Duce gave an evening party at the Palazzo Venezia in honour of his distinguished visitors. The whole staff of the British Embassy together with the most important British residents in Rome were invited; Mussolini spared nothing in his efforts to be friendly with MacDonald – perhaps in gratitude for Jubaland in 1924. The next morning the Prime Minister visited the Fascist Exhibition and declared he was 'greatly interested'; he also lunched with the King, and saw the Pope.

When the guests arrived in Rome on 18 March they were immediately handed the text of a proposed Four-Power Pact between Italy, France, Germany and Britain, containing proposals to revise the Versailles Treaties within the framework of the League of Nations, and a rider that should the Disarmament Conference lead to only partial results the German army equality of rights 'must be put into practice'.

Mussolini had spent the previous weekend drafting the pact in his own atrocious handwriting in a small village in the hills not far from Rome. It is clear that at this stage he fancied himself as a statesman able to make a major contribution to the future peace of Europe.

The Four-Power Pact turned out to be a classic non-event (although it came into nominal existence). On his way back to London MacDonald stopped in Paris and told Daladier that Mussolini had impressed him with 'his sincere wish for co-operation of the four powers'. Daladier pointed out that the Covenant of the League of Nations already provided for the revision of treaties, and gave qualified consent to further discussion.

In May, at Geneva, the German delegate Nadolny raised his demands about the measure of German disarmament to be allowed, and from the exchanges and the statements in Berlin by von Neurath it became clear that the Germans would never accept the British draft convention. Meanwhile in Rome Mussolini had told Graham he deplored the German attitude at Geneva and disliked Neurath's speech of 11 May which indicated that whatever the result of the Disarmament Conference, Germany intended to rearm with military and naval aircraft, heavy artillery and manpower, saying 'such weapons and armaments as the others hold to be necessary for their security can no longer be dispensed with for Germany's security'. In Rome Mussolini told Graham that he would send a strong message to Hitler urging him 'to pour oil upon the troubled waters'. The Duce also said that he agreed with Lord Hailsham's severe language in the Commons to the effect that if Germany rearmed in defiance of Versailles 'sanctions which the Treaty provided' must be applied. Paul Boncour in Paris made a speech to the same effect. At this stage of 1933 there is no reason to doubt Mussolini's genuine wish for disarmament, or his distrust and dislike of Hitler's policy.

On 7 June the Four-Power Pact was initialled in Rome, but with no enthusiasm on either the German or the French part. The only attempt to make use of the Four-Power Pact was a failure. Complaints were received from the Austrian Government in July 1933 that German subversive activities included pernicious broadcasting and dropping of leaflets from aeroplanes to promote the Nazi cause. The British Chargé d'Affaires in Berlin, Basil Newton, was instructed to make an oral communication to the German Foreign Minister 'in the spirit of the Four Power Pact' that broadcasting and dropping of leaflets by German aeroplanes over Austria was in conflict with the principle of non-intervention with internal affairs of neighbouring countries. It was also difficult to reconcile with Germany's obligation under Article 80 of the Treaty of Versailles, besides being inconsistent with the objectives of the (Four-Power) Pact. Similar protests were made by France and Italy. Suvich in Rome pointed out to Graham that the Germans only came into the Four-Power Pact with 'utmost reluctance, suspecting a trap', and were induced to do so principally by the personal efforts of Mussolini, who telephoned direct to Hitler. For the Germans, von Bülow told the British and French that the statement was 'unfriendly' and 'an abuse of the Four-Power Pact', and the matter was no concern of Britain or France. The Italians phrased their representation more softly and received a more conciliatory answer, which led Vansittart to comment acidly that they thought they had a 'special position' vis-à-vis Germany, which was 'an ultimate delusion which time and Germans – who have never respected them – will cure'. Vansittart had not been pleased when Suvich had suggested to him *orally* that instead of a joint protest in Berlin about Austria, Italy might use her 'special position' for some 'undisclosed whisperings at Berlin while the British press and House of Commons should cry aloud'. However, Mussolini's attitude in 1933 was 100 per cent support for Dollfuss against the Austrian Nazis; his idea of 'a special relationship with Germany' did not imply support for Hitler's policies, only that as they were both dictators governing totalitarian states he could be a bridge between them and the democracies.[1]

When Hitler came to power in Germany he immediately made clear his intention to annex Austria Britain was content to rely on a friendly Mussolini to restrain him. Austria was perhaps the greatest sufferer from Versailles. Under the Treaty of St Germain her dynasty, army and empire were dissipated. A small Republic of 12 million inhabitants was created, and specifically forbidden to join with Germany. Vienna, for centuries the capital of a great empire, was far too large for the hinterland.

In *Mein Kampf* Hitler had written: 'German Austria must return to the great German motherland. . . . Common blood belongs to a Common Reich.' As soon as Hitler came to power in 1933 he gave massive funds to the Nazi Party organization in Austria with the intention of winning elections there and securing a Nazi Austrian Government by legal means, as he had done in Germany. The Anschluss would be automatic. If his plans failed for a constitutional take-over, Hitler's design was to create an Austrian Nazi Party who could seize power by a coup. In the years immediately after the war, during the early years of the Weimar Republic, a majority of Austrians would have been happy to vote for union with Germany, but as the Nazis showed their true vicious colours the Austrians became frightened of their violence.

By 1931 Austrian economic problems were endemic. The former parts of the Austro-Hungarian Empire (Yugoslavia, Czechoslovakia and Romania) put high import duties on Austrian exports, although Austrian industries had originally been developed to produce manufactured goods for these predominantly agricultural regions of the former empire.

Engelbert Dollfuss became head of a coalition government in Austria in May 1932. So severe was the economic depression that Austria was a fertile field for Nazi fomenting of trouble, and to combat it Dollfuss suspended parliamentary government in March 1933, and ruled by decree with the consent of the President Wilhelm Miklas. German Nazi activists were expelled, and in June the Austrian Nazi party was declared illegal, although it continued to operate underground.

Given little hope of real help by France and Britain, Dollfuss turned to Mussolini, who promised to protect Austria from the Nazis. When Dollfuss suspended the Constitution there were three Austrian political groupings in existence, bitterly opposed to each other. On the left were the Social Democrats, ranging from socialist to neo-Marxist; they governed the capital, and their powerful army was known as Schurzbund (Defence League). It was so popular that it reduced the Communists to impotence. On the right was the Nazi Party, becoming increasingly belligerent after Hitler's rise to power in Germany. In the centre were the Christian Socialists, who had a paramilitary formation known as the Heimwehr under Prince Starhemberg. Starhemberg, a wealthy, aristocratic landowner, was right-wing and monarchist, but he abhorred Nazism and Hitler. He was a great patriot, enamoured of an independent Austria, and a ruthless opponent of the Anschluss. He became friendly with Mussolini, who supplied generous subsidies for the private army which was Austria's bulwark against Nazi aggression.

British support for Dollfuss was lukewarm. On 3 April 1933 the British Ambassador in Berlin, Phipps, wrote: 'Italy will presumably continue to support Dr. Dollfuss and the Starhemberg Heimwehr in their fight on two fronts against Socialists and National Socialists alike, and so I think will France, and so I hope will HMG in a spirit of benevolent neutrality.' However, on 2 June a statement by Eden in the House of Commons gave little indication that England was on Austria's side in the quarrel with Germany. In August the Foreign Office did consider hurrying up an authorization of an increase in the Austrian army in excess of the Versailles limit, but nowhere in the Foreign Office files is there any indication that keeping Hitler out of Austria was a priority if the peace of Europe was to be maintained. It is true that Orme Sargent sent a minute to Eden on 13 October which said that Hitler was counting on the gradual undermining of Dollfuss's authority until such time as Austria would fall into his lap. On 24 October 1933 Britain even urged moderation on Dollfuss in his battle against Nazi infiltration, and Simon expressed minimal interest in Austria.[2]

In June 1933 Dollfuss came to London for the World Economic Conference. He was well received, and Vansittart in particular gave him the impression that Britain would back him in his struggle against Hitler. Dollfuss made a strong appeal for British help and departed believing that he would receive much more support than in the event he did.

On 19 and 20 August 1933 Dollfuss met Mussolini at Riccione. The two heads of state became firm friends. Dollfuss told Mussolini that considerable numbers of Austrian Nazis were encamped inside Germany, just over the Austrian frontier, and had formed a Legion to attack as soon as Hitler gave the order. Mussolini's plan to save Austria from Hitler was to set up a pro-Italian fascist bloc with Austria and Hungary. Mussolini agreed to financial subsidies and rifles and machine-guns to arm the Heimwehr, and promised economic aid. In return Dollfuss promised very secretly to allow 5000 Italian troops to cross the Brenner to the Kufstein area in Austria if Hitler attempted a coup. The visit boosted Dollfuss's morale at a moment when France and Britain were cold towards him, antagonized by his unconstitutional and fascist-style methods. The Austrian Chancellor was immensely relieved at the promise of Italian armed assistance in the event of a German attack.[3]

By the beginning of 1934 Hitler was threatening Austria, with outbursts against Dollfuss. This united Starhemberg and Dollfuss in defence of

Austrian independence, and Dollfuss ordered that Starhemberg's Heimwehr should be the only paramilitary formation permitted by the Austrian
police, and that not only the Nazis but also the Schurzbund should be
prohibited. Mussolini made it a condition of his financial support for
Starhemberg that the Austrian Government tried to suppress the Schurzbund after he had sent his Foreign Secretary, Suvich, to Vienna in January
1934.

In January 1934 Dollfuss announced that he was going to appeal to the
League because of the criminal agitation by Nazis in Austria which was
clearly engineered by Hitler. One bomb tragedy succeeded another, with
Hitler trying to prove that Austria wanted to become Nazi and that Dollfuss
could not control the situation.

Dollfuss asked for full support from Britain in his appeal to the League of
Nations. This was not forthcoming, although he had sent a long and
convincing dossier of German misdeeds which was discussed exhaustively
by British Ministers on 9 February. All he obtained was a statement that
when his complaint was before the League 'His Majesty's Government
would consider it judicially.' The strong warnings of the Nazi danger to
Austria by Walford Selby (British Minister in Vienna) were almost ignored
by Simon, although Selby stressed that if Austria fell to Hitler all Eastern
Europe would be at his mercy.

Instead a discouraging instruction for Dollfuss was sent by Simon to
Drummond for onward transmission to Mussolini to 12 February 1934, just
when Austria was hoping for the maximum help from Italy at the League of
Nations; this stated that if Dollfuss established a fascist or quasi-fascist
regime 'there would be in Britain, and probably in France,' a very marked
cooling in the unanimity of the support hitherto given to Austria by the
press and public opinion, and further attempts by the British Government
to assist Dollfuss might be 'rendered increasingly difficult'.[4]

The suppression of the Socialists by Dollfuss was having such an adverse
effect on public opinion in England and France that the Austrian
Chancellor was finding it difficult to persist in his appeal to the League over
German subversion of the Austrian Government. Major Fey had become
Austrian Vice-Chancellor in place of Starhemberg; he was a much less
satisfactory individual, and he established paramilitary organizations to
establish fascist measures of which Dollfuss did not approve. Dollfuss was
left feeling that he could only count on help from Rome.

During Dollfuss's absence in Budapest in the second week of February
Fey took a 'fatal' decision to order a search for arms held by the Socialists.
At that time the rival private armies of the Schurzbund and Heimwehr were
deadly rivals and the whole of Austria was at their mercy. On 12 February
the exasperated Socialists resisted by force Fey's efforts to take away their

arms, and a rebellion began in Linz and Vienna. There were four days of fighting in Vienna with all the streets barricaded. Dollfuss ordered the Heimwehr to put down the rebellion by force, but the Schurzbund barricaded themselves inside enormous council-house blocks just outside Vienna, while many fought from their own flats. Fearful of a Nazi coup if he could not restore order, Dollfuss ordered this workers' housing complex to be shelled, and the revolt was put down with fatal casualties. Dollfuss promised a free pardon to all the rebels who surrendered, but also ordered the dissolution of the Socialist Party. However, nine death sentences were carried out, and 1500 insurgents were imprisoned. This vengeance against the Socialists produced strong criticism of Dollfuss in Britain, and he ignored strong pleas for clemency made by Selby on behalf of the British Government.

However, on 17 February the British, French and Italian Governments issued a joint declaration emphasizing their joint interest in the preservation of Austrian independence. For all that, the Austrian appeal to the League was not proceeded with, and Dollfuss and the Socialist opposition remained bitterly opposed to each other.

When Simon and Mussolini had met in Rome in January 1934 Mussolini had reminded the British Foreign Secretary that Italy was shouldering the full burden of preventing Hitler's seizure of Austria. Simon in reply said Britain supported Austrian independence 'but we could not, of course, intervene more actively'. This typified Simon's reluctance to face the Austrian problem.[5]

Mussolini, concerned at the vulnerability of Dollfuss's government and British indifference to the danger of an Anschluss, conceived the idea of a number of agreements between Italy, Austria and Hungary with a view to strengthening all three governments and preventing Hitler's expansion to the east. Accordingly he invited Dollfuss and Gömbös the Hungarian Prime Minister, to Rome on 14 March. Mussolini's plan was to keep both Austria and Hungary under his influence, and he believed France and Britain would co-operate in his design because of the dire danger of Hitler seizing Austria. On 17 March the tripartite agreements were signed which became known as the Rome Protocols. These provided for military combination in case of need, and for economic help. Walford Selby has commented that Mussolini 'came forward nobly in the matter of economic help to Austria' by allowing imports from Austria to be allowed into Italy on specially favourable terms. This came at an opportune moment to aid the stricken Austrian economy because Britain with Imperial Preference and the tariffs of the 1932 Import Duties Act was denying Austrian products access to the British market.

The Rome Protocols did not establish any formal alliances against Germany, but Hitler was furious. Bülow declared that as far as Austria was concerned 'the main impression is its anti-German character'.

Theo Habicht, the Austrian Nazi leader, claimed Dollfuss, Starhemberg and Fey had wrested Austria from 'the German community of destiny', and 'had integrated her into a ring of states hostile to Germany; for this treachery to the German cause there could be no excuse and no pardon'. He made the bare-faced threat 'for the Austrian who signed it, it was the end'. Hitler's immediate reaction was to step up his economic warfare against Austria, banning Austrian key exports to Germany of timber, fruit and livestock, and by continuing the 1000 marks fine for a visa.[6]

On 14 June 1934 Hitler and Mussolini had their first meeting in Venice. It was not a success. Mussolini was furious because Hitler indulged in a monologue. The bad effect of this was aggravated by the Duce refusing to use an interpreter – he was conceited, and would not admit his imperfect knowledge of German. Although the German documents tell a different tale, it is indisputable that Mussolini told Hitler firmly that there could be no negotiations over Austria unless Hitler called off his terror campaign. The two dictators did not get on well together, and were at daggers drawn over Austria, with Hitler fruitlessly demanding the admission of Nazis into the Austrian Government. Suvich told Starhemberg that Mussolini had afterwards referred to Hitler as a *polcinella* and had made fun of him, complaining of the German's incessant talk.[7]

On 1 June Dollfuss made Starhemberg Vice Chancellor instead of Fey. This was a move for the better, and shortly afterwards Starhemberg defied Hitler by holding a provocative rally on Hitler's birthday at his birthplace Braunau-am-Inn after a fresh wave of Nazi bomb attacks; here Starhemberg attacked the Nazis and proclaimed Austrian independence.

Hitler then decided to try to take over Austria by force. He had drawn up plans well in advance. Captured German documents disclose details of the plan to capture the entire Cabinet after a Nazi raid on the Chancellery, seizure of the Vienna radio station, and a simultaneous propaganda campaign which would lead to a popular Nazi uprising, plus the assignment of a special commando force to arrest the Federal President, Miklas, and then to coerce him into legitimizing a new Nazi regime. Already Hitler was developing the technique for state takeovers with which he was to be so successful later. But this time his attempt ended in ignominious failure.[8]

According to General Adam, Commander of Military District VII in Munich, Hitler told him at 9 a.m. on 25 July that 'the Austrian Government will be thrown out today. Rintelen [a leading Austrian Nazi] will be Chancellor', and ordered Adam to arm thousands of Austrian Nazi legionaries and facilitate their crossing the frontier from Germany into Austria.

Dollfuss had been invited to spend his holiday with Mussolini at Riccione, and to bring his whole family. He had accepted, and his wife and children had already gone on 25 July. On that morning a convoy of trucks carrying 150 armed men, all Nazis, arrived at the Chancellery in Ballhausplatz. They were disguised in Austrian army uniform and rushed the guards, immediately shooting and mortally wounding Dollfuss. Simultaneously armed Nazi guards tried to take over Vienna and other centres. In the fighting there were over a hundred deaths, while over two hundred were severely wounded.

Starhemberg was in Venice on 25 July. On hearing of the attempted coup he immediately telephoned to Vienna and ordered the Heimwehr headquarters to call out all their private army to put down the Nazis on their own. He feared that the regular army would contain too many Nazi sympathizers. Mussolini sent a Italian military plane to Venice to fly Starhemberg back to Vienna, where he arrived on the morning of 26 July, having been held up by bad weather. President Miklas authorized Starhemberg, as Vice Chancellor, to take all possible steps to put down the Nazi rising in consultation with Schuschnigg (a Cabinet Minister) and to head the Government temporarily.

Mussolini gave Starhemberg full support and moved Italian troops to the Brenner frontier in accordance with his agreement with Dollfuss, sending a telegram to Starhemberg promising military aid. However, Italian intervention was not needed, as Starhemberg quickly put down the revolt and restored order. It is estimated that around 52,000 Austrian volunteers fought against the Nazis and the army was hardly used.

The part played by Fey in the revolt is obscure. There is reason to believe that he had contacts with the Nazis, and knew in advance the date of the coup. He did not inform the Government; he was smarting from his dismissal from the post of Vice Chancellor, and may well have hoped that he might be the hero of the hour for defeating the Nazis. Alternatively, he may have hoped for a Nazi victory, and in either case may have wanted to be the next Austrian Chancellor. He has left no memoirs, and he was killed by the Nazis on the day of the Anschluss in 1938.

Patriotic Austrian resistance to the Nazi takeover was much helped by Dollfuss having created a new identity for Austria based on attitudes and values peculiar to the Austrian people, and which emerged again in a striking form after the Second World War. The suppression of Hitler's revolt was a personal triumph for Starhemberg and the loyalty of his Heimwehr. However, the President did not ask Starhemberg to become Chancellor. Miklas feared that although Starhemberg had great personal popularity, he would be too right-wing and too intent on a Habsburg restoration. Instead he asked Schuschnigg (who had been Minister of Justice) to be Chancellor. This was a wise choice. Schuschnigg was a great patriot and much liked for his honesty although he lacked charisma. He did much in his four years as Chancellor to further the sense of national pride which Dollfuss had been building up, and this damped down enthusiasm for Nazism.

Hitler's reaction to his defeat in Austria in July 1934 was dramatic. He felt he had not only been defeated in the confrontation, but personally humiliated by the unexpected strength of Austrian resistance and the bold move by Mussolini to support Austria. He immediately made a U-turn, and stopped all further political interference in Austria's internal affairs. Not only was the Nazi propaganda campaign abandoned but the murders and bomb attacks were abruptly ended.

It was Hitler's first trial of strength in his effort to overcome the status quo of Versailles. Like most bullies, when his opponents stood up to him with success, he climbed down abjectly. This leads one to believe he might have climbed down as abjectly if the French had started to throw German troops out of the Rhineland by force in March 1936. So complete was Hitler's U-turn that on 1 August he stated that he 'intended to wind up the National Socialist Party in Austria and disband the Austrian Legion, merely retaining a charitable organisation for the care of Austrian refugees under the impeccable cover of the Red Cross'. Papen was appointed as the new Ambassador in Vienna, and on 28 September the German Embassy in Vienna told the Foreign Ministry that the German press had been ordered to refrain from hostile propaganda. On 13 August 1934 Hitler ordered all aggressive press and wireless programmes to cease and, although many Austrian Nazis had died on 25 July shouting 'Heil Hitler', he ordered the 'exclusion from the leadership of the Austrian Party of all persons compromised by having been leaders of the fight', and that such persons must not be 'rewarded for their services by being given important posts in the Reich.'[9]

The failure of the Nazi revolt in Austria in July 1934 was the sole foreign policy defeat for Hitler from his accession to power in January 1933 until the outbreak of war in 1939. Mussolini, Miklas, Starhemberg and Schuschnigg emerge as clear winners of one round in the struggle to prevent Hitler 'becoming master' of Europe. But Hitler would lose no more rounds until 1942.

Mussolini in the autumn of 1934 approached Britain and France for a three-power guarantee of Austrian independence. The British – not wanting continental commitments – demurred and the disappointing outcome was a meek joint declaration by France, Britain and Italy reaffirming the Declaration of 17 February about the independence of Austria.

In 1934 a combination of Austrian and Italian firmness proved that united and determined opposition to Hitler could prevent Nazi aggression. Mussolini and Starhemberg set a fine example to Britain and France. It was a tragedy that British statesmen ignored their success, and during the coming years continuously capitulated to Hitler.

Austria would have fallen to Germany in 1934 had it not been for Italian opposition to Hitler's aggression. The British should have learnt the lesson that despite all the defects of Mussolini's authoritarian regime his co-operation was vital if Hitler was to be kept out of eastern Europe.

CHAPTER SIX

HITLER REARMS

WITH THE collapse of the Rearmament Conference and evidence that Hitler was creating an efficient large army, navy and air force the MacDonald Government faced a dilemma. Should it legalize German rearmament in return for some undertaking by Hitler to limit his forces, or should it join with France in invoking the League of Nations and threatening to use force to stop German rearmament? The Foreign Office brief for the Cabinet stressed the power of Germany's new forces and emphasized that it would be difficult 'to carry France with us' in legalizing German rearmament. Yet the British Government decided to try to legalize Hitler's forces by fresh negotiations for arms limitation with both France and Germany.[1]

The pacifist mood of Britain was an important factor in the Government's refusal to stand behind Clause 5 of Versailles and invoke it to stop Hitler's rearmament. In 1933 and 1934 by-elections had gone badly for the National Government; rearmament (which would be needed on a massive scale to stop Hitler) was unpopular; opposition to it was swinging many voters to Labour. At Fulham in October 1933 the Labour candidate, John Wilmot, made disarmament the major plank in his campaign, and he transformed a Conservative majority of 14,000 into a Labour one of 5,000 – an unprecedented by-election swing in those days. Lansbury, Leader of the Opposition, said in a message to Wilmot that he would 'close every recruiting station, disband the army and disarm the air force'. In September Arthur Henderson won the by-election at Clay Cross. As President of the Disarmament Conference he had great personal popularity, but because of his position he did not attack Government foreign policy.

In November 1933 at Kilmarnock and Skipton there was a swing against the Government of around 25 per cent; similar swings were repeated in 1934, which made it seem as if the National Government's huge majority might be wiped out in a General Election. The Conservative Party managers warned Baldwin that Germany *must* be brought back to the Disarmament Conference and the League, and that plans for rearmament were a vote-loser.[2]

Wilmot's victory in the by-election at East Fulham occurred ten days after Germany had walked out of the World Disarmament Conference at Geneva on 14 October 1933 when Simon, as we have seen, outlined a new plan for progressive general disarmament down to the level imposed on Germany by the Treaty of Versailles. Vernon Bartlett, an appeaser and sympathetic to Nazi rearmament (although five years later he was to win the Bridgewater by-election on the anti-appeasement ticket), was then a popular broadcaster. On the evening of 14 October he made a strong appeal for sympathy with Hitler in response to Simon's speech at the Disarmament Conference in Geneva refusing arms equality. He claimed that it was less favourable to Germany than MacDonald's draft convention of March 1933. He implied that Britain and France were the potential threats to peace, and included the words, 'We can swallow a little of our pride and meet the German point of view. It is worth swallowing any amount of pride if peace is at stake; civilisation is more valuable than prestige.' According to Bartlett any rearmament by Britain would be an unhelpful and provocative act. This broadcast, which he admitted in his autobiography was 'a very strong criticism' of Simon, resulted in him being sacked by the BBC.[3]

There was emotional opposition to militarism, but it was confused with the League of Nations preventing war by a police force and controlled disarmament. However, any talk of building bombers or equipping an expeditionary force was a vote-loser.

Social issues were also important in all the 1933 and 1934 by-elections, although in the heat of the controversy about Germany's withdrawal Wilmot may have secured a greater-than-average swing by claiming the Conservatives were warmongers. However, it must not be overlooked that Wilmot also engaged in muck-raking about housing conditions, on which issue his

Conservative opponent, as a prominent local councillor, was particularly vulnerable.

Neville Chamberlain believed social issues were the more important factor in the by-election result, writing to his sister Ida on 17 October: 'I did not lose a moment's sleep over it. The Press put it all down to housing and lies about war. Both no doubt were factors, but I heard yesterday from a friend who had been talking to a speaker (street corner) from Fulham what I had all along suspected, that the real attack was on the means test.' Baldwin, however, took the pacifist undertones seriously, and the cumulative effect of Fulham and other by-elections made him a reluctant rearmer.[4]

Baldwin was very conscious of voting swings because he had a shock when he lost the autumn 1923 general election after he had dissolved Parliament unnecessarily and held the election to obtain a mandate for tariff protection. This was an act of gratuitous folly from which the Conservative Party were lucky to recover, and Baldwin from then on decided he would never rush his fences, by which he meant he would wait to educate public opinion before putting an issue to the electorate. Hence he dragged his feet on rearmament, although he was personally convinced of its necessity.

The East Fulham result received world-wide publicity and influenced Baldwin, but it had no effect on the rearmament programme because at that moment there was no such programme.

However, the by-election helped to convince the Conservative leaders that for electoral reasons they must leave no stone unturned to persuade the French to overcome their fears and make an arms agreement with Hitler.

With the final breakdown of the World Disarmament Conference in May 1934 the British Government had to face the fact that British disarmament had been carried too far, and the national defence forces were dangerously weak. They continued with their policy of condoning German rearmament and searching for an agreement with Hitler, while they were rigidly opposed to extending any British military guarantee to France beyond Locarno, and they would not consider enlarging it to cover the situation if France was involved in war with Germany because of her guarantees to Czechoslovakia and Poland. Nor would Britain support France in invoking Part 5 of Versailles to arraign Germany before the League of Nations for illegal rearmament. This policy drove Britain and France apart, and France in despair turned towards Russia with the Franco-Soviet Pact. This was signed on 2 May 1935, much against the wishes of Baldwin and the Conservative Cabinet Ministers.

The Government was faced with a difficult debate in the Commons on rearmament on 28 and 29 November 1934. Simon and Baldwin mismanaged it, and gave the impression (eagerly taken up by Hitler) that they wanted to legalize German rearmament. Baldwin was viciously attacked by Churchill for allowing Hitler to rearm while Britain did not, so that Germany had obtained parity. He was compelled to say he knew what was going on in Germany, and this simple admission of 'knowledge' was rephrased to imply 'approval'. Hitler genuinely believed that the Commons debate had given him the green light to go ahead with his rearmament on the scale which he had fruitlessly claimed earlier in the year, and as Phipps pertinently reported, there was an immediate rise in the value of shares of German arms firms on the Berlin Stock Exchange. A mild note from Britain to Germany did nothing to undo the effect of the Debate, while the French were appalled.[5]

The Paris press expressed disappointment at the 28–29 November debate, applauding Churchill's views and deriding Baldwin's. Laval and Flandin, according to Campbell (Minister in Paris), 'looked down their noses and seemed disinclined to discuss the subject', but he managed to talk with Léger on 3 December, who told him there was a feeling of uneasiness lest Germany should seize the opportunity to put forward fresh proposals 'of an unacceptable character designed to drive a wedge between Britain and France'. Campbell added there was no inclination in Paris to resume disarmament discussions with Germany in the absence of evidence of 'a real change of heart'. Léger was a hundred per cent correct. Hitler's plan was to divide Britain and France, and he set about it cleverly.[6]

★   ★   ★

Hitler by now hardly cared whether his rearmament was legalized or not; he took the indecisive British attitude as evidence that Britain would never support France if she arraigned Germany under Part 5 of Versailles before the League of Nations. In the event the situation 'was allowed to drift', as the Ministers feared.

The minutes of the Cabinet Committee on Disarmament (later changed to Defence Requirements) reveal the Government's lack of policy and its readiness to pander to Hitler, in stark contrast with their firm line towards Brüning and von Papen. It dithered in face of the mounting national peril.

A Foreign Office memorandum dated 29 November 1934 for the Disarmament Committee put forward as one solution that far from legalizing German rearmament, and allowing Part 5 of Versailles to lapse,

Britain should join with France in arraigning Germany before the League for its violation. This, it was noted, would have the full support of France "but probably

not that of Italy." However with the rapprochement between Laval and Mussolini it
is well on the cards that Italy would have supported such a move.

But after examining this possibility the Foreign Office pusillanimously went
on that if Germany defied the League and repudiated Part 5

we and the League should have to acquiesce in this defiance, for the coercion of
Germany in such circumstances would be inconceivable. And as an inevitable
corollary the question of French and British security could be raised at once in an
acute form. The situation might then rapidly develop in the direction of an Anglo-
French Alliance coupled with special arrangements for the defence of Holland and
Belgium.[7]

There is no need to blame the diplomats. Foreign Office memoranda are
written to conform with the known views of the Foreign Secretary and not
to provoke argument, and a military guarantee to France was taboo in
Whitehall.

The Committee also had before them two memoranda from Phipps
which described trenchantly how during the seven months since Barthou
had terminated the Geneva disarmament negotiations Germany had been

feverishly rearming on land and in the air without protest on the part of Barthou or
anyone else. The impression left by the summer and autumn is one of incessant
marching and drilliing . . . While other countries enjoy playing football or sipping
coffee under trees German youth is happiest playing at soldiers, and German
manhood is happiest on the barrack square.

Here Phipps was correct, but he was wrong in holding out hopes that Hitler
still wanted an armaments agreement, and on being called to London
misled the Cabinet by stating that Hitler would honour his signature if 'he
signed a document'.

After a lengthy discussion by the Disarmament Committee, in a
memorandum for the Cabinet Simon wrote that he 'tentatively' proposed

the best course would be to recognise that Germany's rearmament in breach of the
Treaty is a fact which cannot be altered . . . and this had better be recognised
without delay in the hope that we can still get in return for legislation some valuable
terms from Germany . . . the main condition would be that Germany would return
to Geneva both for the Disamament Conference and for League purposes. I do not
think it would be possible to get Germany to return to the League on the basis she
was still bound by Part 5 of the Treaty of Versailles.[8]

Simon continued that Part 5 should be abandoned and equality of rights
offered to Germany; he admitted that 'to all this the French will cry
security', and 'protest that wrongdoers and blackmailers should not be given
the fruit of their wrongdoing', but this would have to be rejected because

'British opinion would not stand for it and the practical results would be disastrous.' Simon stated also that France would be left with the Franco-Russian Agreement.[9]

Here was appeasement in full cry, and an admission that by-election results precluded a firm stand; it also ruled out either a British guarantee to France of immediate military aid if she was invaded by Germany or support in arraigning Germany before the League, while recognizing that a Franco-Soviet Pact would be the only recourse left to the French in their fear of Hitler.

Simon's memorandum was approved by the Cabinet, and France, left with no alternative, drifted into a pact with Russia. Simon had ignored an important communication from Phipps on 27 November which said that Hitler had flown into a rage during an interview over the question of a Franco-Soviet Pact, declaring that because of it 'he was determined to proceed with his rearmament as if he was attacked by Russia or France nobody would come to his assistance'. On this letter Sargent minuted: 'I do not think we need take this outburst of Hitler's very seriously', and Eden minuted a fatuity which showed how much he misjudged Hitler at this stage.[10]

Simon told his Cabinet committee colleagues (MacDonald, Hailsham, Hoare) on 11 December 1934 that as a result of the Commons debate 'Hitler was now saying the British Government's announcement was tantamount to a legalisation of German rearmament', The Committee decided to make the point that they were convinced of Germany's rearmament, but they considered it had reached the stage when its recognition had become inevitable. They recorded that they wished 'to press strongly that it is far better that this armament should be controlled rather than that it should remain uncontrolled, and if the French Government should raise the point that Germany had in fact succeeded by a policy of blackmail we should perhaps not dissent, but we should ask France what are the alternatives'. They concluded:

> It is not proposed to legalise what Germany has done but rather to recognise the fact of her rearmament up to date, but there should be no question of at present recognising any further developments before and until the whole matter is negotiated at Geneva.
>
> We realise there is always a risk that Germany may free herself from the restrictions of Part V of the Treaty of Versailles and that no bargaining with her may be possible, and in consequence no general agreement. Such a situation would be very serious, but there does not appear to be any alternative. If the situation is just left to drift Germany will continue to rearm to whatever degree she may ultimately desire.

Simon now suggested he and Eden should go to Berlin to see Hitler in pursuit of an arms agreement. The Cabinet authorized the visit. Surprisingly MacDonald at last had become realistic about Hitler; after Baldwin said in Committee on 19 December it was 'really very little use talking to anyone except Hitler and nothing would happen if his representatives came over here', Ramsay retorted that he thought 'it was a profound mistake for us to visit Berlin', and he did not want two Ministers to go. He was 'very anxious' that the Germans 'should not be too flattered', but he would not press his views if his colleagues thought otherwise. Their more appeasement-minded colleagues agreed that both Ministers should go to Berlin early in 1935.[11]

Simon paid a preliminary visit to Paris in January. In his talks with the French leaders there was no meeting of minds, and they are best passed over in silence.

Meanwhile the British had pleased Hitler by contributing the largest contingent to a small international force which supervised the plebiscite in the French-occupied Saar on 13 January 1935. Under the Treaty of Versailles a plebiscite was to be held there after fifteen years. France hoped that a substantial majority would vote for a continuance of French rule, but in January 1935 an overwhelming majority, almost 90 per cent, voted to return to Germany. Phipps – as so often a correct prophet – feared that the big Saar victory 'will whet not only the German armaments, but also the territorial appetite'; MacDonald, unlike his colleagues, agreed with Phipps, noting 'the Saar vote brings war nearer'.[12] From the Paris Embassy came the news that the German Ambassador in Paris after the Saar decision adopted 'an increasingly aggressive attitude'.

Barthou was assassinated in October and succeeded by Laval as Foreign Secretary, who continued his policy of seeking security from Germany by means of an alliance with Russia. The omens were not good for the Simon–Eden visit to Berlin. The British wanted to act as 'brokers' between Germany and France over legislation to authorize the German rearmament and a general accord on limiting further rearmament by all countries. The French had no faith in any agreement signed by Hitler, and were intent on a British guarantee of armed assistance. Thus they were annoyed when Simon in December 1934 rejected a proposal for Anglo-French staff talks which the French felt should be held because of new blatant evidence about German rearmament.

Flandin told Campbell in Paris on 22 January 1935 that 'he was ready to agree to almost anything' provided Britain would assure him of immediate military assistance in case of need. However, the next day, after a Cabinet meeting, Flandin said that two of his Ministers were 'almost irreconcilable to *any* form of agreement with Germany' although personally he would be prepared to replace Part 5 of Versailles if there was some limitation agreement which included both French superiority in men and materials plus 'adequate guarantees of execution with automatic supervision', combined with agreement with Britain on 'the exact form and time of assistance' they would furnish.[13]

There was no chance of Hitler agreeing to French superiority, and Flandin's statement was evidence that no *modus vivendi* with France was on the cards. Campbell had been instructed by Simon to make it clear 'there was absolutely nothing doing in London on the lines of a military agreement'. Yet a military agreement was the sticking-point for France, and without it French leaders were adamant they would not contemplate legalizing Hitler's rearmament. The omens were poor for Simon's trip to Paris.

Foreign Office and Cabinet hopes that France would approve a general settlement with Germany on rearmament and disarmament lingered on despite dramatic events which overtook the negotiations and which proved the French had been more realistic and correct than the British in their distrust of Germany. It was a pity that staff talks with the French and a British guarantee to France in case of a German attack did not appeal to the British Cabinet; they might have conceivably brought Hitler to reason, but the British archives show this was considered almost sacrilege in Whitehall.

There is a mass of archival material about the 1934–35 negotiations with the French and Germans but the great bulk of it can be disregarded. The French proposed an Eastern Pact (known as the Eastern Locarno) under which France and Russia would guarantee Germany, Poland, Czechoslovakia and the Baltic states against any aggression. This was never a runner; one important factor for its failure was that if Germany attacked Poland, Russian troops would have to be allowed to cross it to confront the aggressor. Poland would never agree to this, mainly because they felt that if Russian troops were allowed into Poland they would never depart.

As prospects became dim for the success of the Eastern Locarno, France became more and more attracted to a simple Franco-Russian Alliance as a defence for France against Germany.

The first concrete result of this French diplomatic move was that Russia returned to the League of Nations. There she could have been a strong force in restraining Hitler but as will be seen, Britain and the Poles foiled this.

Considerable efforts were made by the British and French to negotiate a Convention with Germany to outlaw aerial bombing. Hitler even gave this lip-service, although he had no intention of observing such an agreement if it was reached. Under the proposals France would have to accept cancellation of Part 5 of Versailles, and Britain would be obliged to bomb

Germany if she attacked France, and France to bomb Germany if she attacked Britain. Prolonged international negotiations on an Eastern Locarno and an Air Pact can best be categorized in Robert Blake's phrase as belonging to the 'debris of history'.[14]

The long-awaited Anglo-French conversations took place at Downing Street between 1 and 3 February 1935. MacDonald, Simon and Eden represented the British; Flandin and Laval, the French. They discussed Eastern Locarno, a Convention to stop bombing (the British naively expecting that in return for this the French would legalize German rearmament, including recognizing their illegal Air Force), the dangers arising from German rearmament, and the possibility of Germany returning to the League. Britain wanted a formula to legalize Hitler's rearmament; the French categorically refused. The stumbling-block was Britain's refusal of a guarantee of military aid to France in the event of a German attack; without this the French Government declared (correctly) they could not carry public opinion with them if they agreed to cancel Part 5 of Versailles. As a result the discussions were abortive, as were those when John Simon visited Paris on 28 February. He told the French that he would probably visit Berlin at the end of the following week.[15]

On 4 March 1935 the actual British White Paper on Defence was published. This drew attention to German rearmament, which it declared might 'produce a situation where peace will be in peril', and announced that the British Government had given up hopes of international disarmament and intended to start rearming. The date of the issue of the White Paper had not been influenced by Simon's proposed visit to Berlin; the Estimates debate was scheduled for 11 March, and it was inevitable that the White Paper appeared seven days before.

Reaction from Berlin was swift. Before lunch on 5 March the Foreign Office received a telegram that the British visit must be postponed and no alternative date could be fixed because Hitler had become 'hoarse'. Later Ribbentrop admitted to Phipps that Hitler's malady was 'half throat and half White Paper'. On the other hand, there was jubiliation in Paris.[16]

The Labour Opposition jibbed at the White Paper on the grounds that British rearmament would imperil disarmament negotiations, and this was contrary to the 'Covenant spirit' of the League of Nations; Philip Snowden told the *Manchester Guardian* that the White Paper was the most tragic document since the war. Not surprisingly, Snowden's statement was given prominence in the German national press.

A swift counter-strike came from Hitler. On 9 March Goering announced the existence of an illegal German air force, and on 16 March Hitler decreed German conscription and an army of thirty-six divisions and 500,000 men in peace time. The Treaty of Versailles had been breached.

Italy and France wanted Simon's visit to Berlin cancelled; so did Eden, Under-Secretary for Foreign Affairs, but he was not in the Cabinet and was overruled by Simon, with whom he was on bad terms. Britain sent a note of formal protest to Berlin without consulting either France or Italy. This was a grave mistake, and the inclusion in the Note of a request to be informed whether the German Government still wanted Simon and Eden to come was resented by the French and Italians. The Italians and French wanted the British trip to Berlin cancelled as a rebuke to Hitler.

The French press commented that the British were 'dupes of Hitler'. Simon and Vansittart erroneously thought the Note would not be unsatisfactory to the French and Italian Governments, but were soon disillusioned by the British Ambassadors in Berlin and Rome, who both stated forcibly that the Italians and French were interpreting the British note as dividing Britain from France and Italy. According to Phipps, Hitler took the Note as evidence that France was unable to form a common front with Britain against Germany.

German conscription was applauded in the German press, so that Hitler's popularity rose. Hitler explained to Phipps that he had to introduce conscription as France had increased the length of her compulsory service to two years, and he must have parity with France on land, sea and air.[17]

The proposed British visit to Berlin took place on 25 and 26 March, and four meetings with Hitler were held. Eden noticed a marked 'deterioration' in the German dictator. His favourable impression of twelve months ago was reversed. Now Eden found Hitler 'negative and shifty, his tone conspicuously hostile, even contemptuous', and noted in his diary: 'results bad . . . Prussian spirit very much in evidence'. Hitler offered no concessions, and no progress was made. Simon spent considerable time explaining to Hitler involved legal arguments about colonies and the League of Nations which Hitler clearly did not understand; while Eden reported to the Cabinet that there was 'no basis for agreement with Germany in view of her demands on land and sea'.[18] This was accurate but alas Eden did not stick to this view later.

However, there *was* one sinister result. At the third meeting Simon said the British Government 'earnestly desired' an agreement with Germany on naval power. On 16 March Hitler had told Phipps he would be content to have 35 per cent of the strength of the British fleet. Hitler and Simon agreed to naval negotiations in London* on that basis, although Simon indicated that 35 per cent might be too high. Meanwhile Hitler told Simon that Germany had reached air parity with Britain; Simon made no protest.

---

*This had been suggested by Sir Robert Craigie, Assistant Under-Secretary, in a Foreign Office memorandum dated 14.3.35.

To make a bilateral agreement with Germany divorced from one on general disarmament, and to permit the conquered power 35 per cent of the strength of the British fleet, would be a gross breach of Part 5 of the Treaty of Versailles. On top of that, such an agreement without consultation with the other powers would be a breach of Locarno. Unfortunately, Simon and the Cabinet did not see it that way; nor did the Chiefs of Staff. The Royal Navy was experiencing an acute shortage of ships, for it needed to police at the same time the Far East, the Mediterranean and the German coastal waters. The Admiralty thought that by an agreement limiting Germany's fleet they would need to station fewer British ships around the German coast and the Mediterranean so that it would be easier to fulfil their commitments in the Far East and for the defence of India. The main impulse for the 1935 Anglo-German Naval Agreement came in fact from the Admiralty. The negotiations were based, of course, on allowing Germany to free herself from Part 5 of Versailles, and were a single-handed effort by Britain to legalize on an ad hoc basis German rearmament.[19]

The official historian suggest that it was not Simon but Hoare who was responsible for Britain agreeing to the Anglo-German Naval Agreement. This is incorrect. The formal agreement was made on 6 June, which was Simon's last day as Foreign Secretary, and he signed the Aide Mémoire. He originally had misgivings, and had warned on more than one occasion that he thought the 35 per cent ratio was too high, and also of the dangers of concluding a separate Treaty with Germany to supersede the Naval Accords of Washington and London. The author has been unable to find any record that Simon expressed a view on the inherent drawback that the Agreement breached Part 5 of Versailles or Locarno, which should have been important to him with his lawyer's mind.[20]

Unfortunately, all issues of naval disarmament were dealt with in the Foreign Office by the American Department, not the Central Department, which was responsible for the mainstream of British relations with Germany. The Central Department was opposed to the negotiations, recording (with good reason) that they were 'gratuitously providing the German Government with just the kind of opportunity they so much relished to drive a wedge between her and her closest friends'.

The Naval talks began in London on 4 June. Ribbentrop was the chief German negotiator, and he began by declaring that he would stop the talks unless Britain conceded from the outset the principle of the 35 per cent ratio claimed by Germany to which Simon had demurred in Berlin. The British negotiators explained to the Germans that they would have to give other governments an opportunity to express their views before giving a final answer, but they reported to the Cabinet Committee responsible that 'it would be a mistake to withhold acceptance merely on the ground that other powers might feel some temporary annoyance at our action', and warned that 'if we now refuse to agree the offer for the purpose of the discussions Herr Hitler will withdraw the offer and Germany will seek to build up to a higher level than 35%'. This take-it-or-leave-it diplomacy was typical of the Nazis. Simon and his colleagues meekly accepted it.

After a brief informal discussion in the Cabinet Room on 5 June following a lunch at 10 Downing Street for the British and German delegations, the Ministers responsible agreed that Simon should be authorized to accept the German offer. After the lunch Simon told the Germans 'we had decided in favour of the Agreement, but for courtesy and for fairness we must inform other Governments of our decision'. Simon went on: 'we could congratulate ourselves that our two nations should have been able to make this great contribution to the limitation of armaments, the promotion of peace and the confirmation of the friendship between our two peoples.'

At a meeting on the previous day Ribbentrop had reiterated that he wanted 'a formal appreciation by the British Government of Herr Hitler's acceptance of the 35% ratio'. Simon confirmed on 5 June that His Majesty's Government agreed 'to a permanent relationship between the two fleets in the proportion of 35 for the German Fleet and 100 for the British Fleet'. Simon emphasized that it was 'extremely important that we should officially inform the other Governments before anything at all appeared in the press'.

The news was immediately sent to the Ambassadors in London of other governments. The Japanese had no objection; the Italian Government were not openly hostile; but the French deplored it as an unilateral revision of the Treaty of Versailles and a serious blow to the common front of Stresa six weeks before (see chapter 7), saying it had 'prejudiced the prospect of reaching an acceptable solution of armament problem as a whole'. There were rumours in diplomatic circles from Rome that Mussolini 'nearly went through the roof of the Palazzo Chigi when he heard of it, and that it was a contributory factor to deciding him upon his Abyssinian venture'.

Litvinov said Hitler had won 'a great diplomatic victory' (true) which implied the end of Anglo-French co-operation (untrue) and that Germany would now hasten to build as quickly as possible up to the limit which afterwards she need no longer observe (true); the Belgian reaction was also bad. Britain obtained no advantage in naval security, and it did not improve relations with Hitler. The truth lay rather in Churchill's words 'What had in fact been done was to authorise Germany to build to her utmost capacity for five or six years to come'.[21]

Eden took no part in the negotiations and probably was not even consulted by Simon, during the vital two days 5 and 6 June, when the momentous decision to abandon Part 5 of Versailles was made unilaterally by Britain. Thus no blame can be attached to Eden for this folly.

On 19 June Ribbentrop said details of German construction must be kept secret. Here he was trying to drive a wedge between France and Britain. Corbin (the French Ambassador) went to see Vansittart on 25 June, and alarmed him by saying that the French were disturbed because the Germans refused to give them full details of their ship-building programme. Vansittart minuted 'This has the making of an ugly situation because we had promised the Germans to keep it secret.' Because of this and a burst of indignation from Paris, Eden was sent there to try to placate the French. Laval told him that the Agreement was a breach of Versailles, and reminded him that at Stresa (in April) he had been told that the British would not accept the German claim of 35 per cent, Laval added that the united front of Stresa was broken into pieces, and claimed that it 'released them [Germany] from Part 5, and the German Government were delighted while the French had been given no chance to influence the Agreement'. Eden – himself unhappy about the Pact – did his best to calm Laval, and was successful in that on 27 June the French put out a helpful press statement.[22]

On 19 June Hoare brought the Agreement to the Cabinet and told them he and the First Lord of the Admiralty (Eyres-Monsell) had thought it

> important to conclude an Agreement which would enable us to control German programmes of naval armaments, instead of the probable alternative of an Anglo-German competition in naval armaments. In recent years many opportunities of achieving disarmament had been lost through delay in seizing the favourable moment. It had been clear to the two Ministers that a better agreement could not be obtained from Germany and that it was essential to seize the present opportunity and secure the German signature to an Agreement. Everything possible had been done to obtain the good will of France and Italy. Nevertheless the French had started a press campaign on the subject, and the French Government had sent a Note which could be described as one of criticism rather than of outraged surprise.

Eyres-Monsell (First Lord of the Admiralty) said

> the naval staff were satisfied and had been anxious to bring about an agreement, more especially as they rather suspected that if there had been any delay the German Naval Staff would have tried to whittle away what was proposed. The arrangements as to submarines were the most likely to be criticised.

Well might Eyres-Monsell say the submarine arrangements were 'the most likely to be criticised'. The Anglo-German Naval Agreement laid down that, as long as Germany did not exceed 35 per cent of Britain's *total* tonnage, she should have the right to *submarine* tonnage equal to the total possessed by the British Commonwealth. However, 'unless there were special circumstances, which would be discussed in a friendly manner with the United Kingdom,' Germany's submarine tonnage would not exceed 45 per cent of that of the British Commonwealth. Over submarines Ribbentrop was telling one lie after another. The Versailles Treaty had laid down that Germany should not build submarines, or train personnel to man them, but both the Weimar Republic and the Nazi Government had been contravening these provisions (this was always vehemently denied). Germany from the start evaded these clauses; the full story came out at the cross-examination of Admirals Raeder and Doenitz at the Nuremberg Trials in 1946.[23]

★　　　★　　　★

It is strange that Naval Intelligence did not discover that the German *U–1* submarine was commissioned on 29 June, nine days before the Anglo-German Naval Agreement was officially signed, and was joined at approximately eight-day intervals by *U–2* and *U–12*. Admiral Doenitz reported to Admiral Raeder on 10 October 1935 that the German navy had twelve submarines ready for combat, and on 7 March 1936 (when the German army reoccupied the Rhineland) there were seventeen submarines ready for deployment off France. It is difficult to believe that British secret-service agents failed to report anything about German illegal submarine-building; if they did, it was conveniently ignored.

Lies were told by the Hitler Government about the existence of submarines and the training of their crews. On 9 April 1934 Captain Muirhead-Gould R.N., the British naval attaché in Berlin, called on Captain Densch, Chief of Staff to the head of the German Admiralty, Admiral Raeder, after an article published in the *Daily Telegraph* on 4 April alleged clandestine German naval rearmament. The German naval estimates for 1934 jumped by 100 per cent in 1933, which, according to the *Telegraph*, was because of 'new construction and research'. Captain Densch stated that only one cruiser, four reserve destroyers, eight minesweepers, and two fleet tenders were under construction. When submarines were mentioned Densch said Germany would have to have submarines, but did not admit they already had them. Instead he said it would take three years to build up an adequate submarine service, as although there were still a good many officers with submarine service in the Navy, there were no young officers and no men; he also volunteered that no personnel had been trained in Russian submarines.[24]

In fact the German naval staff had been training submarine personnel, and a training school had been set up under the camouflage of an 'anti-submarine' school. Here mock-ups were provided for training purposes, and assembly and repair work was performed by the students on equipment that was later to be installed in the boats under construction. Thus at the time of the Anglo-German Naval Agreement the German navy had a practical knowledge of submarine operations, and she was in a position to launch a fully fledged submarine fleet in 1935.

There had been a French scare about German submarines on 13 May 1934, when the French radio reported that German submarines had taken part in manoeuvres off Kiel. This was true, but the German Admiralty declared they had no submarines. Phipps accepted this and wrote on 22 June 1935 that 'Germany, having destroyed 315 submarines, had waited for sixteen years for the abolition of submarines by other powers, and not until April 1935 did she determine to build twelve boats of the smallest displacement.' This shows how the Germans had pulled the wool over his eyes.[25]

There was another French scare in December when Muirhead-Gould was told by the French Deuxième bureau (Military Intelligence) that Germany was secretly building five submarines in Krupp's yards at Kiel on covered slipways. Muirhead-Gould went to Kiel but could not get close enough to find any evidence, and on 15 December 1934 Sargent minuted: 'I would prefer to say nothing to the Germans until we see a little more clearly how the general question of German rearmament is going.' The Foreign Office obviously felt that as the Cabinet were considering legitimizing German naval rearmament it was not worth while making a fuss about infringements of Versailles. Thus the French got no support, although as will be seen, their news was correct.

Even if the Admiralty were unaware of Hitler's clandestine building of submarines, journalists of the *Daily Mail* were better informed. The proprietor, Lord Rothermere, wrote to Ramsay MacDonald on 30 September 1934:

> the Germans are engaged in the intensive manufacture of submarines. . . . [One great British] business had large frozen assets in Germany. With a view of realising this money they decided to build tramp steamers in Germany. On applying to Blöhm and Voss, Germany's biggest shipbuilders, they were told they were fully engaged and could not tender for the work, although on an inspection of their works at Hamburg there was not one single ship on the stocks. There was, however, great activity under cover and it was learned that the work in hand was the building of a new type of submarine.[26]

In 1920 the international Disarmament Commission set up by the Treaty of Versailles had ensured that all existing German submarines were destroyed, but they failed to destroy the engineer design team. In 1920 the Japanese Navy purchased from the Germanis Dockyard Company and Vulkan Dockyard Company the plans for three types of submarines which became the prototypes for those of Japan, and both firms sent German construction teams to Japanese shipyards. The Japanese navy would not retain the German submarine design team once its own personnel were trained, and the Germans set up a Dutch firm, Ingenieur voor Scheepbouw I Voors at The Hague to secure contracts to develop submarine design for foreign navies. This firm was secretly subsidized by the German navy.

In 1925 I Voors secured a contract for two Turkish submarines after the German navy gave the firm a million marks to ensure they underbid the British and French yards; in 1927 the Reich Finance Minister loaned 12 million Reichsmarks to I Voors. Because of leaks to the press about I Voors a new firm, Ingewit, was set up by the German Government and charged with developing an efficient German submarine arm for wartime. I Voors won orders for submarines from Argentina and Sweden. These submarines were built in Finland with technical supervision provided by German specialist officers and German naval engineers, who were assigned to the Finnish yards to gain experience.

In 1927 Admiral Canaris, through his personal influence with King Alfonso of Spain and Prime Minister de Rivera, secured a Spanish order for a 750-ton submarine which was to be built at the Ecgevarritta Dockyard at Cadiz under the supervision of the German staff of I Voors. This Spanish shipyard went bankrupt, and 80 per cent of the cost was paid by the German navy, while German technicians and shipwrights went to work in Cadiz. When completed the submarine was placed under the command of a German officer, Lt Braetigan, and with a crew composed mainly of German officers and seamen it carried out its trials under the authorization of the Spanish navy but directed by the German navy.

In March 1929 Austen Chamberlain decided *not* to make representations to the German Government about the reported construction of a submarine at Cadiz with material supported from Germany. Chamberlain told the Admiralty he was reluctant to take the lead in accusing Germany of breaches of the Treaty because of reports in foreign newspapers.[27]

Because of the civil war and the overthrow of the monarchy Spain refused to pay for the ship, and the Germans negotiated her sale to Turkey in 1934, where she was renamed *Gur*. The Germans could not own the submarine openly, but they considered the monetary loss more than offset by the experience gained in submarine-construction, and in the use of splashless torpedoes.

In 1930 Admiral Raeder called for the design of a submarine with components unrecognizable as those of a submarine before construction. In response to Raeder's directive I Voors and Ingewit designed a 250-ton submarine, and agreed with Finland that it should be built at Abo for the Finnish navy. 1 1/2 million Reichsmarks was allocated by the Germans navy. The vessel was assembled in Finland, and was the first submarine to be officially planned and constructed by the German navy since the First World War. It was the prototype for the German *U–1 – U–24* class.

Capitalizing on its clandestine knowledge of submarine construction, the German navy placed orders within Germany for twenty-four 250-ton submarines as soon as Hitler came to power. This was in flagrant violation of the Treaty of Versailles. A warehouse at Kiel was used for Ingewit to store engines, apparatus and spare parts for twelve submarines, and a construction shed was erected. In this, hidden from public view, six 250-ton submarines were partially assembled during 1934–35, though the French obtained information of this manoeuvre. Orders were also placed for parts for two 712-ton submarines *U–25* and *U–26*, and enough parts were officially ordered for these boats eventually to be commissioned within nine months of being laid down. Further clandestine designs were made by I Voors and Ingewit for two 500-ton submarines, but both companies were dissolved after the Anglo-German Naval Treaty, and the personnel and the work in progress incorporated directly into the German navy.

It is difficult to believe that nothing of this was known to the British Admiralty, and that they were unaware that Ribbentrop was lying about German submarine construction during the negotiations for the Anglo-German Naval Treaty. Did the Admiralty ignore German submarine construction because it was keen to conclude the Agreement and make more of the British Fleet available for the Far East? It is a fascinating question.[28]

As a result of the Anglo-German Naval Agreement and the previous secret submarine-construction activities, the German navy had 56 submarines in operation when the war started on 3 September 1939. This was far in excess of the number permitted under the Anglo-German Treaty, and a figure which could not possibly have been attained if before 1935 Germany had not built submarines or trained crews to man them.

By agreeing to the Anglo-German Naval Pact the British Government took a reckless gamble, believing it could rely on Hitler's signature (despite overwhelming evidence to the contrary), and irresponsibly turned its back on the provisions for German disarmament in the Treaty of Versailles – which in 1935 could still have been invoked to preserve peace. The members of the Cabinet were also heavily influenced by electoral considerations. They knew vast sums would be needed for naval rearmament without the specious protection of the Agreement with Germany, and that this would be ill received by the voters; instead of facing up to their responsibilities and risking electoral defeat by doing what was right for the nation, they opted out of their responsibilities.

If the British Government had abandoned the League of Nations it would have been justifiable and realistic. Equally justifiable and realistic would have been to take the Covenant at its face value and invoke it against Germany for her transgressions against Versailles, calling on France and the smaller countries to risk a preventive war in which Germany could have had no chance of prevailing. Instead Britain hesitated between the two courses. This was fatal.

When Hitler tried to force Nazism on Austria in 1934 and was ignominiously defeated he changed course and ate humble pie. There is reason to believe that if confronted in 1935 with the power of France, Britain, Italy and the smaller countries after being arraigned before the League of Nations for illegal rearmament, he might have done the same and followed the road of caution. Then his armed strength would never have reached the stage where he could conquer all Europe.

During 1934 and 1935 the National Government with a steam-roller Commons majority had surprisingly little difficulty in persuading its back-bench MPs to support its appeasement policy. Winston Churchill and Austen Chamberlain in their speeches continually emphasized the dangers of Hitler's rearmament and the importance of keeping step with France and guaranteeing French security. Neither carried much weight with Tory MPs. Churchill was looked on as wild, and the Government whips consistently told the younger MPs that he was an alcoholic, while he spoilt his own case by personal abuse. His influence also diminished because of his unorthodox stand during the abdication crisis of 1936, and his obstinate refusal even to discuss Dominion status for India.

One young Conservative MP of the 1931 intake told the author that Austen was not taken seriously by the younger MPs. His clothes and manner were Edwardian, and he talked with the language of the past. This MP, T. B. Martin, also stated that Simon was most unpopular with Conservative back-benchers and that they would have had little confidence in his appeasement policy if it had not been strongly endorsed by Eden. He recalled that Eden spoke in the House lucidly and with conviction, and was frank and forthcoming in private conversation. Simon's other Under-Secretary, Robert Cranborne (later Lord Salisbury) also belonged to the traditional aristocratic landowning section of the Conservative Party and was friendly and likeable. In the Commons smoking-room both put the points in favour of Simon's policy forcibly and enthusiastically.[29]

It is hard to discover why Simon was pro-Hitler as Foreign Secretary. The most convincing explanation comes from Richard Griffiths in his book *Fellow Travellers of the Right*. He alleges Simon was affectionate to Mrs Ronnie Greville (Maggie), widow of the heir to the Earl of Warwick, who had died in 1909. She was the daughter of the Glasgow brewer and Conservative MP Sir William McEwen. Immensely rich, she was a grand political hostess both in Mayfair and at her country house Polesden Lacey.

After a visit to Germany in 1934 she became a Hitler-lover and radiated pro-Nazi views at her parties. Lord Home told the author she was a political busybody who collected many enemies. Towards the end of the First War she and Simon (whose wife had died in childbirth) had considered marriage, but Simon instead married an Irish woman Katharine Manning (described to the author by Viscount Hailsham as an 'Irish bigot).'. According to Viscountess Simon her stepmother-in-law resented Simon's friendship with Maggie Greville.

In July 1941 Leo Amery recorded in his diary that he had met the Simons at lunch and the Viscountess was 'an incredible woman!' while Maggie Greville told him that when she rejected John Simon he wrote her a letter in which he said he 'would marry the first woman he came across'. Viscountess Simon told the author that it was Maggie who had suggested marriage to Simon, and when he refused they had a quarrel during which he proposed to his second wife, but they never got on and he remained fond of Maggie Greville, managing to see her every week without his wife knowing. Harold Nicolson was 'always amazed' how the mischievous and venomous Maggie Greville managed to command the affection of so many friends, writing 'How comes it that this plump and venomous bitch should hold such social power'.[30]

By April 1935 the Conservatives had had enough of Simon as Foreign Secretary and wanted one of their own party. Those who favoured the League blamed him for the failure of the Disarmament Conference and the impotency of the League over Japanese aggression in Manchuria from 1931–33. The right-wingers criticized Simon for subservience to the League, which they thought diminished Britain's sovereignty, and 'the final straw' for them was Simon's approval of the admission of the Soviet Union to the League in September 1934. In April 1935 70 Conservative M.P.s protested to Baldwin against Simon staying at the Foreign Office, and Baldwin admitted to Austen Chamberlain that the Cabinet no longer had confidence in Simon as Foreign Secretary.

Lord Home told the author that the request to Baldwin to remove Simon was due more to Simon's personal unpopularity, than to his policy, and in his view few Conservative M.P.s wanted strong action after the reintroduction of German conscription and the announcement of the creation of an air force in 1935 and the remilitarisation of the Rhineland in 1936.

Julian Amery recalls how in the late 1930s when he was dining at All Souls with his father, Simon and Brüning. Simon expressed hope to Brüning that Britain might reach a satisfactory agreement with Hitler. This produced the dusty response from the former German Chancellor that any agreement which Britain got from Hitler would be on Hitler's own terms.

In his autobiography Walford Selby comments that Simon's tenure of the Foreign Office was 'a calamitous passage indeed', while Lord Gladwyn writes that 'it was generally alleged in the Foreign Office that Simon was a terrible Foreign Secretary often going back on his decisions and not really trusted by his own side or the other.'[31]

CHAPTER SEVEN

STRESA AND THE ABYSSINIAN WAR

'It would be a truly meritorious action if the Great British people in a spirit of fraternal accord would realise by peaceful means the legal aspirations of the Italian people.' (Pope Pius XI in a confidential memorandum on Mussolini's plan to take over Abyssinia.)

FRANCE AND Italy were both so alarmed at the German reintroduction of conscription and the announcement of the existence of a German air force that they delivered notes of protest to Berlin in March 1935. Britain did the same, but less enthusiastically. These notes were clearly insufficient in face of the blatant and illegal German rearmament, and accordingly as a result of the initiative taken by Drummond and Mussolini in Rome, a three-power conference was called at Stresa in Northern Italy from 11 to 14 April to discuss further steps.

The Cabinet was in cowardly mood when on 8 April it held a special meeting to consider policy for Stresa. It was agreed that Britain should avoid a complete breach with Germany and take no action except to threaten her. She should decline to join in an undertaking 'that we would be prepared to take forcible action anywhere. Germany was in a volcanic mood and not inclined to yield to threats. We ought not to agree to such a proposition unless we were prepared to take action anywhere, e.g. in the event of trouble in Memel.* There was general agreement that we ought not to accept further commitments . . .'[1]

At Stresa MacDonald and Simon represented Britain; Flandin and Laval were sent by France, and Mussolini and Suvich (Under-Secretary for Foreign Affairs) came for Italy. Vansittart and Strang were the British advisers; Léger and Noel the French, and Baron Aloisi the Italian.

The records of the Stresa discussions reveal clearly the attitudes of the respective governments, but have been neglected by most historians. Mussolini was forthright and frank and much more supportive of the French in their desire to restrain Hitler than were the British, who demurred at all suggestions of resolute action. The British deceived the other powers because when Simon gave an account of his trip to Berlin he failed to mention his discussion with Hitler about an agreed figure for the German Fleet (35 per cent of the British), or the Anglo-German naval talks which were scheduled to begin in London soon. Baldwin's telegram to Simon when the Conference concluded is revealing:

> We understand that it was not possible to mention to French and Italian Governments at Stresa proposed informal exchange of views in London between British and German Governments (re Naval Pact); and we do not know if it is intended to do this at Geneva . . . It is evident that announcements of naval programme outside treaty limits on eve of London discussions would greatly complicate the situation . . . (because) we should, whilst theoretically reserving the treaty position, be discussing with a Germany which had already broken the Treaty.

Simon replied that we were pledged to discussions (on a naval agreement) 'with a Germany which had already torn up the Treaty (Versailles) by her air and land rearmament.'

The French might well have broken up the Conference if they had known Britain's intention to condone and legalize German naval rearmament. Vansittart did mention to Italian and French diplomats at Stresa that 'we were proposing to discuss naval questions with Germany', but neither the French nor the Italian statesmen had any idea of the enormity of the proposed breach of Versailles.[2]

Only two important issues were discussed at Stresa. They were Hitler's designs on Austria, and how the League of Nations could prevent illegal German rearmament. On both issues Britain dragged her feet. She lagged behind France in supporting Italy over Austria, and behind Italy over France's appeal to the League. This appeal (due to be heard on 18 April)

---

*Memel was the largest port in Lithuania, with a predominantly German population. It had been taken away from Germany in 1923, but Hitler was agitating for its return. He seized it in March 1939. It is now again in Lithuania, and thus part of Soviet Russia, being known as Klaipeda.

protested about Germanys' conscription and her creation of an air force in violation of Versailles.

Mussolini realistically told the Conference that the situation in Austria was 'not good'. The present Government had not the prestige of the Dollfuss Government. The youth of the country was in favour of the 'Anschluss' while if conscription was introduced 'the majority of the army would be Nazi'. He declared that the Anschluss would not be a direct threat to Italy, but Germany in Vienna 'meant Germany on the Bosphorus, and the revival of the Berlin-Baghdad drive'.

He was right. Once Hitler had Austria his road to the east would be open, and justifiably Mussolini said Stresa must do 'something for Austria', which was awaiting the results 'with anxiety'. Mussolini and Laval wanted a Central European Pact under which the defeated powers of the First World War, Austria, Hungary and Bulgaria, would be freed from the restrictions of Versailles and permitted to strengthen the armed forces of the Little Entente against Germany. He was enthusiastically supported by Laval.

Laval complained that Britain 'had no intention of taking any part in the effective defence of Austria'. Simon could not deny this, and replied Britain would 'support' the pact but could not 'contract into it', and it might cause misunderstanding if Britain supported a declaration about Austria in the same way as France and Italy, while MacDonald said they 'blessed and approved' the independence and integrity of Austria without being committed further. MacDonald insisted that he would not be shifted into more positive support of Austrian independence. In the statement issued after the Conference the three powers stressed their 'desire' for continued Austrian independence. However, the statement – it read: 'The Three Powers recognised that the integrity and independence of Austria would continue to inspire their common policy' – would have been stronger if it had not been for the British intransigence.

Of great importance were the discussions over German illegal rearmament and the forthcoming French appeal to the League over Germany's repudiation of her international obligations. The French circulated a paper by their representative at Cologne which can have left the delegates in no doubt about Hitler's intention to remilitarize the Rhineland, either by agreement or unilaterally in the near future, and the consequent likelihood of an early German denunciation of Locarno. This resulted in the Stresa powers reaffirming their obligations under the Treaty of Locarno, and declaring their intention 'should the need arise faithfully to fulfil them'.

Over armaments Simon reminded the Conference that Germany 'was ready to apply a system of permanent and automatic supervision'; if other countries did the same; it is hard to believe he was genuinely convinced of this; and in any case the great stumbling-blockage (as he more than anyone else knew) at the Disarmament Conference at Geneva had been this precise point. Mussolini was right again when he suggested they might say that the Disarmament Conference had been stricken with 'paralysis' as a result of German rearmament.

The sole concrete result of the discussions on rearmament was agreement on the text of the French resolution for the Council of the League of Nations at Geneva about German rearmament. The French produced a memorandum on economic sanctions which might be applied to Germany by the League. Simon did not applaud, and instead emphasized the difficulties about applying sanctions, citing Japan. Laval saw this as obstructive because he had only suggested sanctions should be 'studied' in the event of any further violation, and explained that at Geneva he would not be asking the League to take sanctions but only to study them, declaring that unless he proposed this he would be 'covering himself and the Council with ridicule'. Mussolini agreed with Laval, but not MacDonald, who was unable to reply when Flandin asked him if he had 'any firm proposal to make which would avoid the future danger of violation'. The draft French resolution proposed that as 'the extent of the vast and uncontrolled rearmament was a threat to security', the Council of the League condemned the failure of Germany to honour her undertakings and requested the League to take action.

This would mean appointing a committee to study sanctions. As the discussion developed the British baulked at the clause relating to sanctions, but Mussolini supported the French against Simon, who deployed a blocking legal argument to the effect that there was nothing in the Covenant providing for coercive action merely on the grounds of violation of a Treaty, and this was 'entirely new'. MacDonald said it was impossible to commit the British Government.

Flandin 'begged' the British to co-operate for the sake of European peace, but MacDonald was adamant that the draft resolution must be watered down. The British also objected to the draft press statement on the conclusion of the Conference as being too provocative to Germany. Eventually, in order to avoid a breakdown of the Conference Simon and MacDonald compromised on both points.

The discussions reveal that Britain was more sympathetic to Hitler than were Flandin, Laval and Mussolini. Simon and MacDonald had their hands tied because they were committed to talks with Germany about legalizing German naval rearmament, and it is extraordinary how they could have sat through seven sessions at Stresa without letting their allies know what they intended to do as soon as the Conference was over.[3]

In a telegram to Baldwin after the Conference Simon laid bare his difficulties over the Geneva Resolution. He wrote (author's italics):

It became in fact clear at an early stage in the Stresa negotiations that no such
solidarity could in fact have been maintained except on condition of collaboration at
Geneva on French reference. It should be added moreover that I succeeded in
considerably *attenuating terms* of resolution agreed at Geneva.[4]

Mussolini (whose subsequent conduct it is impossible to defend) emerges
with shining colours from Stresa. The eminent Oxford historian R. B.
McCallum writes that then: 'Italy with her military force and strong and
virile Government held the balance of power in Europe.' His words were ill
received when published during the war, but no one reading the small print
of Stresa can doubt that Mussolini then was ready to use his power sensibly
to curb Hitler while Britain was not. The three participants at the
Conference had ample forces to impose peace and stop German rearmament. Any chance of them doing so was dissipated by Britain.[5]

Nevertheless, the Conference set up what became known as the Stresa
Front against German rearmament and Nazi aggression in Austria, and for
the last time the three victorious allies of the First World War were in
agreement. Had the Stresa Front held, Hitler's plans must have been
thwarted.

A grave setback for the German dictator was the British–French–Italian
resolution condemning his rearmament which was passed by the Council of
the League at Geneva on 17 April, two days after the conclusion of the
Stresa Conference. The condemnation of Germany was unanimous, with
only Denmark abstaining, and a committee of 13 members including Russia
was set up to consider sanctions. This was the high tide of League
resistance to German rearmament.

In spite of Britain being lukewarm, France had established a solid three-
power front against Hitler, and at the League Council the other nations of
the world had supported France and given effect to a resolution under
which concrete measures to restrain Hitler's rearmament could be expected
to flow after the League Committee of 13 had studied the feasibility of
sanctions.

The importance of this 17 April 1935 condemnation of Germany has
been largely overlooked. Within the Foreign Office doubts were expressed
about the Stresa French Memorandum on sanctions against Germany. In a
minute on 15 April Creswell summarized them: 'It is not certain that an
embargo on certain exports to one specified country can be simultaneously
efficacious and peaceful; it will either do little or nothing to hold up
German rearmament, or may lead Germany, with her complete control of
public opinion, to risk striking a blow.' It was referred to the CLD, who
received a long report from a sub-committee on 6 June stating that the
French proposals would not only cripple Germany's munitions output but

would also disrupt her ordinary economic life, and they regarded it as 'almost inconceivable that Germany would be prepared to remain passive under the threat of such continued control'. By the time the report was received the focus of attention was on Italy and not Germany, and Whitehall was to take a different stand about sanctions against Italy.[6]

Phipps reported German alarm over the Geneva Resolution; it might have 'far reaching consequences in Germany' and would probably 'put an end' to Germany's return to the League . . .' German public opinion is so hostile to the League that it will support Herr Hitler unreservedly in any action which he may choose . . . Moderate opinion in military and official circles is unanimous in regarding the League's attitude as the acme of hypocrisy . . . Hitler may now press on rearmament with increased speed.'[6]

R. F. Wigram had a firm reaction to Phipps' telegram. On 17 April he minuted; '. . . we must stand firm now. As to the League I don't know that we want Germany back while she is trying to blackmail us about colonies and no doubt other things. Perhaps Hitler will "associate further negotiations on disarmament with other European questions" but there too we must not be blackmailed. The possibility of a further expansion of the Air Force is not surprising. It is inevitable as long as Germany is not convinced that the other powers cannot expand quicker than she.'[7]

It would have been a different story if more in Whitehall had taken Wigram's strong line. Unfortunately, Wigram's was almost a lone voice and his view did not appeal to either Simon or Eden.

From Paris, Clerk reported that the Resolution had been received 'with considerable gratification by the French Press which is full of tribute to M. Laval. This is held to be the first fruits of the new solidarity established at Stresa . . . Fortune favours the brave and the resolute tactics adopted by the three sponsors of the Resolution were thus crowned with success.'[7]

However, in London reaction was mixed, and sympathy for Germany was strong. A clearly Government-inspired *Times* leader said on 18 April 1935:

> It is regrettable that no allowance should have been made by a body like the League Council for the special circumstances in which Germany incurred her obligations. It would have enhanced the reputation of the League for impartiality if one voice at least had been raised to recall the manner in which this particular Treaty had been imposed. Germany signed it literally at the point of the bayonet. At the time of signature her representatives made explicit protests that they would be unable to carry out all of its provisions . . . The procedure in Paris was a complete departure from recent practice. At all the previous great Peace Congresses of modern times, the representatives of vanquished countries, though obviously at a disadvantage, were free to negotiate their treaties article by article . . . Far different was the treatment of the Germans in 1919. They were not invited to Paris at all for the first months of the Treaty making, and then it was to receive the Treaty already fully drafted . . . When they signed, they signed, as has been said, under protest . . . The

facts of the conclusion of the Treaty of Versailles, however little they are remembered by most governments today, are not only familiar to Germans – they are burnt into their minds.

Such an article in *The Times* (which was believed on the Continent to be almost a Government organ) was an incitement to Hitler to disregard Stresa and Geneva and go on repudiating his Versailles obligations. A few days later King George V telephoned congratulations to the Führer on his birthday. This was unusual, and it was interpreted by some leading diplomatic correspondents in London as reassuring him that he need not take the Geneva resolution seriously, and implying that Britain had only supported it to please France.[8]

This 'high tide' of resistance to Germany was quickly washed back. On 18 June, as has been seen – eleven days after Baldwin succeeded MacDonald as Prime Minister – Britain violated the Treaty of Versailles by signing the Naval Agreement with Germany. At the same time Mussolini intensified his preparations to attack Abyssinia.

Unknown to Britain, the Duce had sent a memorandum to Marshal Badoglio, commander of the Italian Army, on 30 December 1934:

MEMORANDUM BY MUSSOLINI FOR MARSHAL BADOGLIO, CHIEF OF THE GENERAL STAFF: DIRECTIVE AND PLAN OF ACTION TO SOLVE THE ABYSSINIAN QUESTION.
The problem of Italian-Abyssinian relations has very recently shifted from a diplomatic plane to one which can be solved by force only. The Negus has aimed at centralising the Imperial authority and reducing to a nominal level, through continuous violence, intrigue and bribery, the power of the *Rases* (Chieftains) living in the peripheral areas. A long period will be needed before Abyssinia can be described as a state in the European sense of the word.

Abyssinia is equipped with really modern arms, the number of which is beginning to be considerable. Time is working against us. The longer we delay the solution of this problem, the more difficult the task will be and the greater the sacrifices. I decide on this war, the object of which is nothing *more nor less than the complete destruction of the Abyssinian army and the total conquest of Abyssinia.* In no other way can we build the Empire.

For our arms to achieve a rapid and decisive victory, we must deploy on a vast scale the mechanised forces, which are now at our disposal, and which the Abyssinians either do not possess at all or do so only in an insufficient degree, but which they will possess within a few years. The speedier our action the less likely will be the danger of diplomatic complications. In the Japanese fashion there will be no need whatever officially for a declaration of war and in any case we must always emphasize the purely defensive character of operations. No one in Europe would raise any difficulties provided the prosecution of operations resulted rapidly in an accomplished fact. It would suffice to declare to England and France that their interests would be recognised.[9]

Mussolini genuinely believed his statement 'No one in Europe would raise any difficulties.' The only power which might object was Britain, and Mussolini had grounds for believing that she would condone the annexation. He completely overlooked the delicate question of Abyssinia being a member of the League of Nations; it did not occur to him that after their failure over Corfu and Manchuria the League would take a less generous attitude to Italy than to Japan and Germany.

Foreign Office files for the previous ten years show that Britain consistently took the line that Italy ought to colonize Abyssinia and be the dominating power in that area. They stress that the only British interest was in the headwaters of the Nile. In 1934 Sir John Maffey wrote a long report reiterating this; it was immediately conveyed to Mussolini by the Fascist spy in the British Embassy in Rome, but it said nothing that had not been known to the Italians for years.

The Abyssinian crisis began in December 1934 on the badly defined border between Italian Somaliland and Abyssinia at Wal Wal. Italian troops fought Haile Selassie's for possession of the wells. The Italians demanded compensation from the Abyssinian Government; the Abyssinians invoked the arbitration procedure provided by the 1928 treaty. When the Italians rejected this Abyssinia applied to the League of Nations. No friendly solution of the dispute could be found, and the Abyssinians tried in vain to get the dispute put on the agenda for the session of the League Council following the Stresa Conference on 18 April, but Britain and France shied away from this because of the importance of a solid front with Italy on the much more important question of German rearmament.

Mussolini had begun to fear that as part of Britain's appeasement of Hitler and search for a 'general' settlement with Germany that African colonies would be offered to Hitler, and a likely candidate was Abyssinia. He believed that as a victor Italy should have been given a colonial mandate at Versailles similar to the French mandate in Morocco and the British mandate in Egypt, and that the Ethiopian part of Abyssinia – to which Haile Selassie had little legal claim – would be an ideal colony to be exploited economically by Italy. Abyssinia was landlocked and had no exit to the sea except through French Somaliland. Mussolini in making his plans for the invasion could not believe that Britain would want to take sanctions against Italy at the same time as she abetted the German breaches of Versailles by blatant rearmament.

All might have gone well for Mussolini if it had not been for the Peace Ballot in Britain. This during 1935 became a crusade for the Covenant of the League of Nations. Half a million people acted as canvassers, and memories of the First World War were still vivid, and with Hitler raising the threat of another war emotions were aroused. Public controversy over the

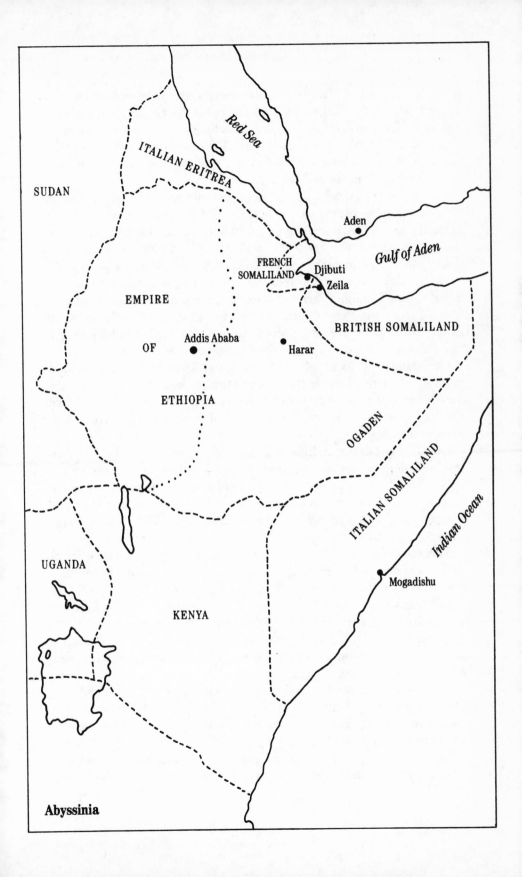

Abyssinia

role of the League of Nations on maintaining peace was sustained for eight months, and 11½ million filled in the ballot forms. An overwhelming majority answered 'Yes' to the question whether if one nation insists on attacking another the other states should combine to compel it to stop. However, three million more voted in favour of economic and non-military measures than 'if necessary military measures'.

Lord Robert Cecil did not announce the results until 23 July, but feelings had been running high since the beginning of the year. Pacifism was rife, especially in the universities, the Liberal and Labour Parties, and among those of all parties who had lost near-relations in the war. The organizers skilfully contrived to make the progress of the ballot into a propaganda exercise which in the last few weeks focused on Italy because of Mussolini's threat to attack another member-state of the League, Abyssinia. Baldwin found it more and more difficult to envisage a satisfactory solution to the Abyssinian crisis in face of this proof that public opinion would not tolerate any defiance of the principles of the Covenant of the League.

On 7 January 1935 Laval and Mussolini in Rome had agreed to minor ratifications of the French and Italian frontiers in Somaliland; they also made a secret arrangement under which France would condone an Italian attack on Abyssinia. Mussolini was now subsidizing both Laval and certain French newspapers.

On 17 May Drummond was called to the Cabinet, when he told them that he understood from a conversation with Laval that France would give Italy 'a free hand' over economic questions, but not territorial ones. An exchange of letters between Laval and Mussolini in December 1935 makes it clear that Laval had agreed to a virtually 'free hand' in all spheres, although he did not approve a war.[10]

Mussolini knew, as has been seen, that Britain believed Abyssinia should never have been admitted to the League, and Britain's attitude for many years had been that Italy ought to control Abyssinia.

Also, he was conscious Britain had not pressed the case for sanctions against Japan for her aggression in defiance of the League in Manchuria four years before, while the Foreign Secretary and his wife were heads of the British pressure group to abolish slavery, and were continually citing Abyssinia as the worst offender.

Simon's support for the Anti-Slavery Society received much publicity. For example, on 9 May 1933 at the City Temple Lady Simon made a speech to the effect that there were 'five million slaves – their cry comes to you to help them to abolish a great crime . . . In Abyssinia and elsewhere these human chattels are marched down to the coast never to see their families again.' John Simon announced that he had asked permission from the Opposition to wind up the debate early, especially to allow him to be present, and added 'Both my wife and I have this subject deeply at heart.'

Viscountess Simon told the author that her late stepmother-in-law was a very strong character absolutely dedicated to the anti-slavery cause, and that she would have impressed on Simon on every possible occasion the iniquities of Haile Selassie and the slavery in his Empire.[11]

Abyssinia was not put on the agenda for Stresa by either Britain or France. This extraordinary omission has never been properly explained. Neither MacDonald nor Simon raised Abyssinia in private conversations with the Duce. Afterwards MacDonald wrote to Vansittart that

> he could not understand why Mussolini had not said a word about Abyssinia at Stresa, and that it had never come to his ears that the delegates had even mentioned it. Mussolini had privately mentioned various things to me that had not come before the official conference; I could not understand why he never whispered Abyssinia in my ear.

But why, oh why, did MacDonald not whisper 'Abyssinia' to Mussolini? And why did Vansittart not tell the Prime Minister he must talk about Abyssinia to the Duce?

MacDonald was well past his best then, and about to resign.[12] It is alleged that at Stresa Mussolini, who had previously had a high opinion of him, called him in Italian 'an old dotard', and that on one occasion the interpreter found it impossible to make sense of what MacDonald had said and had to invent some phrases. But Simon was at the peak of his intellectual powers. Future generations may well ask what was he up to then as they analyse the causes of the disaster that overtook Europe between 1939 and 1945.

As the British Prime Minister and Foreign Secretary ignored the Abyssinian problems in their conversations with Mussolini he was justified in concluding that this silence gave him a welcome nod to go ahead with his invasion. He was soon to have a rude shock. Simon's telegram to Drummond dated 16 January 1935 is clear evidence he was well aware of the dangers of the Abyssinian crisis:

> We must make last attempt to prevent matter going before the Council of the League. The Italian attitude as you forecast it may provoke a lamentable crisis at Ceneva in which the blame would not be put on Ethiopia . . . This appears to be the last contribution that we can make to assist in bringing about the amicable settlement which Italy desires; and if Signor Mussolini rejects it there will be nothing further that I personally, or this country individually, can do to avert a crisis which may be disastrous for the League.[13]

Mussolini had taken pains to let the British know his intention to annex Abyssinia. On 16 February Drummond was given inside information in an interview with Marchese Theodoli, an Italian diplomat and President of the League of Nations Mandates Commission, who said that Italy was planning a military conquest and domination of Ethiopia, and later in conversation with Drummond Mussolini said 'If, however, the League took action contrary to Italian interests he would know what conclusion to draw,' adding that until a *modus vivendi* was reached he would continue to send troops up to half a million.[14]

Simon brought the problem before the Cabinet on 27 February, telling them 'the situation has deteriorated', and he felt it necessary to put on record to Mussolini in the friendliest manner 'our misgivings'; Simon added that the choice of de Bono to command the Italian army on the Abyssinian frontier 'caused concern' because he had acted with great severity in Libya. The Cabinet did not discuss Abyssinia again for four months during which much happened. On 9 March Vitteti, Counsellor at the Italian Embassy, told Ronald Ian Campbell that since their agreement with France on 7 January 'they now felt able to embark upon a more imprudent policy than had previously been possible'. Campbell minuted 'this is most unpleasant'.[15]

According to Geoffrey Thompson, head of the Foreign Office Abyssinian Department, Simon said to him at Geneva in January 1935: 'You realize, don't you, that the Italians intend to take Abyssinia.' Thompson minuted on 17 March that the Italian Foreign Office had let it be known that they considered Stresa an opportunity for informal talks (on Abyssinia) 'between Italian, French and British statesmen which should not be missed'.

Mussolini brought his Abyssinian experts Signori Vitetti and Guarneschelli to Stresa. Simon brought Thompson. Thompson had at least four cordial talks with Guarneschelli and Vitetti. Guarneschelli told Thompson that the Duce regarded a settlement of the Abyssinian question as urgent, and that he did not consider it could be settled by the Conciliation Committee of the League as Britain wanted. Abyssinia, according to the Italians, was a fourteenth-century state with a continuing tradition of slavery and cruelty. She had failed to develop her resources, whereas Italy was denied the opportunity for constructive work in her colonies because they consisted only of arid stretches of coastline.

Thompson warned the Italians of the dangers of a 'forward' military policy in Abyssinia, the consequences of which would be impossible to foresee. The Italians countered by expanding on Italy's need for more colonies – especially as Germany now wanted overseas possessions in Africa. Thompson evaded this point, but when Guarneschelli suggested that Britain should aid Italy in her Abyssinian adventure he told the Italians it was useless to expect it. He had no authority to warn the Italians that Britain would treat an attack on Ethiopia as a breach of the Covenant of the League of Nations, with its attendant dire consequences. They agreed that the Italians and French would exchange views in Geneva with Jèze, the French legal adviser to the Emperor.

Thompson wrote four long memoranda in his hotel bedroom which explained why he was deeply concerned at the danger of an Italian attack on Ethiopia with the resultant menace to the League and collective security. Simon invited him to breakfast on 14 April to discuss these.

After five minutes the Foreign Secretary's private secretary came in and interrupted the tête-à-tête. Simon did not refer to Abyssinia again, and immediately after breakfast said it was time to go to the island on the lake for the main conference. Thompson described it as 'a sad anti-climax'. Simon's conduct at Stresa was to be a major factor in bringing about the Second World War.[16]

MacDonald held a press conference at the end of the Stresa talks and said Locarno was reaffirmed and the policies of the three countries aligned. He said nothing about Abyssinia. When Alexander Werth of the *Manchester Guardian* asked whether Abyssinia had been discussed, the Prime Minister replied, 'My friend, your question is irrelevant.' This was widely reported, and Mussolini thought it another nod to go ahead.[17]

To the world it seemed that a united front against Hitler had been formed, and this impression was heightened when the joint French/Italian/ British Resolution condemning German rearmament was passed at the Council of the League three days later. On the way from Stresa to Geneva, Laval and Simon were applauded at the opera in Milan. However, very soon Mussolini realized he had been deceived, and the Italian press became anti-British.

According to Guariglia, during a long talk Vansittart told Grandi that Simon and MacDonald were very pleased that Mussolini had not forced them to discuss Ethiopia at Stresa, and Grandi got the impression that Simon was taking a weaker line in the summer of 1935 than he had done three months before.

The best comment probably came from Phipps, who wrote to Hankey (Secretary of the Cabinet): 'How could MacDonald, Simon and Vansittart have gaily omitted even to mention Abyssinia? . . . all the Ethiopian imbroglio sprang from that hideous error . . . Naturally Mussolini thought he could go safely ahead despite what Drummond and Grandi may have told him.'

Lord Gladwyn, then at the British Embassy in Rome, wrote in his autobiography that they were amazed that Abyssinia had not been discussed at Stresa, and that in his view Mussolini should have been 'tipped the wink' to go ahead with his adventure. That view was widely held in Whitehall,* but it must be remembered this was before the Peace Ballot had made its full political impact.[18]

On 21 May Drummond had an alarming talk in Rome with the Duce. Mussolini told him he did not want to damage the League, but if it became hostile and supported Abyssinia, he would leave. Drummond tried to find out if the Duce would be satisfied with an Italian mandate or protectorate for Abyssinia, such as Britain had in Egypt. The Duce replied that Abyssinia might come under Italian influence, as Morocco was under French and Egypt under British. He cited Egypt as a country with a king who was more or less independent, but who would not be allowed to do anything to endanger the Suez Canal or other British vital interests while Britain had there a High Commissioner, the head of the Army, the Chief of Police, and various advisers. Vansittart on 22 May minuted on Drummond's report: 'There is one ray of hope in this: the analogy of Egypt with her "King and political independence'. We ought to bear this in mind, and explore it further. It is probably the least that the League (& the peace of Europe) will get away with. We ought to think of this seriously & in advance.'[19]

A mandate that put Abyssinia under Italian control presented a good chance of both satisfying Mussolini and preserving the vital Stresa Front. However, Vansittart quickly changed his mind, minuting on 12 June:

> I also at one time had played with the idea of the Egyptian analogy. I have now abandoned it. If therefore we cannot satisfy Italy at Abyssinia's expense we are as before confronted with the choice of satisfying her at our own (plus some eventual Abyssinian frontier rectification) or letting things drift on their present disastrous course.

On 8 June Vansittart had minuted to the Foreign Secretary:

> Italy will have to be bought off – let us use and face ugly words – in some form or other, or Abyssinia will eventually perish. That might in itself matter less if it did not mean that the League would also perish (and that Italy would simultaneously perform *another volte face* into the arms of Germany) . . . we cannot trade Abyssinia. The price that would now satisfy Italy would be too high for Abyssinia even to contemplate . . . either there has got to be a disastrous explosion – that will wreck the League and very possibly His Majesty's Government – or else *we* have got to pay the price . . . with British Somaliland . . . Personally I opt unhesitatingly for the latter . . . We are grossly over-landed (and British Somaliland is a real debit).

---

*This was Leo Amery's view, and Amery put in his diary that later Churchill told him he regretted supporting the Government over Abyssinia.

This realistic suggestion might have solved the crisis. Eden did not agree. Instead he wanted to support the Covenant of the League, and minuted his agreement when Owen O'Malley of the Italian Department wrote on 3 June 'We must stick to League principles and stand the racket and the sooner that this is made plain to Signor Mussolini, the better.' Eden and Vansittart were at cross-purposes, as they had been over Hitler the year before.

A constructive suggestion came from Ronald Campbell, who minuted on 12 June that Mussolini's colonial ambitions might be satisfied through 'an international conference' which would redistribute colonies as part 'of a readjustment of the colonial and mandatory settlements' after the 1914–18 war. This possible escape route did not appeal to Vansittart, who minuted: 'I don't think we can follow this. In any case it would be too indefinite to produce any effect on Signor Mussolini.'

Mussolini early in 1935 had instructed Grandi, his Ambassador in London, to make his intentions in Abyssinia known to the British Government, and Grandi reported to Rome that Vansittart saw merit in the Italian argument that Britain 'should collaborate with Italy to hasten as much as possible the Ethiopian affair instead of encouraging by its vacillating policy in Geneva the resistance of Ethiopia'.[20]

Thus before Stresa Grandi had made clear the stark options before the British Government. Either they plumped for the League of Nations and sanctions to stop Italian aggression – thus making impossible the Stresa front against Germany – or they had to condone aggression against a member state of the League, weakening its prestige to such an extent that in future it would be impotent to stop any war. Simon set it out clearly in a Cabinet Paper on 15 May:

We now have the clearest indication from the Italian government, that they contemplate military operations on an extended scale against Abyssinia as soon as climatic conditions permit and Italian preparations are complete . . . it is probable that the advance will take place in October . . . The choices facing the British government were unpalatable. 'If they support against Italy a practical application of League principles, their action is bound greatly to compromise Anglo–Italian relations and perhaps even to break the close association at present existing between France, Italy and the United Kingdom,' a state of affairs which could hardly be more welcome to Germany. 'On the other hand, if the UK acquiesces in a misuse of League machinery, His Majesty's government will undoubtedly lay themselves open to grave public criticism . . .'

Germany was rearming and if 'substantial Italian forces would be locked up in North East Africa, Italy's strength in Europe [would be] correspondingly weakened'. Simon concluded, Italian co-operation in Europe was more precious than Abyssinia's sovereignty. He advised the Cabinet that

Britain and France recommend to Abyssinia 'to follow a policy more in accordance with modern conditions by recognising Italy's claim to taking fuller part in increasing the trade between Abyssinia and the outside world and in assisting the development of the economic resources of the Abyssinian Empire.'[21]

If Simon's view that Italian co-operation in Europe was more important than 'Abyssinian sovereignty' had prevailed the Stresa Front could have been held and Mussolini kept out of Hitler's arms, so the course of history might have been different. However, during the next crucial three weeks Simon allowed the Abyssinian crisis to drift, while with his usual ambivalence he concluded the Anglo–German Naval Agreement.

In the reshuffle when Baldwin replaced MacDonald as Prime Minister on 7 June Hoare replaced Simon as Foreign Secretary, and Eden – disappointed at not becoming Foreign Secretary himself – got a seat in the Cabinet as Lord Privy Seal with special responsibility for League affairs.

Hoare brought the Abyssinian crisis to the Cabinet on 19 June when the crisis erupted. Vansittart had briefed Hoare that Italy might take military action against Abyssinia at the end of June 'at which point Italy will leave the League and thereby throw herself into the arms of Germany . . . The League and the Stresa Front will thereby be simultaneously broken and all our past policy shattered, and our national future will be in clear danger.' He suggested giving Mussolini 'definite and concrete inducement'. Therefore we should cede Zeila [a port in British Somaliland] to Abyssinia, and in return ask her to cede territory in the Ogaden to Mussolini.'

Hoare found it tough going to persuade the Cabinet to accept Vansittart's policy. He told them that there was no sign of Mussolini's 'enthusiasm waning', while the French showed every sign they would be on the side of Italy and not the League, and there was every prospect of 'our being placed in a most inconvenient dilemma . . . either we should have to make a futile protest to the League, which would irritate Mussolini and perhaps drive him into the arms of Germany, or we should make no protest and give the appearance of pusillanimity'.

By 1935 the prestige and potency of the League as a peace-keeping institution had been gravely dented by Japanese aggression in Manchuria following incidents on the South Manchuria Railway in September 1931. The Japanese had occupied the Chinese town of Mukden, and from then on waged what was in everything but name a war against China. The Chinese appealed to the Council of the League, but mainly because Simon acted as advocate for Japan (strongly supported by the right-wing *Daily Mail* and *Morning Post*) no decision was taken. The National Government hoped that the Japanese would attack the Soviet Union, and preferred Japanese to Russian influence in Asia.

Instead of citing Japan as an aggressor and taking sanctions against her the Council of the League appointed in January 1932 a Commission to report on what had happened (disregarding the fact that meanwhile Japan and China were fighting each other). The Commission under the Chairmanship of Lord Lytton reported that a large area of what was indisputably Chinese territory had been forcibly seized by the armed forces of Japan. The Assembly of the League met on 6 December 1932 to consider the Lytton report. Simon then whitewashed the Japanese, being congratulated by the head of the Japanese delegation, Mr Matsuoka, for saying in excellent English in a half-hour 'what I have been trying to say in bad English for ten days'. Largely because of Simon, the League of Nations capitulated to Japan. It was strongly believed by British enthusiasts for the League that if the League Council had ordered Japan to withdraw her troops from Manchuria as soon as the aggression was reported to Geneva, the Japanese would not have dared to risk economic sanctions. Whether this is true or not, it is indisputable that the Manchuria precedent coupled with Simon's behaviour convinced Mussolini that it was unlikely sanctions would be taken by the League against Italy if he invaded Abyssinia in 1935.[21]

Hoare told the Cabinet on 19 June that the Foreign Office did not want to countenance any proposal that involved the sovereignty of Abyssinia ('some partition of Abyssinia' has been erased in ink from the record, probably at Eden's request) which had, despite our opposition, become part of the League. In searching for other alternatives a proposal had been suggested that we should cede a part of British Somaliland; he was not prepared to propose it at present, but he asked permission for Eden to go to Rome to approach Mussolini on the basis of some such agreement, and there was ample cover for his visit in the Naval Agreement and the Air Pact. Some members of the Cabinet suggested that it must be made clear that 'this was a sequel to long negotiations; otherwise we might be confronted with an early demand by the Germans for colonies'.

The Cabinet were reluctant to take a decision involving cession of a British Protectorate at short notice. They maintained that 'there should be no question of concluding any agreement involving the cession of British territory except as part of a complete settlement which had ruled out every prospect of war, and that every precaution should be taken to avoid facilitating the slave trade'.[22]

Drummond was asked if Mussolini would be pacified by Abyssinia ceding territory in the Ogaden to Italy in return for the port of Zeila, together with economic concessions in favour of Italy. Drummond telegraphed that it was worth trying the proposition, but after talking to Suvich he changed his mind. The message had been leaked to Mussolini by the spy in the British Embassy, and Suvich had found out the Duce would not agree, so that the Ogaden suggestion was dead before Eden left London. Eden was the wrong person to send on this assignment. He was on bad terms with Vansittart and the most enthusiastic in the Cabinet supporter of the League; the opposition to the proposal expressed on 19 June was almost certainly largely due to Eden.

Eden saw Mussolini on 24 June. The Duce rejected the Zeila–Ogaden proposal out of hand, saying it would shift much of Abyssinia's trade towards Zeila, taking it away from the Italian territory in Eritrea and Italian Somaliland. Mussolini told Eden that although he foresaw a crisis, both with the League of Nations and with Britain, he was determined to go ahead with the annexation of Abyssinia. Either there would be a peaceful solution with outright cession of the territories surrounding Abyssinia to Italy, plus Italian control over Addis Ababa and the central nucleus, or a war which 'would wipe Ethiopia off the map'. Eden replied that 'the difficulty of the situation was Abyssinia being, through no fault of England's, a member of the League of Nations'.

When the Duce told Eden that Laval had promised him 'a free hand' the row started. Eden interjected that Laval had only said France gave Italy a free hand in economic matters. At this Mussolini flung himself back in the chair with a gesture of incredulous astonishment. Later Mussolini showed Eden on a map the parts of Abyssinia where he insisted on direct dominion and where he would allow the Negus nominal sovereignty subject to Italian control. Eden did not refer again to the Zeila proposal.

Eden returned to London fully aware that nothing but control over Abyssinia, either by surrender of sovereignty or an Italian mandate, would satisfy Mussolini. In the House of Commons on 1 July he described his offer to Mussolini and its rejection. The occasion was a humiliation for Eden which gave him a lasting dislike of Italy. His parliamentary statement aroused strong opposition at home: Anglo–Italian tension increased, and British press comment was hostile to the Government – mainly because the Zeila offer looked like pandering to a potential aggressor, while ignoring the Covenant of the League of Nations.

Rumours that Mussolini and Eden had had a violent quarrel spread like wildfire through the embassies and seminaries in Rome. The Italian diplomatic historian Mario Toscano wrote: 'The dictator was said to have used violent language and after this visit Eden was the symbol of blind opposition to Italy's legitimate right to a place in the sun in Africa'. Samuel Hoare has recorded that Eden and Mussolini did not conceal the personal dislike they felt for each other.

Professor Camillo Pellizi of London University – an Italian – told Tower (diplomatic correspondent of the *Manchester Guardian*) that the general view in the Italian Foreign Office was that Eden felt personally insulted by

Mussolini's remarks and his subsequent behaviour at a luncheon, and that as a result he had adopted an almost vindictive attitude to Italy. Tower informed the Foreign Office, and Eden minuted:

> Pure balderdash. There was nothing in my reception at which I could have been offended even if I were an Italian and therefore susceptible to such feelings at the dinner table. Mussolini was definitely cordial throughout – our final interview was, of course, gloomy – it had to be – but sad rather than bad and there was no personal feeling whatever.[23]

This strange language is further evidence that Eden had taken offence.

Austen Chamberlain and Winston Churchill in the Commons argued with passion and conviction that sanctions must be instituted against Mussolini if he violated the Covenant of the League by attacking Abyssinia. However, most Conservative MPs were lukewarm, while Mussolini had strong support from the monthlies *English Review* and *Saturday Review*. The *Daily Mail, Morning Post* and *Daily Telegraph* were pro-Mussolini. The League of Nations Union organized their members so that every MP was bombarded by letters demanding sanctions. Lloyd George, nearly all the Liberal and Labour MPs, and the *Daily Mail, Manchester Guardian* and *Daily News* took the same line.

In France, although Laval was able to dominate foreign policy, he had to look over his shoulder at the French League of Nations lobby which still looked on the League as their best guarantee against a German attack. On 8 August Corbin, the French Ambassador, came to see Vansittart and made it clear that France would not back Britain in demanding sanctions in the event of an Italian attack on Abyssinia unless they could have a firm assurance that Britain would in turn support sanctions against Germany if that country violated the Covenant by attacking Austria, or resorted to force in Europe. The Cabinet would not give such an assurance in terms that were satisfactory to France.[24]

By August the crisis was acute. Italy had an army of 800,000 on the Abyssinian borders, and Mussolini was making clear his intention to invade. On 22 August Hoare told the Cabinet 'there would be a wave of public opinion against the Government' if we failed to stand by the League and take sanctions against Italy in the event of an invasion.' The Cabinet agreed reluctantly, with the reservation that we 'must keep in touch with the French and avoid trying to force nations to go further than they wished'.

Armed with this cautious mandate, Hoare and Eden went to Geneva at the beginning of September, where Hoare astounded the world by a firm speech in which he promised 'Britain would back the League in steady and collective resistance to all acts of unprovoked aggression'.[25] It was interpreted as meaning that Britain had decided to stop Mussolini even if it meant war. The smaller European states were delighted, as was the peace lobby in Britain. However, the speech had been written by Vansittart, and Hoare went further than he intended. The British Cabinet had not the resolution to carry out the threat. On 2 September Hoare undid what he had said by sending a personal message to Mussolini that there had been 'no discussion on closing the Suez Canal or military sanctions'; Laval had already told Baron Aloisi, head of the Italian delegation at Geneva, the same thing.

In May the League had set up a Committee of Five to try to make a compromise solution between Italy and Abyssinia. The Romanian Titelescu and Russia's Litvinov were opposed to any large cessions of Abyssinian territory, so progress was slow. However, the Committee of Five reported on 18 September, and recommended a system of League supervision and control of Abyssinian territories, which obviously would have almost amounted to a mandate for Italy. Privately, Mussolini was told that it was intended that Italy should have the lion's share of control. Abyssinia was ready to agree, and the Italian diplomats at Geneva were conciliatory. Mussolini was on the brink of acceptance. The Report stated: 'The representatives of France . . . and Britain are prepared to recognize a special Italian interest in the economic development of Ethiopia. Consequently these Governments will look with favour on the conclusion of economic agreements between Italy and Ethiopia.' Laval had been prepared to go further, but Titelescu and Litvinov made this impossible.[26]

Aloisi, in despatches on 18 and 19 September, implored Mussolini to accept the proposals of the Committee of Five. He pointed out that Britain would never agree to any solution which did not provide for the nominal continuation of the Abyssinian empire, and that the advantage of the present proposals was that they could be revised in five years. Italy could then make another leap forward, as the French had done with their Protectorate of Morocco after the Treaty of Algeciras in 1906. Aloisi also cited the advantages of reconcilation with the rest of the League in 'the deplorable circumstances of an Anschluss between Germany and Austria'. He held a meeting of all his delegation and the Italian politicians in Geneva, who unanimously supported his entreaties to Mussolini to agree to the Committee of Five's solution 'in principle'.

Aloisi also pointed out that once Italy had accepted in principle, pressure could be put on Britain and the other powers to allow a working Italian majority on the League institutions who would administer Abyssinia. Baron Astuto, a member of the Italian delegation at Geneva, telephoned to the Foreign Office in Rome and spoke to an official who was a dedicated Fascist. He tried to persuade him of the advantages of Italy's accepting the Committee of Five's proposal. The official replied: 'Yes, the frame is excellent, but there is no picture of the man inside' – which meant Mussolini would not get enough personal glamour. To this Astuto responded: 'We are in Geneva to look after the interests of Italy, not to make collections of family pictures.' He was sacked for this remark.*[27]

Mussolini hesitated on the brink of war. Then there was a much–publicized leak in a London newspaper suggesting that he would refuse the Committee of Five's proposal. Instead on 3 October he ordered his armies to invade Abyssinia across the frontiers of Italian Eritrea and Italian Somaliland, and Addis Ababa was bombed. It was a mad-dog act, especially because he could have achieved the important parts of his colonial ambitions through diplomacy, as Aloisi was urging him. Seven months after the Stresa Accord looked like checking Hitler's aggression, Europe was sliding fast down the slope to war, and even if Mussolini could be placated he would never be trusted again. As Gladwyn puts it, 'A successful violation of the Covenant implied a collapse of the whole system of collective security laboriously built up since 1918. This gave frightening opportunities for aggression to Hitler. Therefore the willing participation of Italy in a security system with France and Britain was essential'.[28]

Like all dictators, Mussolini felt that he needed a military triumph to seal his popularity, and he knew the Italian nation wanted some dividend from the economic sacrifices they had made to pay for rearmament; certainly a successful war would make the Fascist regime more popular and crush the anti-Fascists both within and outside Italy. Mussolini felt confident that Britain would not risk going to war with Italy because she had indicated she wanted him to exercise an economic overlordship over Abyssinia, while Laval had virtually promised him that France would not support Britain over sanctions.

Fascist propaganda had convinced a large proportion of the Italian nation that Britain, with her rich African colonies, was trying to deny Italy her right to a similar African empire.

The League of Nations assembled on 5 October, and on 9 October agreed, with Hungary and Austria abstaining (because of their special position *vis-à-vis* Italy), to apply sanctions against Italy. Hitler was delighted. However, it was agreed at Geneva that negotiations with Mussolini should proceed in the hope that an agreed settlement would make sanctions unnecessary.

Laval's loyalty to Britain was suspect. When Laval had met Eden in Paris on 1 October the French leader said he favoured a League mandate to Italy for all the non-Amharic part of Abyssinia and League assistance for

---

*Aloisi was, in his own words 'driven out of the service' as soon as the Ethiopian problem was not on the agenda at Geneva.

Abyssinia proper with Italian participation. Eden replied that it would be 'scarcely possible' to put this forward as we would be rewarding an aggressor. Laval replied that it went no further than the Committee of Five proposals amended and approved by Britain at Geneva on 16 August. Here the Frenchman was not far wrong.

Eden told Laval he was most disturbed at the hostile attitude of the French press to Britain, and that in Britain there was 'grave anxiety about the French attitude', although it was found hard to believe 'the French would not stand shoulder to shoulder with us'. Laval's reply was that France must not be judged by the press: 'French opinion was much divided.' However, he promised mendaciously to seek a mandate for economic sanctions.

On 24 September Hoare had asked Corbin, the French Ambassador in London, whether Britain could count on military support from France if Italy attacked after sanctions started. Corbin did not deliver the reply until 8 October, and it was that Laval would need *'consultation et accord'* before rendering assistance. Vansittart minuted that it was not an honest reply and that Laval wanted 'a loophole for French inaction if we got into trouble'. On 7 October Flandin had told Lloyd Thomas, the British Minister in Paris, that the average Frenchman had no faith in the League and that no French Government would risk war to carry out obligations under the Covenant. Vansittart minuted: 'This is an exceedingly grave statement coming from the late French Prime Minister . . . he is probably speaking the truth.'

Even more worrying was a request by Laval to reduce the British concentration of the Fleet in the Mediterranean because Italy could allege it was unjustified. Laval said he reserved his right not to come to the help of Britain if Mussolini attemped a wild attack on her, although he would honour his obligation once British forces were normal, thus denying the Duce 'his specious plea that our ships constituted a menace to Italy'.

Hoare reported this to the Cabinet on 16 October, adding that the French Admiralty had refused to discuss co-operation with the British naval attaché in Paris. The Cabinet, already lukewarm about sanctions, understood that this meant Britain might have to take the lead over sanctions at Geneva without proper backing from France. Worse was the doubt whether France would come to Britain's aid if she were attacked by Mussolini.

At this Cabinet meeting Hoare and other members claimed that Eden was 'giving the impression' at Geneva that he was making all the proposals for sanctions and the French were constantly wrangling with us. Accordingly the Cabinet authorized Hoare to send a message to Eden in Geneva that the Cabinet was extremely worried by Laval, and 'ask you to go as slow as possible'.

Hoare was also authorized to tell Laval that had Britain felt confident of French naval co-operation, and the use of French ports in the event of Italian aggression, she would have sent fewer reinforcements to the Mediterranean. The Cabinet recorded that if Italy attacked Britain in the Mediterranean, France might refuse co-operation on the grounds that the British Fleet had been 'provocative'. Accordingly it was decided that until the French situation was cleared up no new sanctions would be applied.[29]

The same day (16 October) the British Government repeated a request for a plain and unequivocal assurance of full support by France against any attack. In return they would assure her that they had no intention of attacking Italy except in accordance with a League decision approved by France. If France would give the required assurance Britain was prepared to withdraw two battle-cruisers from Gibraltar, provided Italy reduced her Libyan forces to approximate parity with the British garrison in Egypt. The British Note ended with the tough statement that failing a French assurance the consequences would be grave and would imperil Locarno. Just as in this case the French described British precautions as provocative, so in a number of imaginable contingencies it would be easy for the British to make similar reservations which would render Locarno ineffective. This tough Note marked the lowest point in Anglo–French relations between the two wars, but Laval's conduct had forced the British Cabinet to play on France's fear that she might be left to face a German attack without British support. It worked. The French reply received on 18 October was considered satisfactory:

> In the concrete case . . . that is to say a possible attack by Italy upon Great Britain by reason of the latter's collaboration in the international action undertaken by the League of Nations . . . French support of Great Britain is assured fully and in advance.

A few days later France agreed that Britain could use the ports of Bizerta and Toulon if she was attacked by Italy, and the Cabinet decided that Laval must be asked to tell Mussolini that war with Britain meant war with France, and at the same time Laval should be asked to resume naval staff talks. Laval replied with a categorical undertaking to co-operate, which he repeated to the Italian Ambassador in Paris. A nasty breakdown in Anglo–French co-operation, had been narrowly averted. Soon military considerations were overshadowed by promising peace negotiations in Paris.

On 18 October the Cabinet approved a General Election to be held on 19 November, with a dissolution on 19 October. The honest course for Baldwin would have been to tell the nation that his sanctions policy was subject to French support. Instead he launched the Conservative Party into the election on a prospectus of all-out support for League sanctions.

At the next Cabinet meeting, on 23 October, Hoare said he had received a very lengthy answer from Laval (heavily leaked to the French press) and that it was satisfactory, although it required Britain to reduce her forces in the Mediterranean. Hoare also told the Cabinet that he had sent an official (Maurice Peterson, Head of the Abyssinian Department) to Paris to help the Ambassador to work out a settlement with Laval which would satisfy Mussolini.[30]

A fortnight after the invasion had begun, on 17 October, Mussolini became propitiatory. He told the French Ambassador in Rome that he would settle if the Committee of Five's plan applied to the old Kingdom of Abyssinia, and that for the non-Amharic part (e.g. Ethiopia, the conquered territories) 'instead of international help, the help would be Italian'. In addition he stipulated a reasonable and generous rectification of the frontiers in Ogaden and Danakil in Italy's favour. Peterson minuted: 'Signor Mussolini's latest ideas appear to me much more encouraging than anything we have before had.' Vansittart added 'This seems to me a distinct step in advance . . . we should endeavour to give an encouraging tone to our communication'.[31]

Mussolini thought he could strike a bargain with Britain on the unwritten understanding that he should have a free hand in Abyssinia provided Bari Radio – which continually broadcast propaganda complaining viciously of British activities in Egypt – ceased to interfere with British interests in the Middle East. For a few weeks he tottered on the brink of such an understanding.

In the House of Commons on 22 October Hoare emphasized that Britain would support the League although our involvement would be limited to no military measures, only economic sanctions, and no blocking of the Suez Canal, while Baldwin reiterated the Government's support for the League although he also argued for rearmament.

Ignoring the fact that the Cabinet had authorized negotiations in Paris with Laval for a deal which would favour Italy at Abyssinia's expense, Baldwin opened the election campaign with a broadcast endorsing the Government's support for collective security through the League of Nations, although he pointed out the risks inherent in sanctions. This remained the Conservatives' line during the 1935 Election, and Government spokesmen emphasized their commitment to the Covenant of the League and their determination not to allow Italy to reap the rewards of aggression.

Peterson after discussion with Laval and St Quentin, Head of the French African Department, produced an agreed draft plan which gave Italy a large slice of Abyssinian territory for exclusive economic development. Peterson had been told to use the Committee of Five's proposals (nearly accepted by Mussolini on 18 September) as his text, but he went beyond and produced a draft by which the British and French would suggest a settlement with a special regime for the non-Amharic territories (which were defined as 'depressed by wars, slavery and famine, so that the Central Abyssinian Government had been unable to administer them properly'). The draft pointed out this would virtually amount to an Italian mandate, but it would be difficult at Geneva to get agreement on a mandate. So instead the area would nominally be under League supervision but security would be assured by a Foreign Legion under Italian command. In addition Italy would have exclusive economic development in the south and the con-quered territory, and sovereignty of the Danakil and Ogaden; country south of the 8th parallel was to be ceded to Italy by Abyssinia. The Abyssinian army was to be disbanded. As recompense Abyssinia was to be given a port in British territory, either at Assab or at Zeila.[32]

Hoare told Laval that he did not want exclusive Italian control but he was ready to concede to Italy an appropriate share 'in the personnel both of the Central Commission in the capital and of the administration of the provinces', and that he was agreeable to the proposed boundary changes. He did not want a Foreign Legion but a gendarmerie, and thought Abyssinia would not want a port and corridor enclosed by Italian territory. This meant Zeila and not Assab. Hoare concluded: 'To sum up, we feel the right and least complicated road to a solution is by a simple exchange of territory, which on this basis clearly entails a large advantage to Italy.' In the end the only difference between Laval and Hoare was over 'exclusive control' by Italy, or 'a major share of the officials'.[33]

During the election campaign Hoare and Eden met Laval in Paris on 1 November. Laval told them he was disappointed at the British reply to the draft agreement, but that he had found out from Mussolini that he was anxious to settle, with the British giving Zeila to Abyssinia. Hoare stated that he favoured the Committee of Five's proposals for the central part of Abyssinia (this meant virtual Italian control), and to settle the rest by territorial concessions to Italy. Eden did not protest at this reward to Mussolini for his aggression.

Hoare said that he hoped Italy would as a gesture withdraw one division from Libya, where Italian troops threatened the British in Egypt. How well the Laval–Mussolini bush telegraph worked is shown by the fact that two days later the Metauro Division began embarking for Naples from Tripoli. Baron Aloisi in Geneva saw Hoare, who told him that Britain was anxious to continue talks, and the prospects for an agreed settlement were good. The

Italian press commented that Laval was being stopped by the British because of electoral reasons.

At a meeting in Hoare's room on 11 November the Foreign Secretary told Peterson that as soon as the General Election was over negotiations with Laval would be resumed for a simple exchange of territory and a plan of assistance for Abyssinia – amounting in effect to something near an Italian mandate.[34] On 14 November the Conservatives were returned with another steam-roller majority. Hoare and Eden retained their former posts.

Meanwhile a thunder-cloud had appeared on the horizon. For some unexplained reason Dr Riddel, the Canadian delegate to the League of Nations, raised at Geneva the possibility of oil sanctions against Italy. This scared Mussolini, who suddenly became belligerent. He threatened to break his alliance with France and leave the League, and hinted that he might bomb the French Riviera. At the same time he moved troops to the French frontier. The Foreign Office became apprehensive that while relatively little separated Britain from agreement with Mussolini, the two countries might drift into war. Drummond's signals from Rome were more and more disquieting.

From Berlin too, on 13 November, Phipps reported that Germany was living in a state of war, and that military expansion would be followed by territorial expansion and we had 'no policy to stop them,' complaining that 'Abyssinia was not the only pebble on the beach . . . the present Ethiopian imbroglio is mere child's play compared with the German problem that will in the not very distant future confront His Majesty's Government'. Vansittart told Hoare 'There is not a moment to lose'.[35]

League officials began to plan oil sanctions. The Committee of Five had been instructed by the Council to consider them. On 23 November Vansittart had told Eden and Hoare 'We must not have the oil sanction or the Duce will make war on us' and followed it up by saying it would be 'suicidal' to proceed with oil sanctions unless 'we have full and concrete arrangements with the French' (for military support).

On 30 October Drummond reported that the Duce had told him that if Italy were faced with the choice of being forced to yield or war, he would definitely choose war, even if it meant that the whole of Europe went up in a blaze. Drummond repeated this message weeks later. Baldwin's fears are betrayed in a letter to the Cabinet's Deputy Secretary, Tom Jones:

> If Mussolini broke out there would be more killed in Valetta in one night than in all the Abyssinian campaign up to date and until we got agreement with the French we would have to go single handed fighting Italy for a month or so. French mobilisation would have led to riots. They are not ready in the air for mobilisation. Malta is the only harbour apart from those of the French where you can take ships with our wounded.[36]

The British Cabinet were so alarmed by threats of an Italian attack in the Mediterranean that in view of the possibility of an Italian attack on Egypt from Libya, the War Office on 26 November dispatched tanks and an infantry brigade, with supporting troops from home reinforcements, to Egypt and authorized the calling up of some volunteers and reservists. Two days later the Chiefs of Staff reported grave shortages of anti-aircraft ammunition and no hope whatever that any would become available within a reasonable period of time.[37]

On 21 November Hoare and Eden had authorized Peterson to go back to Paris to continue his quest for a compromise peace plan with Laval. With Eden present, Hoare had told Peterson not to engage in tripartite talks with Italian diplomats but to confine himself to the French. Hoare and Eden were agreeable to an 'exchange' of territory, but Peterson was told to be cagey about Italian personnel participating in the League's plan for assistance. If pressed on this point Peterson was to refer home for instructions.

On 25 November Peterson reported from Paris that the minimum terms which Laval expected Mussolini would accept were: 1) Outright cession to Italy of the whole of the Tigre including Makale; 2) Frontier rectification of Ogaden and Danakil which 'would probably not, at least in the case of Ogaden, involve cession *in toto*'; 3) Creation of a very large special zone in southern Abyssinia bounded by the 8th parallel on the north and the 37th meridian on the west. This zone was to remain nominally under the 'Emperor's sovereignty', but 'Italy must be assured of complete control from the point of view of economic development and colonial settlement'. It meant the Emperor giving up an enormous amount of territory, and Peterson stated that although in theory it was to be administered by an Italian chartered company, in fact it meant cession to Mussolini.

In return the Emperor was to receive the port of Zeila in British Somaliland. It was to be a 'carve up', with Mussolini receiving what he wanted of the Emperor's territory. Peterson wrote that 'the present suggestion completely eliminated League control while making maintenance of Ethiopian sovereignty no more than a transparent fiction'. Scrivener, who had recently returned from Addis Ababa, minuted on Peterson's memorandum: 'One wonders whether in the light of Laval's evident intentions to be more Italian than Signor Mussolini, the continuation of these conversations will serve any *really* useful purpose.' And Oliphant commented: 'It has all along been decided that we should try and hold the scales between Rome and Addis Ababa and not expose ourselves to a possible charge of tilting them in favour of Rome.'

Instead Vansittart was enthusiastic. He considered

the terms were the best we can hope for; we should be very happy if the Italians accepted . . . We shall never get the Italians out of Adowa (the S of S. has always been convinced of this too, I think) and we ought not to try . . . I would authorize Mr. Peterson to go ahead at once . . . If we can convince the French I would be prepared to go to Rome next . . . we, I think, might use General Garibaldi here.

Eden ignored Scrivener's and Oliphant's reservations, minuting:

I agree with Mr Peterson's (1) and (2) (cessation of Tigre and Manakele plus Ogaden and Danakil to Italy) subject of course to the proviso we have always made and must always maintain that a settlement must be acceptable to the three parties, Italy, Abyssinia and the League. How large the area might be for the Italian chartered company would have to be a matter of bargaining. The Emperor could never agree to one third of his territory, or more, being so dealt with, and such a proposal would certainly have to be combined with non-Italian League control.

A.E.   26.11.35.

This Eden minute is conclusive evidence that he agreed in principle to the Hoare–Laval proposals. Hoare took it that Eden was in agreement, minuting on 28 November: 'I agree. Let us proceed for the present on the lines of the last two minutes which might satisfy Mussolini'. This telegram was circulated to the Cabinet.[38]

In an effort to retain British friendship and finalize the Paris negotiations, Mussolini sent General Garibaldi to London as his personal emissary. Bypassing Grandi, he saw Vansittart on 28 November, telling him that Mussolini wanted a mandate for Italy over all the non-Amharic territory (exactly what Peterson had been told to suggest in Paris) and in return Britain would cede Zeila or Assab to Abyssinia; on top Mussolini asked for a League of Nations mandate to be created over the Amharic nucleus with the majority of League officials to be Italians. Here was a promising gambit.

MacDonald also saw Garibaldi at Vansittart's suggestion. After the interview MacDonald tried to see Hoare, but Hoare said he was too busy. By now MacDonald had almost no influence in the Cabinet; he had only been retained to give the impression that the Baldwin Government was 'national' during the General Election. MacDonald favoured a compromise, and wrote to the Foreign Secretary that at Stresa Mussolini had indicated to him that he had no confidence in France and 'longs to keep up the old Anglo-Italian traditions', and expressing his own (MacDonald's) fears that although Mussolini was no mad dog, if he came to regard 'us' as an enemy it would change the diplomacy of Europe, bringing Germany in as a deciding factor. Garibaldi gave MacDonald and Vansittart Mussolini's proposals in writing. A note of the Garibaldi proposals was circulated to the Cabinet, where they were favourably received, and no objection was recorded to an Italian majority on the staff of the League of Nations team to administer the mandate over the Amharic nucleus. The crisis was almost solved. Mussolini wanted little more than Britain was prepared to concede, although it would shock the pro League of Nations British public if an aggressor was to be so palpably rewarded for his attack on another member of the League.[39]

By 30 November Peterson had reported from Paris that he and the French were agreed on the cession of Adowa and Adigrat to Italy, and for a large zone in the south to be put under Italian control; Peterson stated Laval was sounding out Mussolini over this plan. A Foreign Office memorandum for the Cabinet supported the Peterson-Laval proposals, provided that the Tigre area was not ceded formally to Italy for two or three years, and that it should in the interim remain indeterminate under a League Commission, which obviously would be Italian-dominated. Eden agreed, and clearly a period nominally under the League fully met the reservations in his 26 November minute.[40]

Baldwin was on the horns of a dilemma. He had just won an election on the sanctions ticket, although he was aware that the Foreign Office right through the election campaign had been negotiating a solution favourable to Italy in Paris. He knew too that there was strong opposition to sanctions within the Conservative Party. This had come to a head a few days before the election campaign started when a Conservative Parliamentary delegation (the Imperial Policy Group), headed by Leo Amery (former First Lord of the Admiralty and Secretary for the Colonies) and Lord Milne (CIGS from 1926 to 1933) and comprising twenty MPs (including Alan Lennox Boyd, a rising star after being President of the Oxford Union), and influential peers, came to see Baldwin and Stanhope.

Amery contended that British policy over the Italian–Abyssinian crisis was 'a complete and inexplicable reversal of what it had been since Austen Chamberlain made his statement in Geneva in 1925 rejecting the Geneva Protocol and with it the whole sanction system. Instead the Locarno method had been adopted and by the spring of this year British foreign policy was on the verge of a happy fruition' (cf the Stresa reaffirmation of Locarno). According to Amery, the Government was now being accused of pursuing a 'peace ballot policy', and he referred to a letter in *The Times* in which Colonel Gerogellerbet gave the reasons why the Conservative Party could not assist in it. Amery appealed for the Government to make a declaration now that it would neither advocate nor be a party to any sanctions that could lead to war. He said this was the policy of Laval, who had given us the 'opportunity of making it our own'.

Baldwin was in grave difficulties. Personally he agreed with the deputation, but he was on the brink of calling a General Election in which he would seek votes on the Peace Ballot policy. His reply as recorded betrays his indecision: 'There were obviously very great difficulties in saying now in public how far he would go'.[41]

By 22 November Vansittart was in a state of near-panic. He feared that Mussolini would expect that an embargo on oil supplies to Italy to be imposed at Geneva on 29 November, and would be crazy enough to attack Britain. He sent an urgent note to Simon and Eden saying that the paper on the oil embargo ought not to go to the Cabinet until he had an opportunity of discussing it with them, and that we 'ought to walk very warily'. He continued by hand-written minutes to stress that he 'earnestly pressed' not to proceed at Geneva with the oil sanction because 'our measures of defence and supplies of munitions are startlingly deficient' and that

> we should only take part in an oil sanction if France, Spain, Yugoslavia, Greece and Turkey would put in hand their military preparation so that the consequence, if any, will be shared . . . it must be clearly understood that we are neither the League's policeman nor its whipping boy . . . I beg you and Mr. Eden . . . to modify your oil paper to the Cabinet in this sense. We are getting very near the knuckle; we must have time and a big spurt at home immediately. To run the risk alone and unprepared would surely be unthinkable.

After seeing General Garibaldi, Vansittart wrote a further minute to the effect that the General had told him definitely he feared Mussolini would go to war if 'oil goes on the list' and 'he thinks Mussolini is in despair and has lost his head'. As a result of Vansittart's entreaties Hoare agreed to the postponement of the meeting at Geneva about oil sanctions which had originally been fixed for 29 November.

From Rome Drummond reported that he 'did not believe that Mussolini would attack Britain to avoid being starved into surrender', but considered that the Duce might well believe that Britain intended to force him to make terms which were 'humiliating' and the possibility that he 'would prefer to fight us must not be excluded'. Grandi had contributed to Vansittart's alarm with 'very pessimistic' language and by remarking on leaving the Foreign Office on 22 November 'that would probably be the last time he would come there'.

On 18 November the Grand Fascist Council had met in Rome, and according to the account given to Drummond by Theodoli (President of the League of Nations Commission on Mandates) only three members (including Grandi) had been moderate. All the others were extreme, taking the line that 'if Britain thinks she can compel us to submit by sanctions we would rather die fighting'; while the Grand Council had left the decision about war with Britain in Mussolini's hands. Theodoli thought it would be a great mistake to assume that Mussolini and the Grand Council were 'bluffing'.

On Drummond's letter Vansittart minuted 'We are not in a position to call bluffs. We had better get on with peace-making (our own peace-making) as soon as possible . . . we are pushing on with · Peterson's proposals.' He also noted that 'Grandi is an unsatisfactory channel' and that was why he was using Garibaldi. Hoare agreed with Vansittart's minute, and saw Garibaldi twice (Hoare was favourably disposed to him, since he had been friendly with his father Ricotti Garibaldi, son of the Liberator) and assured him that he could tell Mussolini that Britain was ready to co-operate if the Duce was ready for a serious negotiation. Garibaldi told Hoare that Mussolini fully admitted the need for some kind of concession to the Emperor, 'and did not object to the cession of an outlet to the sea at Zeila'.[42]

Meanwhile the British Legation to the Holy See had reported the reactions of the Italian bishops to the sanctions policy as 'very strong' and 'strengthening the hand of the Duce' while the Cardinal of Milan 'had been crusading with fervour' and the Pope was not checking him. Previously the Legation to the Holy See had sent a message that the Pope in a confidential memorandum had written it would be 'a truly meritorious action if the Great British people in a spirit of fraternal accord would realise by peaceful means the legal aspirations of the Italian people,' and that the Pope obviously disapproved of Mussolini's methods but was against 'unequivocal support of the League'.

Hugh Montgomery, Counsellor at the British Legation to the Vatican, reported on 21 November that the British Consul's reports revealed widespread Church support for Mussolini and dislike of 'iniquitous sanctions' and he concluded that 'the Pope while personally disapproving of the Abyssinian adventure abstained from discouraging the "martial ardour" of his bishops since a national clergy must be allowed to espouse a national cause if they consistently feel able to do so.'[43]

According to Drummond, 'the Italian nation in the face of sanctions is today united as it has never been before', and a well-known senator had said to one of the Embassy staff 'You have achieved the miracle of uniting the whole of Italy behind Mussolini,' and unless Mussolini got the type of settlement he wanted 'the Italian people under his direction will be prepared to fight until the last man'. Drummond in a private letter to Vansittart reiterated that Mussolini was reaching the end of his tether owing to sanctions, and was 'determined to perish gloriously . . . by attacking us'. Vansittart insisted on Hoare reading this, noting gloomily 'No-one doubts that Italy is behind Signor Mussolini'.

Vansittart's alarm at the likelihood of a war between Italy and Britain communicated itself to Eden, who had once been the keenest supporter of the oil sanction, but who now even told some of his Cabinet colleagues on 29 November that oil sanctions should be postponed until the result of the

Peterson–Laval negotiations in Paris were known. A special meeting of the Cabinet was called on 2 December to deal with the escalating crisis.[44]

In papers circulated to the Cabinet Vansittart warned: 'We must be sure of our ground i.e. Italy not making war on us before we embark on oil sanctions . . . suicidal to press on with oil sanctions unless we come to a full and concrete agreement not only with the French, but with other military powers concerned,' while Hoare had warned 'No AA guns available for defence of Alexandria . . . the only thing that could deflect an Italian attack would be to attack Italian bases in North Italy. We should require not only facilities for our own aircraft, but active cooperation [of French] airforce in attack and defence.'[45]

Hoare told the Cabinet on 2 December that an embargo on oil raised the risk of a 'mad dog' act by Mussolini, and he had received a number of alarming reports that Mussolini would regard an oil embargo 'as rendering defeat inevitable'. He might use it as a pretext for attacking the British 'in the Mediterranean, although it was tantamount to suicide', while Imperial Defence was weak as compared with an Italy 'mobilised for war'. He pointed out that there were now a barrage of peace moves on behalf of Italy, including those of General Garibaldi in London (who had been disowned by Grandi, though there was no doubt that he came from Mussolini), and now those of Grandi himself, who despite his previous gloom was now 'an enthusiast for peace negotiations'.

Hoare did not want to announce that Britain had abandoned the principle of oil sanctions, but said we must press on with the negotiations by Peterson in Paris, and then when the League Committee met they might be told that peace talks were going on satisfactorily. 'For that reason we and the French were not asking for the immediate imposition of an (oil) embargo.' The Cabinet endorsed the Foreign Secretary's proposal that if peace talks showed a reasonable prospect of success oil sanctions should be postponed. Hoare said he himself would go to Paris.

There was general agreement and the Cabinet were given secret information indicating that 'the Italian threats of an active retaliation to an oil embargo had been implemented by actual preparations'. Duff Cooper, Secretary of State for War, played down the shortage of AA ammunition by saying 'clouds' would render AA guns of little value. Baldwin asked every member to give their view.[46]

Eden on 2 December was apparently sufficiently impressed by Vansittart's alarming minutes about an imminent Italian attack to withdraw his demand for an immediate oil sanction; previously he had had reservations about the correctness of Vansittart's views, and in his autobiography he quotes the following internal Foreign Office minute, which he wrote, as evidence of his attitude:

... this danger (an Italian attack) has always seemed to me very remote and I am quite unimpressed by the threats of such persons as Marchese Theodoli who has clearly been instructed to frighten us as much as possible ... In calculating the likelihood of a mad dog act the isolation of the Italian forces in East Africa should not be overlooked.

Moreover Signor Mussolini has never struck me as the kind of person who would commit suicide. He has been ill informed about our attitude in this dispute and while he may well be exasperated there is a considerable gap between that condition and insanity.[47]

Baldwin summed up the 2 December Cabinet discussion by stating there would be 'strong criticism of the Government unless it had done its utmost to avoid war', and 'criticism would be all the more bitter once the details of our defensive preparations became known' and it should be remembered that, whatever was done to try to ensure collective League action, Britain would almost certainly have to withstand the first shock of hostile Italian reaction to sanctions. Finally, if anything went wrong with Mussolini 'no one would be willing to tackle Hitler'. Baldwin displayed his caution by telling his colleagues that he refused to fix a date for the oil sanction in advance.

In his memoirs Hoare writes that he made a mistake in not calling for a special Cabinet to discuss the Paris negotiations. His memory was at fault. As has been seen the Cabinet on 2 December gave its imprimatur to the Hoare–Laval plan in advance. Fortified by the support he had received from the Cabinet, in the morning of 2 December Hoare wrote to the King in the afternoon asking for permission for himself and Vansittart both to be out of the country together. In the letter he said 'If, as I hope, M. Laval and I agree upon a basis for a peace negotiation Vansittart will stop on in Paris for a day or two to clinch details.' The protocol was that the Foreign Secretary and his Permanent Under Secretary were not allowed to be out of the country at the same time without special Royal permission. On 6 December Vansittart told the French Ambassador in London 'The problem is to find reasonable and even generous terms to Italy'.[48]

Hoare and Vansittart reached Paris on 7 December. Laval made it clear Mussolini was happy with the new suggestions. Hoare agreed to surrender to Italy more territory in Tigre, and to offer Abyssinia a port either at Assab or Zeila. Hoare further agreed to an economic monopoly for Italy under League supervision in a large zone in the south and south–west. Laval then telephoned to Mussolini, who replied the proposals were acceptable. An agreement was typed out and initialled by both Hoare and Laval. Vansittart congratulated Hoare on having stopped the Abyssinian war and re-established the Anglo–French front, and also on having brought Mussolini back to the Stresa front.

Hoare also agreed under pressure from Laval that the terms should be transmitted immediately to Mussolini, but only later to the Emperor Haile Selassie. It was agreed that Abyssinia should not be allowed to build a railway from Addis Ababa along the corridor carved out of British Somaliland to the port. This became the subject of hysterical press comment in Britain, but was no surprise to Haile Selassie.

Hoare telegraphed an account of the talks to the Foreign Office on 8 December, and Vansittart reported by telephone. Thus the Foreign Office was well briefed, but in his autobiography Eden writes that he was 'astonished' when on the morning of 9 December Peterson brought him a four-page document in French initialled SH-PL giving the details of the agreement. This document is in the Public Records Office, and is the agreement to be expected after the Cabinet discussion on 2 December.

In 1972, as soon as the archives for 1935 were available under the 30-year rule in the Public Record Office, R.A.C. Parker, the historian of Queen's College, Oxford, exhaustively researched the Hoare–Laval Pact and wrote: 'After the Hoare–Laval Plan was condemned and abandoned, other members of the Cabinet began to treat it as a strange and personal aberration of Hoare's. In fact the Cabinet gave him a free hand and afterwards approved of what he had done'. No researcher can come to any other conclusion.

★ ★ ★

Eden has distorted history by writing in his autobiography 'We did not discuss any possible terms of peace either at Cabinet or between Ministers before the meeting with Laval', and that he was astonished at the 'Peace Plan' because he could not reconcile it with the instructions given to Peterson, and 'I knew of no other basis agreed in London' . . . and these terms 'went beyond anything which Peterson had earlier been authorized to accept when he left for Paris.' Eden's memory was sadly at fault, and he cannot have had access to the relevant documents.

Unfortunately, Eden's official biographer (Robert Rhodes James) writing thirteen years after Parker, ignored Parker's research and reiterated Eden's false claim, writing: 'Hoare had no instructions to negotiate with Laval.'[49] Another special Cabinet was called on 9 December to deal with the Hoare–Laval Plan. Before Hoare went on from Paris to Switzerland he had written a letter to the Prime Minister strongly recommending the proposals. In Cabinet Eden did not tell his colleagues of his 'astonishment'. He asked only for 'two amendments'.

One was that Haile Selassie should be informed simultaneously with Mussolini; the other was minor, concerning procedure at the League. Eden told the Cabinet he expected the question of oil sanctions would now be 'postponed', and explained to his colleagues with the aid of maps that the whole of the territory Abyssinia was to cede was non-Amharic, and that the Emperor was receiving compensation by the outlet to the sea.

Eden supported the Foreign Secretary's proposals although he stated some features might prove distasteful to some countries at the League – adding 'Laval wanted to interpret the proposals as generously as possible for Mussolini, and there were doubts whether French co-operation over sanctions could be relied on, if Mussolini accepted but Haile Selassie refused. The Cabinet agreed with Eden that the Emperor must be informed of the terms at the same time as the Duce, and that the Emperor should be 'strongly pressed' to accept them.

That evening Hoare and Eden spoke on the telephone after Hoare had received a message the Cabinet had unanimously approved the proposals subject to their simultaneous transmission to Italy and Abyssinia. Eden, while clearly unenthusiastic about the furore in the Paris press, according to Hoare 'did not seem much worried. The only part of the scheme he disliked was the big economic area in the South. I told him to repudiate me (on the extent of the area) if he wished, and that I fully agreed with Cabinet decision to inform Abyssinia and Italy simultaneously'.

The next day, 10 December, Vansittart telephoned from Paris and told Eden Laval would agree to send the text of the proposal to Addis Ababa only on the understanding that if Haile refused there would be no question of oil sanctions.* Eden replied the Cabinet insisted on the terms being sent immediately to Addis Ababa, adding 'It seems very unlikely that oil sanctions would now materialize unless Italy refused the proposals,' although the Cabinet would not pledge themselves to oppose further sanctions under new conditions. Laval eventually agreed to what Eden asked, but with bad grace because he wanted to be able to tell the Duce that oil sanctions were dead provided Italy accepted the Hoare–Laval terms. The proposals officially went to Rome and Addis Ababa simultaneously but Mussolini, of course, had already known about them at the weekend from Laval.

On 10 December the Cabinet were informed that Laval wanted an 'engagement' between the UK and the French that if the peace proposals were refused by Abyssinia 'with a view to bringing an oil sanction into play' fresh sanctions against Italy need not be imposed. Peterson had been called to the Cabinet and told them Laval had taken 'soundings' in Italy, and as a

---

*Laval told Vansittart that if Abyssinia refused the terms 'his colleagues' would not accept 'bringing into play' further sanctions.

result he was confident the terms would be accepted. He went on that Laval had in mind bringing the Italians 'back to the Stresa Front'. The Cabinet decided it could not give the engagement asked for by Laval but if the 'anticipated refusal' by Abyssinia materialized there would be no question of imposing petrol sanctions. When Eden asked if he were 'to support' the proposals at Geneva the Prime Minister replied this 'would have to be done', and there might be some plain speaking about the military situation. The Cabinet recorded that they were 'the best terms which could be obtained from the Abyssinian point of view from Italy', and if Britain had rejected the terms France would not have gone on with sanctions. Eden concurred and signalled to the British Ambassador in Addis Ababa that he should urge Haile to accept, and was 'on no account lightly to reject them'.[50]

In 1906 the tripartite treaty between Britain, France and Italy committed Britain and Italy not to build a railway line in competition with the French line from Djibouti to Addis Ababa. Laval and Peterson considered it reasonable that Abyssinia should join in this guarantee if she acquired a port in British Somaliland, Peterson pointed out on 16 December that 'the world has suffered enough from superfluous railways in the last six years without setting up a duplicate system in East Africa'. He also disclosed that Haile Selassie held a 'substantial shareholding' in the Djibouti line and thus an interest in higher profits. Anyway, Abyssinia was at liberty to construct a line from Zeila, the most probable port, to join the French railway at Djibouti, and the two ports were not far apart. Haile Selassie had bought his shares in the French railway knowing it would have a monopoly, and there is no evidence he objected to this clause.

Advised by Peterson, neither the Cabinet nor Eden thought the prohibition of the railway of importance. In Cabinet on 17 December Eden said 'there was a good case for not allowing a railway because we were committed by the 1906 Treaty not to build a "rival" railway to the interior, and Djibouti must not be "threatened." ' However, *The Times* produced a leader 'Corridor for Camels' which incensed the pro-League lobby in Britain. It was a brilliant headline but the writer was not briefed about the prohibition in the 1906 Tripartite Agreement, nor about the Emperor's large shareholding in the existing railway. The *Times* leader was written by Robin Barrington-Ward, then deputy editor and later editor. The leader said:

> Emperor to be informed at a convenient moment (probably when he had recovered from the shock of dismemberment) that he was forbidden to build a railway along the corridor. It was apparently to remain no more than a patch of scrub, restricted to the sort of traffic which has entered Ethiopia from the days of King Solomon, a corridor for camels.

Barrington-Ward ignored that Zeila was quite unsuitable as a rail-head. It only had a jetty where dhows could tie up, and ships up to 2,000 tons had to moor two miles out.

According to Sir George Clerk, the British Ambassador in Paris, on 15 December Laval was sure that if the oil embargo were imposed Mussolini would fight. Clerk claimed that the 'sober and reasoned' reports of Drummond pointed to some desperate act of war by Italy if the oil embargo came into effect, and emphasized that public opinion in France was getting more and more opposed to the 'exercise of pressure on Italy'. The French press was becoming 'poisonously anti-British, while France was determined not to go to war with Italy, and for Britain to try and force France to fight against her will would have risked a break with France with disastrous consequences'.[51]

Unfortunately, French journalists immediately obtained full details of the Hoare–Laval plan from a leak in the French Foreign Office, and published the details. This produced a public outcry against the proposals in Britain. From the news leaked in Paris *The Times* wrote on 14 December 1935: 'It is proposed to hand over to Italy effective ownership and control of a good half of Abyssinian territory'. But public opinion would not accept it without a resolute and convincing defence of the proposals by Baldwin and the rest of his Cabinet. This they never got. Without a proper lead from the Government it was hailed by a large majority of the British public as an outrage and an abandonment of the election pledges. Thus was the Hoare–Laval plan killed.

There was a storm of protest from Conservative MPs, who were inundated with complaints from constituents declaring that their votes had been obtained under false pretences in the General Election. Thousands of voluntary workers for the League of Nations Union organized the writing of these letters and whipped up indignation against the Government.

Pressure from Conservative backbenchers brought, in the words of Professor Toynbee, 'the Government to their knees' and 'the mastery of the people over the Government was proved by the sensational demonstration of the prevailing public opinion, while *The Economist* wrote on 14 December:

> Conservative members were perplexed, confounded . . . for many of them a few weeks ago won their seats no doubt in all good faith – largely on the strength of assurance to the electors that the Government, if returned, would stand firmly for vindication of the League covenant in accordance with both the spirit and the letter of Sir Samuel Hoare's September speech at Geneva.

Seventy MPs who took the Government Whip put their names to a critical motion in the Commons. One junior Minister, Geoffrey Shakespeare (a

National Liberal), threatened to resign, and Harold Macmillan has recalled: 'MPs supporting the Government could not reconcile themselves to so rapid a change so soon after the election with their election speeches still warm on their lips.'[52]

In America responsible newspapers condemned the proposals – in the words of the British Ambassador – 'unanimously, completely and unequivocally'. It was called 'an iniquitous bargain' and 'a plan which must bankrupt the collective system and act as incitation to other ambitious states . . . It is a vindication of the Italian Government's aggression, and represents such terms as might have been exacted after victory'; and 'an international disgrace'. In America it was accepted that this was the end of the oil embargo.

Little account was taken of the fact that the Hoare–Laval talks were conditioned by Britain's own naval, military and air weakness, and by Laval's support for Mussolini and the fear France would refuse both to support Britain's demand for oil sanctions against Italy and to give military support if Italy attacked Britain.

Samuel Hoare, within minutes of skating on to an ice rink kept empty for him at Zuoz, in perfect sunshine fell down and broke his nose in two places. The doctor told him he must not travel for fear of infection. Seldom had a Foreign Secretary been so urgently required in London, but Hoare stayed in bed in Zuoz while Baldwin told him not to interrupt his holiday. It was a decision both were to regret.

Parliament was perplexed when it met after the General Election. Baldwin told the House of 'hidden truths' and said it was premature to disclose anything until the matter had been before the League and examined by Italy and Abyssinia. His lips were 'not unsealed' but he could have made a case and 'guaranteed that not a single member would go into the Lobby against us'. Eden said the League of Nations had asked France and Britain to find such a solution. The Opposition correctly seized upon the fact that the Government had abandoned the policy on which they had been elected.

Afterwards Hoare was sure that Mussolini would have agreed, and that Laval had a definite nod from the Dictator. Drummond saw the Duce on 11 December and telegraphed:

> Mussolini has not yet made up his mind what to do and feels very keenly his responsibility . . . I still think, although I cannot be certain, of course, that we shall secure his acceptance in principle if the question of oil embargo threat can be overcome. If Committee of 18 (responsible for sanctions) were to adjourn . . . he would, I believe, consider such an arrangement sufficiently satisfactory.

Unquestionably Mussolini was on the brink of accepting the Hoare–Laval proposals which he had told Laval met his aspirations. It can be argued that the Italian–Abyssinian war would have then been over, and Italy would have returned to the Anglo–French camp leaving Hitler isolated again, and the slide into the Second World War might have been halted.

At Geneva the plan had a poor reception. Smaller nations felt that if Mussolini was rewarded for aggression the League would be powerless to save them from Hitler's attacks later. Besides, Eden had changed his line and had become an opponent of the Hoare–Laval Plan. From Geneva he reported on 12 December: 'Impression which Paris proposals have made upon public opinion here is even worse than I had anticipated'.[53]

Hoare arrived back in England on 16 December and went home to bed. In his absence Eden had drafted what amounted to the death warrant of the plan. The Cabinet on 17 December, with almost incredible disloyalty to Hoare, authorized Eden to go back to Geneva with a message that the Government was no longer pressing acceptance of the Paris terms. At this Cabinet Eden explained that

> there was a good case for not allowing the construction of the railway because we were committed by the Treaty of 1906 not to construct from Somaliland ports a rival to the French railway from Djibouti . . . economically the construction of a railway was unlikely since no-one would be anxious to find the money and the Emperor himself was a large shareholder, but the Abyssinians would be entitled to build a railway from the port to link up with Djibouti'. It is unfortunate that in his memoirs Eden gave a contrary impression, writing incorrectly that he knew nothing about this proviso in advance and that he was responsible for having it struck out.[54]

On 18 December the Cabinet met without Hoare, and decided they could not back France in banning Abyssinia from building a railway down the corridor to their new port. Chamberlain advocated a strong defence of the Hoare–Laval plan, arguing that it followed the lines of the Committee of Five's proposals. After the Cabinet, Chamberlain saw Hoare in bed and warned him of the Cabinet's doubts in face of the public outcry. Hoare stuck to his guns and said he wanted to make a vigorous defence of his plan in the Commons, which he claimed did not depart radically from the Peterson agreement reported to and approved by the Cabinet, and it was the alternative to war or the abandonment of oil sanctions. Chamberlain agreed. Then Baldwin and Eden followed to the bedside, both now strongly opposed to the plan, and Hoare reluctantly agreed to Eden's draft for Geneva which destroyed his plan. Hoare accepted that the Cabinet had reneged on him, and that he must resign.

Baldwin was in a panic. It looked as if the Government might fall. Elliot, Ormsby-Gore, Stanley and Duff Cooper told Baldwin that Hoare should resign, but Chamberlain was furious at this. On 18 December the Cabinet was in perhaps the most complete disarray of any Cabinet in this century.

Not until twenty years later, on 4 November 1955, was a Conservative Cabinet to be in a similar predicament. Then it dithered for hours over whether to cancel the attack on Port Said while its troop convoys were on the open sea. Eden was the only Minister present on both occasions.[55] The record of the 18 December proceedings is preserved but the key points were left blank in the typescript and written in by Hankey, the Secretary to the Cabinet, in his own hand. Only a week before the Cabinet had approved both the draft Peterson proposals and the agreed Hoare–Laval text and submitted it to Mussolini, Abyssinia and the League for acceptance, so that the Government's only honest course if it were to be repudiated was resignation. This Baldwin would not do. Attlee pointed out that he had won the election on one policy and immediately carried out another.

Baldwin stressed his worries to the Cabinet about a sudden Italian attack on Britain, and his fear that Laval would not come to 'our' aid. Chamberlain made it clear that Hoare would never change his mind about the correctness of his action in Paris, although he agreed that because of public opinion the Government could not stick to the plan. Chamberlain added that Hoare had been greatly misled by his staff (meaning Vansittart), and had made an error of judgment.

Halifax (Education), MacDonald (Lord President), Kingsley Wood (Health), Stanley (Labour), Thomas (Colonies), and Elliot (Agriculture) all wanted Hoare to resign forthwith and speak from the back benches during the forthcoming debate in the Commons. Only Lord Zetland (India) backed Hoare in a woolly statement, while the former Foreign Secretary, Simon, was adamant that the plan must be repudiated. As all these Ministers had approved Hoare's intentions seven days before, it was a strange, hypocritical performance.

Finally Baldwin said he was not 'rattled' although it was a worse situation in the House of Commons than he had ever known. His final remark was that he 'had not yet made up his mind'. However, he soon did, and sacked Hoare, giving the impression that Hoare had no mandate to come to the agreement with Laval and that Eden had opposed it all along. Baldwin would have liked Hoare to recant and remain in the Government, but the Foreign Secretary courageously refused. He contended for the rest of his life that nothing else would have satisfied Mussolini and stopped him joining the Hitler front.[56]

Meanwhile Mussolini in Rome arranged a meeting of the Grand Council of the Fascist Party for 18 December, obviously intending to accept. As soon as Hoare resigned, Mussolini cancelled this meeting because there was no point in it if Britain was going to back out (as Eden's attitude in

Geneva had indicated), and announced he would not accept. Hitler was enormously relieved; the prospect of the agreement had been an unwelcome shock, as it was crystal-clear that it would recreate the Anglo–French–Italian united Stresa front against him.

Hoare was only a short-stay tenant at the Foreign Office – less than six months. However, he showed a sensible appreciation of the menace posed by Hitler and the need to keep Mussolini's friendship to preserve the balance of power and prevent Hitler's rearmament continuing. Baldwin considered replacing Hoare by Austen Chamberlain, who unfortunately rejected the idea on the grounds of health; instead Baldwin chose Eden. Austen would have been better, but he did not have long to live. Eden was to continue the same policy of appeasement of Hitler and condonement of his rearmament which had done so much harm in the days of MacDonald and Simon.

Baldwin felt that he treated Hoare unfairly, but he could do so with impunity because Hoare did not have a strong following amongst Conservative MPs. His ability and lucidity were appreciated, but his manner of speaking was pompous and he made himself a figure of fun by constantly referring in his speeches to his wife as 'Lady Maud'. Baldwin relieved his conscience by appointing him again to the Cabinet as First Lord of the Admiralty within a few months. He had been made the scapegoat for the Cabinet's change of mind, while Eden was the knight in shining armour. It was blatant hypocrisy.

What would have happened if the Cabinet had stood by Hoare? Almost certainly Mussolini would have accepted the plan. It is unlikely that public opinion could have ousted the Conservatives from Government. The Conservative Party managers with their steam-roller majority and determination to cling to office could have prevented a dissolution, and the political crisis could have been solved by a reshuffle, and possibly a change of leader. More probably Baldwin (who was very popular) could have made the country believe that in spite of brave talk at Geneva no other country was prepared to risk war with Italy while the real danger came from Germany. Sanctions, apart from oil, would never halt Mussolini – and oil sanctions meant war.

CHAPTER EIGHT
RHINELAND DISASTER
1936

'We had occupied the Rhineland with three divisions, and
had only three battalions west of the Rhine. Our occupation
was symbolic.' (General Jodl in evidence at Nuremberg.)

WHEN EDEN became Foreign Secretary in December 1935 he was
anxious to push on with an oil sanction and still be confident that he could
bring Mussolini to heel. He went to Geneva on 21 January and talked to
Laval, who was on the brink of resignation. He found the Frenchman
opposed to the oil sanction, but Titulescu and Litvinov in favour. On his
return to London the new Foreign Secretary was annoyed to read Foreign
Office minutes by Vansittart, Peterson, Sir George Mounsey (a senior
assistant under-secretary) and Eden's parliamentary colleague Lord Stanhope, expressing concern at the likelihood of an early oil sanction and
casting doubts on the efficacy of the sanctions already in operation.

The ever-faithful Cranborne was obviously putting Eden's views as much
as his own on the file when he wrote:

I cannot agree with Sir G. Mounsey . . . All the indications are that existing
sanctions are more successful than could possibly have been expected. Indeed the
chief argument against the oil sanction is that it is no longer necessary, as Italy is in
any case finding it difficult to buy oil, so effective have been the embargo on loans
and the refusal of League States to take Italian exports. If that is already so practical
an oil sanction in operation, it is certainly doubtful whether it is worth while giving
Signor Mussolini the excuse the commit a mad dog act. But HMG have already
accepted the sanction in principle, and they can hardly refuse to cooperate in it if
other nations, members of the League, agree, and the expert committee reports that

166

it is practicable . . . the latest Board of Trade information indicates that, in view of the League control of long distance tankers the cooperation of the USA may be unnecessary to make the sanction effective.   C   27.1.36.

Cranborne was quite wrong; Italy was importing all the oil she needed, and the other sanctions were only an irritant. Colonel Donovan had come as Roosevelt's emissary to Europe to try to find a solution of the Abyssinian dispute, and Vansittart minuted the fact that Mussolini had informed Donovan 'he did not see how a war could be avoided' if the oil sanction was pressed.

Eden minuted crossly 'I hope that nobody here is placing any credence on Colonel Donovan and his reports. They deserve no credence, of course, though they may be useful to Mussolini and Rothermere. I disagree with Sir G. Mounsey's view that existing sanctions are failing.   A.E.'[1]

Laval had emphasized to Eden in their talks at Geneva his grave fear that Hitler would remilitarize the Rhineland and the corollary was that Mussolini must be placated. Thus Eden was burying his head in the sands. However, he was cautious at his first appearance as Foreign Secretary in Cabinet. He told them that at forthcoming meetings in Geneva of the Committee of Eighteen the United Kingdom would not oppose the opening of discussions on oil sanctions, and would support setting up an expert inquiry into their probable effectiveness, although he would not want to propose it himself if it could be avoided.

On 26 February he told the Cabinet he thought 'we should support an oil sanction' even if it did not prove completely effective about which evidence was 'inconclusive' because 'it was bound to add to Italy's difficulties'. The Cabinet felt that the risk of an alliance between Italy and Germany was 'small' because of the 'contempt' in which Hitler held Mussolini. Some Ministers, who had little confidence in the efficacy of an oil sanction, stated that they supported it on the grounds that it was impossible 'after all that had been said at the General Election and before and since not to try [it] out . . . To repudiate an oil sanction after the statements that had been made in the Debate on the Hoare–Laval peace proposals would be politically disastrous.'

There was disagreement, and Runciman and Eyres-Monsell registered dissent. However, the Cabinet decided that Eden should support an oil sanction at Geneva, and try to secure its application at as early a date as possible.

Baldwin's contributions was that he agreed 'in the general view that an oil sanction ought now to be imposed. In this respect his view had changed owing to the altered political situation of the day'. Hitler's threats of aggression were well known, and at this moment of dire danger for Britain it was playing with fire to antagonize Mussolini 'with an oil sanction whose efficacy was in doubt'. The British Prime Minister had changed his view because of internal political considerations typical of Prime Ministers in moments of crisis.[2]

Oil sanctions were anathema to the new French Government under Sarraut who wanted to patch up the quarrel with Italy; they insisted there must be efforts at peace talks before oil sanctions were considered in Geneva. As Mussolini's troops had been advancing solidly since January, the victorious Duce was now little interested in a negotiated peace.

Meanwhile Hitler's threat to remilitarize the Rhineland began to dwarf the Abyssinian crisis. However, Eden did not consider illegal German military occupation of the Rhineland would be anything like the disaster it appeared to the French on 14 February, telling the Cabinet Committee on Germany in a Memorandum:

> Taking one thing with another it seems undesirable to adopt an attitude where we would either have to fight for the zone or abandon it in the face of a German reoccupation. It would be preferable for Great Britain and France to enter betimes into negotiations with German Government for the surrender on conditions of our rights in the zone while such a surrender still has got a bargaining value.

Eden's Memorandum was approved by his colleagues. It is hard to justify his attitude over the Rhineland because he had told the same Committee on 17 January that Hitler's foreign policy may be summed up as the destruction of the peace settlement and re-establishment of Germany as the dominant power in Europe and he showed how well briefed he was on Hitler's aggressive intentions by circulating for the 29 January meeting extracts from all Phipps' alarming reports (which have been seen above), and including

> On every side giant military establishments are springing up . . . Enormous aerodromes either finished or under construction march, sometimes for miles, with the main road . . . military cars and lorries painted in camouflage colours mix with civilian traffic. In the air the ceaseless hum of aeroplanes bears witness to the expansion of the German air force . . . That military expansion will be followed by territorial expansion goes without saying.

Eden told the Cabinet rearmament should be hastened and an effort made for a '*modus vivendi* with Germany'.[3]

Vansittart on 3 February 1936 wrote an important memorandum in which he suggested that German aspirations might be satisfied by the gift of certain colonies. This was illusory. Hitler was not interested in colonies except for propaganda purposes. However, the Memorandum should have brought realism to the Cabinet. Alas, it did not. Vansittart declared that the Versailles system had broken down. Until the Abyssinian crisis Hitler had professed his desire for friendly relations with Great Britain and France repeatedly, but as soon as the Abyssinian crisis arose Hitler 'at once drew in his horns and discouraged any further change of views'. He went on: '. . .

little or no latitude can be allowed to Germany for expansion in a densely peopled Europe, where expansion, in fact, really means both robbery and murder . . . We cannot make a stand for Abyssinia and connive at the spoliation of Lithuania, or Czechoslovakia, or Austria.' (This was in the event exactly what the British Government did.)

Vansittart wanted to

> try and come to terms with Germany before, as is otherwise eventually certain, she takes the law into her own hands . . . Hitler would have been far more likely to be reasonable and forthcoming in negotiation if faced by the Stresa unity. It is to the recent disintegration of this 'front' that we must in large measure attribute the sudden change of tone . . . we *are* committed to resist by sanctions the modification by force of the status quo; and sanctions in the case of Germany mean war, a land war.

He concluded that it would be well to come to terms with Germany, but no lasting bargain could be made 'without the payment of a high price – that is, provision for territorial expansion,' and Britain could not 'immorally seek that price, or connive at it being sought, at the expense of others . . . in Europe.' Therefore he argued that it must be provided 'at our own expense, that is, in Africa by the restitution of the former colonies of Germany.' Before being seen by the Cabinet this paper was discussed at an internal Foreign Office meeting which did not accept Vansittart's arguments about colonies, and suggested other possible bases of agreement. Baldwin appointed a Committee consisting of MacDonald, Chamberlain, Eden, Halifax, Simon, Thomas and Runciman to consider the paper. Although Chamberlain and Thomas favoured offering Tanganyika to Germany, the Committee could not agree.[4]

On 24 February Eden wrote to Phipps 'It seems to be becoming clearer and clearer that before long we shall be making a supreme effort to reach an understanding with Germany' and on 2 March he submitted a further paper to the Cabinet Foreign Policy Committee suggesting an Air Pact with Germany, negotiations for the remilitarization of the Rhineland in return for concessions by Hitler, and recognition of the special interests of Germany in Central and Eastern Europe. It is difficult to understand how Eden believed he could satisfy Hitler's ambitions in Eastern Europe without 'the dismemberment of territory of other European nations' which Vansittart had ruled out.[5]

On 27 January Eden had seen Neurath, the German Foreign Minister, who was in London for the King's funeral. Eden told him it was most important that 'we should strive for air limitation'. In chasing this will of the wisp Eden was ignoring previous negotiations which had got nowhere, and also that (according to the German account of the interview) Neurath told him the Franco-Russian Pact made an air pact 'considerably more difficult' and that if a signatory of Locarno concluded a bilateral agreement contrary to the spirit of Locarno Hitler would reconsider his attitude. This was a threat that Hitler would remilitarize the Rhineland if the French Parliament ratified the Franco–Soviet agreement. In his memoirs Eden writes: 'There was nothing in this interview to arouse any undue alarm.' A strange judgement! The same afternoon Flandin told him that it looked as if Germany intended to remilitarize the Rhineland. He was right. Hitler had already ordered his Ambassador in Rome to tell Mussolini that he intended to denounce Locarno because of the Franco–Soviet Pact and send German troops into the Rhineland.[6]

Acting on these instructions, on 22 February Hassell (German Ambassador to Italy) saw Mussolini, who told him Stresa 'was dead', and that he expected the Russo–French Pact to be ratified, and that Italy would take no part in action by Britain and France against Germany 'occasioned by an alleged breach by Germany of the Locarno Treaty'. This meant that Mussolini would condone remilitarization of the Rhineland by Hitler as a counterstroke to ratification of the Franco–Soviet Pact. If the British Cabinet had known of this Hassell–Mussolini conversation would they have approved the oil sanction on 26 February? It is unlikely.

Diplomatic secrets were not well kept in Rome, and soon it was known throughout Europe that Flandin's fears expressed to Eden about an Italian–German rapprochement were abundantly justified. At this period the Franco–Russian Pact had been signed but not ratified by the French Parliament – a most unsatisfactory state of affairs which heightened the tension. The Pact was finally ratified by the Chamber of Deputies by almost two to one on 27 February.

On 15 February, as Eden was too busy, Cranborne saw Prince Bismarck, Counsellor at the German Embassy. Cranborne emphasized that the British Government attached 'quite exceptional importance' to cultivating friendly relations with Germany – in particular the Foreign Secretary himself was making this one of the guiding principles of his policy.' Eden minuted: 'This interview . . . should have a good effect.   A.E.'

No specific mention of negotiations for German remilitarization of the prohibited zone was made either by Eden or Cranborne in these talks with Neurath and Bismarck, but it was well known that Hitler was contemplating this step, and it was implicit that Anglo–German relations could only be improved by an agreement condoning it; Eden intended the Air Pact as a quid pro quo, and despite German reluctance wanted negotiations to start as soon as possible.

On 27 February Eden told the German Ambassador (Hoesch) that he was 'particularly anxious to make progress with an Air Pact and air limitation' and had 'said so more than once'. Again there was no specific reference to throwing in remilitarization of the Rhineland as a make-weight, but the Germans knew exactly what Eden had in mind, and rumours were circulating freely in London about British intentions. Eden told Hoesch that the British desired 'closer collaboration between France, Germany and Britain', and that after a discussion with Flandin he would discuss ways and means with Hoesch. Hoesch received the impression that Eden was 'devoting himself most actively to trying to find a basis' for German, French, and British co-operation and would himself be glad if the French did not ratify the Russian Treaty.[7]

In Geneva on 3 March Flandin told Eden he was 'most fearful' that Hitler would invade the demilitarized zone, and the French appeared to have information about the Hassell talk with Mussolini in Rome and an Italo–German rapprochement, because they stated that they expected Mussolini would stand aside from Italy's Locarno obligations in the event of a German coup in the Rhineland. Flandin added that should the coup take place France would immediately inform the League Council and consult Great Britain, Belgium and Italy, but France reserved the right to take 'preparatory measures including measures of a military character'. Eden was thoroughly alarmed at this talk of preparatory measures of a military character, and decided to do his best to prevent them.

As a result a special meeting of the Cabinet was called on the evening of 5 March. A long discussion took place about British obligations under Locarno, and it was suggested that it had never been contemplated that one of the signatories might 'run out'. Flandin's intention to consider the immediate use of force if the Rhineland was invaded was acutely embarrassing to the Cabinet. It made Ministers feel they must urgently conclude an agreement with Hitler so that his military occupation of the Rhineland could be legitimized, and thus prevent precipitate use of force by France. It was agreed that Eden should follow up his approaches to the German Ambassador and begin formal negotiations for an Air Pact. Eden said the question of the remilitarized zone was bound to be raised in the discussions. However, by 5 March it was too late. Mussolini's nod had decided Hitler to order his troops to march.[8]

Eden summoned Hoesch the next morning (6 March) and asked him to tell Hitler that Britain wanted to negotiate an Air Pact urgently through diplomatic channels. Hoesch had tried to put off the interview until the next day (7 March), but so enthusiastic was Eden to make overtures to Hitler that he insisted Hoesch came to the Foreign Office on 6 March. Hoesch listened in silence to Eden's advocacy of a bilateral Air Pact with Germany which according to Eden would 'create an atmosphere of greater confidence'. Ominously, Hoesch stated that he would have an important message to deliver the next morning.[9]

This was Eden's least successful diplomatic move ever because the next day, 7 March, Hitler's troops entered the Rhineland amid the applause of the population. Simultaneously Hitler stated that Germany was ready to join the League of Nations and to make 25-year non-aggression pacts with Belgium, Holland and France. Hitler's alleged excuse for the invasion was the 'abrogation' of Locarno through the Franco-Russian Agreement being ratified by the French Parliament.

Paradoxically at the same moment any need for further sanctions against Italy was postponed. Abyssinia agreed to peace negotiations on 5 March, and Italy in principle on 8 March. But it was too late; Mussolini was taking Hitler's side and it would take a lot to detach him.

On 7 March at 9 am Hassell informed Mussolini of the invasion. Mussolini immediately said Germany had gone too far. Hassell upset, thought the Duce disapproved of the coup, but all Mussolini meant was that Hitler had been much too accommodating to France and Britain in his proposals which accompanied the invasion. He was particularly incensed at the suggestion that Germany would return to the League of Nations, because this would give renewed prestige to the League and diminish the effect of the threats Italy was making to leave. However, on the main issue Mussolini sided decisively with Hitler and confirmed that he had no objection to the military occupation.

Hassell made the perceptive comment 'the Palazzo Chigi [Italian Foreign Office] on the other hand welcomes everything that might strengthen Italy's shady connections with the League of Nations which is apt to recreate something like Stresa. This school of thought has now got the upper hand, and France's hope of putting Italy once more in her debt by means of a peaceful settlement of the Abyssinian conflict has been revived . . . We have provided this school of thought with a splendid alibi.' The 'splendid alibi' was a promise by Hassell that if Germany returned to the League she would always support Italy and oppose further sanctions. Hassell had correctly discerned that Italian diplomats were anti-German and trying to bring Mussolini back to the Stresa Front.

Three days later Mussolini emphasized to Hassell that Italy would take no part in sanctions against Germany (*Sanzionati non sansiano altri*). However, on 12 March Hassell reported that Mussolini was wavering and 'unwilling to burn any boats', and was 'unwilling to decide whether his way is ultimately to lead back to Stresa or to cooperation with Germany; he would like to keep his options open'. He was correct. For the next four years Mussolini had second thoughts from time to time about whether or not to stay in Hitler's camp.[10]

The reaction of Baldwin and Eden to Hitler's coup was not dissimilar to Mussolini's response. Baldwin's most trusted adviser was Thomas Jones, former Deputy Secretary to the Cabinet. On 7 March Jones was staying with Lord Lothian at his Norfolk country house, Blickling. After discussion with Lothian and Walter Layton (now Chairman of the *News Chronicle*), Jones telephoned and advised Baldwin to 'welcome wholeheartedly' Hitler's proposals, to play down the fact that the entry of German troops was a breach of Versailles, and to accept Hitler's declarations of peace as being made in good faith. Jones told him 'England would not dream of going to war because German troops had marched into their own territories' and Britain had better accept the situation and 'start making a new Locarno with Hitler *vice* Stresemann'. This was just the advice Baldwin wanted, and he was adamant that nothing must be done which might result in war.[11]

This was disastrous. The last opportunity to stop Hitler dead in his tracks was in March 1936, when the German army was too weak to fight the French.

The British archives and the French and German documents reveal that if the French had attacked the German troops Hitler would have withdrawn ignominiously from the Rhineland. Humiliated again as in 1934 over his attempted Austrian coup, Hitler would have lost popularity and there would have been a chance of the overthrow of the Nazis and their replacement by a democratic government with peaceful intentions.

The German generals were opposed to the Rhineland coup because of the weakness of the German Army. There is every reason to believe that Poland and Czechoslovakia, France's allies, would have attacked Germany simultaneously with the French, and the strategic outlook for Hitler would have been appalling. On 7 March the Czech Foreign Minister stated that his country would do whatever France did, and Beck, the Polish Foreign Minister, told the French Ambassador in Warsaw that Poland would honour the Franco–Polish Alliance. All the Petite Entente was horrified at the lack of action by France and Britain.

Churchill had contacts with many in high places in France, and his judgement is, 'If the French Government had mobilised there is no doubt that Hitler would have been compelled to withdraw and a check would have been given to his rule.'[12]

In his evidence at the Nuremberg Trials, General Jodl stated that Germany would have surrendered the area west of the Rhine 'in case of a French occupation'. In all respects where it can be checked Jodl's evidence is truthful, and there is no reason to doubt what he said about 1936. He went on that 'we had occupied the Rhineland with three divisions, and had only three battalions west of the Rhine. Our occupation was symbolic. Blomberg and I suggested to the Führer withdrawing the three battalions if the French withdrew from their borders. He turned it down.'[13]

Jodl also stated that in 1935 Germany had 36 divisions while France, Poland and Czechoslovakia possessed 90 divisions 'for times of peace, and 190 divisions for war. We had hardly any heavy artillery and tank construction was in its earliest stages.' If Eden ever read Jodl's authoritative description of Germany's military weakness it must have made him rue more than ever his policy of placating Hitler in March 1936.

Eden must have been taken completely by surprise, as the day before he was confident negotiations for air disarmament in return for an agreement over the Rhineland would start shortly. When Hoesch delivered the bombshell to him on the morning of 7 March, Eden told the Ambassador he was impressed by the importance of the offer to return to the League, but stressed Germany had unilaterally repudiated a treaty, which would create a most deplorable impression everywhere. When Hoesch said France had destroyed Locarno by her alliance with Russia Eden replied that if Germany believed this, the course provided for in the Locarno treaties was to appeal to a court of arbitration, and that she was not justified in a unilateral denunciation.

By giving the impression that Britain had doubts whether the Franco–Soviet Pact was a breach of Locarno, Eden was flouting the facts and pandering to the Germans. Action under the Franco–Soviet Pact was strictly limited by the League covenant and by the Treaty of Locarno, and had to be compatible with Versailles and Locarno. Laval, who negotiated the pact, took every precaution in that direction. Even when there was no unanimous decision by the League Council to whom the dispute had first to be submitted, France would still have to make sure that any aid she rendered to Russia did not constitute a violation of the Treaty in the eyes of the Locarno guarantors. Laval had been in constant touch with London during the negotiations, and after the pact was signed the British Government formally agreed with the French that it was compatible with Locarno. Thus Eden's admission that the Franco–Soviet Pact could be a matter for legal debate amounted to a nod to Hitler that Britain would neither use force nor take sanctions against Germany over the Rhineland.

Eden saw the French Ambassador on 7 March, and tried to limit French reaction by saying he felt sure the French would not do anything to 'render the situation more difficult'; there must be a steady and calm examination and 'we must not close our eyes to the fact that a *contre partie* was offered' which would have 'a very considerable effect on public opinion', and we could not leave this side of the situation 'unconsidered'. It was not what the French wanted to hear.[14]

On 8 March the French and Belgian Governments asked for an immediate meeting of the League of Nations Council, and that evening the French Prime Minister, Sarraut, rejected outright on French radio Hitler's memorandum as a basis of negotiations. Over the weekend Eden consulted with Baldwin at Chequers and they agreed that there would be no support in Britain for military action against Germany. They overlooked Baldwin's immense popularity, which meant he could have swayed public opinion if he exerted himself. Eden in Cabinet on 9 March betrayed more irritation than apprehension about the new military situation. He admitted that in his 6 March talk with Hoesch he had in mind the surrender of the Rhineland to Hitler, and 'by reoccupying the Rhineland [Hitler] has deprived us of the possibility of making to him a concession which might otherwise have been a useful bargaining counter in our hands in general negotiations with Germany which we had in contemplation'. He argued that 'it was in our interest to conclude with her (Germany) as far reaching and enduring a settlement as possible whilst Herr Hitler is still in the mood to do so. . . . condemnation by the League Council should be accepted only on the understanding that it would not be followed by a French attack on Germany and a request for our armed assistance.' This was slamming the door on the French, who wanted to throw Hitler out by force regardless of whether it meant war or not, and also naïvely inferring that Hitler would honour any peace agreement which he signed, although he had torn up Locarno after solemnly promising he would abide by it.

The Cabinet accepted Eden's proposals, ignoring both the French viewpoint, and how acquiescence must increase Hitler's popularity at home. Baldwin pursued the idea of further appeasement. On the next day, in response to a suggestion by Eden that a colony should be offered to Hitler as a quid pro quo for Germany returning to the League, he appointed a Departmental Committee under the Earl of Plymouth to consider giving Germany a colonial mandate.[15]

Hitler's action had violated both Locarno and Versailles, and if France had mobilized and Hitler had not immediately withdrawn his troops, under the terms of both treaties Britain would have been obliged to go to the help of France. The divided French Cabinet, however, never put Britain's treaty obligations to the test. The division in Sarraut's Cabinet was disastrous, especially as Gamelin too became irresolute. Unfortunately, the French seriously overestimated the German strength in the Rhineland, putting it at six to seven divisions (140,000 men) whereas the German archives disclose it was only 36,000, including police.[16]

The French Chiefs of Staff were still blithely hoping for Italian aid in throwing Germany out of the Rhineland. At a Chiefs of Staff Conference on 8 March 1936 Gamelin said, 'We can only enter the Rhineland at the same time as the guarantor powers of Locarno [England and Italy]. British and Italian contingents must be with us,' and General Pujo thought 'the Italians might send us 100 bombers', while Gamelin said 'it would be most important that English and Italian troops should immediately be sent to France . . .' These were vain hopes, although twelve months before Mussolini would have willingly obliged with his troops and aircraft.

As it was, Hoesch sent warnings of 'the grave danger from London'; these were not entirely justified. The three military attachés at the German Embassy, including General Geyr von Schweppenberg, sent a personal message to General Blomberg on 13 March that the situation 'should be regarded as extremely grave. An extremely unfavourable development may occur in the next few days'.[17]

Hoesch reported with disquiet an interview with Austen Chamberlain on 10 March. Austen declared that Germany should have sought arbitration about the legality of the Franco–Soviet Pact, and reproached Germany with having announced judgement on her own case and having committed a 'brutal' breach of Locarno, so that in future German undertakings would be distrusted. Austen became heated, and raising his voice repeated twice that France must decide whether she wished to reply by force, and that Britain would be 'dishonoured' if she did not support France 'with the whole of her fighting forces'. One can only lament that Austen had not been made Foreign Secretary by Baldwin three months before, as he so nearly was. Unfortunately, his views had no effect on Eden and Baldwin, and Eden was allowed to conduct affairs as a one-man-band.

Robert Cecil, who Hoesch also saw, in contrast to Austen told Hoesch that he did not consider immediate military counter-action would be justified, while Hoesch was able to report that Lord Duncannon, Lothian, General Sir Ian Hamilton, Thomas Moore MP and Londonderry were on Hitler's side. Londonderry sent a pro-Hitler letter to *The Times*. From Buckingham Palace came news to Hoesch that the new King was very understanding about Hitler's action.[18]

On 8 March Eden and Halifax went to Paris to meet the French, Belgians and Italians – the signatories of Locarno. The Italians did not send a delegate; their Paris Ambassador attended. Flandin said the French Government wanted to put all possible pressure on Germany to withdraw, including military force, and expected the other Locarno powers to co-operate. Both Eden and Halifax said economic and financial sanctions would not be effective, and they were surprised French public opinion would support the use of force. Flandin replied that this was so, and that 'everything was at stake'. Flandin insisted that German withdrawal must be a preliminary to negotiations. The French and British were poles apart, with Eden telling the French not to take action without prior consultation, although the French and Belgians argued strongly that Hitler would withdraw if the Locarno powers took a firm and united stand. Hitler would have been reassured if he could have read an account of these talks.[19]

Eden was confident that he could wring concessions out of Hitler, and as soon as he got back to London late on 11 March he persuaded the Cabinet to give him permission to approach the Führer secretly with a view to a token German withdrawal while negotiations took place. Again this diplomatic ploy by Eden was abortive. After the Cabinet meeting Eden sent for Hoesch and told the German that 'the atmosphere during the previous day's negotiations in Paris had been so impossible that the British representatives had decided not to continue the discussions and had succeeded in having them transferred to London'. This was strange language to use about Britain's allies to the aggressor, and Eden clearly wanted Hitler to know that Britain sought a negotiated settlement in which the remilitarization would be condoned. Hoesch noted that Eden hoped Hitler would offer some compromise, and in doing so emphasized to his master that Eden was resisting the French demand for Britain to honour her obligation to support France's use of force. Hitler refused any compromise or climbdown then, and he never compromised until the outbreak of war.[20]

Eden told Hoesch he wanted to be 'an honest broker' between Germany and France, and suggested that Hitler withdrew part of his troops in the Rhineland and left only a token force there while negotiations took place. He should also undertake not to construct fortifications while the negotiations were in progress. Hoesch told Eden that this was 'unrealistic', but promised to transmit the proposal to Hitler. This was leaked to the newspapers. Hitler must have been delighted at Eden's attitude, and the difference between the British and the French at this moment of crisis.

Eden was ready to go to any lengths to give the impression that Britain was not repudiating Locarno, but he had made Hitler aware that any sign of firmness by Britain would be bluff and would not be followed by action. Eden told the Cabinet on 11 March he and Halifax had found in Paris to their surprise that France and Belgium would not agree to Eden's suggestion of a constructive policy to re-establish the European situation, and in their view the French alternative of forcing the Germans out of the Rhineland 'would not produce a satisfactory settlement'. Baldwin's reaction on 11 March was significant. He told the Cabinet: 'At some stage it would be necessary to point out to the French that the action they proposed would not result only in letting loose another great war in Europe. They might succeed in crushing Germany with the aid of Russia, but it would probably only result in Germany going bolshevik.' Baldwin's fear of Stalin seemed greater than his fear of Hitler.[21]

On 7 March 1936 Albert Sarraut made a firm speech to his Cabinet which he intended to be followed by partial mobilization of the French army. General Gamelin, the French Commander-in-Chief, said it would be six weeks before he could be ready to send an army adequate to expel the Germans; this, and Flandin's reminder that in Geneva Eden had refused to give an assurance of military help, caused Sarraut to find himself in a Cabinet minority. The Minister of War, General Muarin, said military intervention was impossible without mobilization. This split the Cabinet. Flandin described it as being in pathetic confusion (*lamentable dèsarroi*). Some members declared apprehensively that it would be courting electoral disaster because a General Election had to be held in six weeks' time. After bitter controversy Sarraut, Mandel, Flandin and Boncour voted for immediate military action but were a minority. The French Cabinet would have been unanimously in favour of the use of force if British military support had been forthcoming. Instead the French Cabinet decided to await the result of negotiations with Britain and the League of Nations, while each day's delay made it more difficult to dislodge Hitler's troops.

In his broadcast on the evening of 7 March Sarraut had said, 'We will not allow Strasbourg to be within range of German guns.' For this he was heavily criticized in the right-wing press, and many French were confused because they had been indoctrinated into believing that the Maginot Line was invulnerable, so they did not understand the real threat from the presence of Hitler's troops in the Rhineland. Sarraut and Flandin got little help from van Zeeland, the Belgian Prime Minister. Although Zeeland was appalled, he always waited to see what the British would do. Much respected as a banker and pacifist, Zeeland was not a strong politician, and was the wrong man to be in charge of Belgium at this moment.

When Flandin and Boncour arrived in London they met hostility. Much to their annoyance, Germany was allowed to be represented at the League of Nations Council. The snakelike Ribbentrop promised a great deal, saying the military move was only a symbolic gesture, and he attacked France viciously for wanting an exclusive right to a strong army, adding that the reason behind the Franco–Soviet Pact was that France wanted to have her frontier on the Rhine, and Britain ought not to accept the encirclement of Germany by France, Russia and her satellites. The Council ruled that Germany had broken her international obligations but took no action; other member countries were wary of sanctions against Germany because they had failed against Italy. Only Belgium and France demanded action.

Flandin had come to London with high hopes that he could persuade Britain to back a French military move into the Rhineland. Van Zeeland had emphasized in Paris that all depended on Britain, and that Belgium would take military action if the United Kingdom 'joined in'. Baldwin told Flandin categorically that he would not involve Britain in any measures which might lead to war, adding, 'Britain is in no state to go to war.' It is alleged that when Flandin found the British politicians were determined to repudiate their Locarno obligations he burst into tears.[22]

At a Cabinet meeting on 12 March Eden stated that he thought

> at some stage it would be necessary to point out to the French that force would not result only in letting loose another great war in Europe. They might succeed in crushing Germany with the aid of Russia but it would perhaps only result in Germany going bolshevik and the French should be told military action was inappropriate as being "out of proportion to what Germany has done" and the Council of Locarno Powers should give Britain, France, Belgium and Italy a mandate to negotiate with Germany an air pact, settlement in eastern and central Europe (it won't amount to much) on the basis of unilateral non-aggression pacts offered to Hitler and Germany's unconditional return to the League . . . the essential thing will be to induce or cajole France to accept this mandate . . . The strength of our position lies in the fact that France is not in the mood for a military adventure.

This amounted to capitulation to Hitler and abandonment of France. What Eden meant by settlement in eastern and central Europe 'not amounting to much' is anybody's guess, and such woolly thinking in the moment of crisis detracts from his reputation. Furthermore, what value had 'unilateral non-aggression pacts' signed by Hitler after he had broken his word over the Rhineland? However, Eden stuck to this position.

Previously he had gone more than half-way towards justifying Hitler's action, telling the Cabinet:

> although I deeply deplore repudiation of a Treaty freely negotiated, yet it is clear to me that there are certain very important offers contained in the German communication – notably the non-aggression pact with France and Italy to be guaranteed by Great Britain and Italy, and the offer to return to the League. I told the French Ambassador and the Belgian Chargé d'Affaires we should say and do nothing to make the situation more difficult pending the consultation.[23]

The British Chiefs of Staff's pessimistic report on 18 March reinforced the Cabinet in their view that military action must be ruled out:

Possible Despatch of an International Force to Rhineland

> It would be purely symbolic; infantry would be peace strength, e.g. no anti-tank guns, armoured cars, tanks which they would need for war . . . 5 Brigades, 20 Battalions could be sent . . . if war broke out we should not with this prior commitment be able to mobilize any troops to refortify France or Belgium on land for a considerable time.

The Chiefs of Staff ignored the fact that the French army could easily throw the Germans out of the Rhineland and the Germans were too weak to start a war. Twenty British battalions would have delighted the French and completed the discomfiture of Hitler, but neither Baldwin nor Eden wanted this.

With the aid of van Zeeland a middle course between the French and British was found after a series of Locarno Council meetings between 13 March and 23 March, and this resulted in condemnation of Germany's act and a call for reference to arbitration on the compatibility of the Franco–Soviet Pact with Locarno, a proposal for an international force to be stationed on either side of the frontier, and suspension by all the countries of military activities in the frontier zones. However, the official proposals drawn up on 19 March included a British promise of immediate military assistance to Belgium and France if the need arose.

Britain and France signed the London Agreement on 18 March; it was a vague guarantee by Britain to France, subject to League strings. This agreement could have been invoked by the French when Hitler began to build the Siegfried Line, but the French knew only too well that the British response would be negative. Flandin was bitterly disappointed. He told Eden his mission to London had been a failure; France and Belgium, the injured parties, had been classed with Germany, the guilty party, and the proposals were 'impregnated with this unjust assimilation of guilt and innocence'.

In London Ribbentrop had protested with insufferable insolence against the League Resolution condemning Germany, claiming that France, not Germany, was responsible for the termination of the Locarno Treaty. Sarraut told the British Ambassador in Paris he feared French confidence in British policy had been destroyed, and had made 'a breach between the two great peoples on whose union depended the safety of Europe'. Clerk warned Eden that if Britain could not calm French fears the effect on British prestige and Anglo–French relations might be disastrous. On Clerk's despatch Eden minuted: 'We should not allow French politicians to speak like this without reacting.' He did not realize that this was the inevitable corollary of Britain failing to honour her Locarno obligations.[24]

Hitler ignored the request that he should agree not to fortify the zone or reinforce his troops, or agree to an international force, and sent Ribbentrop back to London on 1 April with a 19-point Peace Plan. He had no intention of honouring any of the promises in it, so it does not merit detailed examination. However, it affected British opinion in German favour because of the hypocritical emphasis that Germany intended to return to the League, and the promise not to strengthen Germany's military position in the Rhineland for four months. Eden told the Cabinet that Hitler's Peace Plan was evidence conciliation was succeeding, whereas threats of sanctions had failed. He was deluding them.[25]

Inset: David Lloyd George as Prime Minister wanted to wipe out German reparations. (*Barnaby's Picture Library*)

Poincaré, an implacable enemy of Germany, insisted on her paying heavy reparations. (*Press Association*)

Robert Cecil (Viscount Cecil of Chelwood) believed Abyssinia would abolish slavery once she was admitted to the League of Nations. (*Associated Press*)

Andrew Bonar Law as Prime Minister wanted to continue Lloyd George's soft policy towards Germany but was overruled by Curzon. A portrait taken in 1922. He died in 1923. (*Press Association*)

Austen Chamberlain's five years as Foreign Secretary was a happy period for Anglo–French–German relations. (*Press Association*)

Gustav Stresemann, (*left*), German Foreign Minister, with Austen Chamberlain; they were firm friends. (*Press Association*)

Left to right, front row: Sir John Simon, Ramsay MacDonald and Mussolini in 1933. (*Associated Press*)

Left to right, front row: Lord Curzon, Benito Mussolini and Poincaré at the Lausanne Peace Conference, 1923. (*Associated Press*)

Arthur Henderson, the Foreign Secretary, in Paris, in 1930. *Left to right:* Lord Tyrrell, British Ambassador in Paris, M. Briand, French Minister for Foreign Affairs, Arthur Henderson and M. Leger, secretary to M. Briand. (*Associated Press*)

Left to right, front row: Scialoja (Italy), Vandervelde (Belgium), Dr Luther (Germany), Briand and Gustav Stresemann at the League of Nations meeting at Geneva. (*Associated Press*)

Ramsay MacDonald is greeted on arrival at Friedrichstrasse Station, Berlin, by the British Ambassador and Drs Brüning and Cürtius (German Chancellor and Foreign Minister respectively). *Left to right:* Sir Horace Rumbold, Ramsay MacDonald, Dr Brüning and Dr Curtius. (*Associated Press*)

Ramsay MacDonald with General Dawes, the instigator of the Dawes Plan. (*Barnaby's Picture Library*)

Anthony Eden with French Premier Laval in 1935. They did not get on together. (*Associated Press*)

Stanley Baldwin en route to Buckingham Palace to resign in May 1937. (*Associated Press*)

The German Army crossing the Rhine. March 1936. (*Associated Press*)

Laval (*left*), pro-Fascist and probably in Mussolini's pay, with the Russian Maxim Litvinov who wanted to make an alliance with Britain. (*National Archives, Washington*)

Lord Londonderry, Secretary of State for Air, with Winston Churchill. Pictured in 1919. (*Press Association*)

Overleaf: Sudeten Czechs give a rapturous welcome to German troops, October 1938. (*Associated Press*)

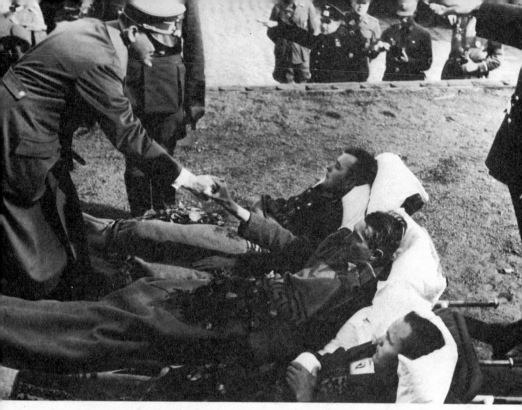

Hitler with alleged German casualties in Czechoslovakia in 1938. Possibly a propaganda picture. (*Barnaby's Picture Library*)

Hitler greeted by Henlein on his arrival in the Sudetenland, 1938. Goering is on the extreme right. (*Associated Press*)

Lord Runciman and Ashton-Gwatkin about to leave on their abortive mission to Czechoslovakia, 1938. (*Associated Press*)

Czech Nazis tearing down the Czech frontier emblem from the frontier post at Grottau, 2 October, 1938. (*Associated Press*)

Josef Beck, Polish Foreign Minister, arriving at Victoria, March 1939. (*National Archives, Washington*)

Ulrich von Hassell, Hitler's anti-Nazi Ambassador in Rome, being condemned to death, 1944. (*The Weiner Library*)

The King granted Lord Halifax, the Foreign Secretary, and Sir Alexander Cadogan, the Permanent Under-Secretary at the Foreign Office, a special concession and allowed them to walk through the gardens of Buckingham Palace, en route to the Foreign Office. This picture was taken on 8 September 1939. (*Associated Press*)

Hitler bids goodbye to Mussolini in Berlin. (*Barnaby's Picture Library*)

Carl Goerdeler, the anti-Nazi German politician, being condemned to death, 1944.

Adam von Trott, the anti-Nazi conspirator, with his wife Clarita. (*From author's collection*)

Viscount Runciman with President Benes in Prague, 1938. (*Associated Press*)

Leslie Hore-Belisha, Secretary of State for War 1937–40. 1940. (*Associated Press*)

Hitler and Chamberlain at Munich during the crisis of September 1938. (*Barnaby's Picture Library*)

Chamberlain and Mussolini at Munich in 1938. (*National Archives, Washington*)

Eden decided to reply to the Peace Plan with a carefully drafted questionnaire to Hitler asking him to define his foreign policy. Eden justified this questionnaire to the Cabinet on the grounds that it would buy enough time through a *détente* with Germany for British rearmament, but the Foreign Office minutes show the officials feared its conciliatory language would only encourage Hitler to commit further excesses. No reply was ever given by the Führer, and he finally buried the questionnaire in a speech to the Reichstag on 30 January 1937.

Hitler's Peace Plan was discussed by the British and the French at Geneva on 7 April. The French asked for an immediate study of 'all measures of coercion which could be applied to Germany', and gave Eden a Memorandum. Eden was uncooperative. Then at a meeting on 8 April, Flandin and Boncour made a last-ditch stand trying to persuade the British to co-operate with France in bringing Hitler to heel. Eden declared categorically that Britain would not 'prepare sanctions in advance' against Germany should the case arise, and she would not even study them as suggested in the Memorandum, and asked whether France would herself 'be in a position to apply sanctions against Germany' if the zone was fortified (meaning would French public opinion stand for it?). Boncour assured him that France would.

Eden then said that if sanctions against Germany were threatened it would prejudice discussions at the League on the German and French plan. However, Flandin calmed the meeting down by saying the French had made a great concession by saying they were ready to regard the reaffirmation of Locarno and the Staff talks as 'a kind of compensation' for the reoccupation of the zone, and he wanted 'some general security arrangement going beyond the terms of the Covenant . . . to balance . . . the refortification of the zone'. Eden in reply proposed that both Hitler's Peace Plan and the French Memorandum (advocating the study sanctions) should be considered by the Council of the League, with Germany represented.

This stung Boncour, who asked Eden what France should do if at the same time Germany refortified the Zone. That would affect not only the security of France but that of Europe as a whole; and 'from behind her concrete fortifications [Germany would] threaten the whole of Europe, including Great Britain'. Eden asked what France would do in that eventuality, and Boncour snapped back that in that case sanctions ought to be applied against Germany as they had been against Italy. Eden commented facetiously that 'Germany had not yet invaded France', which produced the angry response from Boncour that Germany was doing something much worse than Italy – 'she was preparing the invasion of

Europe. Precautions ought therefore to be taken by the most energetic means.'

This tense Geneva meeting on 8 April was France's final effort to persuade Britain to take firm measures against Germany. It failed, and left Hitler not only in possession of the Rhineland but, as he had hoped, with the victorious allies of the First World War bitterly divided. Eden had played into Hitler's hands by his technique for postponing and avoiding decisive action.[26]

Flandin was ready to consider German refortification as part of a general settlement, but he would not start negotiations unless the Locarno powers made preparations for sanctions if the talks broke down. This Eden adamantly refused. However, Eden, using the questionnaire as his main argument, managed to persuade Flandin on 22 April to postpone any further meetings of the Locarno Powers – and thus any threats of action against Germany – until after the French elections in the first week of May. Then much to Eden's relief the tough anti-Hitler Sarraut and Flandin were replaced by the Blum Popular Front Government. Blum was less resolute against Hitler.

Eden expressed regrets in his memoirs that he had not followed the hard French line against Germany in March and April 1936, writing: 'Hitler's reoccupation of the Rhineland was an occasion when the British and French should have attempted the impossible.' This was eating the words he had used to Flandin and Boncour at the decisive Geneva meeting on 8 April 1936.

Although the offer of Staff talks had done much to soothe the French, the Cabinet, influenced by back-bench opinion, thought they were going too far in pandering to their allies. Baldwin became worried, telling Eden that Kingsley Wood had been to see him, saying 'the boys will not have it' while, as would be expected, Simon objected strongly. Eden, to his credit, stood firm and convinced the Commons of the desirability of Staff talks. All that was achieved was five days of such talks with the French and Belgians beginning on 15 April, which laid bare Britain's abject military weakness and the ponderousness of the French army. Talks were not resumed until 1939. Meanwhile the remilitarization and refortification of the Rhineland became a *fait accompli*.[27]

The Foreign Office backed Eden over the Rhineland, although Vansittart was apprehensive of Hitler's intentions. Orme Sargent, his Assistant Under-Secretary, was influential, and advised:

> if we tried to stop the Germans refortifying the Rhineland by threatening economic sanctions, such a system would mean sanctions by Great Britain alone for it is only the British trade which is of value to Germany . . . even if we succeeded in

preventing Germany now from refortifying the Rhineland, the time is past when we can hope to maintain such a servitude indefinitely, and it is quite obvious that so long as such a servitude was maintained it would be impossible to negotiate any general settlement with Germany.'

Vansittart agreed that British sanctions were 'out of the question', although he wrote to Hankey on 16 April: 'The Germany of today has no intention of remaining within her present boundaries or respecting the integrity of her smaller neighbours *NO MATTER WHAT PAPERS SHE MAY SIGN.*' When Sargent minuted 'One cannot help being struck once again, a review of the German plans and ambitions makes those of Italy look comparatively insignificant,' Eden wrote 'But what are they?'

On 18 April the British Ambassador in Paris reported that the French were likely to mobilize as soon as Germany 'begins to fortify the Rhineland'. This produced a minute from Vansittart: 'A disquieting despatch . . . but the existence let alone prevalence of the idea does not account for our anxiety to liquidate Abyssinia.'[28]

Meanwhile Abyssinian resistance to the Italian army was collapsing, and the Foreign Office pressurized Eden for a speedy removal of sanctions in the belief that Mussolini's antagonism to Britain was encouraging Hitler to be aggressive. In Cabinet on 19 March Eden asked his colleagues for their views about raising sanctions in the event of a truce, saying that in his view they should not be raised 'merely in return for a truce, and that we must be assured of peace being in sight'. Chamberlain suggested that 'if sanctions were taken off before peace were in sight, there would be political trouble'. Electoral considerations were always important when the Cabinet considered key international problems, and it was the height of irresponsibility for Britain to antagonize simultaneously both France and Italy at a time when German aggression had produced the worst threat to peace since 1918.

Now Eden's Cabinet colleagues mistrusted his sanctions policy. On 6 April Eden asked the Cabinet to consider closing the Suez Canal, when Baldwin emphatically refused to consider it because it would involve war with Italy Eden said he was 'still hoping that the Italians might be defeated by the rain'. When Roger Makins (Lord Sherfield) wrote a minute on 19 April advocating the closure of the Canal Eden commented: 'This is stimulating,' but he did not mention it again at the Cabinet on 22 April, when the others were pessimistic about sanctions.[29]

Eden clung to his now vain hope that sanctions against Mussolini might succeed. In Abyssinia by 28 April Haile Selassie had been hopelessly defeated by the Italian General Graziani, and on 3 May he fled from Addis Ababa. It is hard to follow Eden's reasoning, for there was now no stopping an Italian victory. He must have hoped to deny Mussolini the fruits of his conquest in order to show the world that defiance of the Covenant of the League could not pay off. He kept to this unrealistic view as late as 22 May, after the Italians had occupied Addis Ababa and life there was returning to normal. On a despatch from Phipps which claimed the belief in British circles that successful League action against Italy would have induced Hitler to change his policy was 'completely fallacious' Eden minuted:

> Sir E. Phipps does not appear to understand (and it is perhaps natural enough, for it is not his business to do so) the importance for this country and *for France* of a League success over the Abyssinian affair. British opinion will not take a part in Europe sans through the League, and if the League suffers, as it has done now, the cause of peace will suffer also. If France had been wise enough to see this, all our present troubles could have been avoided, and at least we could have been in better form and spirit to meet the German challenge if and when it came. However, apparently the French Government took a different view and so does Sir E. Phipps.   A.E.   May 22.

This petulant minute shows Eden at loggerheads not only with the French and the Foreign Office but also with his Cabinet colleagues over sanctions. Lord Stanhope, his under-secretary, minuted: 'I must agree with Sir E. Phipps. The most that I thought a successful application of sanctions to Italy might have done to Germany would have been to make her pause. Now that sanctions have definitely failed Germany . . . may strike them out of her war book altogether.' Although his other under-secretary Cranborne as usual agreed with Eden, Vansittart minuted the despatch 'had been written with Phipps' habitual realism'. Wigram wrote: 'I can't see how anybody can still believe sanctions against Germany to be a practical proposition,' and O'Malley: 'Phipps' despatch is full of hard common sense.'[30]

On another message from Phipps of 27 May that 'If Anglo–Italian relations do not soon improve, events will indeed by playing into the hands of Herr Hitler' Eden wrote: 'this may be true, but it is not we who have broken the Covenant, & the British public is not prepared to sit round the table on friendly terms with the aggressor for many a long day – nor can I blame them.' Cranborne as ever supported him, but Wigram, Vansittart and Stanhope wrote minutes which aggravated Eden, to the effect that they wanted sanctions lifted.

On the same day after Grandi had told him that Mussolini had realized his colonial ambitions, and wanted to open as soon as 'practicable a chapter of collaboration with England and France' Eden minuted '. . . we are not in a mood to be blackmailed by Italy. Some constructive contribution by her is also called for . . . If Mussolini thinks she has only to beckon and we will open our arms, he is vastly mistaken.'

In spite of Eden's desire to humiliate Mussolini, the end was in sight, and only two days later on 29 May Eden admitted defeat, telling the Cabinet, 'it was not practicable by the maintenance of sanctions to ensure the withdrawal of Italy from Abyssinia' and promised to circulate a memorandum suggesting the end of sanctions.

Baldwin then said the 'difficulty' now was 'one of face saving in the country'. Hitler had by now profited to the hilt from Eden's intransigence over sanctions against Italy, and it was too late to put the clock back.[31]

Chamberlain felt this strongly, and after the Cabinet had considered sanctions again without making any decision because they awaited a memorandum from Eden on 11 June jumped the gun, and without informing Eden in advance in a speech which obtained great publicity stated that the continuance of sanctions was 'midsummer madness'. Baldwin ineptly dissociated himself, but this was a silly move because the Cabinet were about to approve the immediate raising of sanctions. Chamberlain noted in his diary: 'I did it deliberately because I felt the country and the party needed a lead . . . I did not consult Eden because he would have been bound to beg me not to say what I proposed.' However, Chamberlain wrote to Eden that he had been so occupied on the Treasury bench that 'he had had not enough time to put his thoughts in a form which he could show me'. On 17 June the Cabinet announced the end of sanctions after considering a long memorandum from Eden which, while admitting sanctions were dead, advocated that Britain should not recognize the Italian conquest of Abyssinia because 'it would be bitterly unpopular at Geneva'. This refusal by Eden to be generous to Mussolini after sanctions had failed, and to recognize the conquest, was to be costly.[32]

At the beginning of August Vansittart went to Berlin during the Olympic Games – not to join in Nazi junketing, but to inform himself about German intentions. He liked von Neurath, whom he thought 'lazy and good natured' and peacefully inclined. He saw too much of Ribbentrop for his taste, and described him as 'shallow, self-seeking and not really friendly' and likely to be a trial when he became Ambassador in London.

Vansittart was cynical about Hitler's policy and doubted if the Five Power meeting would ever take place and whether Hitler intended to act up to his March offers respecting pacts with Germany's neighbours in Central Europe and 'still more important whether they truly meant business as regards a fresh Locarno'. He found the danger of Communism the dominant theme in Berlin, but got the impression that Hitler himself had no fear of it because of his immensely strong hold over the German people and the more stable German economic situation. Hitler told him that German workmen were not demanding higher wages.

185

Perceptively he thought Germany was ruled by 'talented and almost purely political adventurers'. Surprisingly he got on best with Dr Goebbels – 'much charm; quick as a whip, with a really nice wife.' (Sir Ivo Mallet and his wife also told the author of Goebbels' charm.) Vansittart thought Germany wanted to come to an understanding with England on its own terms, and no longer had any serious hope of dividing us from the French but that (contrary to Eden's continual optimism) there was 'no hope of any acceptable limitation of air forces'. He thought England would be committing suicide by any agreement which meant curtailing British rearmament. He had one interview with a prominent Jew who had to come in and out of the Embassy by the back door and was very frightened. He asked Vansittart to intervene on behalf of 'his co-religionists, but Phipps said any intervention would do more harm than good to the victims. But Vansittart did not think a German–Russian rapprochement was feasible; (at that time perhaps it was not even in Hitler's mind). It was a pity his perceptive views were not accepted by Eden, because they turned out to be correct.[33]

Whereas in October 1935 an overwhelming majority of the British public became anti-Italian, in March 1936 a wave of pro-German feeling swept Britain. Simon wrote to Baldwin on 25 March that he thought an expeditionary force should not be 'the way in which we might make a contribution if war returned'; instead our contribution should take 'the shape of an air contingent. I cannot believe that if London was being heavily bombed we should send regiments of soldiers to the Low Countries.' He felt it was vitally important that we made no promise of sending an expeditionary force because of 'the instinctive revulsion of public opinion and that the British people do not really contemplate sending their sons to fight on the continent'. Simon also emphasized doubts as to whether Britain's obligations under Locarno were still binding after the Franco–Soviet Pact, and 'Locarno was most definitely not an Anglo–French Alliance.'

Simon was exerting his baneful influence on foreign policy from his new post as Home Secretary. Perhaps this letter was inspired by his friend Mrs Greville. He was always apt to look at matters from a lawyer's standpoint, but as Foreign Secretary he had never expressed the view that the Franco–Soviet Pact was a breach of Locarno. His concluding paragraph, bitterly anti-French, probably delighted Mrs Greville, as it would have done Hitler.

> The French now feel pretty sure that they have got us so tied that they can safely wait for the breakdown of discussions with Germany. In such circumstances France

will be as selfish and as pigheaded as France has always been and the prospect of
agreement with Germany will grow dimmer and dimmer.

Baldwin and Eden were in the spring of 1936 wedded to this approach, and
Baldwin must have been as pleased with this advice as he was with that of
Tom Jones.[34]

Two meetings of the Conservative back-bench Foreign Affairs Committee are revealing. (Reports to the Prime Minister were made by Lord
Home.) At the first on 12 March, which was not well attended, Lord
Winterton, Robert Boothby, Austen Chamberlain, Churchill and Sir
Edward Grigg wanted action to force Germany to withdraw; Churchill
painted a romantic picture of all the countries of Europe 'hurrying' to assist
France and ourselves against Germany. However, Nancy Astor and Hoare
thought it would be 'criminal' to embark on war, and had the support of
almost the whole meeting after Hoare had sobered them down by saying
there was 'a strong pro-German feeling in this country', and that as regards
Winston's reference to all the nations of Europe coming to our aid, 'these
nations were totally unprepared from a military point of view'. Hoare was
distancing himself from his fervent support of the Covenant of the League
in his September speech.

Even stronger evidence of pro-German feeling came at the next meeting
on 17 March, which was better attended. Victor Raikes thought to
discontinue sanctions upon Italy in order to apply them to Germany would
be 'intolerable,' and 'would make the League of Nations a mockery . . . he
did not believe there would be any support for action which might lead to
war'. He was echoing the feelings of the majority of MPs.

Although Harold Nicolson and Anthony Crossley contradicted Raikes
'the general feeling amongst the Tory MPs present was that Britain would
not have signed Locarno if the Franco–Soviet Pact had been in existence'.
However, Patrick Donner took the French point of view and voiced his
suspicions that Germany was building submarines secretly – which, as has
been seen, was true. Arnold Wilson declared Britain had 'no sympathy with
France'; and Austen Chamberlain, milder on this occasion, contented
himself with 'We must obtain some redress from Germany for breaking the
Locarno Treaty.'[35]

In Parliament on 26 March Neville Chamberlain stated that 'the German
Chancellor had declared that he has no other intentions other than peaceful
intentions at the present time. Personally I believe that.' Unfortunately, he
held this delusion too long and it resulted in fatal mistakes when he became
Prime Minister. In the 26 March debate Nicolson, Boothby, Churchill and
Austen Chamberlain argued for firm action in support of France.

This was one hundred per cent sound, but on that day they were a tiny minority among both Government supporters and Opposition in the Commons. Nicolson said:

> When Dr Brüning, that most admirable man, was engaged in a final struggle to save Liberal Germany we turned our shoulder on him. Now when Germany is strong we fall upon our knees, we bow our head in the dust and we say 'Heil Hitler'. There is a great wave of pro-German feeling . . . we should enter into a precise agreement with France that pending a final solution we will without question come to her assistance with all our forces; but we should say that only applied to the west. It has nothing to do with the east.

Austen Chamberlain said, 'You can find plenty of reassuring words from Hitler. What we want is reassuring acts.' He took a strong line, Boothby echoed Nicolson, saying:

> Instead of making a real practical gesture to Stresemann by offering one-quarter of what we have now allowed Herr Hitler to take, we kept on the armed occupation which ought to have been removed immediately if Locarno meant anything, and we kept on those ridiculous reparations which finally had to be paid for by means of loans made to Germany by the City of London . . . it was not until the economic crisis which really swept the Nazis into power that we began, when it was too late, to take steps which earlier might have stabilized a great political system and created a great country out of the Weimar Republic . . . I feel that if we talk to the Germans under the present duress without their having made a single gesture at all force will have won . . . and the whole system of collective security and international law endangered . . . we must stand in with the League . . . and the principle of collective security.

Winston told the House that German rearmament was 'an even greater threat' and was rebuked by Attlee for implying that we should remove sanctions from Italy and put them on Germany, while Dalton from the Opposition front bench said a mixed British and Italian force stationed on German territory 'is fantastic and absurd', and Eden told Sinclair, the Liberal leader, that 'Staff talks committed us to nothing.'

Eden's official line for the Government was 'Our policy is the Covenant.' However, he made a nonsense of the Covenant by declaring, 'The French said the Germans must withdraw, and if they refused they must be made to withdraw by progressive pressure beginning with financial and economic sanctions. We did not take that view . . . we thought it our imperative duty to seek by negotiation to restore confidence,' while Cranborne confirmed that the Government still wanted the oil sanction against Italy.

Although the Government line was that it 'stood by the Covenant of the League of Nations', it argued that that need not apply to this particular German breach. Hitler must have been delighted with the Commons debate on 26 March and need not have been worried by the Lords debate on 8 April when Robert Cecil declared that in France the Rhineland was more important than Abyssinia, 'but we are right in thinking that the Abyssinian issue was the more important issue of the two'. Cecil was right about British opinion; the warped view in Britain was that the Rhineland was minor compared with Abyssinia. In the Lords' debate Lothian argued that 'France, Yugoslavia, etc.' had enough troops to rearraign Germany and because of our commitments in the Far East 'we should not be lured into further commitments' because of the immense reserves available for maintaining the status quo. Thus influential British statesmen gave comfort to Hitler and none to the French; their lack of realism is inexcusable.[36]

At a distance of over fifty years it is difficult to understand why so many Conservative politicians should have given such support to Hitler and the Nazis, but the Liberal and Labour opposition also supported Eden in his policy of pandering to the Nazis and turning his back on the French.

In another Commons debate on 9 April Boothby said that although he had been very opposed to the Hoare–Laval Pact,

> Britain was not prepared to fight Italy on behalf of Abyssinia . . . the chance of unanimity and effective action at Geneva had gone; it could only be kind to the Abyssinians if we faced that fact instead of leading them up the garden path; (one can hardly call it through this hell) in the absolutely vain hope that somehow in some way at some time effective assistance will be given them by Geneva . . . I cannot understand what was the point of Eden's speech at Geneva yesterday (a report of Eden refusing to consider sanctions against Germany) which can have no other effect than of prolonging this ghastly war and still worse the effect of severing us from France at a moment of very grave crisis in Europe.[37]

Alas, his sensible arguments fell upon stony ground.

The majority of the nation supported Eden and Baldwin in their pro-Hitler and anti-French attitude. It looks as if Hitler through some uncanny instinct had gauged likely British reactions correctly, and by harping on the Franco–Soviet Pact he triggered off fears of Bolshevism among the right wing which made them anti-French. On the other hand, many on the Left resented France's lukewarmness over sanctions against Italy. The furore over the Hoare–Laval Pact had diminished France's popularity in Britain, and the Franco–Soviet Pact was made out to be both an unfair plan to encircle Germany and a threat to unleash Communism on western Europe. The prevalent feeling was that as Germany had only 'marched into her own backyard' there was little to worry about. On 10 March *The Times* headline was 'British view of the Crisis: Condemn the Past; Rebuild for the Future'. *Headway*, the League of Nations magazine, said it was a turning-point in history, and the *Spectator*: 'discussion must start on Hitler's positive proposals . . . in a spirit of sympathy and goodwill.' The Liberal *News*

Chronicle and the Labour *Daily Herald* joined the *Daily Mail* in approval of Hitler's coup.

The Observer published an article by Garvin approving of Hitler's action, and his view was repeated in Rothermere's *Sunday Despatch*; mainstream public opinion in Britain was that French reaction must be toned down. *The Times* found it hard to find enough anti-German letters to balance their correspondence column. A letter to *The Times* on 27 March from five young men with well-known names said: 'the Powers should immediately open negotiations upon the terms which Herr Hitler offers' and although existing undertakings should be honoured 'our Government should rigorously refrain from involving this country in fresh commitments to France for which there would be no popular support'. The five had been friends in the Oxford Union, and were Patrick Heathcoat Amory, uncle of Derek, post-war Chancellor of the Exchequer; Jan Smuts, son of the Field Marshal; John Boyd-Carpenter, later a Conservative Cabinet Minister; Arthur Greenwood, son of Arthur Greenwood; and A.J. Irvine, who had been President of the Oxford Union and later became a Labour Minister. Baldwin, egged on by Tom Jones, considered visiting Hitler or even inviting him to Chequers. Ribbentrop was enthusiastic for this. This project was under consideration before Eden vetoed it.

Ribbentrop showered hospitality on all influential British people who accepted invitations to the Olympic Games in Berlin in August. As part of his propaganda for this event the persecution of the Jews in Germany was temporarily slowed down. Lord Monsell, recently retired from the Cabinet, went to the Games; so did the press barons Rothermere, Camrose and Beaverbrook, together with the Conservative Lords Redesdale, Mount Temple and Rennell. Other important guests were Lady Ravensdale, Admiral Sir Barry Domville, the influential former MP Sir Harry Brittain, and sitting Conservative MPs 'Chips' Channon, Lord Apsley, Sir Thomas Moore, Sir Frank Sanderson, Sir Arnold Wilson and Admiral Sir Murray Sueter. Beverley Nichols attended, and wrote glowingly in the *Sunday Chronicle* of 'the new Germany'.[38]

By May 1936 the dramatic end of the Abyssinian war displaced the Rhineland as the main news in the national press. There were headlines about Mussolini's surprise victory and evidence of Fascist brutality, including the use of mustard gas. In the eyes of many France had let the side down, and anti-French feeling swelled with the victory of the Blum Government on 3 May, when an alliance of Radicals, Socialists and Communists came to power in the Popular Front. Although the Communists declined office in Blum's Government, the idea of a French Government kept in power by Communists was disliked in Britain. The bogey of Communist infiltration into western Europe was strong.

In this climate controversy over the Rhineland petered out. The official historian has written 'But the process of talking out the crisis, or as Bismarck would have said, drowning it in ink continued.'[39]

With Sarraut as Prime Minister and the militant Flandin as Foreign Secretary a military counter-move by the French was always on the cards, but with the Blum Government there was no chance of this. British historians have made much of French public opinion being opposed to military action, and how this hamstrung Flandin. It should be remembered that the Sarraut Government would have had no trouble with French public opinion if Britain had openly backed them in the use of force. Equally, the argument that British opinion would not have supported the Baldwin Government if they had encouraged the French to use force is false. Eden and Baldwin were a hundred per cent opposed to a French military move, and manipulated British public opinion to support this negative policy. If they had desired they would have had no difficulty in whipping up British opinion in the opposite direction in favour of a combined British and French military operation in the Rhineland. They were determined to appease Hitler, and did not care about the resulting division of Britain and France.

As the crisis evaporated Hitler failed to follow up his peace plans; the Plymouth Committee rejected any colonial transfer to Germany, so that Eden's and Vansittart's hopes that a durable European settlement with Hitler could be reached on the basis of giving Germany colonies became a non-starter. An Anglo–French–Belgian meeting was held in London on 23 July after Blum had retreated from Flandin's demands for German concessions over the Rhineland, and issued an invitation to Germany and Italy to negotiate a new agreement to take the place of the Rhine Pact of Locarno, together with 'a general settlement essential for the peace of Europe'. Hitler did not accept the invitation, and this 23 July London meeting marked the end of the Rhineland crisis with Hitler the undisputed victor.

On 20 May 1936 the Italian victory in Abyssinia was complete, and Baldwin told Eden he wanted better relations with Hitler than Mussolini. Baldwin has left behind in the archives an authentic account of his views. On 28 July a high-powered deputation of out-of-office Conservative top brass talked with Baldwin, Halifax and Inskip. The delegation consisted of:

House of Commons
The Rt. Hon. Sir Austen Chamberlain, former Foreign Secretary
The Rt. Hon. W.S. Churchill, former Chancellor of the Exchequer
The Rt. Hon. Sir Robert Horne, former Chancellor of the Exchequer
The Rt. Hon. L.S. Amery, former Sec. of State for Colonies

The Rt. Hon. Sir John Gilmour, former Home Secretary
Capt. the Rt. Hon. F.E. Guest, former Sec. of State for Air
The Rt. Hon. Earl Winterton, former Under Secretary for India
Brig. Gen. Sir Henry Page Croft, M.P. since 1910
Sir Edward Grigg, former Governor Kenya Colony
The Rt. Hon. Viscount Wolmer M.P. since 1918. Former Asst. Postmaster
    General
Lt.-Col. J.T.C. Moore Brabazon, former Parliamentary Secretary for
    Transport
Admiral Sir Roger Keyes, former Commander Mediterranean Fleet
The Rt. Hon. Sir Hugh O'Neill, former Speaker Ulster Parliament

House of Lords
The Rt. Hon. the Marquess of Salisbury
Lord Trenchard
Lord Milne
The Rt. Hon. Lord Lloyd
The Rt. Hon. Viscount Fitzalan

First Baldwin stated that (unlike Eden, who was still in favour of sanctions against Italy) he had no faith at all in League of Nations sanctions, saying that by trying them out (against Italy) we showed 'the people' that they were 'butting their heads against a brick wall'.

He went on that Hitler did not want to move west but east, and 'If he should move East I would not break my heart.'

The Labour and Liberal Opposition had refused to join the deputation and Baldwin – obviously feeling he was among friends, and so could be frank – went on with an indiscretion which the author feels almost embarrassed to repeat:

> I am not going to get this country into a war with anybody for the League of Nations
> . . . There is one danger, of course, which has probably been in all your minds –
> supposing the Russians and Germans got fighting and the French went in as the
> allies of Russia owing to that appalling pact they made, you would not feel you were
> obliged to go and help France, would you? If there is to be any fighting in Europe to
> be done I should like to see the Bolsheviks and Nazis doing it.

Baldwin also told the deputation that we had no engagement with the French to send an expeditionary force to the Continent, and he wanted at all costs to avoid any such engagement as we had with France in 1914. This encapsulated British policy in 1936. Baldwin's views were quickly repeated in that Tory gossip shop White's Club, and other West End clubs frequented by foreign diplomats, so that Stalin and Hitler knew that he had abandoned hopes of peace-keeping through the League and wanted Germany and Russia to fight each other.[41]

CHAPTER NINE

EDEN QUITS AS
FOREIGN SECRETARY
1938

A myth has been perpetrated that Eden resigned in protest
against Chamberlain's appeasement of Hitler. This is false.
Eden held it was more important to curb Mussolini's support
for Franco in Spain than to persuade the Duce to prevent the
Anschluss. For this reason Chamberlain sacked Eden.

MUSSOLINI'S BEHAVIOUR over the abortive Nazi coup in Austria in
1934 makes it clear that he looked on Austria's independence as the
linchpin of Italian policy in Eastern Europe; while anti-Nazis in Austria
looked on Mussolini as their saviour. However, with the traditional enmity
between Austria and Italy throughout the nineteenth century and during the
First World War, it was difficult to establish a stable Austrian regime based
on Italian influence. Fortunately, the fascist Starhemberg, and the new
Austrian Chancellor Schuschnigg, agreed to share power. Starhemberg
continued as Vice Chancellor, but the position was complicated because
both he and Schuschnigg were leaders of rival private armies. Schuschnigg
headed the Sturmscharen, and Starhemberg the Heimwehr, which he
wanted to enlarge into a single Mussolini-style fascist militia under his own
complete control. Schuschnigg would not allow this; and also went to
considerable lengths to make sure that the regular Austrian army was kept
out of reach of Starhemberg and under his own direct control as
Chancellor.

When Mussolini embarked on the invasion of Abyssinia in October 1935
he had no intention of allowing Hitler to increase his influence in Austria.
However, the tough British line against Italy and the threat of an oil

The Drift to War

sanction (which became increasingly acute as Eden, more hostile to Italy, succeeded Hoare as Foreign Secretary in December 1935) so embittered Mussolini against France and Britain that he began reluctantly to consider reorientating his foreign policy towards Germany. Hassell reported to Hitler on 7 January 1936 that the Duce had told him that Berlin and Vienna should settle their relations 'on the basis of Austrian independence'. Then came ominous words: 'If Austria as a formally quite independent state were thus in practice to become a German satellite he [Mussolini] would have no objection.' Mussolini told Hassell to report this direct to the Führer emphasizing that he wanted to improve German–Italian relations and to dispose of their only dispute, 'the Austrian problem,' while he regarded Stresa as 'dead and buried'.

A German Foreign Office internal memorandum suggested that Mussolini wanted to divert the attention of the Great Powers towards Central Europe in order 'to influence favourably' their attitude to Italy over the Abyssinian war, and that Mussolini's proposal should be rejected politely. However, Hitler took a more optimistic view after talking to Hassell, and sent word to Mussolini that his overtures were accepted subject to 'the certainty' that Italy did not wish to return to the Stresa Front, and would promise to give instructions to Vienna that an understanding with Berlin must be facilitated, and that the Duce no longer saw any reason to stand by Austria.[1]

As the Austrian problem was overtaken by the Rhineland crisis, Mussolini faced the dilemma whether he should repudiate Locarno as well as Stresa and commit himself irrevocably to Hitler. Ciano at this stage wanted close ties with Germany, as did Alfieri and Attolico (Italian Ambassador in Berlin) but Suvich resisted a pro-German policy stubbornly, while Mussolini became apprehensive about Hitler's aggressive intentions. Starhemberg visited him in Rome shortly after the Rhineland coup and found the Duce angry about Hitler's (bogus) offer to return to the League. According to Starhemberg (and there is no reason to disbelieve him, although there is no other record of the talk), the Duce talked of reviving the Stresa Front and stated that he would defend Austria come what may against Germany.

Schuschnigg followed Starhemberg to Rome and found Mussolini ambivalent. Contrary to some accounts, Mussolini did not urge Schuschnigg to begin direct talks with Berlin. Mussolini was trying to be all things to all people and wanted to play Germany off against the Western Powers in order to find a favourable solution to his Abyssinian adventure. However, he cajoled Schuschnigg into an anti-League attitude; Schuschnigg for his part thought Mussolini would return to the Stresa Front. In this Front, not the League, lay the best hope, both for Austria's security against Hitler and for

194

a revision of Versailles to restore to Austria former territory now incorporated in Hungary and Czechoslovakia. Here Schuschnigg made a fatal mistake, for he antagonized Britain, and he made an equally grave one in reintroducing conscription to the Austrian army. This emasculated the Heimwehr, since it produced a large influx of Nazi sympathizers into the army. It also deprived Starhemberg of much of his political power, and Mussolini to his annoyance found he was losing his influence in Austria, so that on 16 April he suspended financial aid to the Austrian army.[2]

Schuschnigg, like Baldwin and Eden, thought erroneously he could make a settlement with Germany which Hitler would honour, so that the two separate German cultures could co-exist. Instead Hitler's sole aim was to conquer Austria. Starhemberg was more realistic about this than Schuschnigg and refused to disband his Heimwehr, which provoked a clash on 10 May 1936 when the Sturnscharen and Heimwehr came to blows during a parade in Vienna. Schuschnigg then marched with the Sturmscharen leaders, and Starhemberg, with his political power much reduced, refused further co-operation with him. Starhemberg's final gesture was a message praising Italy and Fascism for conquering 'barbaric' Abyssinia. It was an affront to Schuschnigg and also to France and Britain, whose continued support against Hitler was vital for Austria. Accordingly Schuschnigg sacked Starhemberg. On 15 May 1936 Starhemberg went to Rome, where Mussolini told him he was on Schuschnigg's side in the dispute. This was the end of Starhemberg's political career.

Starhemberg asked Mussolini point-blank whether or not he intended to make an agreement with Berlin at the expense of Austria. Mussolini replied that 'the survival of Austria was essential and Germany must not have a common frontier with Italy for that would prove to be Italy's worst hour.'[3] Starhemberg was convinced that Mussolini held this view right up to the rape of Austria by Hitler: certainly he was always ambivalent towards the Führer. Austria had consistently taken Italy's side in the negotiations over sanctions at the League of Nations, and Mussolini preferred to see Austria drawn closer to Germany than for her to be aligned with Britain and France through the League of Nations which he now so hated.

Schuschnigg was free to start talks with Hitler without opposition from Starhemberg in Cabinet. Before doing so he went to see Mussolini at his Adriatic home on 5 and 6 June. Mussolini was cynical, telling Schuschnigg to be cautious about bringing Nazis into the Cabinet, saying 'They tend to create not a *modus vivendi* but a *modus moriendi.*' The Duce told Schuschnigg that Italo-German relations were better because of sanctions, and that Austria must not count on either France or Britain to save her from Hitler, and only Italy would stand by Austria if negotiations with Hitler failed. According to Schuschnigg, the Duce told him: 'In view of Italian commitments elsewhere Austria must now stand on her own feet . . . it will be easier to help Austria if both Italy and Austria are on good terms with Germany.' According to Ciano, Mussolini advised Schuschnigg to reach an agreement with Germany because Austria was a German country and too weak to pursue an anti-German policy.[4]

Accordingly Schuschnigg started negotiations with Papen, the German Ambassador in Vienna, and on 11 July 1936 Germany and Austria signed an agreement to re-establish 'normal and friendly relations'. Hitler promised to recognize the sovereignty of Austria, but Schuschnigg had made the significant concession that Austrian policy would be 'based always on the principle that Austria acknowledges herself to be a German state'. Each Government promised not to interfere in the other's domestic policies.

After the murder of Dollfuss, both Austrian Nazis and Socialists had been forced underground by typical fascist methods and relations with Germany remained bad despite the July agreement. Schuschnigg was treading a difficult road, relying on the protection of Mussolini but seeking the favour of the Duce's enemies France and Britain to preserve Austrian independence. However, the Austrian Chancellor had suffered a rude shock when he found the League was impotent not only over the Abyssinian war, but also over Hitler's illegal conscription and his remilitarization of the Rhineland. Thus Austria turned more and more to Mussolini, continually taking Italy's side in the sanctions discussions at the League of Nations.

Despite the provisions of the agreement, Hitler had no intention of banning Nazi activities in Austria; propaganda for the Anschluss continued almost unabated, while the 1,000-mark fine on tourist visas was not lifted. Austria, however, obtained economic advantages through concessions on the export of forestry and agricultural products to Germany, and these economic considerations may have been Schuschnigg's main reason for concluding the agreement; he may also have thought it would make it easier to control the subversive activities of the troublesome Nazi minority. He, Schuschnigg had high ideals about Austria, deeming it the second German cultural state, and he hoped friendship with Germany would help him to establish a strong Austrian national identity. The British Foreign Office treated the 11 July Agreement as unimportant. This was correct.

Schuschnigg had assured Sir Walford Selby, the British Ambassador, shortly before the Agreement was signed, that he would maintain three points: 1) No Anschluss. 2) No compromise with the Nazis. 3) No interference in Austrian internal affairs; and after the *modus vivendi* was agreed Schuschnigg repeated that he had in no way modified his conditions. The Chancellor also told Selby that he did not expect too much because the Germans had disregarded every undertaking given to the Austrian Government during the preceding three years. Selby noted that relations between the Austrian and German Governments did not improve after the July Agreement.

On 1 April 1936 Austen Chamberlain issued a dire warning:

> The independence of Austria is a key position. If Austria perishes, Czechoslovakia becomes indefensible. Then the whole of the Balkans will be submitted to a gigantic new influence. Then the old German dream of a Central Europe ruled by and subject to Berlin will become a reality from the Baltic to the Mediterranean and the Black Sea with incalculable consequence not only for our country, but for the whole Empire . . . if we mean anything by all the declarations that our policy is founded on, the League may have to intervene at any moment.

Unfortunately, this was not Eden's view. As will be seen, he was not opposed to the Anschluss, although Neville, Austen's brother, realized the implications for Czechoslovakia and Eastern Europe and was horrified when the Anschluss took place. By then Austen was dead.[5]

In July 1936 the Spanish Civil War captured the headlines and became a major preoccupation of the Cabinet and the Foreign Office. The French were on the side of the Spanish Government; the Germans and Italians sided with the insurgents. The left-wing Blum Government did not dare to send help to the Spanish Communist Government for fear of provoking a civil war in France, but Hitler and Mussolini had no such inhibitions, while Soviet Russia openly aided the Spanish Government with shipments of weapons, crated aeroplanes and lorries. (At France's instigation an Anglo--French non-intervention Pact was signed).

After six years of dictatorship under Primo de Rivera unrest became so great that King Alfonso advised Rivera to resign. Elections were held in 1931 and the King left Spain, after which a new constitution was proclaimed, but the Communists caused grave trouble. In February 1936 the General Election was won by the Left. Strikes, riots and disorder followed. In July there was a revolt in Spanish Morocco led by General Franco. Franco's forces crossed to the mainland. Madrid, Barcelona and Valencia stayed loyal to the Republic, but by mid-August the rebels had united their southern and northern armies and in November the siege of Madrid began. The war was ruthless on both sides, with murders of clergy and Communists. Franco's supporters maintained more unity than the Republicans, and although a negotiated peace was possible he insisted on unconditional surrender, so that the war did not end until April 1939, after almost three years of bitter fighting.

Hostilities started on 19 July; on 22 July Franco sent a letter to Hitler asking for transport planes and other assistance. Hitler, without consulting his Foreign Office, sent thirty-nine Junkers which solved the problem of transporting Franco's troops (mainly Moroccans) from Morocco to Spain. Italy sent considerable help with 'volunteers' to Franco.

Baldwin was worried by Eden's attitude to the outbreak of the Spanish Civil War, saying to his confidant Tom Jones on 27 July 'I told Eden yesterday that on no account, French or other, must he bring us to fight on the side of the Russians.'[6]

It was claimed that the Spanish Civil War was a conflict between Fascism and Communism. This is untenable; it was a conflict between the Socialists and Communist factions and the conservatives who were backed by the majority (but not all) of the Church and the Army. The British Cabinet, apart from Eden, wanted the insurgents to win, and were appalled by Russian Communist infiltration into Spain, but decided on a policy of strict neutrality.

Britain took the lead in setting up the Non Intervention Committee which met first in London on 9 September 1936. It held fourteen meetings up to the end of the year and considered complaints against Germany, Italy and Portugal from the Spanish Government; complaints by Russia against Portugal; and accusations against Russia by Germany. It was ineffective, although Eden attached great importance to its deliberations.

The Spanish Civil War produced a further deterioration in relations between Britain and Italy. Eden told the Cabinet that Mussolini was intervening because he wanted to dominate the Mediterranean, and looked on the Civil War not just as a struggle between Communism and Fascism, but as a means of weakening British sea-power in the western Mediterranean. However, Ciano gave a specific assurance that Italy would not make a deal with the Spanish insurgents for the cession of Ceuta, Spanish Morocco or the Balearic Islands, which were being used as bases by the Italian navy, air force and troops. On 12 September 1936 the British Government sent a firm note to Italy: 'Any alteration in the status quo in the western Mediterranean must be a matter of the closest concern to His Majesty's Government.'

Meanwhile Hitler looked on the Civil War as a distraction which would help him to obtain a free hand in the east where, after he had taken Austria, he intended to occupy Czechoslovakia and impose his will on Hungary and Romania regardless of Russia. A revealing Foreign Office minute dated 19 August 1936 said: 'We should decline to disinterest ourselves from the East and Centre of Europe and continue to insist on the need for a general settlement, while urging France not to wreck a Western settlement by maintaining impossible demands in the East and Centre.' France had treaty obligations to Czechoslovakia and the Little Entente which Eden firmly refused to underwrite, but he accepted the Foreign Office view that concessions to Germany should be limited to colonies and guarantees in the west while leaving German expansion to the east an open question. However, as the official historians have written, the Foreign Office did not believe invasion and dismemberment of western Russia as envisaged in *Mein Kampf* was likely, although they were under no illusions as to Hitler's ambitions to push east his country's boundaries. Vansittart and the Foreign Office thought that a settlement which Hitler would adhere to was 'improbable' but 'not quite impossible'. Eden was more optimistic.

Equally difficult were problems with France and Italy. Sargent wrote in a memorandum on 12 August: 'All these considerations seem to indicate the importance of (1) our preventing France by hook or crook from 'going Bolshevik' under the influence of the Spanish civil war; and (2) our freeing Italy from the feeling of isolation and vulnerability which the Abyssinian affair has left her with.' This was correct but neither Cadogan nor Mounsey were able by their minutes to show Eden how it could be done, and Sargent's final comment was that he was 'not greatly comforted' by their observations.[7]

In October 1936 there was evidence that Mussolini was wobbling between friendship with Hitler and the Stresa Front, and did not want the Spanish Civil War to be a barrier. Drummond wrote on 21 October:

> In my view few things would give Italian Government at the present moment greater pleasure than to return to really friendly relations with His Majesty's Government . . . If however we show no visible signs of an advance on our present attitude Italy may soon think that a choice is being forced on her between France and Germany, in which case she will certainly prefer to choose the latter. Any concrete sign from us that we are ready to go back to a pre-Abyssinian world would at present be most welcome to Italy; if no such sign is forthcoming she may well think we are not interested, and in these circumstances there is I believe real danger of her running out of the course and coming to some definite political arrangement with Germany . . . What is necessary in order to dispel the present Italian suspicions is some definite and early indication that we are ready to discuss the Mediterranean with them within a reasonable time.

The same line was taken by Grandi when he saw Eden on 13 October, and said Mussolini was anxious to let bygones be bygones and desired nothing more than to return to a period of full co-operation such as existed before 1935. Grandi asked if Eden could not make some small gesture of goodwill 'which would have a psychological effect on Italian opinion'. What Grandi was asking for was recognition of the conquest of Abyssinia. Unfortunately, this turned out to be Eden's sticking-point, with fatal consequences for British-Italian relations.[8]

In the Commons on 5 November Eden had said 'The differences that have existed between us and Italy have been due to our differing – I regret to note still differing – conceptions of the methods by which the world should order its international affairs . . . For us the Mediterranean is not a short cut but a main arterial road.'

The next day Vansittart saw Grandi, who looked on Eden's speech as unfriendly. The Italian Ambassador, according to Vansittart, had never been so cast-down or spiritless; Grandi complained he had no instructions from Mussolini to do anything, so that he was forced to stand by and see Anglo-Italian relations deteriorate 'to the profit of Germany in a manner that filled him with gloom and nearly with despair'. Vansittart thought the rapprochement between Rome and Berlin had been 'practically, if not quite, completed'.

Grandi made it clear to Vansittart that Mussolini insisted on the recognition of the Italian conquest of Abyssinia before he would halt negotiations with Hitler in favour of France and Britain and return to the abandoned Stresa Front. Eden's uncooperative minute on the account of this talk was 'I am told that Grandi shows no signs of "drooping spirits" at the non intervention cttee. I sometimes wonder whether he is not merely a very good Ambassador, first class at raising his country's value?' This remark displeased Vansittart.[9]

On 12 November 1936 Baldwin referred to the 1933 Fulham by-election in the Commons: 'when a seat which the National Government held was lost by 7000 votes on no issue but the pacifist . . . Supposing I had gone to the country and said that Germany was rearming and that we must rearm, does anybody think that this pacific democracy would have rallied to that cry at that moment? I cannot think of anything that would have made the loss of the election from my point of view more certain.' He then pointed out that by biding his time he later won a General Election with a large majority and a mandate for rearmament, 'a mandate for doing a thing that no-one twelve months before would have believed possible'. Churchill in his memoirs called this statement 'carrying naked truth about his motives into indecency'.

This speech by Baldwin has been widely quoted and has done infinite damage to his reputation, but its historical importance is to show how far past his best he was in the autumn of 1936, and not surprisingly leaving the whole conduct of Britain's foreign policy to Eden.

On 18 November, much to Eden's displeasure, Germany and Italy officially recognized the Spanish Government of General Franco and removed their diplomatic representatives from the Republic.

Eden's chief concern was for what he termed 'a general settlement with Germany'. Although Hitler would not reply to the British questionnaire, the

Cabinet and the Foreign Office refused to admit that this was the end of the dialogue, and in July had invited Italy and Germany to a Five Power conference (without Russia) to negotiate a new agreement to replace the Rhine Pact of Locarno which might facilitate a general settlement. The German and Italian Governments accepted the invitation to a Five Power conference in principle, but then stalled indefinitely by saying there must be previous diplomatic negotiation. Finally in March 1937 both Germany and Italy turned the proposal down. Hitler was prepared to discuss a *modus vivendi* only as a screen to cover the speed of German rearmament. The British Cabinet was divided as to whether it should use the temporary lull in 1937 as a device for 'buying time' for British rearmament to make her comparatively safe by 1939, or whether there were reasonable hopes of an Agreement with Germany which would be a genuine satisfaction of Hitler's ambitions. Eden tried to convince them that a far-reaching settlement with Germany was possible; and that this was the way to preserve peace. Foreign Office appeasers were strengthened when Ralph Wigram, Chief Adviser on German Affairs, a firm opponent of Hitler, and an intimate of Churchill's, died on 31 December 1936.

1937 was a year without a major international flare-up. However, the European situation was tense, with Italy and Germany intervening in Spain on the Franco side, and Russia and France on the Republican. Chamberlain replaced Baldwin as Prime Minister on 28 May, but it made no difference to Britain's foreign policy. Like Baldwin and Eden, Chamberlain wanted to appease Hitler. The policy remained to seek peace in Europe by satisfying the German dictator, and the vain hope was cherished that this could be done while Germany was confined within her Versailles frontiers, whereas Hitler was determined to seize Austria, Czechoslovakia, and great chunks of Poland and Eastern Europe. Baldwin, Eden and Chamberlain had a blind spot here. Vansittart continually warned them they were unrealistic, but he spoilt his own case by using extravagant language.

Eden thought Vansittart and Phipps were blocking friendship with Germany, and both were replaced. In April 1937 Neville Henderson was sent to Berlin in place of Phipps (who went as Ambassador to Paris) with instructions to placate Hitler; and on 1 January 1938 Vansittart, having misguidedly refused the Paris Embassy, was 'kicked upstairs' to be the Government Adviser – a post which effectively removed his influence, while the compliant Alec Cadogan became Head of the Foreign Office.

In one of his last reports from Berlin, Phipps wrote that Hitler looked on Britain 'as the one country who blocked his territorial ambitions, and that he might take "the final gamble of war".' This truth was lost on Eden.[10]

In reponse to Downing Street requests *The Times* continually took a pro-Hitler line. Plaintively the Editor, Dawson, wrote to Lothian on 23 May:

I simply cannot understand why they [Germans] should apparently be so much annoyed with the Times; at the moment I spend my nights in taking out anything which I think will hurt their [German] susceptibilities and in dropping in little things which are intended to soothe them.[11]

On 26 September 1937 Chamberlain even wrote to Roosevelt 'At the present moment as far as Europe is concerned I think I may say that it is far less menacing than it has appeared for some months past.' The lull was illusory. German rearmament was proceeding so much faster than British or French that the balance of power in Europe was swinging fast in favour of Italy and Germany. British defence preparations, to the dismay of the French, had culminated in abandoning plans for an expeditionary force of five divisions in favour of reliance of bombers and sea power for a war of defence and siege. Defence costs – largely because of Simon's firm stand as Chancellor of the Exchequer – were actually cut in the 1937 Budget, and the Cabinet accepted the delusions of the Chiefs of Staff that our rearmament would reach a level of 'comparative safety' by 1939.

On 18 March 1937 Baldwin took the chair at the Cabinet Committee on Foreign Policy. He said nothing. Eden proposed that 'discussions for a general settlement with Germany' should be carried on with Hitler or Neurath, and indicated that he wanted a Western Europe Treaty to replace Locarno, guarantees to the East European powers, a return of Germany to the League of Nations, and international agreement on the limitation of arms. Eden stated that if Germany agreed to most of this then we ought to consider returning colonies to her. The Cabinet concurred.[12]

Eden was ignoring a recent report from Phipps which stated that until Mussolini's victory in Abyssinia Hitler had wanted an understanding with Britain. Then British prestige fell so rapidly that Hitler thought agreement unnecessary, and had decided to push on with his plans to conquer Austria and the Sudentenland 'while the question of the colonies was a sideline'.

The term 'General Settlement with Germany' was in continual use in the Foreign Office and in Cabinet discussions. Eden liked it and believed assurances of British sympathy and economic advantage would tame Hitler, whereas Hitler's territorial ambitions could only be satisfied by the rape of Czechoslovakia and Austria. Sir Ivo Mallet, then in charge of the German desk at the Foreign Office, told the author he and his colleagues constantly pointed out that the phrase was 'meaningless' and requested clarification, but Eden would never give his definition.

Eden's hopes of a deal with Hitler had been raised by a German aproach in February 1937 through Hitler's Economic Minister, Dr Schacht, who stressed to Sir Frederick Leith-Ross, Chief Economic Adviser to the British Government, that Germany needed colonies because of her shortage of raw materials, foodstuffs, fats and oils. Schacht, an able economist like Leith-Ross, understood perfectly well that this was a Balance of Payments problem incapable of solution by the gift of colonies. However, Eden and Chamberlain naively believed the effect on Germany's prestige if she acquired a colony would satisfy Hitler.

This view was not shared by Vansittart, who called it 'Schacht's little bluff' – which angered Chamberlain. The Government seriously considered the return of the Cameroons and Togoland to Germany, although they were mainly under French rule. The Imperial Conference in London in May and June considered colonies for Germany, but came to no conclusion.

Although he made no headway with Hitler, Eden remained anti-Italian. A typical minute from him was on 5 November 1936:

> Does anybody in the Foreign Office really believe that Italy's foreign policy will at any time be other than opportunist? Any agreement with Italy will be kept as long as it suits Italy. Surely nobody can now place any faith in her promises?[13]

Eden was correct that little faith could be placed in Mussolini's promises, but beggars could not be choosers, and the experience of 1934 had shown that only Mussolini could save Austria from Hitler, and that once German armies were in Austria Hitler's road to Eastern Europe would be open. It was folly not to try to placate Mussolini to ensure he would keep Germany out of Austria. Eden persisted throughout 1937 with this anti-Mussolini attitude, remarking half jokingly to Oliver Harvey, his private secretary, on 23 December that he must prevent his personal prejudice against Mussolini colouring his attitude too much, and that he looked on 'Musso' as 'anti-Christ'. Harvey abetted his chief by saying 'I do too.'[14]

However, while Baldwin was still Prime Minister, Eden had improved Anglo-Italian arrangements by signing the 'Anglo-Italian Gentleman's Agreement' in January 1937. In this both sides recognized the importance of free transit through the Mediterranean for both countries and disclaimed any desire to change in any way the national sovereignty of territories in the Mediterranean area. Both powers agreed to co-operate to limit intervention in the Spanish war. To Eden's intense irritation, Mussolini consistently ignored this clause.

The success of these negotiations produced a string of optimistic minutes in the Foreign Office. Vansittart's was:

> This is all most successful and gratifying. The Italians – in particular Mussolini – have behaved very well and accommodatingly . . . If we never *talk* of detaching them from Germany, but merely exploit this success . . . we shall automatically loosen the Italo-German tie, so have a more reasonable, or anyhow tamer, Germany to deal with.

This did not appeal to Eden, who wrote:

> Let us bear in mind during our new relations with Italy that the latter has at least as much to gain from this better state of affairs as we. We shall lose nothing in Italian eyes by continuing to *nous faire valoir*.[15]

However, immediately after signature 3000 Italian troops landed at Cadiz, violating the spirit of the agreement, and Mussolini publicly praised the role of Italian troops in capturing Malaga while the Italian press became violently anti-British and Radio Bari stepped up anti-British propaganda – all on Mussolini's instructions.

When the British Government invited Haile Selassie to King George's Coronation, Mussolini refused to allow Umberto, the King of Italy's heir, to attend. On Mussolini's orders the Italian press boycotted the Coronation celebrations. Then press comments on the defeat of the Italian attack on Guadalajara in Spain and a sermon by the Dean of Winchester at a service for the victims of Italian rule in Ethiopia – in which the Dean inferred that Mussolini was a madman – worsened relations to the point that the Foreign Office again seriously considered that Italy might go to war with Britain.

On 23 March 1937 Drummond recommended granting Italy 'de jure' recognition of her conquest of Abyssinia. Then, according to Drummond, Mussolini would be generous. Eden refused on the grounds that 'de jure' recognition was too important a diplomatic bargaining point. Vansittart wanted 'de jure' right away.

On 4 May Drummond pointed out that if Italian sovereignty in Abyssinia still went unrecognized at the League of Nations Council and Assembly at the end of May the Duce would conclude definitely a complete alliance with Germany as her only true friend. This should have been the red light. Vansittart endorsed Drummond strongly, and for once Cranborne went against Eden, but Eden would not have it, minuting: 'Mussolini is a gangster'. On 25 May Sargent and Cadogan minuted that 'a decision to recognise 'de jure' would by September have lost much, if not all, of its value'. Vansittart agreed emphatically, but not Eden.[16]

Eden must have known he was playing with fire. On 2 July Drummond had written:

> Is Mussolini working up public opinion for an eventual war with us? I frankly do not know, but if this is his intention he would hardly go about it otherwise than the way he is at present doing. It is unpleasantly reminiscent of the technique used in the early months of 1935 to bring Italian public opinion up to pitch for his Abyssinian adventure . . . Talk about war possibilities was very prevalent in Italian circles 4 or 5 days ago; fathers and mothers were resigned.

Eden immediately wrote to Inskip:

I am sorry this letter was not in my hands for C.I.D. [Committee on Imperial Defence] meeting last week.

I was not altogether happy even then at our excluding from our hypothesis the possibility of a single handed war with Italy. Had I been in possession of Drummond's letter I would have felt this even more strongly.

At this Imperial Defence meeting on 5 July 1937 Eden had urged that 'Italy should be treated as a potential enemy against whom the C.I.D. should make certain preparations.' At the same meeting the Prime Minister argued Germany was our greatest danger and should have priority in our defence preparations – 'Defence preparations against Italy should be considered of secondary importance.'[17]

With the Rhineland crisis there had been a strong and growing demand for a single Minister to be responsible for defence. Churchill was the favourite choice both in and outside Parliament. Instead Chamberlain appointed Sir Thomas Inskip, easy-going and popular and at the time Solicitor General. Chamberlain in his diary noted that Inskip would create no jealousies, although he would excite no enthusiasm. On the other hand, appointing Churchill – with his known views on Europe – would be 'dangerous for the Cabinet'. Macmillan writes that the appointment was 'astonishing', and recalls that the common phrase then was that there had been nothing like it since Caligula made his horse consul. Inskip was a pedestrian and uninspiring Minister for the Co-ordination of Defence. But the Archives show him to have been less of an appeaser than the majority of his colleagues.[18]

On 21 July Grandi told Eden that Mussolini had sent a message for the Prime Minister and allowed him discretion to choose the moment at which to deliver it, and as he was returning to Italy at the end of the month he would like the interview arranged now. Eden agreed, and Chamberlain and Grandi met without Eden at 10 Downing Street on 27 July. Grandi told Chamberlain that Mussolini attached 'immense importance to 'de jure'. The Prime Minister replied that this would give rise to very 'strong hostile criticism in this country, and could only be justified as part of a great scheme of reconciliation.' Grandi aroused Chamberlain's enthusiasm so that in Grandi's presence the Prime Minister decided to make a dramatic gesture, dictating a warm letter to Mussolini saying conversations could begin as soon as the Duce wished:

I have been having a long talk this morning with Count Grandi who brought me the message you were good enough to send me. No doubt he will report to you what I have said to him, but I should like to send you a personal note, and Count Grandi has encouraged me to write.

Although I have spent some of my happiest holidays in Italy it is now some years since I visited your country, and to my great regret I have never had the opportunity

205

of meeting your Excellency. But I have always heard my brother, Sir Austen, talk of you with the highest regard. He used to say "you were a good man to do business with."

Since I became Prime Minister I have been distressed to find that the relations between Italy and Great Britain are still far from that old feeling of mutual confidence and affection which lasted for so many years. In spite of the bitterness which arose from the Abyssinian affair I believe it is possible for those old feelings to be restored, if we can only clear away some of the misunderstandings and unfounded suspicions which cloud our trust in one another.

I therefore welcome very heartedly the message you have sent me and I wish to assure you that this Government is actuated by the most friendly feelings towards Italy and will be ready at any time to enter upon conversations with a view to clarifying the whole situation and removing all causes of suspicion or misunderstanding.

Believe me, Yours sincerely, N.C.[19]

In his memoirs Grandi wrote that he exceeded his instructions by giving Chamberlain the impression that Mussolini was keener than he really was on returning to the Stresa Front. However, there is no doubt that Mussolini was ambivalent and wobbling at this moment because of the imminent danger to the independence of Austria, and he was being pushed away from Hitler and towards Britain by Ciano and his Palazzo Chigi officials.

Chamberlain did not send a copy of this letter to Eden because he had 'the feeling he would object to it'. This was a repeat of his failure to tell Eden in advance of his speech describing sanctions as 'Midsummer Madness' for the same reason. It was a strange situation, with the Prime Minister refusing to communicate with his Foreign Secretary. It is stranger still that Chamberlain put up with Eden for another six months which effectively ruined the chances of keeping Mussolini out of Hitler's embraces.[20]

Chamberlain's reference to his brother must have struck a happy note with Mussolini who like all Italians had a strong feeling of the importance of the family. Anyway, he replied warmly three days later:

I remember with the greatest sympathy Sir Austen – the nobility of his mind and his broad and clear intelligence, and I cherish the recollection of the work we accomplished together in the interests of our two countries and of the political reconstruction of Europe.

I am glad to agree that conversations be entered upon in a spirit of sincere collaboration in order to ensure the understanding we desire between our two countries.[21]

Grandi told Vansittart he was 'elated' after his Downing Street talk, and Vansittart wrote to Chamberlain that Grandi was 'completely sincere' and 'his whole political life had been founded on the policy of intimate relations with this country . . . he is a very close personal friend of mine'.

Eden was alarmed at this prospect of negotiations leading up to 'de jure' recognition, and wrote to Vansittart on 4 August: 'I am presuming that there will be no further correspondence between No. 10 and Rome without my seeing it . . . by all means let us show ourselves ready to talk but in no scrambling hurry to offer incense on a dictator's altar,' and he insisted that negotiations should not take place until his holiday was over.[22]

Eden during these approaches to Mussolini was in fact on holiday; he had rented a large country house, 'Stanswood', near Southampton, for his son's school holidays. Lord Halifax (Lord Privy Seal with responsibility for foreign affairs) had been left in day-to-day charge of the Foreign Office in London. Halifax, unlike Eden, thoroughly approved of Chamberlain's overture to the Duce.

Drummond was ordered by Chamberlain to tell Ciano in Rome, to Eden's displeasure, 'We hope discussions will start towards the end of August or the beginning of September.' The imponderable is to what extent Mussolini was really considering turning his back on Hitler. The evidence either way is scant. However, Eden vetoed the overture, to Chamberlain's intense irritation.

Drummond again urged 'de jure' recognition on 5 August, writing: 'The essential condition for any successful negotiations with Italian Government for a general *détente* is recognition on our side of Italian sovereignty over Abyssinia.' Chamberlain agreed, and wrote to Vansittart:

> We should give 'de jure' recognition while it has some marketable value, but we must not offend the French or shock League friends at home. Italians will be quite satisfied if Abyssinia is declared no longer an independent state. These dictators are men of moods. Catch them in the right mood and they will give you anything you ask for. But if the mood changes they shut up like an oyster. The moral of which is that we must make Musso feel that things are moving all the time.[23]

Chamberlain was right. Mussolini was not only the lesser evil but 'a creature of moods' who by immediate 'de jure' recognition might still have been won back to the Stresa front in 1937, whereupon he would have used his power to prevent Austria falling into Hitler's clutches. Eden, alas, rejected 'de jure' out of hand. This difference of opinion between Eden and Chamberlain as to whether it was Mussolini or Hitler who was public enemy number one was to prove disastrous.

As Eden was at loggerheads with his Prime Minister over 'de jure' recognition, he should have considered resignation. Alternatively, Chamberlain should have sacked him. Halifax realized the two were on a collision course, but did not have the strength of mind to bring the matter to a head. If only the dispute between Chamberlain and Eden had reached crisis point in August 1937 Mussolini would probably have been kept out of Hitler's arms.

It was not to be. In Eden's absence by the sea a long meeting under Halifax was held in his room in the Foreign Office on 10 August. Drummond had come back from Rome, and, fortified by his advice, Halifax and the others agreed that the status of Abyssinia should be put on the agenda of the next meeting of the League Assembly, and that Britain ought to start talks immediately with Ciano in Rome about 'de jure' recognition as part of a general settlement with Italy. In return Italy should be asked to reiterate the Stresa accord to keep Austria safe; to reduce her Libyan garrison; to withdraw volunteers from Spain; to exchange military information; and to stop anti-British propaganda on Bari Radio.

Halifax sent the Foreign Office note of the meeting to Eden the next day, writing with it: 'When we talk we shall liquidate the Abyssinian position. We must in some form grasp the Abyssinian nettle.' Eden replied immediately:

> I disagree with the Office note. It would be difficult to put all my objections on paper. I will put them to you when we meet . . . we should decline to be rushed into conversations. I am very reluctant to recognize 'de jure' conquest. I do not think I could bring myself to any kind of approval of what Italy has done. You will see how strong I am feeling after ten days of sea breezes . . . Come and stay and walk in the pine trees by the sea or play tennis.

On receiving Eden's reply Halifax wrote to Vansittart: 'This letter disquiets me . . . His attitude is dangerously divergent from the Prime Minister's . . . onus is on me to say something to Anthony . . . Time is running out.' Halifax had correctly diagnosed the danger, but there is no evidence that at 'Stanswood' he had the courage to suggest to Eden he should resign, or to tell Chamberlain he must sack his Foreign Secretary.

After his visit to 'Stanswood' Halifax failed to grasp the nettle. On 19 August he wrote a letter to Chamberlain, but it was weak and inconclusive:

> I found him [Eden] as I expected, rather apprehensive about the procedure proposed in the long office discussion [10 August] of which I sent you a note, and the principal heads of his anxiety might I think be summarised thus:
>
> (1) He was very sensitive on the point of our appearing to make recognition of the Italian conquest part of a bargain against advantages that we hoped to receive for ourselves.
>
> (2) He was dubious about the value that we should be likely to get in return, and feared that once having given Mussolini what he principally wanted our relations would in a short time with Spain and other complicating factors still in our flank, be no better than they had proved to be after the Gentleman's Agreement of a few months ago.

Halifax blithely thought that the dispute could be solved by a talk between Chamberlain and Eden, although the Office discussion had made it clear that acceptance of the principle of 'de jure' was essential before negotiations started, and time was running out if conversations were to be opened in Rome before the meeting of the Assembly of the League of Nations.

Chamberlain wrote to Halifax on 15 August that he agreed with the Office view expressed at the meeting with Drummond on 10 August, but he did not press Eden on the urgent need to rebuild Britain's bridges with Mussolini.[24]

On 8 September Eden circulated a memorandum to the Cabinet stating that 'de jure' recognition must await a general settlement with Italy. He stressed the Spanish War iniquities of Mussolini, and ignored the threat to Austria from Hitler. The Cabinet gave him discretion to choose the moment when he would raise 'de jure'. This delay had disastrous effects on Mussolini during the following six months, while the rift between the Prime Minister and Eden widened.

Chamberlain made his attitude clear to the Cabinet, emphasizing that the important thing 'was to strive for a change of heart and attitude on the part of Italy'.[25]

The critical date before which it was essential to start discussions with Mussolini was 13 September. Then the League met without any British initiative over recognizing Italy's conquest of Abyssinia. As a result when in the last week of September Hitler and Mussolini met in Berlin they agreed that Italy would give Germany a free hand in Austria, and in return Mussolini could do what he liked in the Mediterranean, including approving Mussolini's designs on French Tunisia, Djibuti and parts of Egypt. The Stresa Front was shattered.

After his meeting with Mussolini, Hitler started to whip up agitation over the treatment of Germans in Czechoslovakian Sudentenland. Here a large German population had been incorporated in Czechoslovakia by the Treaty of Versailles, and they had not been treated well by the Czech Government. Henderson, in Berlin on Eden's instructions, took the side of the Sudeten Germans.

Halifax saw Goering and Hitler in Germany in November 1937. He made a grave mistake by telling Hitler that there could be possible alterations in the European order and 'amongst these questions' were Danzig, Austria and Czechoslovakia. Halifax did say that alterations should come through peaceful evolution, and that methods should be avoided which might cause far-reaching destruction. However, he failed to tell Hitler that Britain might use force to oppose him if he attacked in the east. A fortnight before Halifax's visit Hitler had told his Foreign Office and War Office that subjugating Austria and Czechoslovakia would be his first step in conquering more territory in the east, and the Führer interpreted Halifax's visit as meaning that the British Government were likely to condone these proposed annexations.[26]

Halifax reported to the Cabinet on 24 November that he found in Germany 'friendliness and a desire for good relations', and had seen no signs that the Germans were planning any immediate adventure. This was what Chamberlain wanted to hear, and he wrote to his sister that Halifax's visit had been 'a great success' and created 'an atmosphere in which it is possible to discuss with Germany the practical questions involved in an European settlement'. Nevertheless, both Vansittart and Eden were extremely worried by the words Halifax had used to Hitler and Goering.[27]

The French Prime Minister, Camille Chautemps, and the Foreign Minister, Delbos, came to London in November 1937. Eden and Chamberlain made it clear to the French statesmen that they were lukewarm about resisting Hitler if he tried to annex the Sudetenland, and they agreed with the French that the map of Africa could be redrawn to give Germany back colonies in the hope of the longed-for 'general settlement'. In these talks Eden was as appeasement-minded as the French and Chamberlain.[28]

Nothing was done to try to satisfy Mussolini over 'de jure' recognition of Italian sovereignty in Abyssinia for the rest of 1937. On 11 December Italy left the League, and this intensified Eden's belief that 'de jure' must be withheld. On the other hand, it made Chamberlain even more positive that we must make a supreme effort for a reconciliation with Mussolini.

Chamberlain became increasingly concerned at Eden's intransigence, and was very conscious of the threat to Austria, bearing in mind the solemn warning given (as has been seen) by his brother Austen in one of his last speeches before he died (suddenly, in April 1937). Evidence accumulated about Hitler's intention to launch another coup in Austria. On 7 January Chamberlain summoned Cadogan to discuss talks with Italy after a Foreign Office memorandum of 29 December stated that if there were talks with Italy 'de jure' must be on the Agenda. Cadogan warned him 'against opening up with Mussolini with a personal letter and then leaving the break to Eden'. According to Cadogan's diary, Chamberlain saw the force of this and agreed to guard against it.[29]

After seeing Cadogan Chamberlain offered to write a second letter to Mussolini. Eden scribbled on the draft against the reference to 'de jure' the words 'This will set half Europe against the conversations.' Then on 3 January he went to the South of France for a holiday, much troubled by Chamberlain's views on Italy. On 9 January from the luxury Hotel Park Palace at Grasse on the French Riviera Eden sent a long, rambling handwritten letter to Chamberlain which showed that he trusted Hitler more than Mussolini:

> There seems to be a certain difference between Italian and German positions in
> that an agreement with the latter might have a chance of a reasonable life, especially

if Hitler's own position were engaged, whereas Mussolini is, I fear, the complete gangster and his pledged word means nothing. Moreover we mean to get something tangible for any colonial accession . . . What worries me much more is the effect that recognition might have on our own moral position. There is no doubt that such a triumph is just what he (Musso) needs to rally his disgruntled fellow countrymen and maybe to reconcile them to a further expedition to Spain. At the moment the Abyssinian wine of victory is beginning to taste sour on the Italian palate. U.S. have accorded no recognition and we do not want to give offence in that direction.

Eden's contention that Mussolini was less trustworthy than Hitler was flouting the facts. By his militarization of the Rhineland Hitler had broken his solemnly given word that he would respect the Locarno Treaty, and was posing a dire threat to the peace of Europe. Mussolini, on the other hand, from 1922 until 1935 had co-operated loyally with Austen Chamberlain over Locarno, and aligned his foreign policy to that of Britain, apart from the Corfu incident, and had saved Austria from Hitler in 1934. Eden had in mind Italy's breach of the Gentleman's Agreement over Italian volunteers in Spain – but then France and Russia were doing the same, and Spain was outside the mainstream of European politics. Anyway, Chamberlain was unimpressed with Eden's letter and replied:

My plan is as you know to proceed both with Italy and Germany concurrently. I see nothing whatever that is inconsistent in this . . . You say you are worried about our moral position if we give Mussolini a triumph. . . . The one way in which we can maintain our moral position is to make recognition part of a general scheme for appeasement in the Mediterranean and Red Sea.[30]

On 12 January Cadogan wrote to Eden there was little use worrying unduly about 'de jure' recognition, since it seemed likely that members of the League would present the Duce with a series of triumphs: 'the longer we leave it, the more will be the defections from the League front on this question, the more isolated we shall become and the more foolish we shall look.' Cadogan thought Mussolini had made 'a definite advance', and if no satisfactory basis for talks could be found he would be confirmed in his suspicion of British intentions, and would be likely to accentuate 'his nuisance value towards us' . . . failure to begin talks would solidify the Rome-Berlin axis . . . Moreover is not Germany going to ask us a higher price for her friendship so long as we have a frankly hostile Italy on our flank rather than a mere neutral Italy?'

Significantly, Cadogan added 'From the discussions I have had with the Prime Minister I am convinced that he is extremely anxious to reach an agreement if that be at all possible with Mussolini, and that he attaches great importance to it.' This was sensible advice which the Foreign Secretary rejected to his cost.[31]

In the second week of December 1937 Ivy Chamberlain, Austen's widow, had gone to Rome. Her reception is evidence that Mussolini was considering restoring the Stresa Front if Britain held out a friendly hand. In a letter to Eden dated 15 December she reported that Bastianini (Under-Secretary for Foreign Affairs) had said to her that when Chamberlain became Prime Minister and sent his message to Mussolini they were all 'so pleased because they felt that here was someone, a brother of Sir Austen, who understood and sympathized with us' and they could forget all that had gone before, and much looked forward to Anglo-Italian conversations in September. Ciano in August had (to the embarrassment of the Foreign Office) leaked to the press Chamberlain's friendly August letter and Mussolini's warm reply, and the Foreign Office had been constrained to a statement that talks would probably start in September. Bastianini told Ivy that because the conversations had been postponed 'we have the feeling that, and believe that, the Prime Minister has opposition in his Cabinet'.

Ivy also saw Mussolini, who greeted her warmly and talked of his happy times with Austen. Mussolini told Ivy 'We believe Mr. Chamberlain is friendly, but that Mr. Eden is not.' Ivy denied this, and the Duce said: 'I *want* friendship with England, we have always been friends . . . Why therefore can we not commence conversations?' Ivy commented to Eden that he really wants an understanding and 'does not realize why the conversations have not commenced'. She probably made a correct diagnosis. On this letter Eden minuted: 'Lord Lloyd, whom I told of this conversation, remarked that Mussolini will never talk politics seriously to a woman. If this is true, it is none the less useful that Lady Chamberlain should have spoken as she has done.'

Ivy wrote privately to the Prime Minister, pointing out the strong dislike and distrust with which Eden was regarded in Rome and the general belief that he did not want better relations. On 18 January Neville sent her a letter of reply (which he concealed from Eden) praising her efforts, and saying he was going to try again to overcome 'difficulties', and that he expected to have Anglo-Italian conversations started well before the end of February.

During a conversation with Ciano, Ivy emphasized the keen desire of her brother-in-law for an early agreement with Mussolini. Ciano then taxed her with not really believing what she was saying. This prompted Ivy to show Nevillés letter of 18 July to Ciano, although it was intended only for her own eyes, and she had no permission from the Prime Minister to show it to anyone in Rome. The effect was electric ('magical' according to Chamberlain's diary). Ciano immediately said she must show it to Mussolini urgently, and on 5 February Ciano took her to the Palazzo Venezia. Mussolini asked her if he might see the letter, and Ivy said she 'saw no objection'. The Duce told Ivy he was anxious to come to a complete Anglo-

Italian agreement as a tribute to Austen, and dictated five points to be communicated to Neville by Ivy. Mussolini confirmed these points in writing to the British Ambassador (Lord Perth). In this communication Mussolini stated:

> I entirely agree with the Prime Minister's point of view and beg him to remember that I am working in a very realistic spirit and when conversations start I aim at reaching a full and complete agreement. Such an agreement will cover all points including propaganda, Mediterranean, colonies and economics, and it will be the basis of future cooperation between the two countries.

This reveals the definite opportunity existing in Feburary 1938 to bring Mussolini back to the Stresa Front and out of Hitler's orbit. All that the Duce wanted was 'de jure' recognition of the Italian conquest of Abyssinia and a blind eye to the armed help he was giving to Franco in Spain. It would have been difficult to persuade British public opinion to swallow these, but Chamberlain – still in his honeymoon period as Prime Minister, and widely regarded as the apostle of peace – would have had little difficulty in getting them generally accepted. Unfortunately, the opportunity was let slip.

Cadogan was embarrassed at showing Perth's and Ivy's messages to Eden who betrayed extreme annoyance, both in his minutes and later in his memoirs, at Ivy's unofficial diplomacy. Chamberlain wrote in his diary 'This incident produced suspicion in Eden's mind that if the Italians wanted talks there must be some catch in it and we had better hang back.'[32]

Before he went to the Riviera, Eden had written to Chamberlain that he would never resent 'any interest you take in Foreign Affairs'. This admirable statement was quickly overtaken by an irreconcilable quarrel between Chamberlain and Eden over Italy. On 12 January, with Eden still away, Roosevelt suggested to Chamberlain a calling together of the whole diplomatic corps in Washington at the end of the month to try to improve international relations. Chamberlain did not like this. Without consulting Eden, he replied that it was not an opportune moment because we were 'about to start talks with Italy and Germany and this might cut across efforts for quick results'. Chamberlain added that in the forthcoming talks he would be prepared to recognize 'de jure' the Italian conquest of Abyssinia if Italy gave evidence of her desire to restore friendly relations. Eden (immediately recalled from his holiday) was outraged at Chamberlain's reference to 'de jure' recognition for Italy. The two met at Chequers and relations were 'strained'. Eden reiterated that he 'would not have 'de jure' recognition of the Italian conquest of Abyssinia' and bluntly reminded the Prime Minister that immediately after signing the 'Gentleman's Agreement' Mussolini had sent 4,000 more volunteers to Spain. Conceding 'de jure', Eden stressed, would shock public opinion in Britain. Without consulting

the Prime Minister, he sent a wire to Washington saying that Chamberlain
had not meant 'exactly' what he had said.

Eden proposed that the Government should at once call off the idea of
Italian conversations for fear of offending the United States and welcome
Roosevelt's proposal for a diplomatic conference. The Prime Minister, very
put out, said they must take their dispute to the Cabinet's Foreign Affairs
Committee. The Committee decided they wanted talks with Mussolini, but
compromised with Eden by agreeing 'de jure' need only be given as a factor
in general appeasement. Chamberlain wrote in his diary that Eden
threatened to resign over the Roosevelt letter but 'this was impossible
because Roosevelt had "enjoined complete secrecy on us".'[33]

Eden had a rough passage at the FPC over his objection to 'de jure'
recognition, but the Committee felt that they must let Roosevelt go ahead.
Cadogan has confirmed that Eden contemplated an impulsive resignation 'if
the Government repudiated Roosevelt's initiative'. However, because of his
minor success at the FPC, Eden thought no more about it. Cadogan
recorded that although Eden had agreed 'in principle to talks with Musso'
he was 'silly on this question and uses every excuse – clutches at it – to run
out. This makes a very bad impression.'

Eden was extremely angry when he heard that Ivy Chamberlain had
talked to Ciano again in Rome and told him 'N.C. passionately wants a
settlement.' Eden complained sharply to Chamberlain, who agreed to ask
his sister-in-law to stop her efforts, but added 'She must not give the
impression that we do not want to have conversations at all.' Eden then
wrote to the Prime Minister that Ivy's 'unofficial diplomacy' placed him in a
difficult position, and

> Mussolini is in an extremely uncomfortable position. He has commitments in
> Abyssinia and Spain neither of which is turning out well. He now sees a
> Government in Berlin which is comparatively enthusiastic for the Rome-Berlin axis
> but which is also apparently determined to pursue a more active foreign policy in
> Cetral Europe with Austria as the first item of intended victims. In such a position
> we have nothing to gain by showing ourselves too eager [for diplomatic talks with
> Mussolini].

The Foreign Office prepared a memorandum on an agenda for talks with
Italy which emphasized the joint resolution at Stresa about Austria. It read:
'The three Governments examined afresh the Austrian situation, and
recognized the necessity of maintaining the independence of Austria would
continue to inspire their common policy.' Against this Eden pencilled, 'Is
this a concession at all?'[34]

This minute and Eden's letter to Chamberlain are incontrovertible
evidence that the Foreign Secretary misjudged the deadly danger of the
Anschluss for the peace of Europe and failed to consider properly how

Mussolini might, even at this late stage, be cajoled into preventing Hitler from annexing Austria. Chamberlain, on the other hand, kept to his late brother's briefing that at all costs the Anschluss must be prevented, and was becoming increasingly angry at Eden's obstinacy.

In his memoirs Eden emphasizes almost exclusively his concern at Mussolini's intervention on Franco's side in the Spanish Civil War. Alone in the Cabinet Eden wanted a Republican victory, while Chamberlain and his colleagues wanted a Franco victory. This at the time seemed imminent, although it was in fact to be delayed. The disagreement was an important factor in the Eden–Chamberlain quarrel. Eden has left no record to indicate that he appreciated the threat to European peace if Hitler took over Austria, or that he realized that once the German army was in Austria, Czechoslovakia was indefensible. Her defence plans were based on defending her well-fortified and hilly German frontier in the Sudetenland, whereas a German army along the flatter southern Czech frontier with Austria would have an easy passage.

Surprisingly, Eden's intimate advisers shared his view that the Anschluss would be no disaster. Cranborne as usual echoed Eden's views. Cadogan wrote in his diary on 15 February 'Personally I almost wish Germany would swallow Austria and get it over. She is probably going to do so anyhow – we can't stop her . . . What is the good of brandishing Austria under Hitler's nose when we can't do anything about it?'

On 22 April after the Anschluss Cadogan wrote to Henderson: 'Thank goodness Austria's out of the way . . . after all it wasn't our business; we had no particular feelings for the Austrians – we only forbade the Anschluss to spite Germany.'[35]

On 31 January Eden fired off another woolly letter at the Prime Minister which he did not want their Cabinet colleagues to see. In this he said 'I cannot help believing that what the Chiefs of Staff would really like to do is to reorientate our whole foreign policy and clamber on the band waggon with the dictators even though that process meant parting with France and estranging our relations with the United States.' This hypothesis was unlikely to appeal to Chamberlain.

Eden went on that he was convinced that 'the French army is absolutely sound, and surely if we had to choose between France and Italy as an ally we could not hesitate for a moment'. Why he thought such a choice might have to be made is far from clear – except that Delbos, the French Foreign Minister, was objecting to Anglo-Italian talks. Eden was guarded on the Italian conversations.

> As you know, I entirely agree that we must make every effort to come to terms with Germany. The Italian conversations are rather a different matter but, even there, once we have heard what Roosevelt has to say and have agreed upon our own

desiderata which must in my judgement include Spain, there should be possibilities. In contemplating such negotiations we must avoid, I am convinced, the temptation of being led astray by any exaggeration of the weakness of our friends and an unduly high estimate of the strength of totalitarian states which their practice makes only natural.

This letter was hardly calculated to improve the strained relations between the two.

Obviously at Eden's instigation, Cranborne wrote a Memorandum reiterating Eden's views for the benefit of the Prime Minister. It advised 'entering on conversations on the basis of "de jure" recognition . . . would be an error and maybe disastrous error of policy,' and repeated Eden's arguments: 'If HMG today unilaterally and not in conjunction with the United States, grant "de jure" recognition of Italy's title to Abyssinia they will go far to destroy the foundation of the only platform on which Anglo-American cooperation can at present be based. Let us proceed as rapidly as may be with our negotiations with Germany.' Cranborne, like Eden and Cadogan, feared that talks with Italy might be looked on by Hitler as an attempt to detach Italy from him and would annoy him.[36]

Cranborne and Eden need not have worried about the American reaction because Lindsay had reported that the American Under-Secretary for Foreign Affairs 'could think of no reason why they should not go ahead' with conversations in Rome. Chamberlain claimed that this telegram indicated President Roosevelt's willingness for Anglo-Italian talks to begin. According to Oliver Harvey, 'The PM naturally seized on this as entitling us to go ahead, and wanted Eden to summon Grandi at once and tell him we would start conversations. A. E. refused to be rushed.'[37]

Eden insisted on sending a further telegram to Lindsay asking for a clearer statement of what exactly the President meant. On 8 February Lindsay cleared up all doubts by writing:

> In reply to the query I think it hardly necessary to worry much about effects in America of "de jure". No doubt in press and in Congress we shall be to some extent jeered at for weakness and taunted for making friends with unrighteousness, and there will be genuine disapointment among some high minded people, but I hardly expect this would be very important. It is more likely that our action would be regarded as an effort to pay the necessary price of peace. The whole issue has rather faded away into the background . . . I do not think the attitude of the administration would be materially different.

Although Mussolini had told Hitler in September that he would agree to the Anschluss, prompted by Ciano he had second thoughts once it became evident Hitler was poised for action against Vienna. Accordingly, Ciano told Drummond he had instructed Grandi to press for an early start of Anglo-Italian conversations 'in view of possible future happenings' (i.e., Hitler's take-over of Austria). On 17 February Ciano lunched with Ivy Chamberlain and warned her solemnly that she must tell Neville 'time is everything – today an agreement will be easy, but things are happening in Europe which will make it impossible tomorrow'. According to Ivy, Ciano was 'completely changed and intensely worried'.

Chamberlain understood perfectly well that Mussolini and Ciano were frightened of a Hitler coup in Austria, and passed a copy of Ivy's message to Eden, who was very irritated at Ivy's renewed intervention, writing to Chamberlain:

> Mussolini will say "I know that the Prime Minister is determined to open conversations in February so do not pay any attention to any condition Eden may be trying to impose" . . . Already Rome is giving out the impresssion that we are courting her with the purpose no doubt of showing Berlin how worth courting she is. This is exactly the hand Mussolini always likes to play, and plays with so much skill when he gets a chance. I do not think we should let him. . . . The main idea of this letter is therefore to express the hope that you will ask Lady Chamberlain through the Embassy to be careful not to engage in any further conversations with Mussolini for any continuation of them must inevitably confuse the situation, embarrass me, and I suspect Grandi also.[38]

Grandi would not have been embarrassed; instead he would have been pleased.

Eden had had an inconsequential talk with Grandi on 10 February but unknown to him Chamberlain was sending messages to Grandi through Sir Joseph Ball of the Conservative Central Office to the effect that he wanted an urgent agreement with Mussolini, with talks starting at once. As a result Chamberlain fixed a meeting with Grandi and Eden at 10 Downing Street for the morning of 18 February. Eden demurred, and tried to evade the meeting. Chamberlain told him firmly it must take place. Eden shilly-shallied again with a letter stating that he wanted a private talk with Grandi first so that he could ask him about the scheme to withdraw Italian troops from Spain. He also sent a second letter to the Prime Minister imploring him 'not to commit ourselves' in any way at the meeting with Grandi. Chamberlain ignored these requests.

At the Downing Street meeting Chamberlain asked Grandi 'if all was lost in Austria'. Grandi replied that 'they were only at the end of the third act', but if Germany was on the Brenner Italy could not be left alone with two great potential enemies, Germany and Britain. Asked what effect opening of Anglo-Italian conversations might have, Grandi stated 'It would give my people more courage.' Eden inquired if Italy would withdraw volunteers from Spain, and Grandi said 'It would be a mistake to hold up Anglo-Italian conversations because of Spain.'

According to Grandi, there then ensued a lively altercation between Eden and Chamberlain. Chamberlain adjourned the discussion. Then in private Chamberlain told Eden that he had made up his mind to tell Grandi at 3 pm that he would open immediate conversations, and that Drummond should be instructed to come back to London at once to begin preparatory work. When Eden disagreed emphatically Chamberlain said angrily 'Anthony, you have thrown away chance after chance.' Cadogan noted that Eden and Chamberlain had 'a good row' and a 'set to.'[39]

Grandi told Leo Amery that 'if only' the Anglo-Italian talks had begun six months earlier Austria might have ben saved. It is difficult to dissent from this view.

This was the end of the road. Chamberlain had decided to have another Foreign Secretary. Grandi cabled Mussolini that Eden and Chamberlain were completely divided, and without consulting the Foreign Office issued a press statement welcoming 'the new British approach' and stating that the Italian Government thought the talks should embrace every subject including 'de jure' recognition, with which the British Government agreed. Eden was furious.[40]

Chamberlain called a special Cabinet the next day, 19 February, to try to resolve the dispute. He began by putting his case for immediate Anglo-Italian talks. Eden replied (according to Chamberlain's diary, ineffectively), arguing that before talks 'We ought to obtain an indication of Italian good faith and good will. Such an atittude could be found in Spain if the Italian Government would modify their attitude there and agree to the formula that we have proposed for the withdrawal of volunteers.' He stated that his information was that Mussolini had agreed not to oppose the Anschluss in return for Hitler's allowing him a free hand in the Mediterranean. There were twenty Ministers present, apart from Chamberlain and Eden themselves. Fourteen supported the Prime Minister without qualification; four with some qualification. Eden said he could not accept their decision and must resign. There was a gasp of horror, and fruitless efforts were made to persuade him to reconsider his decision. The next day he resigned, to be succeeded by Halifax.[41]

Chamberlain, often wrong about foreign policy, was correct in considering Austria more important than Spain, and that the imperative need was to prevent the Anschluss. However unpalatable it might be, he felt that he had urgently to seek the Duce's support. Eden thought no trust could be placed in Mussolini. Such a view can be justified, but surely it was worth while making an effort to enlist Italian support when Austrian independence was in the balance?

Eden's original biographer (Carlton) many years later was told by Malcolm MacDonald, a close friend of Anthony's (then in the Cabinet as Secretary for the Dominions), that he dined with Eden on 19 February, and that Eden was 'physically and mentally unwell with his thoughts less clear and reasonably coherent than they usually were'. He felt it was better Eden should resign. Too much reliance should not be placed on MacDonald's memory in his old age, because according to Harvey on 20 February MacDonald urged Eden not to resign and instead to agree to the opening of the Anglo-Italian conversations subject to conditions about Spain. Much to Eden's annoyance, Simon and other friends of Chamberlain assiduously circulated rumours that Eden had been having a nervous breakdown. These were false. Eden was under strain, but his judgment was unaffected, and for the rest of his life he justified his conduct.[42]

Eden's resignation created a political storm within the Conservative Party. He was then at the peak of his popularity with back-bench Tory MPs while Cranborne and his private secretary, Jim Thomas – who both resigned with him – were also much liked. The quarrel over the Roosevelt initiative was kept secret, and the Conservative Whips office fanned rumours that Eden's physical and mental health were poor. *The Times* repeated Simon's malicious comments that Eden's resignation was due to bad health, and in the obscurity the impression was created that Eden's resignation was due to his opposition to Chamberlain's policy of appeasing Hitler.

With commendable honesty, Eden in his resignation speech to the Commons stated that he had not resigned on an issue of principle, but on 'whether official conversations should be opened in Rome now'. He devoted much of his speech to Italy's intervention in the Spanish Civil War. Here he lost friends because all that most Conservative MPs cared about the Spanish Civil War was that the Communists should not win. Eden could not speak of the Roosevelt initiative as this was being kept secret even from the Cabinet.

He made a veiled reference saying that the talks with Italy were not 'an isolated issue' in the dispute between him and the Prime Minister, and 'within the last few weeks upon one most important decision of foreign policy which did not concern Italy at all the difference was fundamental'. This, although it was in no way Eden's intention, led to the widespread supposition afterwards that Eden meant he was opposed to appeasement of Hitler. Nothing could have been further from the truth.

Chamberlain has been criticized for his secret contacts with Grandi through Sir Joseph Ball, and behind Eden's back. They were a breach of protocol; Chamberlain was driven to it because he was desperately anxious to get into talks with Mussolini, as each week made it more likely that

Austria would fall to Hitler. Were these contacts a worse breach than Chamberlain's letter to Mussolini in August, sent without Eden's knowledge? It was up to Eden to threaten to resign in August if he objected strongly to letters written behind his back.

Chamberlain should have got rid of Eden in August instead of leaving it until it was too late to save Austria. Undoubtedly he was swayed by the fear that Eden, with his popularity among Conservative MPs, might form a group in the Commons hostile to the Government's foreign policy at a time when it was in difficulties. Macmillan has written: 'In the House the younger members in particular had put their confidence in Eden . . . so had large numbers throughout the nation of all parties and none.' In the event no strong nucleus formed around Eden, and the true reasons for his resignation remained secret. Even the Cabinet knew almost nothing of the dispute between Eden and Chamberlain until 19 February. Macmillan has recalled that when Eden's resignation was announced on 20 February 'the sensation was immense. Yet because of the uncertainty and obscurity as to its real cause 'the debate turned out to be 'something of an anti climax' and 'Chamberlain's position was not seriously shaken'. Macmillan pooh-poohs Simon's allegations that Eden was having a nervous breakdown. As Eden agreed with Chamberlain's policy of appeasing Hitler, and offering him colonies, he did not oppose Chamberlain's subsequent appeasement policy after he had left the Foreign Office. Chamberlain, believing strongly in the urgent need to get into talks with Mussolini, was wrong to allow Eden to hold up conversations for six months, and had the Prime Minister been successful in winning Mussolini over and persuading him to veto the Anschluss (as in 1934) the course of history might have been different.[43]

The drama of Eden's resignation remained obscure. Now from the official documents containing *inter alia* the letters between the two, together with the diaries of Cadogan, Harvey, Amery and others*, the author has been able to reveal the exasperation and stubbornness which caused such bitterness between the two men. It is a sad tale of personal animosity when the peace of Europe was at stake.

---

*The biographers of Eden and Chamberlain have not drawn on the correspondence and minutes in the archives at the Pubic Record Office, and Eden's autobiography does not reveal the full story. An interesting sidelight is that the Astors never invited Eden and Chamberlain down to Cliveden on the same week-end.

CHAPTER TEN

ANSCHLUSS AND BRITISH OVERTURES TO MUSSOLINI

'It is tragic to think that very possibly this might have been prevented if I had had Halifax at the Foreign Office instead of Anthony at the time I wrote my letter to Mussolini [in August 1937]' (Chamberlain to his sister when Hitler annexed Austria in March 1938.)

HALIFAX'S VISIT to Germany produced enthusiasm in the Cabinet for the return of colonies to Hitler in the hope that it would overcome his desire for conquests in Europe. On 24 January 1938 Chamberlain emphasized to the Foreign Policy Committee that 'the colonial question was in German eyes the only outstanding problem remaining between the two countries'. The Prime Minister was ignoring his advisers. When he went on to say that no satisfactory 'general settlement with Germany' was possible without a 'colonial settlement on a broad and liberal basis' he found several Ministers in disagreement. Hoare said that this 'might make the position worse rather than better', and Ormsby Gore (Colonial Secretary) warned that 'the whole of the coloured world would greatly resent the idea'. However, the Committee agreed Henderson should be instructed to start negotiations for a colonial agreement with Hitler as part of a 'general settlement'. When Simon asked Eden (in his last few weeks in office) what were our desiderata in a 'general settlement', and hoped that they did not include a return of Germany to the League (which he regarded as a 'hopeless proposal'), the Foreign Secretary replied that the items would include Air Disarmament, a Western Pact and Eastern Europe. How Eden expected to dispose of territories belonging to other nations in Eastern Europe in order to satisfy

Hitler was a question that was left unanswered.

The Committee wanted to placate home opinion by putting restrictions on the sovereignty Germany could exercise in any colonies that might be given to her, and Britain, France and Belgium were to accept similar qualifications over sovereignty in their own colonies. Henderson was called to the next meeting on 3 February, and reported that 'the German Government would not be greatly thrilled unless they obtained some territory in which they could exercise full sovereign rights and call their own'. Ominously, Henderson also said he had recently seen Neurath, who told him that Austria was behaving 'badly', he could make no promise of any kind with regard to her' and that the German view was that as long as the Spanish troubles continued there was little or no hope of general settlement in Europe.[1]

The outlook was unpromising, but Henderson was told to continue his negotiations in Berlin. On 15 March the FPC Committee met, with Halifax as Foreign Secretary Drummond (now Lord Perth) was called back from Rome so that Italian conversations, for so long blocked by Eden, could be considered. Chamberlain said that agreement with Mussolini must be reached as soon as possible. All members were conscious of the difficulty imposed by Italy's intervention in Spain; Halifax suggested Spain should be placed formally on the Talks Agenda (otherwise 'we might be criticised') but that the subject should not be pursued. This was too weak even for Chamberlain, who said that a settlement of the Spanish question must be a 'fundamental' condition of the agreement. Hailsham pointed out that the Spanish Government was constantly receiving large supplies of men from France, and munitions from Russia. Mussolini had openly told Perth that as long as France and other countries supplied the Spanish Government, Italy would continue to supply General Franco. Perth was alarmed by the suggestion that the Spanish issue must be resolved before an Italian agreement could be reached.

Simon reminded the Committee that public opinion at home would not like an agreement if Spain was not solved.

Halifax sensibly warned the Committee that 'we might have to choose between the dilemma of giving a liberal and practical interpretation to the Prime Minister's undertaking to Parliament on 21 February or 'running a grave risk of losing any results from the Anglo-Italian conversations'; and he favoured 'a liberal interpretation'. However, Chamberlain and the other Ministers would not accept this for fear of public opinion at home. As will be seen, the attempt at a rapprochement with Italy foundered on the rocks of Spain although an agreement of a sort was signed with Mussolini.[2]

On 21 February Chamberlain had assured the House of Commons that the Government would not complete an Anglo-Italian Agreement 'unless the agreement contained a settlement of the Spanish question.' This was instrumental in persuading Mussolini to condone the annexation of Austria. The Spanish War was always the main stumbling-block to the resumption of friendship between Britain and Italy which was the only way to curb Hitler's aggression. Halifax's desire for a 'liberal interpretation' expressed at the FPC on his first appearance there as Foreign Secretary had much to commend itself.

Towards the end of 1937 the Austrian Government found that Germany was conspiring with the Austrian Nazis to overthrow it, and had captured Nazi plans in cypher for nationwide sabotage and provocation by Austrian Nazis to be followed by a demand from Hitler (under threat of a German invasion) for a Nazi-dominated Government. The pretext would be that Germany was preventing a Habsburg restoration; it was entitled 'Action Plan for 1938'. Hitler (an Austrian) had the Anschluss as a sacred date in his political calendar; he had his sights on November 1937. He desperately wanted the 6½ million Austrians incorporated in the Reich, to avenge his humiliation in the failed 1934 Vienna Putsch.

Despairing of help from Mussolini or France, Schuschnigg unwillingly fell back on his last resort – a negotiated compromise with Hitler. He was heartened by talks with von Papen, now German Ambassador in Vienna, who suggested in December 1937 a personal meeting between what von Papen termed guilefully 'the two German Chancellors'. Schuschnigg was to find talking to the civilized von Papen was quite a different matter from talking to his mad master.

On 26 January a formal invitation for a personal meeting at Berchtesgaden arrived. Although Schuschnigg was well aware that Hitler was committing gross breaches of his 1936 pledge of non-intervention, and of his own weakness in comparison with Hitler, the Austrian Chancellor accepted. Schuschnigg thought naively that his best plan would be to attack, and he told von Papen in advance that he would complain of the subversive behaviour of the Nazis within Austria. When von Papen told Hitler this it provoked the Führer to senseless rage. However, before leaving Vienna Schuschnigg had in fact given instructions for fresh discussions to take place with the Austrian Nazis, thus destroying any impression of firmness. He later said that this was 'to show Hitler we had already made of our own accord the maximum internal concessions'. As a bait von Papen promised Schuschnigg that after the meeting an agreed joint declaration would be published, reiterating the basic principles of the July 1936 pact.

It is hard to say whether or not Schuschnigg knew before he went to Berchtesgaden that Hitler was an obsessed fanatic, determined to swallow Austria by hook or crook. Significantly, as he stepped on to the train from the Vienna platform he said to his Foreign Minister, Guido Schmidt, 'It would be better for a psychiatrist to undertake this mission instead of me.'

As soon as Schuschnigg arrived at Bershtesgaden Hitler demanded that the Austrian Chancellor accept a Ten Point Plan which included an amnesty for all Austrian Nazis, and the appointment of Seyss-Inquart – an Austrian Nazi in Hitler's pay – as the Minister of the Interior. This would mean the Nazis could run riot in Austria.

Gone were Schuschnigg's hopes that Hitler might promise to stop the Nazi conspiracy in Austria, and to his horror Hitler threatened him with invasion if he did not sign the document at once. He asked for three days' grace to consult with Miklas, the Austrian President. Miklas at first would not accept Hitler's demands, which he said correctly amounted to the destruction of Austrian independence. After discussing the futile suggestion that instead Austria should offer to cede to Germany the frontier town of Braunau-am-Inn (Hitler's birthplace), Schuschnigg and Miklas with great reluctance agreed to Hitler's demands. They were influenced by fake army manoeuvres on the German-Austrian frontier which gave the impression that Hitler was on the point of invading. Keitel testified at Nuremberg that these were indeed bluff. It was a national tragedy for Austria but Miklas and Schuschnigg still hoped the Agreement would give them time to patch up some agreement by which Britain, France and Italy would promise support.[3]

Alas Mussolini would not help. Ciano recorded in his diary that the Anschluss was inevitable, and the only question was how long it could be postponed. The Duce had promised Hitler to abandon Austria in exchange for a free hand in the Mediterranean.

Schuschnigg told the French Minister in Vienna (Puaux) that Hitler was a madman 'who thinks he is a god'. Puaux was told by the French Foreign Minister he must assure Schuschnigg that 'France looked on the independence of Austria as indispensable to the peace of Europe'. Comforting words, but there was no hint of action in support of them.

Eden had just resigned. Halifax and Butler (who had replaced Cranborne as Under-Secretary) were uneasy, but, they were advised by Cadogan that the Anschluss was nothing to be feared. Chamberlain – who did fear the Anschluss – had no time to concert action against Hitler.

After the Hitler–Schuschnigg meeting the Labour opposition tried to make a major issue out of British policy towards Austria, and 100 Tory MPs at the back-benchers' Foreign Policy Committee, egged on by Churchill and Nicolson, issued an appeal for 'a more positive attitude'. In almost his last statement to the House of Commons as Foreign Secretary, Eden gave a favourable account of the Berchtesgaden conversations; when the Communist MP Willy Gallacher asked 'In view of the fact that Austrian independence has now been disposed of by Germany, is it not necessary that something very urgent should be done?' Eden made no reply. Churchill on 22 February had told the Commons that he would be in favour of concessions to Italy if she would aid France and Britain in maintaining the independence of Austria. This was taking Chamberlain's line against Eden.

Eden and Churchill did not consult together after Eden's resignation. If they had, they would have found they were diametrically opposed, with Churchill supporting Chamberlain's view that Spain was a sideshow and the paramount need was to restrain Hitler from annexing Austria. Churchill was unaware of the real reason for Eden's resignation, and believed erroneously it came about because Chamberlain was keener on appeasing Hitler than was Eden. As a result he used words about Eden at the time which have given the impression that Eden shared Churchill's desire for a firm stand against Hitler. This was a delusion; Eden wanted to appease Hitler and be firm with Italy. Eden and Churchill did not become close political collaborators; as a result no effective group of Tory MPs opposed to Chamberlain emerged before the outbreak of war.

In Austria Seyss-Inquart as Minister of the Interior defied Schuschnigg, indulging in open Nazi propaganda and making speeches before seas of Nazi swastika banners claiming that 'Austria is German . . . the National German Reich has a common destiny which we must uphold.' The Austrian Nazis dictated the pace of events in Austria. Schuschnigg tried hard to compromise with Seyss-Inquart, but in his own words 'Every concession on our part brought an avalanche of new and impossible demands.'

In desperation, deprived of any encouragement from Rome, Paris or London, Schuschnigg decided on a final gamble to redeem the situation and prevent the Anschluss. He called a plebiscite. Austrian Socialists and monarchists applauded. Otto Habsburg offered to take over the Chancellorship from Schuschnigg, and his proposal had considerable support among the Right. Schuschnigg, who until now had flirted with Otto, declined, saying that an attempt at a restoration would mean with 100 per cent certainty the death of Austria.

Schuschnigg consulted Mussolini, who told him the plebiscite would be a bomb which would burst in his hands. This was the last message Schuschnigg received from his former protector, and unfortunately it was a correct prediction. The formula chosen for the plebisicite question was: 'Are you in favour of a free and German, an independent and social, a Christian and united Austria?' On 9 March Schuschnigg launched his campaign for the plebiscite amid enormous enthusiasm.

Hitler reacted with fury. He ordered Keitel to put into operation immediately 'Operation Otto', which was a vague plan for the military occupation of Austria drawn up in case there was a Habsburg restoration. It was only a theoretical staff study, but adequate. Hitler sent Schuschnigg an ultimatum that he must withdraw the plebiscite.

Schuschnigg was an Austrian patriot without political ambition. A lawyer, he was mild and irresolute. On receiving Hitler's ultimatum he telephoned to Mussolini, who ordered his staff to say he was 'not available'. Schuschnigg and Miklas both agreed that a war between Germany and Austria was unthinkable. The French Government of Chautemps had fallen that day, and in London Ribbentrop was lunching with Chamberlain. As the lunch was ending a telegram came from the British Legation in Vienna that Schuschnigg had been given an ultimatum by Hitler that he must resign forthwith. It transpired that Ribbentrop knew nothing of this ultimatum.

No offer of help to Austria came from London, and Schuschnigg resigned. Hitler ordered Miklas to make Seyss-Inquart Chancellor instead. Miklas, made of sterner stuff, defied Hitler and refused. Halifax sent a message that Britain could not take the responsibility of advising 'any course of action which might expose Austria to dangers against which Britain is unable to guarantee protection'. German troops then occupied Austria, arriving in Vienna on 11 March. Thus Austria became the first State to fall victim to Hitler's agression, being wiped off the map and incorporated into Germany. On 7 March Colonel Liebitskt, the Austrian military attaché in Rome, had talked to Mussolini and found him 'not indifferent' to Hitler's insolence but the Duce's mind was made up in Hitler's favour and he was much concerned with the Führer's forthcoming visit to Rome, about which both the King Victor Emmanuel and the Pope were making difficulties.[4]

Hitler was worried by Mussolini's likely reaction to invasion of Austria. He sent Philip of Hesse – married to the King of Italy's daughter Mafalda – with a cringing and untruthful letter alleging that Schuschnigg was drifting into a military alliance with Czechoslovakia aimed at Germany, and a Habsburg restoration. Such tendentious arguments were unnecessary. (The references to Czechoslovakia were deleted in the press version of Hitler's letter.) Late on 11 March after talking to Mussolini, Philip of Hesse telephoned to Hitler that Mussolini had been very friendly about the proposed coup; if Schuschnigg persisted with the plebiscite 'he was finished with Austria' and he condoned the invasion. Hitler was delighted, sending a message to Mussolini that he would never forget this, and that if the Duce was ever in danger he would protect him.[5]

Italian experts agree that Mussolini lost more popularity through his acceptance of the Anschluss than he did over the Matteotti murder twenty-four years before. A promise was given by Hitler to the Italian Embassy in Berlin that the German army would stop at Innsbrück and not appear on the Brenner. This was later ignored. After what Mussolini had enthusiastically said in 1934 and later about Italy's guarantee of Austrian independence, eating his words in face of Hitler's aggression made him look silly, and the whole operation was sprung on the Duce without advance warning. This was an indication of Hitler's contempt for Italy. The Italian port of Trieste was strangled by the loss of its traditional trade with Austria.

Grandi claimed after the war that Mussolini would have acted diffently if it had not been for Eden's intransigence over de jure recognition of Italy's conquest of Abyssinia.

Although only a minority of Austrians were in favour of the Nazis, the German troops – Austria's ally in the First World War – were greeted enthusiastically by the majority of the population, especially in Vienna. One would like to think that if Schuschnigg's plebiscite had been held there would have been an overwhelming vote against the Anschluss but it must not be overlooked that by 1938 many Austrians, cast down by the harsh provisions of the Treaty of Versailles, had come to look on themselves as Germans, while 1918 Habsburg stamps had been overprinted 'Deutschös-terreich.'

Immediately persecutions of the Jews began. These were reported in the British national press, but not in *The Times*, where Dawson stuck to Chamberlain's request not to print anything which might upset Hitler.

The British–Italian entente wanted by Chamberlain and blocked by Eden was stillborn. On 12 March Chamberlain told the Cabinet '. . . it might be said with justice that we had been too late in starting conversations with Italy', and in a letter to his sister the next day 'It is tragic to think that very possibly this might have been prevented if I had had Halifax at the Foreign Office instead of Anthony at the time I wrote my letter to Mussolini' (in August 1937). Chamberlain may well have been correct.

With Austria gone, the spotlight was on Czechoslovakia, where it was clear Hitler would strike next. Czechoslovakia was an artificial state created by Versailles out of the former Habsburg Empire, and its population included Slovaks, Magyars, Ruthenians, Poles and Germans. The German minorities in the Sudetenland had been treated harshly and had legitimate grievances which Hitler now magnified as an excuse to destroy Czechoslovakia and gain even greater popularity by achieving more *Lebensraum* in the east. Chamberlain was under no illusion as to the deadly danger to Czechoslovakia with German armies in Austria – a situation about which his late brother had briefed him so well.

On 14 March Neville's initial reaction in the Commons echoed Austen's views. On the Monday after the Anschluss he expressed anger, saying 'the methods adopted' call for 'severest condemnation' and were 'a profound shock', and that the Government would consider increased rearmament.

Criticism of British policy towards Austria from Government supporters had burnt itself out – apart from Churchill, who stated Britain could not afford to accept the Anschluss and called for urgent discussions with 'our' Allies and through the League of Nations. Churchill emphasized that Czechoslovakia was isolated militarily and economically and that Nazi Germany was now in a position to dominate the whole of South-East Europe. But Boothby – normally Churchill's most vigorous ally – was muted, although Amery said that much as he disliked from an Empire point of view Continental entanglements they were now essential, and 'let us make it plain 'that the first German soldier or aeroplane to cross the Czech border will bring the whole might of this country against Germany'. Like Churchill and Chamberlain, Amery wanted better relations with Italy. Eden was abroad on holiday.

Unfortunately, Chamberlain did not stick by his brave words in the Commons on 14 March, neither did they find favour with his Cabinet colleagues. In Cabinet on 14 March Halifax had said stoutly 'If the Government want to get public opinion behind them they must show they are not afraid to tell the dictators what they think', but the Prime Minister had replied that the crisis 'did not indicate that the events are leading us to war.'[6]

Cadogan attended the meeting of the Foreign Policy Committee on 18 March, and wrote in his diary that the Committee felt 'Czechoslovakia was not worth the bones of a single British Grenadier . . . they are quite right too'. The FPC record bears out Cadogan because they decided they could not have 'recourse to war' against Germany over Czechoslovakia with Chamberlain telling them 'if Germany obtained her *desiderata* by peaceable methods there was no reason to suppose that she would reject such a procedure in favour of one of violence' while Halifax thought 'we must decline any fresh commitment to the Czechs' and the Czechs must make a settlement with Germany if she was to survive and we were 'batting on a very bad wicket'. In March 1939 Chamberlain and Halifax had the same reaction as their predecessors as Prime Minister and Foreign Secretary (Baldwin and Eden) to the militarization of the Rhineland – that on no account would they risk war with Hitler.

Halifax had presented a Foreign Office memorandum which stated that the German Government would 'by fair or foul means' work for incorporation into the Reich of the German minority in Czechoslovakia, and aim at breaking the Czech connection with France and the Soviet Union; it emphasized that Czechoslovakia was weak militarily, with Germany controlling her only communication with the sea. The future was 'black', and a commitment to defend Czechoslovakia would be 'bluff'.

Inskip said he had been struck by the telegram from the British Minister in Prague (Newton) that Czechoslovakia was not permanently tenable, and 'an unstable unit in Europe. At the Peace Conference it had been a toss up whether Czechoslovakia should be treated as belonging to Western or Eastern Europe . . . a highly artificial state which had been created under most favourable and peaceable circumstances.' Hankey pointed out that Czechoslovakia could only exist if the whole territory was kept as one unit because manufacturing and agricultural districts were mutually dependent. Hailsham thought we should only be obliged to come to France's assistance if she was attacked by Germany; and Ormsby-Gore was satisfied that any specific commitment to the Czechs would split public opinion in this country from top to botton. Hoare wanted some commitment to France, but preferred it to be tied up with Central Europe; Stanley (Board of Trade) said it was impossible to argue that the preservation of Czechoslovakia was a vital interest of Britain and our only obligation to Czechoslovakia was that of one League member to another.'

Chamberlain summed up, saying the idea was hopeless that 'any effective help could swiftly be brought to Czechoslovakia in an emergency . . . therefore we should say it was impracticable to aid Czechoslovakia except by making war on Germany'. He wanted direct Beneš–Hitler negotiations. Halifax then said the discussions pointed to Britain declining any fresh commitments to Czechoslovakia, and we must persuade the French and Beneš to make the best possible terms with Germany: 'We should persuade the Government of Czechoslovakia to adopt a fair and reasonable attitude.' Inskip emphasized that 'we could only go to war if France had already got involved in war.' Chamberlain said he disliked the idea that it was left to the discretion of France whether the UK was involved in war or not; 'He intensely disliked the idea of such a situation.' Several Ministers intimated their dissent from 'any conclusion which involved a new commitment to France'.[7]

The logical plan to save Europe from the Nazis was a guarantee to Czechoslovakia, coupled with an all-out drive for rearmament and an alliance with Russia. Vansittart argued for this, and, according to Cadogan, damaged his own case by overstatement. Amery undoubtedly gives a correct impression of Tory MPs' attitude in his diary entry of 21 March, which reveals that after talking to a number of them George Tryon summed up their views: 'We cannot be expected to guarantee the independence of a county which we can neither get at nor spell.'[8]

On 19 March the Soviet Government suggested a Four Power Conference to discuss means of preventing further aggression by Hitler; the British Cabinet rejected the proposal on 22 March.

With the Prime Minister and his colleagues lily-livered about Czechoslovakia it is not surprising that in the debate in the Commons on 24 March Chamberlain was less firm than he had been ten days before. Churchill in an emotional speech said: 'Now the victors are vanquished and those who threw down their arms in the field and sued for armistice are riding on to world mastery. That is the position – that is the terrible transformation that has taken place.' He called for a Danube bloc to arise out of conversations with Mussolini, to include Czechoslovakia, Yugoslavia, Romania, Hungary and Bulgaria – 'an aggregate of fifteen million people with powerful armies animated by a hatred of Nazi rule'.

Chamberlain rejected either 'a commitment to the Czechs direct or to France arising out of the Czech Treaty'. He added that he would not agree to Soviet proposals for mutual pledges against aggression. But he said resolutely that British armament must be accelerated.

The speech has been aptly described by Wheeler-Bennett as a 'masterpiece of obfuscation'. Perhaps the Prime Minister intended it as a guarded warning to Hitler because he also pointed out that if war broke out over Czechoslovakia or some other victim of aggression it was unlikely to be confined to those countries which had undertaken contractual obligations. Nobody could tell where it would end. Other parties might be drawn in. That evening he wrote to his sister:[9]

> The Austrian frontier is practically open; the great Skoda munition works are within easy bombing distance of the German aerodromes; the railways all pass through German territory, Russia is 100 miles away. Therefore we could not help Czechoslovakia – she would simply be a pretext for going to war with Germany. That we could not think of unless we had a reasonable prospect of being able to beat her to her knees in a reasonable time, and of that I see no sign. I have therefore abandoned any idea of giving guarantees to Czechoslovakia or the French in connection with her obligations to that country.

A request by Russia for a Conference on resisting Hitler through the League of Nations was turned down by the British Government.[10]

Hitler with the precedent of British and French weakness over the militarization of the Rhineland, and over the Anschluss, was now sure he could annex Czechoslovakia without war. Konrad Henlein, the leader of the Sudeten German Nazis in Hitler's pay, was summoned, and Hitler told him that in negotiations with Beneš he must always demand more than was likely to be conceded. On paper Beneš was in a strong position. Czechoslovakia had the Alliance for Mutual Defence, together with the Alliance with Soviet Russia of 1935 (which did not come into operation unless France acted first) and the Little Entente Treaties with Romania and Yugoslavia. However, Beneš knew well that he could count on no armed help from the French unless the British would act as well, and he was conscious that a strong faction in Czechoslovakia felt 'better Hitler than Stalin' just as many Austrians had felt 'better Hitler than the Habsburgs'. On their German frontier the Czechs had powerful fortifications and they had a well-equipped army of thirty-four divisions, and the Skoda works, the most modern arms factory in Europe, but there were no fortifications on the Austrian side although frenzied work was begun.

Failing an accord with Russia, the only thing which could stop Hitler's aggression was if Italy, France and Britain jointly agreed they would intervene with force, as they had decided at Stresa three years before.

★   ★   ★

With Eden out of the way and Halifax in the saddle rapid progress was made with Anglo-Italian talks in Rome. Grandi passed a message to Halifax that Mussolini would accept a formula for the progressive withdrawal of the Italian 'volunteers' from Spain. In March 1938 it seemed that Franco's military victories must bring the Spanish Civil War to a conclusion within weeks. This expectation proved false. Negotiations began in Rome on 8 March three days before Hitler annexed Austria; Ciano and Perth held fifteen meetings. Mussolini became wary of Hitler after his Austrian coup, and personally indignant because Hitler had not given him advance warning. This improved the climate for the talks, and for prestige reasons Mussolini wanted to sign an Agreement with Britain before Hitler's visit to Italy scheduled for the first week of May.

The Easter Agreement was signed on 16 April and reaffirmed the Gentleman's Agreement. On paper it disposed of the problems of propaganda, Arabia, Libya, and British interests in Abyssinia. These were peripheral, all that mattered were Spain and 'de jure'. Britain agreed to raise 'de jure' at the League, and Halifax on 12 May secured a vote in the League Council which allowed each member to make his own decision. In return Mussolini undertook not to send new contingents of troops to Spain. In the negotiations Britain had insisted that the Agreement was only to come into force after Mussolini had withdrawn a substantial number of Italian troops from Spain. Suddenly Republican resistance in Spain strengthened. Russia and France supplied them with aid, while Mussolini honoured a commitment to Franco to send around 6000 additional Italian troops in the summer of 1938, together with planes. With the Spanish Civil War continuing, the Easter Agreement did not formally come into force until 16 November 1938, after the Munich Agreement.[11]

There is reason to believe that if Britain had waived her scruples about Spain, Mussolini might have returned fully to the Stresa Front. Unfortunately, public opinion in Britain attached more importance to Spain than to Czechoslovakia. The Government was frightened of hostile public opinion if the Easter Agreement was put into operation while Mussolini's help to Franco was blatant. The minutes of the Cabinet and the FPC reveal that as so often, electoral consideration swayed the Government.

Since the Cabinet and the Conservative MPs wanted a Franco victory, this was inconsistent. Anyway, Chamberlain could have persuaded public opinion to accept implementation of the Easter Agreement without difficulty; he was widely regarded as 'the Apostle of Peace', and took pains to preserve this image. Moreover, he was in his honeymoon period as Prime Minister, but he never pointed out publicly that Spain was a sideshow compared with the threat from Hitler.

When Chamberlain introduced the Easter Agreement in the Commons he described the vigour, vision and efficiency of the new Italy under the stimulus of the personality of Signor Mussolini and declared (over-optimistically) that 'already the clouds of mistrust and suspicion have been cleared away'. He had correctly diagnosed that there was opposition to the Easter Agreement, though, and significantly fifty Government supporters abstained in the division. With Britain withholding 'de jure' recognition pending evidence of Italian withdrawal from Spain, Mussolini's enthusiasm for the Agreement dwindled, although at first he was pleased. His popularity had been dented by Hitler's seizure of Austria, and the Easter Agreement was much applauded by the Italian people.

Leo Amery went to Rome on 20 April. His account of his meeting with Mussolini is evidence of the Duce's enthusiasm. Mussolini told Amery that he intended to keep the Agreement 'in the spirit as well as in the letter, and regarded it as a blessing not only for Italy and England, but for all Europe'. Amery noted that the Italians as a whole were thoroughly bored at the prospect of the Hitler visit, and Mussolini agreed most warmly with Amery when the latter regretted that Neville had not fixed up the agreement six months earlier. Both agreed that Czechoslovakia could not survive.[12]

Unreliable as Mussolini was, with hindsight it was a grave mistake not to condone his intervention in Spain and to grant him 'de jure' recognition when he was in a warm mood towards Britain. When 'de jure' recognition was finally given by Britain in November, after the shock of Munich, Italian volunteers were still pouring into Spain in thousands, but by then Mussolini had moved firmly and disastrously towards Hitler.

★　　★　　★

Hitler visited Italy on 2 May accompanied by a bevy of Nazi leaders and a troop of uniformed German journalists in four special trains. Relations between Mussolini and Hitler were clouded not only by the Easter Agreement but by the problem of the German-speaking Austrian minority in the South Tyrol. The two dictators hoped to solve this problem by a transfer of populations. Immediately after the occupation of Austria the Nazis had begun to persecute the Catholics in Austria, which added to the Pope's indignation over the persecution of the Church in Germany. Italian diplomats had managed to prevent some confiscation of Church property, but Pius XI was bitterly anti-Hitler. When he was told that Hitler was an art-lover and wanted to see the Vatican Museum he firmly ordered it to be closed for the whole of Hitler's stay in Rome, and he removed himself to the Papal Villa at Castel Gandolfo, staying there until the Führer had left. 3 May was the day of the Holy Cross, and on that day Pius XI said with considerable publicity that it was wrong that 'the banner of another cross [the swastika] should have been raised in Rome on that day'.[13]

King Victor Emmanuel also produced difficulties for Mussolini. Because of protocol Hitler had to stay with the King at the Quirinal Palace, but Victor Emmanuel was violently anti-Nazi and furious at having to entertain an ex-corporal who had assumed the birthright of his cousins the Hohenzollerns and Habsburgs. Also, Hitler's table manners were bad. Much to Hitler's annoyance, as soon as the King had finished eating his first course the footmen removed all the gold plates from the guests. Hitler – who liked spaghetti – was making slow progress with a delicious dish when it was whisked away from under his nose. The King also refused to give the fascist salute, but Hitler's main annoyance was when he had to travel in a four-horse carriage from the Terminus Station to the Palace. Hitler was happier when he left Rome for Naples and Florence, but to his intense irritation he was forced to wear a silk hat at the Naples Opera, which he knew always made him look ridiculous.

Mussolini and Hitler talked *à deux* in German without interpreters, so evidence is scanty about their conversation. Undoubtedly Hitler told Mussolini of his intentions in Czechoslovakia which Mussolini approved, and Mussolini agreed to initiate punitive measures against the Jews in Italy which he pursued with little zeal. However, beyond doubt the foundations of the military alliance were laid during their talks. According to Ciano, on 5 May 1938 in Naples Hitler made a definite proposal for a military alliance, although it was left hanging in the air by Mussolini's ambivalence. Much of any good done by the British-Italian Agreement on 14 April was undone during Hitler's visit to Italy.[14]

Hitler's visit to Rome came immediately after Daladier and Bonnet had visited London to seek an assurance from the British Government that Britain would come to the aid of Czechoslovakia in the event of a German attack. She refused out of hand; Mussolini and Hitler were well aware of this pusillanimous refusal, which may have been a factor in persuading Mussolini to take Hitler's side.

In London the French stressed their determination to honour their Treaty obligations to defend Czechoslovakia against Germany, and Daladier stated his belief that if the British Government now spoke firmly Hitler would climb down.

The British emphasized that under the Guarantee of March 1936 they
would come to the aid of France if she was attacked by Germany, but they
could not promise even two divisions for an expeditionary force, and they
refused the French suggestion for naval staff talks for fear of upsetting
Mussolini. Chamberlain said 'If Germany decides to destroy Czechoslovakia I do not see how this can be prevented.' Chamberlain added that he
would urge the Czechs to make concessions to Hitler. All that was decided
was that Britain should ask Hitler what he wanted. Two weeks later
Henderson told the German Foreign Office that Britain was supporting
Germany over Czechoslovakia – only to be rebuked by Halifax, who told
him that whatever he thought he must not let the impression be created that
'we and others [i.e. France] should sit by in all circumstances'.[15]

At the end of April Bonnet sent Leon Noel, former French Ambassador
to Prague,on a special mission to Czechoslovakia. His report was deeply
pessimistic, stating that Czechoslovakia, because of the various national
minorities in the country, was in the throes of disintegration.

Henlein came to London in May on Hitler's orders. The design was to
lull the British into believing that on behalf on his Sudeten Germans he was
genuinely trying for a compromise solution which would satisfy both Hitler
and Beneš. In fact he was Hitler's catspaw. Even Vansittart was taken in. He
described Henlein as 'far more reasonable and amenable than I had dared
to hope', and after his visit recorded: 'If the Germans will desist from
blocking tactics, we may really have turned a crucial corner in European
history.' Vansittart was soon cured of this illusion.[16]

At this stage Chamberlain believed Hitler could be appeased, and
genuinely felt the Sudeten Germans had had a raw deal. At party given by
Lady Astor on 15 May the Prime Minister told foreign correspondents off
the record that Czechoslovakia must give up territory, and that the new
boundaries should be guaranteed by a four-power pact. This was immediately published in Canadian and American newspapers, and Hitler felt the
British Prime Minister had given him a green light. By his 'four powers'
Chamberlain included Italy, not Russia. He was determined there should
be no military agreement between Russia and Britain.

However, the immediate repercussion was that Chamberlain became so
alarmed that he made it clearer than ever in public that he had made up his
mind to sacrifice Czechoslovakia.

On 22 May Halifax – now more resolute than Chamberlain – told
Herbert von Dirksen, the new German Ambassador in London (he had
replaced Ribbentrop on the latter's being made Foreign Minister) that
France would attack Germany if Hitler invaded Czechoslovakia, even after
'serious acts of provocation by the Czechs'. It would then be 'impossible to
see whether Britain would not be drawn into it [a European conflict.]'

Dirksen had already previously reported to Hitler that the Foreign Office attitude was that Britain would agree to the dismemberment of Czechoslovakia, but that if force was to be used they would definitely go to war alongside France.[17]

Henderson now began to exceed Halifax's instruction in his desire to appease Hitler. Halifax's statement of 22 May had received wide publicity in Germany, and on 28 May Henderson told Weizsäcker (Permanent Head of the German Foreign Office) that Halifax had been misunderstood, and that if the Czechs committed unbearable provocation Britain would 'leave them to their fate'. Ribbentrop was so angered by Halifax's statement that he asked Dirksen to try and get him to deny it. Halifax, to his credit, refused. Henderson was trying to pursue Chamberlain's policy in Berlin, rather than Halifax's, and was ignoring reports from the British Legation in Prague that Benes was trying to find a compromise with the Sudeten Germans under Henlein.

A leader in *The Times* inspired by 10 Downing Street on 3 June declared that the Germans of Czechoslovakia ought to be allowed by plebiscite or otherwise to decide their own future 'even if it means secession to Germany'. This, according to *The Times*, would mean rectification of the injustice of the Treaty of Versailles – which was now Chamberlain's policy. But the Sudeten Germans had not gone to the Czech lands because of the Treaty of Versailles. They went voluntarily into the Habsburg Empire from 1839 onward to find well-paid work in the coalfields and other developing industries.

Dawson in *The Times* was Chamberlain's mouthpiece, and Halifax was concerned when *The Times* published another leader advocating the partition of Czechoslovakia. He wrote on 15 June to Dawson that he was 'disturbed' by recent references in *The Times* to the desirability of a plebiscite in Sudetenland, and that Britain had already persuaded Beneš to make 'a really statesmanlike offer' to Henlein who was a 'moderate' and would prefer a 'settlement' to an Anschluss with Germany. Dawson was unrepentant in his reply, so sure was he of Chamberlain's conciliatory attitude to Hitler.[18]

On 30 May and 10 June 1938 Hitler issued Directives to his generals with the headline 'War on two fronts with main effort in South East' which stated that his immediate aim was the occupation of Czechoslovakia, and from 1 October he would make full use of every favourable political opportunity to realize it; 'It is my unalterable decision to smash Czechoslovakia by military action in the near future.' However, he qualified this by stating that he would only invade Czechoslovakia if he was sure (as in the case of the Rhineland and Austria) that Britain and France would not intervene. The German General Staff were nevertheless ordered to make full military plans for both *Fall Grün*, Operation Green (invasion of Czechoslovakia) and *Fall Rot*, Operation Red (defence of the West against Britain and France). Hitler also wrote: 'In all probability attempts by Russia to give Czechoslovakia military support, particularly with her airforce, are to be expected,' and it would probably consist of 'mere reinforcements of the Czech airforce and armaments or even penetration of East Prussia via the Baltic States'.[19]

Hitler's directives and the news of the probable Russian support for Czechoslovakia appalled many of the German generals, who knew Germany was not strong enough for a war on two fronts with Russian participation. Some generals with Weizsäcker plotted the overthrow of Hitler, and started discussions with former politicians of the Weimar Republic including Goerdeler, who had been Hitler's original Price Commissioner but had turned against the Nazis.

On 21 May Halifax received reports from Newton in Prague and Henderson in Berlin that German troops were concentrating on the Czech frontier. These turned out to be bluff to frighten Beneš into acceding to the demands of Henlein, the Sudetenland leader, but they resulted in Czechoslovakia calling up one class to the colours.

Halifax instructed Henderson to tell Ribbentrop that if in spite of His Majesty's Government's efforts

> a conflict arises, the German Government must be well aware of the dangers which such a development would involve. France has obligations to Czechoslovakia and will be compelled to intervene in virtue of her obligations if there is a German aggression on Czechoslovakia. Indeed, French Ministers have repeatedly stated to His Majesty's Government that France would certainly so act. In such circumstances His Majesty's Government could not guarantee that they would not be forced by circumstances to become involved also.[20]

This telegram when read by Henderson put Ribbentrop in a state of considerable excitement. Henderson reported that the German Foreign Minister was 'clearly perturbed', and 'declared if worst came to the worst, Germany would fight again as she did in 1914'. On the same day the French Ambassador in Berlin was instructed to warn the German Government of 'the extreme danger of using force which would probably compel France to come to the help of Czechoslovakia and mean that Great Britain would stand by France'. Phipps confirmed to Halifax that 'it seems certain' if German aggression takes place France will go to the help of Czechoslovakia'.

An even stronger warning was sent by Halifax on 22 May:

> 'Please convey following with all earnestness you can command as personal message from myself to Herr von Ribbentrop.

His Majesty's Government are exerting all possible influence at Prague for avoidance of further incidents and will continue to do so, and I earnestly hope Herr von Ribbentrop will do anything he can on his side to secure patience at this critical time. If resort is had to forcible measures, it is quite impossible for me or for him to foretell results that may follow, and I would beg him not to count upon this country being able to stand aside if from any precipitate action there should start European conflagration. Only those will benefit from such a catastrophe who wish to see destruction of European civilisation.

In any case prospects of understanding and cooperation between our two countries would be gravely jeopardised by any action that would appear to English opinion as wantonly destroying chances of peaceful settlement.

I fully approve way in which you have made official representations but it may perhaps help if you give this personal message on my behalf.[21]

Halifax's firmness had a salutary effect, and the German newspapers carried stories that both the British and French Governments were doing their best in Prague to bring about a peaceful solution.

Hitler had no intention of invading in May. He had created the Czech crisis to frighten Beneš, but national newspapers all over the world – including especially the London *News Chronicle* and *Daily Herald* – applauded Chamberlain for Britain's firmness, and Beneš for his partial mobilization. This made Hitler angry because it gave the world the impression that because of the fear of British and French reaction he had backed down; he felt humiliated, and determined to revenge this by an immediate triumph over Czechoslovakia.

On the same day Halifax told the French Government not to read too much into his warnings to Germany:

His Majesty's Government would of course always honour their pledge to come to the assistance of France if she were the victim of unprovoked aggression by Germany. In that event they would be bound to employ all the forces at their command.

If, however, the French Government were to assume that His Majesty's Government would at once take joint military action with them to preserve Czechoslovakia against German aggression, it is only fair to warn them that our statements do not warrant any such assumption.

In the view of His Majesty's Government the military situation is such that France and England, even with such assistance as might be expected from Russia, would not be in a position to prevent Germany over-running Czechoslovakia. The only result would be a European war, the outcome of which, so far as can be foreseen at this moment, would be at least doubtful.[22]

Chamberlain was trying to undermine the French guarantees to Czechoslovakia; he feared more than anything else that because of the Franco-Soviet Pact Britain might be drawn into a war against Germany on Russia's side. He still looked on the Nazis as a bulwark against Communism. (In a BBC 2

TV programme on Munich on 23 September 1988 Lord Hume said Chamberlain feared Russian intervention on the side of Czechoslovakia against Germany in 1938 would leave Eastern Europe 'wide open to Russian penetration.')

CHAPTER ELEVEN

MUNICH – HITLER'S
BIG BLUFF

'War in 1938 at the time of Munich was out of the question because there were only five fighting divisions and seven reserve divisions on the western fortifications which were nothing but a large construction site to hold out against one hundred French divisions.' (General Jodl in evidence at the Nuremberg Trials)

'In 1938 I had so few divisions on the western front that war would have been sheer "lunacy".' (General Wilhelm Adam, Commander of German troops on the Siegfried Line, in his memoirs).

IN JULY 1938 Hitler sent Fritz Wiedemann of his personal staff to London to see Chamberlain with a message that, if Britain induced Beneš to give in to the demands of the Sudeten Germans, Germany would not attack Czechoslovakia. Chamberlain gave 'certain assurances' about restraining the Czechs. Worried that the French might become involved in war with Germany because of their guarantee to Czechoslovakia and the Franco-Soviet Pact, he conceived the idea that he should send a British mediator to Prague to ensure that Beneš met German demands. He chose Lord Runciman, a former member of the MacDonald and Baldwin Cabinets, who he knew would faithfully carry out any instructions given to him. Neither the French nor the Czechs were asked to agree in advance. The French at first objected, with Daladier saying that such a mission would only encourage the Germans to make unreasonable demands, but faced with a *fait accompli* he agreed. Beneš also reluctantly consented. Had he not,

Chamberlain would have made great play with his refusal as an illustration of Czech unreasonableness.

In Paris Pertinax wrote in *L'Europe Nouvelle* that Runciman's mission was 'a nail in the coffin of the French Treaty with Czechoslovakia', and the influential foreign correspondent of the *Manchester Guardian*, Robert Dell, wrote in the *Statesman* 'Hitler has scored again, thanks to his faithful friend Neville Chamberlain. Lord Runciman has been sent to Prague to try to persuade the Czechs to commit national suicide.' Chamberlain misled the House of Commons on 26 July by saying incorrectly that Runciman had gone at the request of Beneš.

Runciman interpreted his role as being to force Beneš to kowtow to German demands for autonomy for Sudeten Germans within a sovereign Czechoslovakian state. Like Henderson, he was antipathetic to the Czechs. On 5 September he wrote to Halifax about Beneš 'Nothing can excuse his slow movements and dilatory negotiations of the past five months,' and he also wrote 'I have found troublesome fellows' among other Czech leaders and Ministers. Runciman was on a par with Henderson, who complained of Beneš, writing: 'The Czechs are a pig headed race and Beneš not the least pig headed amongst them . . . we shall have at long last to put down our feet very firmly and say to Beneš "you must".'[1]

As has already been seen. Beneš' position on paper was strong because he was backed by the Alliance for Mutual Defence with France of 1925, and the Alliance with Soviet Russia of 1935, but the latter only came into operation if France acted first. Unfortunately, the British attitude was steadily eroding the value of these treaties, and by September his only hope of preventing a German invasion appeared to lie in agreement with Henlein. The latter produced eight points at Karlsbad in April, which demanded recognition of the right of the Sudeten Germans to constitute themselves a totalitarian Nazi state within Czechoslovakia. Prodded by the British, Beneš was painfully moving to acceptance, and trying to bring public opinion with him towards this considerable breach of Czech sovereignty. On 5 September he offered the Germans his 'fourth plan' for the Sudetenland, which would have sacrificed much Czech sovereignty but preserved the integrity of the republic in order to satisfy Hitler and preserve peace. This would have satisfied the Sudeten Germans, but Hitler ordered Henlein to reject it out of hand, to the consternation of Britain and France. This marked the end of negotiations for a reasonable settlement of the grievances of the German minorities in Czechoslovakia, and from then on the situation changed because further negotiations with Sudeten Germans became abortive, with Hitler demanding dismemberment under the threat of war.

Ashton-Gwatkin wrote to the Foreign Office on 23 August after talking to Henlein 'I like him. He is, I am sure an absolutely honest fellow', and he described the eight Karlsbad points as 'quite unobjectionable'.[2]

In April 1938 Goerdeler had two secret meetings in London with Vansittart, who trusted him as a respected politician and a genuine opponent of Hitler. Unfortunately, Goerdeler at the first meeting suggested that the Sudetenland should be surrendered to a new anti-Nazi German Government, which displeased Vansittart. As a result Vansittart did not take Goerdeler seriously when at the next meeting he stated that the German generals were hostile to Hitler and were about to stage a revolt.

Goerdeler was correct, and it was unfortunate that this territorial demand antagonized Vansittart. Goerdeler's message to London was followed by one from a jounalist, Victor von Koerber, who contacted the British Military Attaché in Berlin (Mason-Macfarlane) on 6 August and said the Hitler regime could be overthrown and the only hope of averting catastrophe in Europe was by fostering revolution from outside; otherwise Hitler's troops would march in September. Koerber stated (correctly) that the German army was entirely unfit for war.[3]

Then Ian Colvin, the *News Chronicle* correspondent in Berlin, met Ewald von Kleist-Schmenzin, the conservative politician, who stated that the German General Staff wanted to prevent war but needed a 'sheet anchor' from outside if they were to restrain Hitler. In late July Colvin sent information to the British Government that military action against Czechoslovakia would begin on 28 September. Kleist went to London on 18 August as a secret emissary for the anti-Nazis on the German General Staff. General Beck (Chief of Staff) had told him 'Bring me certain proof that Britain will fight if Czechoslovakia is attacked and I will make an end of this regime.' The 'proofs' he wanted were a declaration of British support for Czechoslovakia and a military demonstration.

Vansittart reported to Halifax that he saw Kleist secretly (not at the Foreign Office) on 18 August. In his note of the conversation Vansittart revealed that he had already received from secret sources a great deal of other information which corroborated Kleist. According to the German generals, only Hitler and Ribbentrop wanted war over Czechoslovakia.

Kleist was surprised that Vansittart did not know the date which had been fixed by Hitler for the war (which was 28 September), and said Ribbentrop keeps on telling Hitler that when it comes to the showdown 'neither France nor England will do anything' and 'you must make him understand that this is not the case'.

Kleist went on that 'a great part of the country is sick of the present régime', and the army is 'dead against war'. 'I wish that one of your leading statesmen would make a speech which would appeal to this element in Germany emphasizing the horrors of war and the inevitably general catastrophe to which it would lead.' Vansittart emphasizd to him that a number of German moderates with whom he had been in touch during the past few weeks had made the same request for Britain and France to proclaim their intention to fight if Hitler invaded Czechoslovakia. Kleist added he had put 'a rope round his neck' by coming, and that 'if war was avoided it would be the prelude to the end of the régime and a renascence of a Germany with whom the world could deal'. Halifax sent Vansittart's report on to the Prime Minister, who ignored it and replied he had had similar information from another source and

> I take it that Kleist is violently anti-Hitler and is extremely anxious to stir up his friends in Germany to make an attempt at its overthrow. He reminds me of the Jacobites at the Court of France in King William's time, and I think we must discount a good deal of what he says.

Kleist also saw Churchill and told him that an attack on Czechoslovakia was imminent and would most likely occur between the Nuremberg Conference and the end of September; he repeated nobody in Germany wanted war except Hitler who still regarded the impression given that on 21 May he had ignominiously reversed his decision to attack Czechoslovakia as a personal rebuff 'whose recurrence he must avoid and whose memory he must obliterate'.[4]

On 18 August General Beck in protest against Hitler's aggressive policy resigned, and was succeeded by General Halder, an anti-Nazi who continued Beck's efforts to prevent war. (He survived the war, living till 1972, and was one of the few witnesses of the plots against Hitler to do so.) Halder sent Hans Böhm Tettelback to London to give similar messages to Vansittart as Kleist's. He only succeeded in sending them second-hand, and they produced no reaction.

Weizsäcker, the permanent head of the German Foreign Office, now conceived the idea of asking Theo Kordt of the German London Embassy to meet Chamberlain and Halifax in secret and give the same message as Kleist.

On the evening of 6 September Theodor Kordt called secretly on Sir Horace Wilson, Chamberlain's chief adviser, after making arrangements to be let into 10 Downing Street by the garden gate. Kordt gave a message that Hitler would invade Czechoslovakia on 19 or 20 September, and urged that Britain should send him the strongest possible warning. The next morning he gave the warning personally to Halifax.

On 7 September the Foreign Office received a message from the British Minister at Berne, Geoffrey Warner, of overwhelming importance. It recounted a long conversation with Karl Burckhardt, the League of Nations Commissioner for Danzig, and one of the most respcted international figures. Burckhardt had recently found Forster, the German Gauleiter in

Danzig, tremendously excited about 'the forthcoming German attack on Czechoslovakia' which he (Forster) described in 'extravagant terms', stating that Prague would be laid in ruins by attacks from 1,500 German bombers. Forster was also trying to remove gold from Danzig and compile a register for military service.

Much alarmed, Burckhardt went to Berlin where he saw Weiszäcker and repeated what Forster had said to him. Weiszäcker threw up his hands and said 'Unfortunately, these are the ideas of the Führer,' and that Hitler was completely under the influence of Ribbentrop and Himmler who wanted war. Weiszäcker said that General Beck had resigned because of Hitler's proposal to start a war, and that he himself had attempted to tell Hitler the truth, which had made his position 'shaky'. Admiral Horthy, Regent of Hungary, had tried to argue with Hitler, but the Führer screamed at him 'Nonsense! Shut up!' Weiszäcker told Burckhardt that the only method of bringing Hitler to see the truth would be a personal letter from the Prime Minister to Hitler, making it plain that if Germany attacked Czechoslovakia 'a war would start with Great Britain inevitably on the opposite side to Germany'. Weiszäcker said he could not possibly suggest this to Henderson, but he asked Burckhardt to act as an intermediary with the British Government, and stressed the extreme urgency and necessity that the letter should reach Hitler before the Nazi celebrations at Nuremberg.

Burckhardt learnt from Weiszäcker that Goering and all the other German Ministers and the General Staff including Keitel were opposed to an attack on Czechoslovakia. Burckhardt was so impressed with the gravity of Weiszäcker's pronouncement that he got in his car and drove 900 kilometres – some 550 miles – in one day to Berne to recount the conversation to Warner, who immediately transmitted it to London.[5]

Here was prima facie evidence of the opposition to Hitler and the importance of warning Hitler that if he attacked Cechoslovakia he would face war. A warning was prepared and sent to Henderson to give to Hitler before his speech at Nuremberg. Almost incredible to relate, Henderson refused to give the warning to Hitler because 'it will drive Herr Hitler straight off the deep end'. He had just made a strange request to Cadogan that *The Times*, Camrose, Beaverbrook Press, etc. should be persuaded to write up Hitler as 'the apostle of Peace'. Weakly Chamberlain and Halifax agreed that the 'warning' need not be given.[6]

Weiszäcker was correct in telling Burckhardt that the German generals were against Hitler, and determined to stop a war breaking out over Czechoslovakia. In mid-September Goerdeler, Witzleben and other high-ranking German army officers, including General Halder, met and concocted a plot to arrest Hitler and force him to resign. Witzleben, who commanded III Corps based on Berlin, agreed to head a raiding party which would go to the Reich Chancellery surrounded by high-ranking staff officers to demand Hitler's resignation. Some members of the conspiracy wanted to shoot the Führer out of hand; others wanted to arrest him and put him on trial. Units of Witzleben's Army Corps already in Berlin would occupy the capital and crush the expected resistance from the SS. Proclamations were ready, and plans made to occupy the radio stations.

Halder was to give the starting order as soon as Hitler ordered the attack on Czechoslovakia. They were waiting for the moment when war would become inevitable. Cadogan and Vansittart received rumours of the plot from Secret Service sources.[7]

On 12 September the Cabinet were informed of Plan Z. This was a solo mission by Chamberlain to Hitler; which Chamberlain hoped would result in not only an agreement on Czechoslovakia, but also a wide general understanding. As he had referred to Hitler as 'half mad', it was an odd decision and flouted the advice from Weiszäcker and Kordt which both Vansittart and Cadogan had told the Prime Minister was being confirmed secretly from impeccable anti-Nazi sources in Germany. Plan Z was enthusiastically endorsed by the Cabinet, and Chamberlain sent a message to Hitler inviting himself on 13 September for a visit by air the following day. Vansittart strongly opposed this tactic; Cadogan favoured the move; Halifax was ambivalent. At first Chamberlain considered Runciman might accompany him, but he abandoned this idea. Hitler invited the British Prime Minister to meet him at Berchtesgaden.[8]

Chamberlain had a good press for his departure to Germany; the country breathed a sigh of relief. Kordt summed it up in his message to Berlin: 'Until last evening the entire British population was sunk in deep depression . . . Now things had taken a completely unexpected turn which offered the hope of peaceful settlement . . . it is no exaggeration when the newspapers report that men and women weep for joy in the streets.'[9]

At Berchtesgaden Chamberlain expected to propose that Runciman should be the arbitrator between Beneš and Hitler, although Runciman said he would only undertake the assignment 'with great reluctance and as the last resort'. On the plane Horace Wilson warned the Prime Minister to be careful not to get into the position of negotiating on behalf of the Czechs. Chamberlain had told the Cabinet that he might most unwillingly have to guarantee the rump of Czechoslovakia. Such considerations were irrelevant because when Hitler met Chamberlain he was not in a negotiating mood. The British Prime Minister received a rude shock when Hitler abruptly refused to discuss a general settlement, but instead demanded an immediate solution of the Sudetenland question, saying 300 Sudeten Germans had just been killed; this was untrue.

Hitler went on that 3½ million Germans in Czechoslovakia must return to the Reich at once; otherwise he would go to war, and he continued with a long and irrational tirade which prompted Chamberlain to ask tartly why Hitler had agreed to him coming to Germany if he was determined on action, not negotiation. Hitler said he would only continue conversations if Chamberlain agreed to the secession of Sudetenland to Germany 'as a matter of principle'. Yielding to this demand was not the price of peace; it was the price of continuing negotiations. Chamberlain had no authority from the Cabinet to make such a commitment; he told Hitler that although personally he had no objection, he must consult the French Government and his colleagues.

Hitler then indulged in bluff, talking about 'the great military machine which Germany had built up' and which once in motion could not be stopped. In fact Hitler's army was too weak to fight in the east and the west simultaneously, but Chamberlain was badly briefed. Chamberlain returned to London, learning before he left Germany that Hitler's tale of 300 Sudeten Germans being killed was false.[10]

That evening, 16 September, the 'inner' Cabinet met at 10 Downing Street. This consisted of Chamberlain, Halifax, Simon and Hoare, together with Vansittart, Cadogan and Runciman. Runciman told them Beneš was dishonest and a prevaricator and Czechs and Germans could never live together, but he favoured a settlement on the basis of the Karlsbad demands and denunciation of the Czech–Soviet Treaty. This was not what Chamberlain wanted to hear because the Karlsbad demands meant preserving the Czech frontiers which had been established at Versailles, and which the British Prime Minister twenty-four hours before had told Hitler he personally was prepared to alter. Chamberlain, before Runciman's arrival, had told the Special Committee that 'the most convenient course' would be an announcement by Runciman that Sudeten Germans and Czechs could not possibly settle down together and that 'a plebiscite was the only way out'. The furthest Runciman would go was to say Czechs and Sudeten Germans could not live together happily unless someone 'who was not a local politician' assumed responsibility for law and order, and once you accepted the principle of self-determination there was no alternative to a plebiscite. This was no support at all for Chamberlain's plan to cede the Sudetenland to Germany.

To Chamberlain's irritation Runciman made it clear to the full Cabinet the next day, 17 September, that he considered there was no case for cession of the Sudetenland to Germany, and that the problem could be satisfactorily solved by an autonomous Sudetenland on the Swiss canton principle within the existing Czech frontiers. Duff Cooper's comment about this Cabinet meeting was: 'Runciman was quite unhelpful as he was unable to suggest any plan or policy. Runciman stated the two sides had been close to agreement, but it had failed because of the influence of Berlin.'[11]

However, Runciman told the Cabinet he was in favour of ceding the small areas of Cheb and Ax which lay outside the Czech frontier fortification, but that the Czech army would certainly oppose any (major) transfers of territory, and Dr Beneš had said they would rather fight than accept it. Runciman finished by telling the Cabinet he was in no position to put forward any further plan at the present time, and that a considerable percentage of people in the German area did not want to be incorporated in the Reich. He then left.

Hitler's bluff about the strength of his army was successful because Chamberlain told the Cabinet the German army was 'a terrible instrument' and he asked for agreement in principle to force Czechoslovakia to cede her frontier territory to Germany, including her fortifications. After Runciman's reservations agreement was not readily forthcoming. Hailsham, Duff Cooper, Stanley, Elliot and Winterton expressed dissent, and after three hours they adjourned without reaching a decision.

When the Cabinet reconvened after lunch Simon and Lord Chancellor Maugham strongly supported Chamberlain over ceding Sudetenland to Germany; this was echoed by MacDonald and Hoare, although they wanted some quid pro quo for Britain. Duff Cooper and De la Warr still strongly opposed cession. De la Warr had just returned from the League of Nations at Geneva, where he had been fortified by a talk with Litvinov who had convinced him Russia would come to the assistance of Czechoslovakia if France and Britain declared war on Germany. Halifax and the other Ministers gradually fell into line with Chamberlain, and the opponents of dismemberment of Czechoslovakia were outnumbered. By the time the Cabinet was over it was past 6 p.m. but Chamberlain went on to see the Labour leaders. Here he had a rough passage with Dalton, the Labour Foreign Affairs spokesman, who sharply disagreed about the usefulness of Soviet support if there was a war. In defence Chamberlain fell back on describing the 'weakness of France' and the 'appalling' state of the French Air Force. He had not expected Labour support, and as the Cabinet had approved his decision he did not anticipate much difficulty in bringing the nation along with him.[12]

On 18 September Daladier and Bonnet came to London. Daladier told the British that if Sudeten Germans exercised self-determination by means of a plebiscite other minorities (Polish and Hungarian) would claim the same right, and that 'Herr Hitler therefore regarded this principle as a weapon to disintegrate Czechoslovakia' (How true!). Unknown to Chamberlain and Daladier, Hitler was already encouraging the Poles and Hungarians to stake claims to parts of Czechoslovakia where they had a substantial population. Daladier continued

> in all honour and morality France had no right to regard her engagements as null and void. Any suggestions in the press that France was not prepared to meet her obligations could be 'ignored'. He did not think (and in this he was expressing the views of the French Government and the French people) that France could desert her ally. No Frenchman would be capable of committing such a crime . . . no Frenchman could avoid doing his duty.

This robust opposition to Hitler was far from Chamberlain's and Halifax's liking, and Halifax replied 'neither ourselves nor the French nor Soviets could give effective protection to the Czechs'. Daladier then said he regarded this less as a Czechoslovak problem than a general problem involving the peace of Europe, and if we accepted German demands 'we should have created a very serious precedent. Further German demands would follow in due course and Germany would conclude that we should give way.'

Chamberlain then produced a secret paper showing how German military preparations were being intensified since his visit to Berchtesgaden. Daladier in reply stressed France's treaty obligations and objected to the suggestion of a plebiscite which had been raised by the British. Eventually Daladier gave way and agreed to some cession of territory provided Britain agreed to join in a guarantee of Czechoslovakia's revised frontiers. Finally he proposed an International Commission to 'lay down a frontier to correspond with the ethnical frontier'. Halifax insisted it was impossible for the direction of British policy to be in the hands of another country; if a guarantee was to be given the Czechs must undertake to accept British advice on issues of peace, and if they did not accept, then Britain would be automatically absolved from their guarantee. Such a guarantee on such terms would be clearly bogus, and as will be seen, six months later Britain gave Poland a firm guarantee which committed Britain to war with Germany if Poland was attacked, and implicitly gave Poland the right to decide British policy on going to war or not. After a long adjournment Chamberlain announced that the British would give the Czechs the guarantee wanted by France without Halifax's reservations. Daladier before leaving London insisted that if the settlement fell through the Franco-Czech Treaty would come into force but 'the strongest pressure' would be brought on Beneš to accept.[13]

At these talks Chamberlain had committed Britain to a Czech guarantee without consulting his Cabinet colleagues. This was ill received in Cabinet; there was an acrimonious discussion, but the dissenting Ministers realized it was too late to renege without forcing Chamberlain's resignation, and reluctantly concurred. Chamberlain immediately sent a telegram to Hitler offering to resume discussions on 21 September. After procrastination and threats from London of abandoning the Czech cause notwithstanding an assurance of military support from Russia, the Czechs accepted the proposition. Their note of acceptance declared that they had been forced to yield by circumstances, and deeply regretted 'their proposal on arbitration had not been accepted; they accepted on the assumption that France and Britain would not permit a German invasion of Czechoslovak territory 'which will remain Czechoslovakian up to the moment when it will be possible to carry out its transfer after the determination of the new frontier by the International Commission'.

The Anglo-French plan for a plebiscite was that in addition to the joint guarantee Germany should agree to the 'mixed districts' being policed by the Czechs with numerous British observers, and only the almost entirely German districts should be occupied immediately by the German army, while a three-member International Commission should be set up under a British Chairman to 'decide' all issues of dispute between Germany and Czechoslovakia. The British decided not to ask Russia to participate in the guarantee, and considered the possibility of British troops or the British Legion policing the Sudeten areas pending their cession. This ran into too many difficulties and was abandoned.[14]

Before Chamberlain set off for Godesberg on 21 September (the venue chosen by Hitler) the Cabinet met. Chamberlain wanted Hitler to be allowed to send his troops into the German areas immediately. This was opposed by several members including Duff Cooper, who said he would prefer going to war if we abandoned the Sudeten Czechs and German Social Democrats 'to the tender mercies of the Nazis'. Hore-Belisha recorded in his diary 'We were all dead against any proposals to allow German troops to cross the frontier during the transitional period.'

At Godesberg on 22 September 1938 the Prime Minister (now accompanied by the German-speaking Kirkpatrick) received another shock because instead of trying to negotiate a settlement Hitler raised his demands and presented an ultimatum. It is strange that after this Chamberlain retained his faith in Hitler's sincerity. Chamberlain outlined the Anglo-French plan which France, Britain and Prague had accepted, and suggested that where there were 80 per cent Germans there should be immediate cession, but where there were only 65 per cent the International Commission should draw the frontier. He also suggested population exchanges, compensation for Czech Government property in the ceded areas, and German assumption of a share of the Czech public debt.

He was wasting his words. Hitler told him curtly 'I am sorry, but all that is no longer any use,' and because of the 'unstable' situation in Czechoslovakia 'the problem must be settled definitely and completely by 1

October at the latest'. Hitler went on that a line must be drawn along the 'language frontier'; the Czech army and police must be withdrawn behind the line, and the area would be immediately occupied by German troops and he would offer no compensation for Czech Government property because the inhabitants had paid for it by taxes. A sharp argument ensued. No agreement was in sight, and Chamberlain adjourned to his hotel, whence he reported to Halifax that he had had 'a most unsatisfactory interview' and ben unable to make Hitler understand that British and French public opinion would not accept such a solution.

With Chamberlain away on Friday, 22 September, the inner group under Halifax became more resolute and authorized a telegram to Chamberlain saying that public opinion was hardening against any more concessions to Hitler and that objections to Czech mobilization could not be sustained. Beneš was so informed, and the Czechs called up all men up to the age of forty.

Wilson demonstrated his dry sense of humour by saying in a phone conversation to London that the message from the Foreign Office about withdrawing the advice to Beneš not to mobilize 'had spoilt our lunch'.[15]

On 23 September a proposed morning meeting was cancelled. Instead Chamberlain sent a letter asking Hitler to put his demands in writing. The reply was received during the afternoon, and reaffirmed Hitler's determination to use force if it proved impossible to have the clear rights of the Germans in Czechoslovakia accepted by negotiation. In the late afternoon Chamberlain sent a note to Hitler: 'Since the acceptance of Your Excellency's proposal is now a matter for the Czechoslovak Government to decide, I do not see how I can perform any further service here.' But he was persuaded to stay another night when Hitler told him he would have a memorandum ready at 10.30 p.m. According to the *Daily Telegraph* reporter Hitler seemed extremely satisfied with Chamberlain's discomfiture and was seen to clap Ribbentrop on the back.

At 10.30 p.m. on 23 September the British delegation went to Hitler's hotel, where they were presented with a fresh memorandum. As soon as Henderson and Wilson read Hitler's document they told Chamberlain it was an outrageous document, demanding in peremptory terms that evacuation of Sudeten German areas by Czechoslovakian troops and police should start on Monday, 26 September (in two days time) and be completed a day or two later. Chamberlain at once said that if this was the nature of the memorandum there was nothing for him to do, and he half rose from his chair to leave. However, instead of leaving he reproached Hitler for having made no concessions despite all that he (Chamberlain) had done, and said the memorandum would have a deplorable effect throughout the world. It would have been better if he had left. When he drew Hitler's attention to the peremptory nature of the document Hitler replied that it was a 'memorandum', not an 'ultimatum', and offered to substitute the word 'proposals' for 'demands'.

Chamberlain said that 26 September was 'quite impracticable'. Then came news on the radio that Czechoslovakia had mobilized. Hitler became excited and said this 'settled' the whole affair, and the only solution was for the Germany army to seize the Sudetenland. The two heads of state wrangled through the interpreter, but finally Chamberlain weakened and asked if this was Hitler's 'last word' and said that provided Hitler 'would hold his hand' he would transmit the final proposal to Prague. Hitler then promised 'not to take action' while the negotiations were in progress, and in a token gesture of conciliation agreed to put back his date for the invasion from 26 September to 1 October, saying Chamberlain was one of the few, or the only man, to whom he had ever made a concession (conveniently forgetting his climb-down after the death of Dollfuss in Vienna in 1934). At Godesberg Chamberlain had not even succeeded in discussing the Anglo-French proposals; all he had accomplished was an apparent 72-hour postponement of the invasion. This was no concession at all because the German Generals had told Hitler they could not be ready for action before 1 October. On returning to his hotel at 1.55 a.m. on 24 September Chamberlain was deeply pessimistic, telling the *Daily Telegraph* reporter: 'You cannot call it a complete breakdown. I am submitting certain proposals to the Czech Government.'[16]

It looked like war. Public opinion had changed dramatically since Chamberlain's visit to Berchtesgaden. A Mass Observation opinion poll showed only 22 per cent in favour of Chamberlain's policy and 40 per cent against. There was a feeling of fatality; a war was being inexorably forced on Britain.

At midday on Saturday, 24 September, Chamberlain was back in London conferring with Halifax and his inner group. After reading Hitler's memorandum Cadogan wrote: 'Hitler's memo now in. It's awful . . . The P.M. is transmitting it to Prague. Thank God he hasn't yet recommended it for acceptance.' But Chamberlain's aim now was to sell Hitler's plan not only to his colleagues, but to Beneš. He told the Cabinet's inner group that as the principle of cession had been granted it was better to get it over as soon as possible; he thought he had established some degree of personal influence over Hitler, while he was also impressed by Hitler saying that if we got this issue out of the way without conflict if would be a turning-point in Anglo-German relations, and (amazingly) 'He was also satisfied that Herr Hitler would not go back on his word once he had given it.'

The inner group, which had been firm in Chamberlain's absence, with the Prime Minister present turned round in favour of capitulation.

According to Cadogan, Simon 'seeing which way the cat was jumping' made no objection, although for the previous forty-eight hours he had been 'as bellicose as the Duke of Plaza Toro'.

The full Cabinet was less compliant. Chamberlain told them he believed Hitler was speaking the truth when he said his policy was racial unity, not domination of Europe, and 'much depends on the answer to this question'. He thought he had now established an influence on Hitler and that the latter trusted him and was willing to work with him.'

Duff Cooper replied 'No confidence could be placed in Hitler's promise . . . He was certain Hitler would not stop at any frontier which might result from the proposed settlement . . . our right course was to order general mobilisation forthwith. He was sure the Czechs would fight.' Duff Cooper was supported by Winterton and Stanley. Faced with this dissent Chamberlain adjourned the Cabinet until the morning of Sunday, 25 September, without any decision being taken. Halifax supported Chamberlain on the evening of 24 September and Cadogan, horrified, set to work to make Halifax change his mind.[17]

When the Cabinet resumed on September 25 Inskip said significantly the latest Chiefs of Staff information showed that Germany had only a thin *couverture* on her western frontier. On 23 September Colonel W. Fraser, the British military attaché in Paris, had reported the most recent information from the French Ministry of War was that Hitler only had twenty-four divisions facing Czechoslovakia, and only nine divisions on the Siegfried Line. Fraser described this as 'a thin *couverture* by no means able to hold the French if they really mean business . . . the *couverture* in the west very thin because Hitler is convinced, in spite of all statements to the contrary, that the threat of his airforce is sufficient to keep the French and consequently ourselves quiet.' Fraser's report also stated that he had evidence from French military sources which led him to believe the French would not fight. This contradicted a statement made by Inskip to the Cabinet that the Chiefs of Staff appraisal was that the French General Staff was ready to fight. Chamberlain ignored the fact that French military intelligence believed Hitler to be in a weak bargaining position.

A heavy responsibility lies on the Chiefs of Staff for their failure to impress on the Prime Minister that military intelligence from the French proved Hitler was in a weak bargaining position.[18]

Halifax told the Cabinet that Eden had asked him for the terms to be rejected, and said that he himself after a sleepless night had changed his mind.

> What made him hesitate was that it might be held that there was a distinction in principle between orderly and disorderly transfer with all that implied for the minorities of the transferred areas . . . he could not rid his mind of the fact that

Herr Hitler had given us nothing and that he was dictating terms just as though he had a war but without having to fight . . . he did not feel it would be right to put pressure on the Czechs to accept. We should lay the case before them. If they rejected it he imagined that France would join in, and if France went in we should join them. His reflections through the night had provisionally led him to think that the present proposals involved a difference in principle, and that pointed tentatively to the conclusion that it would be very difficult to put any pressure on the Czechs . . . if we were driven to war the result might be to help to bring down the Nazi regime.

This showed that Halifax had taken seriously the messages about the German opposition.

Chamberlain, horrified, wrote a note to Halifax: 'Your complete change of mind is a horrible blow.' Halifax scribbled back: 'I hope you do not think I agree with Buck [de la Warr, the leading hawk] . . . but I do not feel entitled to coerce them into it.'[19]

On 25 September Hailsham was adamant that there should be no capitulation to Hitler, saying the

Prime Minister had told the Cabinet yesterday that he was satisfied of the good faith of Herr Hitler's assurances. The Prime Minister had seen Herr Hitler and was in a better position to judge than were his colleagues. Nevertheless, the Lord President continued, he felt that he could not trust Herr Hitler. He quoted in this connection a number of renunciations of territorial claims in Europe which had been made by the Führer or other representatives of the German Government, viz., on the 21st May, 1935, two months after the reintroduction of conscription in Germany Herr Hitler said –

"The German Government has broken away from the discriminatory articles of the Treaty, but it herewith solemnly declares that these measures relate exclusively to the points which involve moral and material discrimination against her people. It will therefore respect unconditionally the articles concerning the mutual relations of nations in other respects, *including the territorial provisions*, and will bring about the revisions inevitable in the course of time *only by the method of peaceful understandings.*"

On the 7th March, 1936, the day of the re-occupation of the Rhineland, Herr Hitler said –

"We have no territorial demands to make in Europe. We are aware, above all, that all the causes of tension which arise as a result either of faulty territorial provisions or of a disproportion between the size of populations and their living space; *cannot be solved by means of war in Europe.* At the same time we hope that human wisdom will help to mitigate the painful effects of these conditions and to remove causes of tension *by way of gradual evolutionary* development in peaceful collaboration."

Again, two pronouncements made on 11th and 12th March, 1938, after the Anschluss. On 11th March Field Marshal Goering assured M. Mastny, the Czechoslovak Minister in Berlin, that Germany had no hostile intentions against Czechoslovakia –

252

"I give you my word of honour", he said, "and I can add that we wish only for better relations".

. . . These undertakings had not been adhered to. He did not feel that we could trust Herr Hitler's declarations in future. The Germans differed from us in that to us a promise was a binding obligation, whereas to them it was a statement of intention.

He thought the right thing to do was to put the facts to the Czechoslovak Government, and if that Government rejected the German demands and France came to Czechoslovakia's assistance we should come to the help of France. No pressure, however, should be put upon Czechoslovakia to accept.[20]

Hailsham was Chamberlain's oldest Conservative friend and his longest-serving Cabinet colleague. This devastating indictment of his policy shook the Prime Minister, coming as it did immediately after Halifax's surprising volte-face. Winterton supported Hailsham and said that otherwise the Government would fall. Duff Cooper said great moral issues were at stake, there was not time to weigh out one's strength too carefully. He discounted Lindbergh who was an admirer of the Nazi regime and had declared the German air force was invincible, and went on: 'We should now tell the Czechs the terms are intolerable and if they refused the ultimatum we would stand by them, and we hoped the French would do the same. The future of Europe and democracy were at stake.' Oliver Stanley said 'War was horrible but it would be equally horrible in six months' time.'

Chamberlain, greatly disconcerted, summed up that we were essentially in the position outlined in his 24 March speech and in discussions with the French he would decline to say whether Britain would or would not declare war on Germany if Prague rejected the terms. His final words were that he was faced with a 'critical situation' and it was important that the Cabinet presented a 'united front'.

Prague categorically rejected Hitler's memorandum, saying in ringing tones: 'It is a de facto ultimatum of the sort usually presented to a vanquished nation and not a proposition to a sovereign state which has shown the greatest possible readiness to make sacrifices for the appeasement of Europe.' Chamberlain, without consulting Halifax, asked Kordt to let Hitler know that he must not think the Czech rejection was the last word, disregarding the fact that the Godesberg ultimatum had also been rejected by his own Cabinet.[21]

The Chiefs of Staff were on the Prime Minister's side. General Ironside declared it 'madness to expose ourselves to annihilation for the sake of the Czechs'. Air Marshal Sir John Slessor has recorded that at the time the Air Staff 'bore heavily in mind what was referred to as the "knockout blow" ' by which he meant catastrophic damage to London from German bombing. In fact the Germans had no bombers capable of reaching London with a full bomb load.[22]

On 25 September the French Cabinet unanimously decided to reject the German demands. By nine the following morning (26th) Daladier was in Downing Street. Daladier reported that the French Cabinet had rejected Hitler's memorandum and emphasized that Hitler's design was to destroy Czechoslovakia by force. Chamberlain tried in vain to persuade him that the German document was 'not too bad'. Daladier disagreed, and then Chamberlain asked whether France would declare war on Germany. Daladier 'implied this was so; he had asked one million Frenchmen to go to the frontier, and France would assist Czechoslovakia by drawing the greater part of the German army against France.' Simon, at Chamberlain's request, then cross-examined Daladier aggressively, asking: 'Was the French army contemplating the invasion of Germany? Would the French simply man the Maginot Line or take active measures? Would the French Air Force be used over Germany? Daladier replied: 'It would be ridiculous to mobilize French land forces to leave them under arms doing nothing, and equally ridiculous to do nothing in the air.' Around midnight it was agreed General Gamelin should come to London on the next day. Then the British adjourned to hold a Cabinet meeting at which Chamberlain proposed he should send Sir Horace Wilson with a letter to Hitler making a last appeal for a German, Czech and British Commission to handle the dispute, and if the letter failed to secure any response from Herr Hitler, Wilson should be authorized to give a personal message from the Prime Minister to the effect that if this appeal was refused France would go to war, and if that happened it seemed certain 'we' should be drawn in. The Cabinet agreed, and Daladier in the early hours of the morning endorsed such a letter.

That evening, 25 September, Halifax with surprising firmness authorized a Foreign Office press statement: 'A German attack upon Czechoslovakia would produce the immediate result of France coming to her assistance, and Great Britain will certainly stand by France.' Chamberlain was much put out, and reproached Halifax for not having submitted it to him before publication. Churchill claims he participated in its preparation.[23]

This was the high tide of Chamberlain's resistance to Hitler during the 1938 Czech crisis. At last an unequivocal commitment to support France if she went to war over Czechoslovakia had been given. This was exactly the commitment that France had sought in vain since the Anschluss. If Chamberlain had stuck to his guns Hitler would have been stopped dead in his tracks. He was too weak militarily to fight Czechoslovakia, Britain, France and Russia simultaneously, and he would have been humiliated by having to call off his campaign for the Sudetenland after so much bombast.

The next day Gamelin in London said in interviews with Chamberlain at 10 Downing Street and with the Defence Ministers and Chiefs of Staff in the Cabinet Offices that the French army would launch an attack in about five days after the outbreak of war, and their air force would attack German industrial targets; Germany and Czechoslovakia each had some 34 divisions facing each other, and the Czech army 'would give a good account of themselves'. (Gamelin exaggerated the number of German divisions both in the east and the west.) Gamelin added that France had 23 divisions on the western front against 8 German, and the Siegfried Line was far from complete, being 'improvised'. Gamelin also said he had 'no intention of sitting behind the Maginot Line waiting for a German offensive. It was his intention to advance immediately into Germany and to continue to advance until he met really serious opposition.'

Meanwhile Phipps discouragingly reported: 'War now would be most unpopular in France . . . all that is best in France is against war.' Cadogan immediately challenged this view, going so far as to give instructions that the British Consuls in France were to report direct to him to prevent the Embassy in Paris 'doctoring their messages'.

Harvey recorded in this diary on 24 September 'I have never seen anything like the defeatist stuff which Phipps is now sending us.' Phipps soon amended his views, writing: 'While there is no enthusiasm for war, people are resigned; while most of the workmen are said to be in favour of France complying with her obligations, many of them believing that help would be forthcoming from Soviet Russia,' and Cadogan minuted: 'these kaleidoscopic changes are too much for anyone as slow witted as myself.' The messages from the British consuls sent in cypher direct to the Foreign Office told a tale of a resolute nation determined to resist German aggression. Sir Ivo Mallet summed them up:

> There is little enthusiasm for war but a growing feeling that it is a question not of fighting for the Czechs but of engaging now in an otherwise inevitable struggle for the very life of France; resignation is the dominant feeling but coupled with one of determination, and the country is falling in solidly behind the Government now that they have made every possible effort to preserve peace.

Sargent agreed.[24]

Nevertheless, Phipps suggested in a message to the Prime Minister on the eve of Munich (28 September) that the only party in favour of war were the Communists, and the Socialists were divided, exactly what Chamberlain wanted to hear. Phipps's career in the Foreign Office came to an end sooner than it might have because these reports made such a bad impression on Cadogan.

Sir Horace Wilson's visit to Hitler was farcical, and should have alerted Chamberlain to the fact that they were dealing with a psychopath. The first message was:

> Very violent hour . . . In view of intense emotion and frequent references to tonight's speech it seemed better not to deliver special message (until the next morning) . . . he would not wait beyond 1 October for complete evacuation. At one stage he intimated that unless evacuation was agreed to by Wednesday afternoon occupation might begin before 1 October.

At the end of the telephone talk Jebb said to Wilson 'Good!' Wilson retorted 'Good is not the word to use.'[25]

The same afternoon 26 September, Wilson had difficulty in transmitting Chamberlain's letter to Hitler because the Führer first refused to listen and then interrupted, to 'vociferate in staccaco accents that the problem must be solved without further delay', making gestures and exclamations of disgust and impatience. When the interpreter read out the phrase 'the Czechoslovak Government . . . regard as wholly unacceptable the proposal' (Hitler's Godesberg Memorandum) Hitler tried to leave the room, muttering that it was no use talking further; the time for action had come. He would not talk sensibly, ejaculating that Germany was being treated like 'niggers' and 'On the 1st October I shall have Czechoslovakia where I want her. If France and England decided to strike, let them strike, I do not care a farthing,' and that Chamberlain might be out of office any day; he wanted action, not words; soon he would have 400,000 refugees from Czechoslovakia in Germany and he must have an affirmative reply by 2 p.m. on Wednesday. As Wilson was going to the door to leave Hitler started inveighing against the Czechs, saying that the Germans had intercepted telephone messages from Masaryk in London to Beneš stating Chamberlain could be overthrown, and abusing Chamberlain and Wilson in terms 'that could not be repeated in a drawing room'.

The next morning, 27 September, Wilson saw Hitler again and told him that Chamberlain had made a press statement saying he felt himself 'morally responsible' for the execution of the obligation which the Czechs had taken upon themselves. Finally Wilson in Civil Service language made clear the key part of Chamberlain's message, which was that if Germany attacked Czechoslovakia France would go to war with Germany and 'Great Britain must be obliged to support her'. Hitler became excited and said that probably in six days we should all be at war with another, and not for nothing had he spent 4½ billion marks on fortifications in the west. This was bluff.[26]

The inner group met as soon as Wilson got back to London on 27 September. Wilson said that morning Hitler had been 'quiet and cordial' and he thought Hitler had given sufficient assurances that this was the last of his territorial ambitions in Europe. Wilson suggested sending a telegram to Prague that the Czech Government should tacitly accept German occupation of the 'red areas' (those demanded by Hitler at Godsberg – i.e., total capitulation) because he thought this was very likely the last opportunity to avoid war. Chamberlain and the others agreed, and decided to call a Cabinet at 9.45 that evening to hear Wilson's account.

Chamberlain summoned Mason Macfarlane to this special committee in order to impress his colleagues with the futility of fighting. Macfarlane said

> 'Czech morale appeared to him poor. The customs frontier guards were obviously scared stiff. On the southern frontier opposite Vienna–Linz the Czechs appeared to him very ill prepared. On the northern frontier opposite Silesia was a piece of the Maginot Line . . . the French military attaché in Berlin was doubtful of the value of the resistance which the Czech army could put. He (Mason Macfarlane) thought it would be very rash to base any policy on the assumption that the Czechs would fight like tigers . . . there was much dislike of war in Germany but Colonel Macfarlane thought there would be more enthusiasm for war than seemed possible a month ago.'

Macfarlane had no business to talk authoritatively about the Czech army as his information was all based on a quick visit, not a detailed inspection. In letters to *The Times* after the war his deputy, General Strong, described the report as 'superficial'; while Brigadier Stronge wrote it was 'typical' of Mason Macfarlane's impulsiveness.' Although it was immediately contradicted by the British military attaché in Prague, the damage was done because it was what Chamberlain wanted to hear, and according to Telford Taylor it was seized on with avidity by those who did not want encouraging news but 'news which would justify capitulation'. In his diary Cadogan wrote: 'What does Mason Macfarlane know about it?'[27]

That evening in full Cabinet Duff Cooper threatened to resign rather than accept Wilson's suggestion. Halifax said there were much greater differences between the Franco-British proposals and the German memorandum than one of time and degree, and 'we could not press the Czechs to do what we believed to be wrong. Nor did he think the present suggestion [Wilson's, of capitulation] would be accepted by the Commons.' The Prime Minister summed up by saying that the Foreign Secretary had given powerful and perhaps convincing reasons against the adoption of Wilson's 'suggestion' and 'if that was the general view of his colleagues he was prepared to leave it at that'. The Cabinet recorded its decision 'not to proceed with the telegram to Prague'. Chamberlain had been overruled, but he refused 'to leave it at that', and behind his colleagues' back without consulting the French he wrote to Hitler at 11.30 a.m. on 28 September in another effort to find a formula for capitulation:

After reading your letter I feel certain that you can get all essentials without war and without delay.

I am ready to come to Berlin myself at once to discuss arangements for transfer with you and representatives of Czech Government, together with representatives of France and Italy if you desire.

I feel convinced we could reach agreement in a week. However much you distrust Prague Government's intentions, you cannot doubt power of British and French Governments to see that promises are carried out fairly and fully and forthwith. As you know I have stated publicly that we are prepared to undertake that they shall be so carried out.

I cannot believe that you will take responsibility of starting a world war which may end civilisation for the sake of a few days' delay in settling this long standing problem.

Simultaneously he wrote to Mussolini:

I have today addressed last appeal to Herr Hitler to abstain from force to settle Sudeten problem which I feel sure can be settled by a short discussion and will give him the essential territory, population and protection for both Sudetens and Czechs during transfer. I have offered myself to go at once to Berlin to discuss arrangements with German and Czech representatives and if the Chancellor desires, representatives also of Italy and France.

I trust Your Excellency will inform German Chancellor that you are willing to be represented and urge him to agree to my proposal which will keep all our peoples out of war. I have already guaranteed that Czech promises shall be carried out, and feel confident full agreement could be reached in a week.*[28]

Thus at the moment when the British Cabinet and the French were about to call Hitler's bluff, Chamberlain sold the pass. If Britain had stayed firm Hitler would either have been defeated in the field or the German generals would have overthrown him. Hitler had staked his reputation on occupying Czechoslovakia by 1 October, and failure would have left him vulnerable.

An influential backbench Conservative MP, Godfrey Nicholson, told the author that Neville Chamberlain was vain, and always thought his judgement superior to that of other people. He attributes this to an inferiority complex arising from jealousy at the favoured treatment given by his parents to his elder brother Austen. Austen had remained in England enjoying the privileges of a rich and influential family, while Neville was shipped off to manage a sisal plantation in the Bahamas, which failed. If this is true, it was a vanity that was disastrous for Europe in September 1938.[29]

On the afternoon of the same day (28 September) Chamberlain made a speech to the Commons describing his negotiations with Hitler, during which he claimed (incorrectly) that a letter he had received from Hitler that

---

*Chamberlain wrote to his sister that he sent these telegrams without consulting any of his colleagues.

morning contained 'reassuring statements'. During this speech a message was brought to him, and he told the House jubilantly that he, Daladier, Mussolini and Hitler would meet in Munich the next day. He was the hero of the hour, as the House dissolved in wild applause. This nation indulged in a hysterical celebration of relief that immediate war had been averted without counting the cost.

Chamberlain the next morning at Heston airport told the press 'It will be all right this time.' It certainly was all right for Hitler; he got everything he had asked for at Godesberg. Around midnight on 29 September the Munich Agreement giving the Czech fortifications and Sudetenland to Germany, and other parts of Czechoslovakia to Hungary and Poland, was signed. Hitler's troops were allowed to march in immediately to give Hitler the triumph he needed to seal his popularity at home.

In his letter to Hitler Chamberlain had said that arrangements would be discussed with the Czech representatives. This did not happen. Instead of Munich being a five-party conference as envisaged in Chamberlain's letters to Mussolini and Hitler, it became a four-power meeting with the Czechs (and Russians) excluded. Two Czechs came as observers attached to the British delegation. They arrived at Munich in the late afternoon while the conference was in progress. They were taken by the Gestapo from the airport to the Hotel Regina where the British delegation were staying, and forbidden to leave their room which was guarded. At 7 p.m. Ashton-Gwatkin, the British diplomat, had a short talk with them. At 10 p.m. after he had dined Sir Horace Wilson handed them a map which marked the areas of Czechoslovakia to be occupied immediately, and said this had British approval. When the Czechs demurred they were told 'If you do not accept you will have to settle your affairs with Germany direct.'

At the start of the Conference only Chamberlain and Horace Wilson represented Britain, but Henderson and Sir William Malkin (FO legal adviser) arrived later in the day. In a caustic note Wilson wrote 'organisation was very imperfect and there appeared to be no arrangements for the taking of notes. A Secretary General had been appointed, but he took no part in the Conference for the first four or five hours and was only one unit in the chaos which ruled for the last five hours.'

Mussolini produced a memorandum which had been drafted in the German Foreign Office, and to Chamberlain's and Wilson's 'relief' Daladier said he was prepared to accept this as a basis for discussion. With some minor amendments over ceding certain areas to Hungary and Poland the Mussolini memorandum became the Munich agreement. It read:

(1) Evacuation to begin on the 1st October.

(2) The Powers, England, France and Italy, agree that the evacuation of the territory shall be completed by the 10th October, without any existing installations

having been destroyed, and the Czech Government will be held responsible for carrying out the evacuation without damage as aforesaid.

(3) The conditions governing the evacuation shall be laid down in detail by an international committee, in which Germany, England, France, Italy and Czechoslovakia are represented.

(4) Doubtful territories will be occupied by international forces until the plebiscite has been completed. Under terms of the Memorandum, the conditions of the Saar Plebiscite shall be considered as the basis of the Plebiscite.

The final determination of the frontiers will be carried out by an international committee.

(5) The occupation, by stages, of the predominantly German territory by German troops will begin on the 1st October.[30]

Chamberlain suggested that damage done to 'installations' could be deducted from compensation due to Czechoslovakia from Germany. This produced an outburst from Hitler, who repeated his Godesberg protests about this property being built out of the proceeds of additional taxation levied on Sudeten Germans during the last twenty years, and he denied any compensation was due to the Czech Government. During the dinner recess the British prepared and sent into the Drafting Committee a short clause providing that financial and currency questions arising out of the transfer of the territory should be referred for settlement to a German-Czech Commission with a neutral chairman. Ribbentrop made it plain to Malkin that this was unacceptable, and the British draft was conveniently 'lost'. Chamberlain did take some sort of stand on this, emphasizing that a number of questions – property, currency, outstanding loans etc. – must be dealt with. Eventually it was covered by a Supplementary Declaration that all questions arising out of the transfer should come within the terms of reference of the International Commission – which as will be seen meant they were left to the whims of Hitler. All Chamberlain earned from this bargaining was a remark by Hitler:

> Daladier is a lawyer [incorrect] who understands the particulars and consequences. With him one can negotiate clearly and satisfactorily. But this Chamberlain is like a haggling shop-keeper who wrangles over every village and small detail; he is worse than the Czechs themselves. What has he lost in Bohemia? Nothing at all! . . . [Chamberlain was] an insignificant man whose dearest wish was to go fishing on a weekend. I know no weekend, and I don't fish![31]

Wilson noted that after very long delays due to 'inefficient organisation and lack of control' it was not until 2 a.m. that the Agreement was ready for signature, and not until 2.15 a.m. was the Prime Minister free to talk to the Czechs. Hitler apparently remained calm throughout the Conference except for the half-hour when he made his tirades about 'compensation and about the Czechs 'destroying existing installations'. The final sentence of Wilson's long note states that Russia 'at no time was mentioned'.

During his conversation with the Czechs Chamberlain yawned without ceasing. The Czechs were told to send a representative without fail to Berlin by 5 p.m. that day for the meeting of the International Commission which was to fix the details of the evacuation of the zone to be occupied. According to Masarick, one of the delegates, 'It was a sentence without right of appeal and without possibility of modification.' The Czech pilots who had been kept under guard at the airport were then freed to make arrangements for the flight back to Prague.

The next morning Hitler and Chamberlain met and signed an agreement that 'consultation should be the method adopted to deal with any other questions that may concern our two countries', and that the agreement signed last night and the Anglo-German Naval Agreement were 'symbolic of the desire of our two peoples never to go to war with one another again'. On his return to London Chamberlain had a tumultuous reception. He waved the bit of paper signed by him and Hitler, and said 'This is peace for our time.'[31]

Alec Home believes that the Prime Minister was persuaded by colleagues to make this last remark against his better judgement, and Home (who accompanied Chamberlain to the morning meeting with Hitler) says he did not himself attach much importance to the 'piece of paper' because Hitler had 'hardly glanced at it'.[32]

Chamberlain who six years before had brought about the downfall of the last non-Nazi German Chancellor by bullying him into resuming payment of reparations had kowtowed to a German Chancellor who was a despot, with a well-known record of brutality and false promises.

The treatment of the Czechs at Munich must have weighed on Chamberlain because he said to the Cabinet on 3 October he had suggested a Czech representative be present at Munich 'but it had been presented to him that the matter was too urgent to permit of the delay [the Czechs could not arrive until the afternoon] because Mussolini had to be back in Rome for a reception'. This was a lame excuse. The Prime Minister also said the guarantee to Czechoslovakia from Britain and France entered into operation 'at once'. This was untrue. He then argued at length that the Munich agreement was a vast improvement on the Godesberg demands and 'a triumph for diplomacy'. Duff Cooper – who had come expecting to offer his immediate resignation – said he would 'probably resign' but Chamberlain had given him grounds for thinking the Munich agreement was more of an improvement on Godesberg than he had previously recognized. After talking to Eden he decided that Chamberlain's arguments were specious, and resigned. In his own words he tried to persuade himself that the terms were good enough: 'I tried to swallow them but they stuck in my throat . . .

after accepting the humiliation of partition she should have been spared the ignominy of invasion'.[33]

★   ★   ★

It has been argued that Chamberlain bought a year at Munich, and that the year was well spent because British and French military strength caught up with Germany's. This view is unsustainable.

General Jodl at his trial at Nuremberg said that war in 1938 at the time of Munich 'was out of the question because there were only five German fighting divisions and seven reserve divisions on the western fortifications which were nothing but a large construction site to hold out against one hundred French divisions. That was militarily impossible.' Jodl explained that in April 1938 the German army had only one Panzer division properly equipped, and two other skeleton ones, and about twenty-eight other divisions ready, whereas a year later Germany had seventy-three divisions.

General Keitel in his evidence at Nuremberg said during the 1938 Czechoslovakian crisis 'We were extraordinarily happy that it had not come to a military operation because our means of attack against the frontier fortifications of Czechoslovakia were insufficient and the Czechs could have deployed an equal number of divisions to us!'

General Wilhelm Adam, commander of the German army on the French frontier, revealed in his memoirs that the troops under his command were completely inadequate to withstand a French invasion, and he considered a war with France and Britain in September 1938 was 'sheer lunacy'. He also revealed the poor state of the partly constructed Siegfried Line.[34]

There is no reason to doubt the truth of these statements. Thus apart from thwarting the plans of the German conspirators attempting to overthrow Hitler at Munich, the French and British threw away an opportunity to inflict a military defeat on Hitler which must have brought about his downfall.

If Gamelin had attacked he would have encountered only slight resistance and the French army could within a short time have occupied much of the Ruhr. Only by withdrawing a considerable number of divisions from the east could Hitler have held up the French, and in that case the German army would have had lost the opportunity of overrunning Czechoslovakia, thus allowing Russia time to come to her aid.

Unfortunately, Gamelin had told the British in London if he met really serious resistance 'he would then, if necessary, withdraw to the protection of the Maginot Line'. This sentence was a disaster because the British, perhaps misled by the interpreter, considered it meant that the French would withdraw to the Maginot Line in the event of any setback. There is no reason to believe Gamelin intended his remark to be received in this way, and he knew how weak were General Adam's troops opposite the Maginot Line. In any case, he could not have evacuated any large area of Germany which the French army had occupied in the initial assault without the permission of his Government. Harvey, who was present when Gamelin spoke, got the definite impression that Gamelin intended to launch attacks from the Maginot Line.

When Churchill went to Paris early in January 1939 after discussing Munich with everyone he wrote to his wife:

> They all confirm the fact that Germany had hardly any soldiers on the French frontier during the crisis. And Blum told me (secret) that he had it from Daladier that both Generals Gamelin and Georges were confident that they could have broken through the weak unfinished German line almost unguarded as it was by the fifteenth day at the latest and that if the Czechs could have held out only for that short fortnight the German armies would have had to go back to face invasion.

Litvinov had made Russia's intention to fight to save Czechoslovakia clear, telling a press conference in Moscow on 15 March that Russia would intervene in defence of Czechoslovakia. When asked 'How, without a common frontier?' he replied: 'Means would be found.' When it was suggested that this must involve 'creation of a corridor,' he assented, actually repeating the words. In a separate interview with the correspondent of *Le Temps* Litvinov again said 'Means would be found.'[35]

As early as 25 April the German Foreign Office had found out that the Russians had been discussing in Bucharest the question of the Romanian Government allowing Soviet troops rights of transit through the country to assist Czechoslovakia if Germany attacked.

The Germans feared Anglo-French co-operation in these talks. A report shortly afterwards was sent to Berlin by the German Minister in Romania that thirty-six Russian bombers were being flown to Czechoslovakia; and later confirmation of flights of Russian bombers to Prague over Romania. Soon after, the Germany Embassy in Warsaw reported that forty Soviet aircraft had been flown by Czech pilots to Prague, and twelve Czech pilots were waiting in Kiev for more aircraft.[36]

On 23 April Stalin had told the Czech Government that Russia would defend Czechoslovakia in concert with France, and on 12 May at Geneva Litvinov asked the French to try to obtain permission for Russian troops to cross Poland or Romania if they needed to defend Czechoslovakia. Litvinov reiterated his March declaration of Russia's intention to honour her obligations to France and Czechoslovakia at the League of Nations on 21 September. He said Russia intended to fulfil her obligations under the pact with France to assist Czechoslovakia 'by the ways open to her', and asked for immediate consultation between the Great Powers of Europe and the interested states to decide on the terms for a collective démarche.

Evidence that Russia had found the 'means' came from De la Warr on 15 September 1938:

> I saw Foreign Minister of Roumania this afternoon . . . he gave me to understand there was no definite agreement between Russia and Roumania but that, in case of war, supplies would probably pass through Roumania to Czechoslovakia and he thought there would be no difficulty in such a case in allowing transit, especially for aeroplanes. He stressed immense geographical difficulties which stood in the way of easy transit of men and materials across Northern Roumania. There were no convenient railways; a single line railway entailed some 500 miles of devious route to borders of Czechoslovakia . . . Russia's natural line of communication with Czechoslovakia lay through Poland and if the latter was willing to allow Russian aid to pass through her territory Romania could then march and if she did so, so could Yugoslavia.

The single-line railway from Russia to the Czechoslovakian border may have been slow, but it existed. The Russian army was mainly horse-drawn, and Romania could supply both unlimited fodder for the horses and plenty of remounts. This is evidence that the Little Entente would have aided Czechoslovakia. On 23 September further evidence of the Russian commitment to defend Czechoslovakia came when de la Warr and Butler met Litvinov and Maisky, in Geneva. The Russians confirmed that if France honoured her obligations to Czechoslovakia, Russia would fight on her side. Litvinov told the British delegates that he wanted conversations away from Geneva – preferably in Paris – with France, Britain and Romania and any other small power who could be considered reliable. Litvinov also confirmed that Russia had told Poland that if she attacked the Czech Teschen area the non-aggression pact between Poland and Russia would lapse.

In his memoirs Butler plays down the genuineness of these Russian intentions to intervene against Germany. The evidence of the British, French and German archives is against him. Telford Taylor describes Butler's account as 'absurdly tendentious'.[37]

Butler is contradicted point-blank by the memorandum of a surprisingly frank and friendly conversation between Marshal Voroshilov and General Doumenc (head of the French mission) after the break-down of the Anglo-French-Soviet military talks in Moscow on 22 August 1939. Voroshilov said: 'Last year when Czechoslovakia was threatened we waited for a sign from France. Our troops were ready; the sign was not given.'

The Special Cabinet Committee was told on 23 September that Litvinov had seen Boothby in Geneva and had told him that he had himself seen the Czechs two or three times in the previous week, and had affirmed to them each time that if they were attacked by Germany 'Russia would give them effective aid. Help in the air would certainly be given although it was more doubtful whether it could be given on land.' Litvinov also contemplated an appeal to the League of Nations, partly in order to assist in securing a passage for troops through Romania.

Evidence that Russia would be likely to be involved militarily only made Chamberlain more anxious to get Hitler's demands on Czechoslovakia accepted.[38]

On 12 September, when Halifax had suggested a four-power conference to solve the crisis which would include France, Germany, Britain and Italy, Vansittart warned

> it would be the thin end of the wedge for driving Russia out of Europe, and would be completely playing the German game . . . it is Germany, not Russia, that threatens the physical existence of this country . . . it would surely be unpardonable folly to assist Germany in driving off the map an associate we need.

Vansittart's view did not appeal to Chamberlain and Halifax.[39]

In their first report in September as the Czech crisis began, the Chiefs of Staff misled the Cabinet: 'In our opinion Germany will be able to spare adequate forces to hold her fortified line in the west against attack,' and 'the most we could provide would be two divisions inadequately equipped'. They also argued against bombing attacks on Germany because of the fear of 'immediate reprisal action on the part of Germany' when our defence measures are very far from complete. However, on 24 September the Chiefs of Staff reported that although they had always assumed the Germans would occupy the Siegfried Line in sufficient strength to balance the French army, 'Our latest information is that the Germans at present have only eight or nine divisions on their Western Frontier.' This intelligence should have been immediately spotlighted to the Cabinet; instead Inskip made his half-hearted intervention on 25 September. Hailsham was probably influenced by it, since he had close connections with the War Office as their former Secretary of State. The Chiefs of Staff did the Government a grave disservice by first misleading them about Germany's strength in the west and then failing to emphasize the importance of the later news about the weakness of Adam's forces.[40]

There can be no doubt that the year's delay of the outbreak of war helped Germany and not Britain. The occupation of the Sudetenland made possible by the Munich agreement gave Germany a present of 1½ million rifles, 750 aircraft, around 600 tanks, and over 2,000 field guns. Czech guns and tanks were superior Germany's, and it has been estimated that every third tank used in the 1940 invasion of France and the Low Countries was Czech-built. The arms production of the Skoda works at Pilzen between August 1938 and September 1939 was almost equal to the whole British weapons output.

Churchill has summed it up correctly: 'the year's breathing space said to be "gained" by Munich left Britain and France in a much worse position compared to Hitler's Germany than they had been at the Munich crisis'. Churchill went on that the alteration in the relative strength of the French and German armies was 'disastrous', and 'the Skoda works – which instead of making arms for the Allies was manufacturing them for Germany – produced in the twelve months between August 1938 and September 1939 as much as the total output of British factories, and although we gained time to build Spitfires and Hurricanes to fight the Battle of Britain, without that year Hitler's ground forces might not have been strong enough to conquer the airfields from which he fought the battle'.[41]

Undoubtedly the French were nervous and irresolute. However, at the start of the crisis they took military precautions; on 4 September troops' leave was stopped, and the next day reservists and men on leave were recalled to man the Maginot Line. Frightened of having to fight alone, France was awaiting a firm lead from Britain, and this she never got.

Shortly after the end of the war General Halder on 1 July 1945 told United States Intelligence interrogators: 'With the Munich Agreement the psychological moment for the elimination of Hitler had passed, never to return. Never has a nation been more betrayed than the Czechs by the British at Munich.' Halder went on that the Czech fortifications along her frontier with Germany were extremely well built, modern and unsurpassed in effectiveness, while 'in addition she possessed a well trained and well equipped army of some thirty-five divisions,' and Hitler could only deploy against Czechoslovakia in September 1938 a total strength of twenty-one divisions with no more than two Panzer divisions, so that 'all German commanders reported unfavourably on the prospects of war, including von Rundstedt':

> The German Generals, convinced that war would be catastrophic, decided to act to prevent what they felt would be inevitable catastrophe by removing Hitler. The leaders of the conspiracy were Halder himself, Witzleben, General Beck, Helldorf (Halder's own predecessor) Police President of Berlin Graf Brockdorf, and Head of the Potsdam garrison Stülpnagel. Von Brauchitsch was informed, and if the conspiracy had taken its course Hitler would have ceased to rule on 14 or 15 September.[42]

Halder as Chief of Staff arranged for a Panzer division to be moved into Berlin ostensibly as part of normal operations, and when this division arrived in Berlin he placed it temporarily under command of Witzleben, which as a routine matter did not arouse suspicion. Witzleben had in addition a number of garrison troops of his own, while Helldorf was confident about the conduct of the police. The plan was to arrest Hitler, not to kill him. Halder said: 'I am opposed to political murder.' Then the generals were to lay the full facts before the German people and say: 'Here is the man who wants to lead us into war, which, in the opinion of all of us, could only lead the nation into catastrophe.'

According to Halder, the general trend of public opinion in Germany was very favourable to such a move, as the idea of war filled everyone with horror and the feeling about Hitler's genius in the political and diplomatic field only emerged *after* Munich. Halder claimed that if Hitler had left Nuremberg direct for Berlin on 12 September he would have been arrested by the generals on the night of 12 September or the morning of 13 September. Instead he went to Berchtesgaden, where they could not reach him. But on Wednesday 14 September, Halder decided to strike, because Hitler was back in Berlin, and he went confidently to Witzleben's office. Everything was in readiness; only the final signal was required, and they were ready to give it. Then as Halder and Witzleben were sitting together came the news Chamberlain was flying to see Hitler.

Hitler immediately left Berlin and flew back to Berchtesgaden; thus he escaped their clutches. Halder told his interrogators: 'This extraordinary coincidence between the imminent execution of this operation and Chamberlain's plan may sound extremely theatrical, but it is true. If Chamberlain had postponed his visit, or rather the announcement of the visit by only a day, Hitler would have been deposed and the subsequent war prevented. But it was God's will, and God's ways are inscrutable.' In addition Halder claimed that Hitler successfully bluffed Chamberlain about the strength of the German army and airforce.

The Foreign Office reaction to Halder's interrogation is shaming. Christopher Steel, later British Ambassador in Bonn and at the time political adviser at British Military Headquarters in Berlin, wrote to London on 11 August 1945 that the first three pages of the Report 'strike me as being very dangerous . . . Halder therefore claims that Germany was really in no position to attack Czechoslovakia at the time of the Munich crisis which was an enormous and wholly undeserved triumph for Hitler's methods of bluff.'

Other Foreign Office minutes betray alarm at Halder's disclosures. It caught them in a sensitive area because as they pointed out after Munich Kirkpatrick had written 'Hitler told us at Godesberg that he could mobilise ninety odd divisions and there was no reason to believe this was incorrect.' Cresswell minuted on the US Report 'All the German Generals . . . spend most of their time white washing themselves and one another to deceive the (as they think) credulous eyes of posterity.'

Michael Vyvyan wrote that the 'best thing to aim at would be to discredit Halder in the course of an interrogation of our own.' Con O'Neill (who had been at the Embassy in Berlin at the time of Munich) was better informed, and wrote: 'I really do not think we can complain about the first allegation relating to the Munich crisis. After all, though no doubt Mr. Steel would think it unlikely, it may have some truth in it . . . I suggest we do nothing but wait and see.'

Another minute was: 'I can imagine nothing more unwise than any attempt to rig a statement on Halder to justify our part in Munich,' and 'many people who should know have always held the view . . . that it would have been to our military advantage to make war at the time of Munich'.

One Foreign Office official wrote: 'It is quite likely that the same type of mischievous evidence will crop up in the course of the war crimes demonstrations unless the mouths of the witnesses are closed by OGPU-Gestapo methods of court management.' The story was leaked to the *Daily Worker*. Kingsley Martin on 22 September wrote in the influential weekly *Statesman and Nation* that he knew throughout the Munich crisis that Goerdeler was desperately trying to get a message through to Chamberlain to the effect that the anti-Hitler coup would be made 'if only Chamberlain stated unequivocally his intention to fight'.[43]

Halder also stated that in response to clandestine peace overtures from anti-Nazis through Switzerland and the Vatican in the winter of 1939–40 Halifax promised Goerdeler, Hassell, Beck and Witzleben that Britain would agree to a non-Nazi German Government keeping Austria, Sudetenland, Danzig and the Corridor. This was true, but the Foreign Office did not want it known.

When Michael Foot put a question in the House of Commons to the Prime Minister (Attlee) the Foreign Office brief for the reply was 'The full statement by Halder is a mischievous document.'[44]

After the Nuremberg Trials of the major war criminals the British withdrew from further punitive legal proceedings, but the USA persisted, with American judges. In 1947 Weiszäcker was prosecuted before an American court, and he requested the British Foreign Office to provide him with statements in his defence about his activities against Hitler in 1938 and 1939. British diplomats were advised to keep quiet, and Vansittart and Cadogan who knew all about Weizsäcker's approaches to Britain refused to help. Only Lord Halifax gave a helpful affidavit, and Weizsäcker was convicted by a majority of two to one by three judges. Evidence from Cadogan and Vansittart about what had happened must have produced a different verdict. It is hard to justify their silence.

Vansittart wrote: 'I can recall nothing that made me believe that Baron von Weizsäcker used his official position to hinder these calamitous courses. To the best of my recollection he was never mentioned or reported to me as being a convinced and active opponent of Nazi policy.'[45]

A. J. P. Taylor has written: 'The settlement at Munich was a triumph for British policy', but as he wrote on the preceding page that Chamberlain 'destroyed' the case for his own policy by speeding rearmament after Munich, he cannot have been serious, and in any case he did not have access to the Cabinet discussions and the Foreign Office files.

The archives reveal Munich was a disaster, because Hitler completely bluffed Neville Chamberlain over German military potential. If the British and French had declared war on Germany in October 1938 Russia would have joined them, and the result must have been an ignominious defeat for Germany, whereupon the dissident German generals and the opposition politicians would have had little difficulty in overthrowing the Nazi regime in the hour of Hitler's humiliation and the unpopularity of a disastrous war.[46]

If Chamberlain had been content to abide by the Cabinet's decision of 27 September – to stand firm, as he told his colleagues he would – Hitler's bluff would have been called and the history of Europe different. A year later Russia was on Hitler's side, the Czech arms and fortifications in German hands, and Hitler's armed forces much stronger compared to the British and French.

★　　★　　★

Munich was debated in the Commons on 3, 4 and 5 October. Chamberlain had an easy passage because of the relief from the immediate threat of war. Opinion polls at first showed a large majority in favour of the Munich settlement, although its popularity declined fast.

The Opposition put down a motion censuring the Government for the harsh terms imposed on Czechoslovakia by the settlement, and Chamberlain devoted the greater part of his speech to claiming (as he had to the Cabinet) that Munich was a great improvement on Hitler's Godesberg demands. Duff Cooper missed the mood of the House in his resignation speech in which he said: 'We have taken away the defences of Czechoslovakia in the same breath as we have guaranteed them, as though you were to deal a man a mortal blow and at the same time insure his life.' Chamberlain, speaking immediately after Cooper, said the real triumph of Munich was that it showed 'representatives of four great powers can find it possible to agree on a way of carrying out a difficult and delicate operation by discussion instead of by force of arms, and thereby they have averted a catastrophe which would have ended civilization as we have known it . . . I feel it may be possible to make further progress along the road to sanity.' He spoilt the effect by saying, in winding up the debate, 'war is coming, broadly speaking the democracies against the totalitarian states – that certainly we must arm ourselves to the teeth.' If Munich was the 'triumph' he made it out to be rearming should have become something less of a major priority.

Chamberlain emphasized the differences between the unacceptable terms of Godesberg and Munich by claiming that Munich allowed the Czechs up to 10 October for evacuation, with the line fixed by an International Commission, not just by Hitler's demands as in the Godesberg Document, and 'on the difference between the Godesberg Document and the Munich Agreement will depend the judgement as to whether we were successful'.

Both the Berchtesgaden and Munich documents were printed as White Papers. The White Paper on Munich published on 28 September included a letter dated 21 September from Runciman to the Prime Minister which proposed the cession to Germany of frontier districts 'with an important German minority'. It became known as the Runciman Report, and contradicted the advice given by Runciman to the Special Committee and the full Cabinet on 16 and 17 September. It was used effectively by the Prime Minister in the Commons on 29 September to give the impression that Runciman had on his return from Prague advised immediate cession.[47]

In fact the Runciman Report was 'rigged'.* On 20 September Runciman sent a letter to Chamberlain beginning in his own handwriting 'My dear Prime Minister.' On Chamberlain's instructions, and with Runciman's agreement, this letter was doctored to become the Runciman Report. Pages 1 to 4 of the letter are identical with the White Paper, but the original page 5 is removed from the Foreign Office archive. It obviously contained proposals in line with Runciman's earlier statements to the Special Committee and full Cabinet.

In place of the missing page 5 in the Foreign Office archives there are five typewritten pages on the characteristic blue Foreign Office minute paper corrected in Ashton-Gwatkin's handwriting criticizing the behaviour of the Czechs, and advocating immediate cession to Germany of frontier districts 'with an important German minority'. The doctored version was good ammunition for Chamberlain over ceding Sudetenland to Germany.[48]

As Runciman agreed to Chamberlain's suggestion of allowing his letter to be rewritten, the Prime Minister was perhaps justified. However, it was unethical of the Prime Minister to say in the Commons on 29 September that on 16 September Runciman had told the Cabinet that the frontier districts must be ceded to Germany. Chamberlain not only falsified the date

---

*The Germans intercepted a call from Masaryk in London to Beneš in Prague on 23 September, in which the Czech Ambassador said 'The old Lord (Runciman) had rung me up and said "he had been slighted in the most shameful manner".'

of this full Cabinet, but he prevaricated because no such advice was given by Runciman until he was put under pressure later by the Prime Minister.

Sir Ivo Mallet (then in charge of the German desk at the Foreign Office) wrote to the author that after fifty years he could not remember the details of this episode but it was typical of the lengths to which Chamberlain would go to make sure the Cabinet and Parliament accepted his policy of the immediate cession of the Sudetenland to Germany; Mallet also wrote he felt if Runciman was agreeable it was not unethical for Chamberlain to instruct Ashton-Gwatkin to tamper with the Report.

Runciman, who was sixty-seven, was very tired when he returned from Prague. Harvey (then private secretary to Halifax) has described him as having been brought in 'to help the Government to do the dirty work' and Runciman told Harvey 'I feel I must do everything to make the P.M.'s position easier.' Harvey commented 'Runciman is quite broken down and is now rather pathetic.'

Keen as Runciman might have been to solve Chamberlain's problems, it reflects no credit on him that at the Prime Minister's request he reversed his considered opinion on the key question of whether cession was inevitable or not. Shortly afterwards Runciman was undeservedly rewarded by being given a place in the Cabinet again as Lord President of the Council when Hailsham resigned at the end of October. It would be bad taste to speculate if this appointment was reward for pandering to Chamberlain over the all-important Report on Czechoslovakia. On 31 October Dorothy Thompson (Mrs Sinclair Lewis) wrote in the *New York Herald Tribune* that the Runciman Report which had been published in the British White Paper on 28 September had been 'rigged' because there was a contradiction between his first part which argued – as did his final statement in Prague – that a solution could be found to the Sudeten dispute by autonomy within the existing Czech frontier, but 'suddenly on the basis of nothing contained in the first part of the report recommendations are made which embody in substance the Anglo-French proposals presented to the Czechoslovak Government on 19 September after Chamberlain's visit to Hitler,' and showing Runciman as in favour of immediate cession of the frontier districts to Germany.

The British Embassy in Washington wrote to the Foreign Office that they were 'particularly concerned' because of the *New York Herald Tribune*'s allegations and that 'surely there was a break or hiatus in the Report'. It is inconceivable that Mrs Sinclair Lewis could have told from the style of the White Paper that Runciman's original letter had been altered. Clearly someone had 'marked her card'. Perhaps it was Duff Cooper, but more likely it was some Foreign Office official whose identity now can never be discovered.

Ashton-Gwatkin, interviewed by a Germany historian in May 1971, remembered Runciman telling him 'as guidance' that he wanted to back up Chamberlain's policy, but afterwards he 'seems to have regretted the degree to which he had become identified with Chamberlain'.[49]

In the Commons debate upon Munich starting on 2 October and the White Papers Dalton spoke forcibly about the Government cold-shouldering the Russians, and Attlee said it was victory for 'brute force'. But the knife was put in by Eden, who in an otherwise moderate speech pointed out that the maps attached to the White Papers were 'deceptive', and that although there was 'a very much smaller area on the Munich map than the Godesberg map, the Munich map did not contain the fifth area to be occupied before 10 October, nor the plebiscite areas'. This was indisputable, and the Government did not attempt to reply. Churchill, who had wished Chamberlain godspeed when the Munich meeting had been announced in the Commons, said: 'We have suffered a total and unmitigated defeat . . . the utmost he (Chamberlain) has been able to gain for Czechoslovakia . . . has been that the German dictator instead of snatching his victuals from the table has been content to have them served to him course by course . . . this is only the first sip, the first taste of a bitter cup.' Churchill also said, with good reason, that 'the system of alliances upon which France had relied for her safety had been swept away and could not by reconstituted', and that 'we would bitterly regret the loss of the Czech fortress army which would have required thirty German divisions for its destruction'. In the ensuing division 31 Government supporters abstained; 13 of them remained ostentatiously seated, including Churchill, Duncan Sandys and Harold Nicolson. Eden, Amery and Harold Macmillan abstained but rose from their seats.

Although Chamberlain staked his reputation in the Commons on his argument that Munich was a much better settlement than Hitler's Godesberg demand, it soon became apparent this was untrue, and that Czechoslovakia was broken strategically and economically. She had lost the Skoda arms factory (almost the biggest in Europe), her main coal-mines, and her railway system was disrupted; she had no choice but to become a satellite of Germany.

In November a devastating pamphlet (written by Professor R. W. Seton-Watson, and published at his own expense for circulation to all MPs and selected peers) demolished Chamberlain's case with unassailable arguments why the 'much vaunted Munich agreement' hardly differed from the Godesberg proposals which the Prime Minister had rejected indignantly as 'unacceptable', and as 'an ultimatum rather than a memorandum'. Seton-Watson, ackowledged to be the leading British academic expert on Central Europe, had kept in close touch with Masaryk throughout the crisis in

London and had considerable political influence because he was friendly and in close touch with Cecil, Lytton, Lord Lloyd, Eden on the Government side, and with Dalton, Sir Geoffrey Mander, and Philip Noel-Baker among the Opposition. He was also in contact with Leo Amery.

The pamphlet stated that the Czechs had argued that a short time-limit for evacuation of their fortifications would lay bare their inner secrets to the Germans, and as these were modelled on the Maginot Line it would cause immense damage to the French; it pointed out the only difference between Godesberg and Munich was that the former insisted on German occupation in one operation by 1 October, while Munich provided for five clearly defined stages between 1 October and 10 October; and that in the event Czechoslovakia had been forced to surrender her vital defences before the future frontier had been defined by the International Commission. It also showed how the International Commission – which had been down-graded into an 'Ambassadors' Conference' in Berlin – had assigned to Germany predominantly or purely Czech areas in excess of the areas demanded by Hitler at Godesberg. The Professor claimed that the Berlin Commission (Ambassadors' Conference) in fixing the Fifth Zone – about whose size Eden had complained in the Commons – had entirely disregarded the principle of ceding only districts with over 50 per cent of Germans. She had ceded some almost purely Czech areas as compensation for the German enclaves or minorities in the 50 per cent German districts already ceded. He commented: 'In view of the Führer's assurance to Chamberlain that he had no wish to include in the Reich people of other races than Germans, it is not clear on what principle the Commission acted, unless economic and strategic interests of Germany were allowed to override Czech national interests, and Germany was acquiring territory containing 2,806,000 Germans and 719,000 Czechs, while in the Czech Republic there remained 6,500,000 Czechs and 250,000 Germans.'

Seton-Watson also pointed out that any improvements claimed by Munich in the Fifth Zone were wiped out when the plebiscite was abandoned, and definition of German areas was left to the Berlin Commission; while Mr Chamberlain had laid stress on Munich rectifying the prohibition on removal of 'foodstuffs, cattle or raw materials' only two days elapsed between the announcement of the Fifth Zone and its actual occupation by German troops, and thus the population was taken by surprise.

About the guarantee Seton-Watson was scathing. In the Commons Chamberlain had stressed that the new system of guarantees was likely to give Czechoslovakia 'a greater security than she has ever enjoyed in the past'. Now, the Professor argued

If we could not help Czechoslovakia when she possessed a splendidly equipped and disciplined army, almost impregnable defences and firm alliances, it may well be asked how we can hope to help her now that she is almost utterly defenceless and robbed of economic resources ... The Minister of Defence was right in announcing that the Government felt 'under a moral obligation to treat the guarantee as being now in force . . . but how the Prime Minister hopes to make this moral guarantee effective in case of further aggression is more easily asked than answered'.

Lord Lytton, a friend of Seton-Watson's, forwarded a copy of the memorandum to Halifax and asked him if Seton-Watson's statements were 'true'. Malkin, the Foreign Office legal adviser, minuted: 'On the whole the Professor's memorandum is a criticism of the settlement which in detail would be difficult to refute and I would not advise that the attempt be made.' Cadogan on behalf of Halifax replied to Lytton admitting the 'general accuracy' of the Professor's facts, but remarking that Seton-Watson had taken no account of what were the alternatives to the proposals accepted at Munich. Thus Halifax was denying Chamberlain's argument that Munich was more favourable than Godesberg.

Lytton replied to Halifax:

The thing that distresses me most is that after the Prime Minister made so great an effort at Munich to prevent the Sudeten German grievance being converted into an injustice to Czechoslovakia, and after he had been so confident that he had prevented the worst features of the Godesberg ultimatum, everything should have been given away.

Lytton's view became more and more prevalent in informed circles as information leaked out about what was happening in the evacuated parts of Czechoslovakia.

The final sentence of Lytton's letter to Halifax said that the International Commission sat in Berlin and conceded every German demand whether they were just and defensible or not; 'I cannot help feeling very bitter about this, I am afraid.'[50]

The guarantee question was soon answered. On 8 December a letter from Halifax to Newton stated that the Czech guarantee against unprovoked aggression would only come into operation when three out of the four powers (Italy, France, Germany and Britain) were prepared to implement it. As there was no possibility of Mussolini making war on Hitler over seizure of the rump of Czechoslovakia, no more bogus guarantee in history has ever been offered. In Cabinet Halifax claimed that the French had argued a guarantee, which could not operate if Germany attacked Czechoslovakia and Italy stood aside, and which did not fulfil the offer made in the Anglo-French proposals, but the British Government were 'not prepared to put themselves in a situation in which they would either have to go to war without any prospect of saving Czechoslovakia or defaulting on their guarantee.' After a short Cabinet discussion in which no opposition was expressed Newton was told to put the following brutal points to the Czech Government:

a) 'His Majesty's Government are not prepared to consider a guarantee which might oblige them, alone or with France, to come to the assistance of Czechoslovakia in circumstances in which effective help could not be rendered. This would be the case if either Germany or Italy were the aggressor and the other declined to fulfil the guarantee.

   It might also be that, if Czechoslovakia thought herself able to count securely upon French and British help, she might be tempted to adopt an attitude towards Germany which would only create the trouble we all wish to avoid.

b) The question arises whether or not the Czech Government should ask or accept a guarantee from Russia. His Majesty's Government consider that, if Russia were brought in as guarantor, it is probable that Germany and Italy would refuse to join in the guarantee. Since the guarantee of Germany is essential, *we should, if matter came to one of clear choice between Germany and Russia, PREFER THE FORMER AT the price of exclusion of the latter.* Moreover, a Russian guarantee would be ineffective in the probable event of Poland and Romania refusing passage to Soviet troops. The attitude of the French Government is, however, that, while they will not impose a Russian guarantee on Czechoslovakia, they will do nothing to stop such a guarantee if the Czechs insist.[51]

Considering Hitler's behaviour, it must have strained Foreign Office loyalty to put down on paper that Germany was preferred as a guarantor to Russia.

In the Commons debate on Munich in October Hoare had been put up by the Government to use his debating skill to reinforce the Prime Minister's arguments about the efficacy of the guarantee, saying 'I myself believe that the international guarantee in which we have taken part will more than compensate for the loss of a strategic frontier'. When asked by Pethick-Lawrence to explain how, if it was not possible to protect the Czechs before, the new guarantee would be any more effective Hoare replied

> The guarantee that I contemplate is a guarantee that I believe will be more effective than either the Franco–Soviet Treaty or the Soviet–Czech Treaty. I contemplate a guarantee in which all the great Powers will in one way or another take part . . . we do not in any way comtemplate the exclusion of Russia . . . it . . . may make the new Republic as safe as Switzerland.

Harold Nicolson commented 'the guarantee was the most farcical piece of diplomatic hypocrisy that has ever been perpetuated . . . it is quite unworkable.'

During the Cabinet discussion of the Guarantee on 8 December Hoare made no effort to justify his arguments in the Commons, and his statement that Russia would not be excluded was conveniently forgotten.

Meanwhile the Ambassadors' Conference was fulfilling Seton-Watson's worst fears, and had proved a sham instead of a worthy substitute for Chamberlain's idea of an International Commission with Runciman as Chairman. As early as November 22 the Germans even suggested it should be dissolved. Ogilvie Forbes, in charge of the British Embassy in Berlin during Henderson's absence on prolonged sick leave, wrote on 3 December:

> I entirely agree with Troutbeck that all questions arising out of the Munich Agreement have been and will be decided at German Nazi dictation. It is pathetic to see the trouble taken by members of the Foreign Office in their correspondence with interested parties on questions of frontiers, economics and options, all in vain. The Ambassadors' Commission might well be dead for all the use it is.

Chamberlain himself was in no doubt about the nature of the creature he had spawned, telling the Cabinet in mid-November that 'the final boundary between Germany and Czechoslovakia had now been agreed, the result being a compromise in which Czechoslovakia had conceded everything and gained nothing.' Yet to the end of his life he would never admit that Munich was a mistake.[52]

When in October Halifax had drawn the German's attention to press reports of ill-treatment of Sudeten Czechs, Hitler replied in a speech at Saarbrücken: 'We cannot tolerate any longer the tutelage of governesses. Inquiries of the Reich concerning the fate of Germans within the frontiers of the Reich or of others belonging to the Reich are out of place.' Sir Charles Petrie (who knew Chamberlain well) had written that in the autumn of 1938: 'Chamberlain entertained a touching belief in Hitler's sincerity.'[53]

However, for the first few months after Munich the easiest way for a Conservative to arouse applause at a political meeting was to say that but for Munich, Britain would be at war, although within Conservative Associations there was bitter controversy over Munich inspired mainly by Churchill and Amery. Had Chamberlain held an election immediately after Munich in October 1938, he would have won an overwhelming majority, but as the months passed his popularity eroded fast.

The result of the Oxford by-election on 27 October showed how popular Munich then was. Quintin Hogg (Lord Hailsham), the Conservative candidate, campaigned almost exclusively in support of Chamberlain's policy, while his opponent A. D. Lindsay, with both Labour and Liberal support, made opposition to Munich his chief plank.*[54] Churchill, Eden, Duff Cooper and Harold Macmillan supported Lindsay, although Macmillan was the only Conservative to go to Oxford to speak. The result in a turn-

---

*Lord Hailsham told the author Munich was the only issue in the by-election.

out higher than in the 1935 General Election was 56.1 per cent for Hogg and 43.9 per cent for Lindsay – a vote of confidence in Chamberlain's appeasement policy.

Soon after, the Conservatives lost Dartford in a by-election, but it was a marginal seat and the swing against the Government was insignificant, 2.9 per cent.

However, the Bridgwater by-election result on 17 November showed a dramatic erosion of support for Munich. The Independent, Vernon Bartlett – who by now was a bitter opponent of appeasement – had his candidature endorsed by the Liberal and Labour local parties. Bartlett concentrated his campaign on attacking Chamberlain's 'weak and vacillating foreign policy' while his Conservative opponent Patrick Heathcote Amory emphasized that he stood entirely behind the Prime Minister's foreign policy. There was an 82 per cent turn-out, and Bartlett got 53.2 per cent against Amory's 46.8 per cent, to overturn the previous Conservative majority of 10,569. Normally British voters pay little heed to foreign-policy issues, but at Oxford and Bridgwater foreign policy dominated.[55]

By the end of 1938 it was being generally realized that Munich was not the success Chamberlain had tried to make out, and he was becoming discredited. Instead of being looked on as an Angel of Peace, he was referred to more and more under his nickname 'the undertaker'. The secrets of the Cabinet at the time of Munich were not well kept. Leo Amery early in October had spent a week-end with Eddie Winterton, who had been present at all the Munich Cabinets, and found out from him that the majority of the Cabinet had been strongly against recommending the Godesberg terms to the Czechs, although Chamberlain wanted to do so.

Amery with his acute political sense wrote in his diary after his talks with Winterton that it was clear

> Neville was determined to have peace on any terms and that when he was frustrated by the Cabinet and by the attitude of the French he found a way round by personal appeal to Hitler and Mussolini which enabled him at Munich to accept practically the same terms with a little sugar coating to the pill long since worn off.

This is the exact story told by the archives.[56]

Amery would have let a great number of MPs know of the Cabinet leak he had obtained from Winterton, and Lytton would have talked in the Lords to other peers about the Foreign Office admision that the arguments in the Seton-Watson memorandum were correct. Not surprisingly, opinion polls which earlier had shown the large majority of the nation in favour of the Munich settlement recorded a sharp dwindling in its popularity as 1939 dawned.

There was a sinister development on 30 October when Hitler expelled 13,000 Polish Jews from Germany. They were compelled to leave their property and money behind, and were taken by special train to the Polish frontier where machine-guns were fired behind them to terrify them into crossing. On Kennard's despatch reporting the steps the Polish authorities had taken to receive them R. L. Speaight minuted: 'This shows that the Poles have done what they could to relieve the sufferings of these wretched people – the behaviour of official circles is in fact all the more creditable in that anti-semitic feeling, particularly in western Poland, is very violent.'

On 6 November a young Polish Jew in Paris, Herschel Grynszpan, received a letter from his sister written on the deportation train, describing the appalling treatment they had received from the Nazis. In revenge Grynszpan went to the German Embassy in Paris on 7 November and shot and wounded a German diplomat, von Rath (a well-known homosexual). Rath lived for two days, and Hitler sent his personal physician to Paris to try to save him. On 9 November the Nazis launched a pogrom against Jews in Berlin as revenge for the murder of von Rath. It has gone down into history as the *Kristallnacht* – a reference to the number of windows smashed. There were 267 synagogues set on fire, thousands of Jewish shops and homes devastated, around 100 Jews murdered, 30,000 rounded up for concentration camps, and innumerable others beaten in a night of savagery organized by the Gestapo. Goebbels was preparing for a show trial of Grynszpan in 1942, but Grynszpan sabotaged it by claiming that he was Rath's homosexual lover and that the shooting was not revenge for the deportation of the Polish Jews, but because they had quarrelled over payments due for services rendered.

The deportation of the Polish Jews was an act of gratuitous hostility to Poland by Hitler, but it was not so interpreted by the British Government, who failed to register the warning that Poland would soon be the next victim of Hitler's aggression.

Ogilvie-Forbes in Henderson's absence wrote that a joint German–Polish attack on the Soviet Union was a possibility, a paradoxical view which ignored Hitler's vicious deportation of so many Polish Jews.

The Foreign Office minutes on Ogilvie-Forbes' letter stated that Polish–German relations had 'cooled off' since Munich, and that any general settlement with Hitler of Danzig and the Corridor was improbable, while the Poles would never give up Gdynia where they had spent so much money in creating a first-class modern port. Sargent pointed out it will 'behove us to examine the situation very carefully with the French and to decided whether we are prepared to become involved in a conflict with Germany similar to that which we so narrowly escaped over Czechoslovakia in order to maintain the Versailles settlement as it affects Poland . . . or whether we are resigned to see this settlement radically revised in Germany's favour in face of Polish opposition'.

Thus Sargent pinpointed in advance the dilemma which was to face the Cabinet in March, but in November his prognostications were ignored.

Instead Kennard was asked to give his views, which were that Poland definitely would not have joined with Germany in fighting Russia if war had come over Czechoslovakia. Instead he thought Poland would have remained neutral, but would have joined the Western powers when it appeared Germany was losing. Kennard thought correctly that closer co-operation between Poland and Germany could not be expected. After Sir Ivo Mallet had pointed out that Poland had always 'eschewed like the devil' any policy of co-operation with Soviet Russia Strang wrote that Poland might be 'Germany's next objective' and that the attack might take place within a few months. This file was read by Halifax without comment.[57]

Strang was correct. Poland was Hitler's next objective. Dark clouds were hanging over the future of Eastern Europe in 1939, but as will be seen in the next chapter Chamberlain and Halifax neglected this Foreign Office warning, and were to be caught by surprise when Hitler's intentions became clear.

CHAPTER TWELVE
FALSE HOPE OF PEACE

'There is no means of maintaining an eastern front against Nazi aggression without the active aid of Russia.' (Winston Churchill in *'Daily Telegraph* May 1939)

'Unless the Poles are prepared to accept the only conditions with which we can successfully help them the responsibility must be theirs.' (David Lloyd George in Commons, April 1939)

CHAMBERLAIN AND Halifax arranged to go to Rome in January 1939 in an effort to bring Mussolini back to the anti-Hitler camp. Jebb sent Cadogan a memorandum stating that Mussolini's bargaining position was much stronger than at Easter 1938, and that only by a really tempting offer would be be persuaded to rejoin the British side. Jebb proposed offering Italy the two Somalilands (French and British), the southern half of Tunisia, a large loan and a seat on the Board of the Suez Canal. Cadogan disagreed, and did not back Jebb's arguments with the Foreign Secretary and Prime Minister.

A section of public opinion in Britain would have resented such rewards to the Italian dictator so soon after the much-disliked Abyssinian war, but alarm was widespread about Hitler's intentions, and in the desperate situation Chamberlain could have convinced the bulk of the nation that Mussolini must be propitiated. Pertinax, the influential French columnist in *Le Temps*, also advocated ceding the Somalilands.

Chamberlain said he intended to hold 'a heart-to-heart talk with Mussolini', but as he came without gifts in his hands the talks were unsuccessful and the dangerous situation in no way alleviated. The mercurial and unreliable Mussolini was now firmly backing Hitler, and the trip was a sad anticlimax after the successful MacDonald–Simon visit four years before and the high hopes aroused by the Easter Agreement of 1938.

The British Ministers spent three days in Rome, but conversations with Ciano and the Duce lasted only two hours and forty minutes. The Rome correspondent of the *Daily Telegraph* on 13 January made the percipient comment: 'It does not appear that the British representatives and the Fascist Government have much in common', and this summed up the position well.[1]

During the period between Munich and March 1939 the Foreign Office left the Government in no doubt about the alarming nature of Hitler's intentions. On 19 January Cadogan noted in his diary that he had passed the papers for circulation to the Foreign Policy Committee 'on the German peril', and they had put the Prime Minister into a highly nervous state. This is not surprising, because the warnings included this:

> All the reports seem to show that Hitler is planning a coup early this year, the danger period beginning towards the end of February. Hitherto it had been generally expected that Hitler's designs would lead him eastwards, and more particularly that he was planning something in the Ukraine. More recently we have been receiving reports showing that he may decide that the moment is propitious for dealing an overwhelming blow at the Western powers.

Cadogan emphasized that all the reports came from sources which had proved reliable and accurate; they completely contradicted Henderson, who from Berlin consistently claimed Hitler intended no more adventures.

Jebb's memorandum stated:

> Germany is controlled by one man, Herr Hitler, whose will is supreme and who is a blend of fanatic madman and clear visioned realist and who regards Germany's supremacy in Europe as a step to world supremacy. Up until December and since Munich he had been peculiarly susceptible to extremist influence.

As long as secret reports indicated that Hitler intended aggression to the east against Russia, Chamberlain and Halifax had not been alarmed, because they did not object to Russia and Germany destroying each other. However, they were most disturbed by the section of Jebb's memorandum

> ... there is incontrovertible evidence that at any rate many of the Führer's entourage are seriously considering the possibility of a direct attack on Great Britain and France during the next few months ... all our sources are at one in declaring that he [Hitler] is barely sane, consumed by an insensate hatred of this country and capable both of ordering an immediate aerial attack on any European country and of having his command instantly obeyed.

281

Cadogan's view was that Hitler reckoned 'we' would not take up arms in defence of Holland and (this is only too likely to be true), that France and Belgium would not do so, and that once in command of Holland and the Dutch coast 'Germany would aspire to dictate terms to us.' Cadogan wanted immediate consultation with the Dutch and an approach to Roosevelt. The Committee decided to approach Roosevelt, but not the Dutch. A British message to Roosevelt stressed the menace of a coup by Hitler against Holland or Britain, and said that Hitler's mental condition, his insensate rage against Great Britain and his megalomania 'are entirely consistent with the execution of a desperate coup against the Western powers', and that no revolt against Hitler could be anticipated in the event of an aggressive war.

According to Jebb, 'secret reports from Germany came pouring in . . . the total absence of any reports that were mildly reassuring could hardly be attributed to anti-German bias in the secret service . . . never could any Government have been more fully warned of the prospective conduct of an adversary.'[2]

Chamberlain told the Cabinet on 25 January 1939 that 'for the moment it would be undesirable that we should enter into a precise and definite obligation to intervene if Holland were attacked by Germany' and the Cabinet agreed there was 'little scope for acceleration of the Defence Programme'. They were fiddling while Rome burnt.

On 28 January the Prime Minister made a speech advocating further appeasement of Hitler and wrote to his sister that he believed Hitler 'had missed the bus at Munich' and that we were in a stronger position than then.[3]

Chamberlain was misled by over-optimistic messages from Henderson in Berlin, who wrote on 18 February 1939: 'In my opinion . . . it would be useful publicly both in press and speeches to stress our full reliance on Herr Hitler's peaceful intentions as it is harmful to show suspicion to them'. On 28 February he wrote that Hitler was so fully occupied with the quarrel between Italy and France that 'it seems that Germany, even if she was so disposed, would find it difficult to embark on a serious venture elsewhere,' and on 9 March: 'Personally, I would not go further than to say that, as an individual, he [Hitler] would be as likely to keep it [his word] as any other foreign statesman – under certain conditions probably more so.'

Fortified by this false optimism, Hoare, at Chamberlain's suggestion, had made a speech on 14 March to his Chelsea constituents glorifying 'the golden age of peace and prosperity' that co-operation would bring to Europe because of Chamberlain's triumph at Munich although Cadogan had reported on 11 March Hitler was on the brink of occupying the remainder of Czechoslovakia, and Chamberlain must have ignored or overlooked this.[4]

The Government's complacency was shattered on 15 March when Hitler broke his solemn promise at Munich that he had no more territorial ambitions in Europe, and occupied Prague and the rump of Czechoslovakia, claiming with demonstrable deceit that he had acted at the invitation of Hácha, the Czech President. Hácha ordered no resistance to the German army, but only after he had been summoned to Berlin and told by Hitler otherwise Prague would be bombed and his country overrun by the German army.

Immediately after the coup in an internal Foreign Office minute Sargent criticized Henderson for his false advice, writing:

> The misleading forecast of 18 February was particularly unfortunate if, as I suppose, it was one of the factors which decided the Prime Minister to issue to the press the *mot d'ordre* to the effect the international position could now be viewed with comfort and optimism.[5]

On 15 March Chamberlain told the Commons 'The course we took at Munich was right' and 'do not let us be deflected from that course'. And on 16 March the Prime Minister continued in the same vein, telling the Commons that he hoped and believed 'the new Czechoslovakia will find a greater security than she has ever enjoyed in the past', while Simon roused the House to anger by saying: 'It is indeed impossible to suppose that in these circumstances the guarantee to maintain the State of Czechoslovakia can have any meaning.' Professor Seton-Watson had been truly vindicated. At Birmingham on 17 March Chamberlain continued with the appeasement line, saying 'I am not prepared to engage this country by new unspecified commitments operating under conditions which cannot be foreseen.' However, he added that the nation had not lost 'its fibre' for war. There was an undertone of petulance and wounded pride in this speech as he repeated the assurances Hitler had made to him at Munich, and said that surely he was entitled to consultation as provided in their joint Munich declaration 'instead of which he [Hitler] has taken the law into his own hands'.

At this stage Chamberlain was arguing that now Britain had no obligation to Czechoslovakia because it was an internal disruption of the State and the guarantee about which he had made so much at the time of Munich related to 'a transitory state of affairs and HMG was no longer bound'.[6]

In the secrecy of the Cabinet meeting on 15 March doubts were expressed about the means used by Hitler to secure Hácha's signature, but no protest was contemplated. Halifax pointed out 'There is no possibility of effectively opposing what was taking place,' and Chamberlain emphasized that Britain had no obligation to fulfil her guarantee to Czechoslovakia,

The Drift to War

saying 'the German action had all been taken under the guise of agreement with the Czechoslovak Government. The Germans were, therefore, in a position to give a plausible answer to any representations,' and the military occupation 'was symbolic, more than appeared on the surface'.

Halifax wanted to withdraw Henderson from Berlin. Chamberlain refused, saying it was 'going too far', but a planned trip to Berlin by Stanley was postponed. Within 48 hours of the occupation of Prague, Tilea, the Romanian Minister in London, panicked the British Government by asserting that Hitler had presented an ultimatum to the Romanian Government demanding that Germany should have a monopoly of the output of the Ploesti oil-field and generally reduce Romania to economic vassalage. The British Minister in Bucharest cabled to London that Tilea's story was untrue, and it was denied by the Romanian Government. However, the rumour had shocked Chamberlain. In Cabinet on 18 March he announced a change of policy from 'appeasement' to 'joining with friends in resisting aggression', and explained that neither he nor any of his colleagues had had time to give the matter proper consideration and he had 'now come definitely to the conclusion that Herr Hitler's attitude made it impossible to continue to negotiate on the old basis with the Nazi regime', and the Nazi leaders did not deserve any reliance. However, neither Chamberlain nor his colleagues contemplated resignation after having let their countrymen down so badly by their mammoth misjudgement of Hitler six months before. On 17 March Henderson was instructed to protest to the German Government against 'the changes effected in Czechoslovakia by military action' and to denounce them as 'devoid of any basis of legality' and 'a complete repudiation of the Munich agreement'.[7]

The enigma was Russia. There was doubt as to how powerful her army was; it had been greatly weakened by purges of the generals. With the Czech fortifications and army gone and Hitler's army fast catching up in strength with the French the only way in which Germany could be now prevented from dominating all Europe was a military alliance between France, Russia and Britain.

Stalin had been appalled by Munich. His allegiance to peace-keeping through pacts with the western powers waned. Forty-eight hours after Munich, Litvinov had told Bonnet in Paris that he was highly incensed at the Munich Agreement, and that 'the Prime Minister should never have been allowed to go to Berchtesgaden, and still less to Godesberg. These two mistakes were as nothing compared to the enormity of what had passed at Munich.' Litvinov declared that 'Hitler had bluffed France and Great Britian completely; he had never meant to risk war; if your two countries had stood firm they would, with Russia's help, have made Germany climb down.' With hindsight no one can cast doubts on Litvinov's claim that

Hitler was bluffing.[8]

At a luncheon on 9 March Maisky had given a serious warning to R. S. Hudson and Rab Butler, saying that Russia no longer believed Britain could be relied on to stand up to the Dictators; as a result Russia was going isolationist, and felt she was militarily invulnerable. Maisky also stated that he was very suspicious of British approaches to Russia, and could not believe friendship with her was part of Chamberlain's policy of appeasement.[9]

Stalin, again shocked by Hitler's occupation of Prague on 15 March 1939, made fresh efforts to stiffen France and Britain against Germany. Within forty-eight hours the Kremlin repeated the proposition made after the Anschluss twelve months before, of convening a conference of Britain, France, Romania, Poland and Russia to plan 'concerted action'. Russia declared that she was ready to give all military assistance, if Britain and France co-operated, to any state in Eastern Europe which might become the victim of German aggression. The British snubbed their powerful potential ally by telling them that the suggestion was 'premature', and Halifax added insult to injury by telling Maisky, 'No Minister of the Crown could spare time to take part in a conference.'[10]

According to Maisky's statements after the war, if this offer had been immediately accepted Russia would have been a firm ally and there would have been a good chance of Hitler being overthrown by the internal German resistance. Unfortunately, in addition Stalin wanted to acquire the parts of Poland which had formerly belonged to Tsarist Russia. He saw Austria and Czechoslovakia grabbed by Hitler with the acquiescence of France and Britain, and did not see why Russia should not have a share of the spoils in Central Europe.

The brilliant, successful Polish campaign against Russia in 1920 had pushed the Russians back far behind the frontier contemplated by the Versailles powers (Curzon Line), and in the Treaty of Riga the victorious Poles had (perhaps unwisely) acquired much former Russian territory. In 1939 the British Government appeared unconscious of Stalin's territorial ambitions, and the furthest the British Government would go in reply to his proposal was to offer Russia 'a declaration of intent' to resist aggression, but no firm agreement.

Stalin had not been pleased when Ribbentrop had visited Paris on 6 December 1938 and concluded an agreement with the French consisting of a declaration of friendship and goodwill, confirmation of the existing Franco-German frontier as final, and an undertaking to consult together. Rumours circulated that the French had also promised Hitler a free hand in Eastern Europe; these were unfounded[11] and France continued to adhere to her pacts with Poland and Russia. Probably the main French motive in concluding the agreement with Ribbentrop was to find a lever against Mussolini, who was demanding Djibuti, Tunis, Corsica and Nice to be ceded to Italy by France.

Chamberlain believed he had established good personal relations with Mussolini during his recent visit to Rome, and he decided to write a personal letter to the Duce to try to enlist his support over the Prague crisis. The Foreign Office wanted him to stress Anglo-French unity, but he would not put this in the letter, which he drafted himself, together with Horace Wilson. Mussolini was asked to do what he could to reduce tension and restore confidence. So keen was Chamberlain that Mussolini should receive his letter immediately that he ordered the British Embassy to pursue the Duce to Southern Italy with it. The Duce's reply was delayed, but it was an unmitigated snub, stating that Mussolini could not take the initiative until 'Italy's rights had been recognized'. ['*prima che i diritti dell'Italia siano stati riconoscuiti*'][12]

On 21 March the French President Le Brun and Bonnet were in London for a previously arranged State visit. A joint plan was produced (probably drafted by Chamberlain himself) by which Britain, France, Russia and Poland should declare their common attitude towards aggression and their intention to consult together if further acts of aggression were imminent. The Russians thought this inadequate but reluctantly agreed, and tried to strengthen it by asking for the signatures of the Prime Ministers in addition to the Foreign Secretaries on the declaration. However, this initiative became abortive because the Poles rejected it out of hand. Significantly, on 22 March Halifax reported to the Cabinet that Litvinov seemed to be 'somewhat perturbed that we have not been more enthusiastic for his proposals for a conference'.[13]

Meanwhile Germany had torn up more of the Treaty of Versailles on 21 March by occupying Memel in Lithuania, and the Slovakian part of Czechoslovakia, which according to Hitler on 15 March would remain an independent state, and over which Poland hoped to exert influence. These coups frightened Poland, so that the Poles ordered partial mobilization and the Foreign Minister, Beck, asked the British Government for an immediate bilateral declaration in the spirit of the five-power declaration which Poland had just declined.

On 21 March there had been a sinister developement in Berlin. Ribbentrop told Lipski that the Danzig Corridor dispute must be solved or 'a serious situation would arise'. This was a threat that Germany would make war on Poland unless Danzig and the Corridor were given up.

On 28 March Ian Colvin, the *News Chronicle* German correspondent, delivered the bombshell that Hitler intended a *putsch* to take Danzig and the Corridor. Colvin knew all about the Lipski–Ribbentrop talk and the

German threat to Poland. He was trusted in Whitehall; he saw Halifax and Cadogan and gave 'hair-raising details of the imminent German thrust against Poland'. Halifax took him to see the Prime Minister.

Colvin explained that the only way to stop Hitler's coup against Poland was to convince him that it was certain that Britain would attack if it happened, and in that case there would be a good chance of the German generals persuading him to stay his hand. Colvin added that he was certain that the generals would have revolted in September if Britain had stood up to Hitler. Almost in a panic, the British Government, for fear of a sudden Hitler attack on Poland, decided on a unilateral guarantee of military help to Poland if she were attacked by Germany.[14]

The fateful decision was made at a full meeting of the Foreign Policy Committee on 27 March. Chamberlain disclosed that Poland insisted any understanding with Russia must be kept secret not only from the public, but also from France for fear of 'detrimental consequences to Poland' (from Germany) and the Prime Minister argued that in face of this attitude 'the best we could hope for would be the public declaration by Great Britain, France and Russia [to consult together] and a secret bilateral understanding with Poland'. Chamberlain feared that 'our attempts to build up a front against German aggression were likely to be frustrated if Russia was closely associated, and intimations had been received from Poland, Roumania, Finland, Yugoslavia, Italy, Spain and Portugal that this would not be acceptable'. The Prime Minister felt that failure to associate with Russia would give rise to 'suspicion and difficulty' with the British Labour Opposition, while on the other hand insistence on association with Russia would destroy any chance of building up 'a solid and united front' against German aggression. Therefore he wanted to abandon the Four Power Declaration and concentrate on Romania, which was the next most likely victim of German aggression. He suggested that we should include Poland and Romania in an Anglo-French agreement and 'leave Russia out of the picture'. Hoare did not agree that Russia should be left out, and said it would be regarded as a considerable defeat for our policy.

Halifax took Chamberlain's line and said 'if we had to make a choice between Poland and Soviet Russia it seemed clear that Poland would give the better value'. To please Poland he wanted to 'camouflage' any inclusion of Russia in the Common Front, although he pointed out that if France was involved in war Russia would have to come in under the Franco-Soviet Pact. Halifax thought Labour would make no difficulty if the Government could satisfy them that the exclusion of Russia was 'no fault of ours', but he had no doubt that 'whatever explanation was given to Soviet Russia about her exclusion she no doubt would make mischief'. Hoare reiterated the importance of bringing in Soviet Russia; Chatfield thought Russia would act as a greater deterrent than Poland (surely only too obvious), and did not think Romania was 'worth the candle' because she was too weak and drew all her military equipment from Czech factories now in German hands.

Stanley hit the nail on the head by saying that the exclusion of Russia was bound to have serious consequences; and 'was it not possible to find some form of declaration in which Russia could join because Russian propaganda was representing our policy as directed to pushing Germany into war with Russia.' He was supported by Hoare. Morrison chimed in that Russia would react badly if she was excluded from the pact, but that was the limit of his opposition. Morrison was a newcomer to the Cabinet, having been promoted Chancellor of the Duchy of Lancaster from being Minister of Agriculture. He was very much a Chamberlain man, which may have accounted for his promotion. However, the Committee unamimously approved the Prime Minister's policy of excluding Russia.

Chatfield, Stanley and Hoare failed to press home their arguments about the need to involve Russia. They did not resign, and must take responsibility with the others for Britain's failure to offer Russia an alliance against Germany.[15]

On 31 March Chamberlain made the dramatic statement to the House of Commons that if Germany attacked Poland, Britain and France would go to war. Germany had a better claim to Danzig, a German town, than she had had to the Sudetenland; the Polish Government was oligarchical and corrupt, and Poland was militarily indefensible whereas Czechoslovakia would in all probability have been too strong a nut for the German armies to crack. The worst feature from the diplomatic point of view was that if Poland refused to negotiate a settlement with Hitler she could force Britain to go to war, and the British guarantee strengthened Polish determination to concede nothing to the Germans. Another unfortunate result was that Russia interpreted it as a declaration that Britain would deny her claims to former Tsarist territory within Poland. Therefore a rapprochement between Stalin and Hitler became more likely, but no suspicion of this crossed Chamberlain's or Halifax's minds.

During the morning of 31 March Halifax had seen Maisky and asked him if in order to avoid 'any unnecessary appearance of divisions' between Britain and Russia the Prime Minister could tell Parliament that the Soviet Government approved of the Commons statement. Maisky indignantly refused, saying soon after to Lloyd George's secretary that it was a reckless gamble by Chamberlain to believe that he could really stop Hitler by combining France, Poland and Britain. Lloyd George agreed and told Chamberlain so in a private talk, but it had no effect.[16]

On the evening of 30 March Chamberlain had seen the leaders of the Labour Opposition (Greenwood, Alexander and Dalton). They said they were 'much disturbed' at the absence of any mention of Russia in the proposed declaration, and warned that if the declaration was limited to Poland trouble might be expected. They stressed that this was on grounds of expediency, not ideology. Nevertheless, they would be satisfied with some reference to Russia, however slight. Chamberlain told them that because of the danger of alienating Poland he refused to insert a reference to Russia, and the Labour leaders leaked this conversation to the Press, which made it doubly clear to the Russians why they had been excluded.

Poland was warned that she must not indulge in 'provocative behaviour or stupid obstinacy either generally or in particular as regards Danzig'. This warning made no difference to the Polish rulers, who fortified by the guarantee from then on refused to discuss the cession of Danzig with Hitler.[17]

Although Churchill, Eden, Harold Nicolson and Lloyd George wanted, like Labour, to include Russia, the bulk of Conservative parliamentarians agreed with Chamberlain. In the Lords the Archbishop of Canterbury was strongly against negotiations with Russia, as were the Conservative peers Hastings, Phillimore and Mansfield. When Snell, the Labour Leader in the Lords, said that the 'key' was Anglo-French-Soviet co-operation Sankey, a National Labour peer (who had considerable influence as a former Labour Cabinet Minister), did some classic fence-sitting by arguing against Russian inclusion but then saying 'If I were shipwrecked in the Baltic I should not refuse a Soviet lifebelt.' Even Plymouth, the Under-Secretary for Foreign Affairs, wanted to avoid Russia, and Haifax's remarks were so guarded that they must have discouraged the Russians.

In the Commons on 3 April Lloyd George said:

> I ask the Government to take immediate steps to secure the adhesion of Russia . . . If Russia has not been brought into this matter because of certain feelings the Poles have that they do not want the Russians there it is for us to declare the conditions, and unless the Poles are prepared to accept the only conditions with which we can successfully help them, the responsibility must be theirs.

This is exactly what Chamberlain refused to do, and Lloyd George's feelings were echoes on the Conservative side only by Churchill, Eden and Harold Nicolson.

In an article in the *Daily Telegraph* on 4 May Churchill urged the Poles to accept the involvement of Russia in European affairs as a decisive factor 'in preventing war', and wanted to impress on the Polish Government that 'from the moment when the Nazi malignity is plain a definite association between Poland and Russia becomes indispensable . . . There is no means of maintaining an eastern front against Nazi aggression without the active aid of Russia.'

There was now a clear-cut division on foreign policy, with the Government and the Conservative parliamentary party opposed to an alliance with Russia but the Liberal and Labour opposition (backed by Churchill, Eden, Brendan Bracken and, Harold Nicolson) advocating a formal military treaty with Russia.

CHAPTER THIRTEEN

BRITAIN'S SLUGGISH REARMAMENT 1936–9

'I view the prospect of the dispatch of a field force to France with the greatest misgivings. We should need, at any rate in the initial stages, all our available troops to assist in the defence of this country.' (Samuel Hoare in Cabinet, 11 April 1938). Only Duff Cooper disagreed, and Halifax told the Germans not to take an exaggerated view of the significance of Anglo-French staff talks.

IT IS difficult to excuse the apathy of the Cabinet over the British Army after Hitler came to power in Germany, and even more so in the months between the Munich Agreement in September 1938 and the German occupation of Prague in March 1939. The Foreign Office made it clear how serious was the German peril in one memorandum after another.

In December 1936 Duff Cooper, Secretary of State for War, had asked approval for the modernization of the twelve Territorial Army divisions and reinforcements for the five regular divisions. In Cabinet Cooper met resistance from the Chancellor of the Exchequer, Neville Chamberlain, who emphasized that 'the political temper of people in this country was strongly opposed to Continental adventures and suspicious of any preparations made in peace time with a view to large-scale military operations on the Continent'.[1] Chamberlain told the Cabinet 'Our aim should be to deter war and that might be better done by increasing the air force', and he doubted whether we 'were right in equipping the Territorial Army for the trenches'.

In their report of 28 January 1937 the Chiefs of Staff threw down the gauntlet, stressing their concern at the serious effect the Government's indecision about the role of the Army was having. When the War Office estimates were presented to the Cabinet on 5 May 1937 Cooper proposed that £43 million should be spent on four Territorial divisions. Chamberlain again opposed, saying the Government should not prepare for and would not be allowed by the country to fight another land war on the scale of 1914–18, and British liability for a 'land contribution' must be strictly limited. As a result, a decision was deferred.[2]

Duff Cooper continued his fight for a decision on the role of the Army in Britain's strategy and hence in rearmament priority, but his views irritated Chamberlain, so when he succeeded Baldwin as Prime Minister in May 1937 Cooper was moved from the War Office to the Admiralty. Despite the obviously dangerous speed of Germany's rearmament Chamberlain and other Cabinet Ministers continued to resist equipping the Regular and Territorial Army to make them capable of intervening promptly in a Continental war. A strong economy was their priority, and they attached a false value to economic strength in a war waged against more powerful armed forces. This strategy in the event of a European war was to prevent Britain succumbing to a knock-out blow from German bombers, and little was done for the Army.[3]

Leslie Hore-Belisha succeeded Cooper in May 1937 at the War Office. He was forty-three, a Jew, flamboyant and keen on self publicity. He had justly acquired a reputation as a man of action when as Minister of Transport where he had initiated the scheme of having Belisha beacons at pedestrian crossings. Although he was a renegade Liberal and not greatly liked by Conservative MPs, he was very much a Chamberlain man.

At first he was popular with the top generals. General Ironside noted in his diary: 'We are at our lowest ebb in the Army, and the Jew may resuscitate us . . . He will probably be our saving.' Belisha's (unofficial) adviser was Liddell Hart, the controversial defence correspondent of *The Times*. Liddell Hart was strongly opposed to a large British Expeditionary Force going to France to take part in a French offensive against Germany. Instead he wanted to provide two mobile armoured divisions as a boost to the attack potential of the ponderous French army.

Simon, as Chancellor of the Exchequer, was as opposed in 1937 to extra spending on the field army as his predecessor, Chamberlain, had been the year before. £1500 million had been inserted in the White Paper of 16 February 1937 as the maximum available for rearmament for the period 1937–42; Simon now reiterated this was the maximum.

In December 1937 Inskip, now Minister for the Co-ordination of Defence, presented to the Cabinet his reappraisal of Defence priorities, saying: 'If France were again to be in danger of being overrun by land armies, a situation might arise when, as in the last war, we would have to improvise an army to assist her. Should this happen, the Government of the day would most certainly be criticized for having neglected to provide against so obvious a contingency.'

His warning fell on deaf ears. On 22 December 1937 the Cabinet laid down that the Army estimates were to be drawn up on the assumption that no field force would go to France in event of a war. Stinginess over money, coupled with the fear of a German bombing attack and obsession with the likely resulting damage to London, were the chief factors in this decision. In Cabinet on 22 December there was little opposition to the Army's Continental commitment being scrapped. Eden did not oppose, merely saying France should be informed. 'Limited liability' had become 'no liability'.

In February 1938 Belisha told the Cabinet that two divisions would be available for Continental commitment but only if the situation in the rest of the world permits,[4] and on 16 February he presented to the Cabinet a Memorandum on the new role of the Army. It was to be primarily anti-aircraft defence of Britain; two existing Territorial infantry divisions were to be converted to AA and searchlights. On 7 March 1938 Chamberlain told the Commons that the White Paper on Defence showed 'this enormous power, this almost terrifying power which Britain is building up has a sobering effect, a steadying effect on the opinion of the world'.* This myth was well received at home, but with scorn by Hitler. However, the Opposition parties welcomed the abandonment of a Continental expeditionary force. The generals were disgusted, Ironside writing in his diary 'the White Paper is truly the most appalling reading'. On 3 February Ironside had commented: 'The air defence of Great Britain is absorbing all the money which was intended for the Field Army. The Air Ministry dictates what it wants and the Army Estimates bear the cost.'

The Anschluss in March 1938 did not produce a dramatic change in British defence policy. Staff talks with the French were, as has been seen, begun, and at a CID meeting on 11 April Hoare said

> the problem is to win the war over London. In order to do so we might have to station certain squadrons of our Advanced Striking Force in France. [Hoare] viewed . . . the prospect of the despatch of a field force with the greatest misgivings. We should need, at any rate in the initial stages, all our available troops to assist in the defence of this country.

---

*He was referring to the RAF strike capacity.

Halifax, now Foreign Secretary, added that 'he was as anxious as anyone that the field force should not be sent . . . but he hoped that we should not categorically say that in no circumstances would a field force be sent to the Continent.' Lord Gort wanted only 5,000 men sent to France to help with the RAF bases there. Only Duff Cooper disagreed. When Staff talks with the French began the Germans were told by Halifax not to take an exaggerated view of their significance.[5]

Despite Chamberlain's statement to the Commons on 5 October 1938, (after Munich) about the urgent need to rearm Britain, there was no sharp increase in spending on the Army. All that the Cabinet considered necessary as a first step was a Ministry of National Service under Sir John Anderson to make a register of manpower. However, the French were no longer content with only two British divisions, and Chamberlain and Halifax arranged for talks in Paris with the French Government at the end of November.

On 22 November Chamberlain told the Cabinet in the forthcoming conversations in Paris that

> if the French took the line that they were relying on us for the defence of Paris then it would be necessary to make it quite clear to them that our airforce was being built for our own defences . . . our attitude would be governed largely by the fact that we did not wish to see France drawn into a war with Germany on account of some quarrel between Russia and Germany with the result that we should be drawn into war in France's wake.

When Hoare said it was 'in our interest to see a strong Russia, and we must not take any action which made it appear we were anti-Russian or indifferent to Russia's future', Chamberlain was obliged to agree although he added '. . . it was desirable to avoid entanglement arising out of a possible dispute between Russia and Germany.' This shows Chamberlain hoping Russia and Germany would fight each other, and Britain could stand aside.

Thus the omens for Chamberlain's and Halifax's visit to Paris were not good, and their visit turned out in Professor Bond's words to be 'a hollow gesture'. Undoubtedly the British policy on sending an expeditionary force to France in the event of a war with Germany undermined the French will to fight against Hitler.[6]

When Chamberlain and Halifax arrived in Paris on 23 November 1938 they became alarmed lest France might do a deal with Hitler at Britain's expense, and Halifax admitted to Phipps that France might become so defeatist as not to defend her own frontiers. Phipps on his side made it clear that French opinion demanded 'an army of a size to do something to redress the balance between France and Germany and 'large numbers of British troops in Europe'.[7]

The British statesmen made it clear that they relied on France to hold the western frontier while they made their own island impregnable to German attacks. They would not budge upwards from their two-division contribution to an Expeditionary Force. It was not lost on Hitler that Daladier's request for an increased land contribution was refused, while Chamberlain completely misled his Cabinet on his return by telling them on 30 November that 'no point of difficulty had cropped up except the Czechoslovak guarantee'. He must have been anxious to stifle discussions about an Expeditionary Force.[8]

When further Foreign Office reports (see previous chapter) made it appear likely that Hitler was about to attack Holland on 1 February 1939, the Cabinet on that date agreed that Britain should assure France that she would go to war if Germany invaded Holland or Switzerland, and that there must be periodical liaison between the British and French and Belgian staffs.

Halifax now showed some conversion. Chamberlain and Simon opposed Hore-Belisha's proposals for increased expenditure on a field force designed for France on grounds of economy. Halifax then said Britain could risk borrowing money in these exceptional circumstances: 'either war would come soon or the Nazi regime would collapse, and he would sooner be bankrupt in peace than beaten in a war by Germany'. When Simon and Hoare wanted air defence to be absolute priority Halifax stressed the sensitivity of French feeling on this subject.

On 22 February 1939 the Cabinet agreed to raising the Expeditionary Force to four infantry divisions and one mobile division, plus four territorial divisions; even then there was 'penny-pinching', and the Prime Minister hoped to save around £5 million by postponing the dates of arrival in France. Professor Bond comments aptly: 'The records leave a strong impression that financial economy counted for more than military preparedness.'[9]

With the occupation of Prague pressure from Conservative MPs for conscription and a much larger army mounted. Hore-Belisha by now was a strong advocate of conscription, but Chamberlain feared it would antagonize the trade unions and check their co-operation in the arms factories. Hore-Belisha on 28 March suggested to Chamberlain the simple expedient of doubling the size of the Territorial Army from 170,000 to 340,000 at a cost of £88 million to the Treasury. Chamberlain liked the idea and immediately agreed, as did Simon. However, a Treasury memorandum was scathing, saying 'it would be no effective military help for twelve to eighteen months'; the large requirement of manpower would have adverse effects on industrial production and Hitler would realize that its 'military value is nil'; adding 'This plan has been invented in the space of a few hours. It cannot be related to anything in particular and must *prima facie* be full of flaws which will reveal themselves in the course of time.'

The Treasury was right. Doubling the Territorial Army impressed nobody abroad; it reduced the ratio of armoured divisions and diverted war material from the field force. In the Cabinet on 29 March Chamberlain suggested that conscription was preferable but said it would be dangerous as it would alienate Labour 'who might go slow in essential war production'. Halifax said he too would have preferred a measure on somewhat wider lines, but the course proposed was the right one and should be taken quickly.

On paper Britian now had thirty-two divisions but there was no chance of making the bulk of them into an effective force for years. By doubling the Territorial Army the Government was able to pacify its own MPs without antagonizing Labour, but Hitler and his General Staff correctly diagnosed that this move did not constitute a more effective deterrent, and the French were not reassured.

This field force was grotesquely and inadequately equipped. By July 1939 none of the new 25-pound field guns had been issued, and only 144 out of 240 anti-tank guns. AA guns were far behind schedule and the field guns were all First World War vintage. In August only 60 infantry tanks were available against a requirement of 1646.[10] Field Marshal Montgomery wrote that when he took 3 Division to France in September 1939 much of the transport consisted of civilian vans and lorries in bad repair and 'the countryside of France was strewn with broken down vehicles . . . it must be said to our shame that we sent our army into that most modern war with weapons and equipment which was quite inadequate'. Only in fighter aircraft and radar was the pace of British rearmament as fast as Germany's between September 1938 and September 1939.[11]

The Government had been consistently misled into giving priority to defence against bombers by false estimates of Germany's air strike-power and gross over-estimation of the damage which would be done. In 1934 the Air Staff calculated that Germany could drop 75 tons of bombs a day on Britain from her home bases and 150 tons if she occupied the Low Countries, with casualties of 50 per ton. By 1936 the estimate was 600 tons with casualties during the first week of war 150,000; by 1939 it was 700 tons with a possible 'knock-out blow' of 3,500 tons in the first twenty-four hours. In the event the heaviest air raid on Britain was on 19 April 1941, when 1026 tons were dropped on London. 500 tons were dropped on Coventry on 14 November 1940, and the weight of major attacks fluctuated between 400 and 500 tons.[12]

The French pressed the British to introduce conscription. On 20 April Chamberlain bowed to the inevitable and the Conscription Bill was announced. In the final phase of preparation for the 1939 war in the Anglo-French staff talks plans were made for four British divisions to go to France if war began.

CHAPTER FOURTEEN

POLISH GUARANTEE AND SOVIET–GERMAN PACT 1939

Chamberlain snatched at any opportunities of reopening negotiations with Hitler. There was a Russian spy in the Foreign Office, so Stalin knew of it. Rab Butler minuted: 'The best hopes of obtaining an approach to Hitler lie in concluding something ANODYNE with Russia.'

THE POLISH Foreign Minister, Beck, came hot-foot to London after the 31 March offer. Now he felt he could cock a snook at Hitler, but was adamant that Poland would make no military alliance with Russia which might mean Soviet troops coming on Polish soil. He also refused to consider any public agreement with Russia for fear of provoking Hitler; he insisted that any understanding with her must be kept secret. This left the British little room for manoeuvre.

On a previous visit to London Beck had rather disgraced himself by excessive drinking, and he was a light-weight politician of dubious reliability who had now become ludicrously over-optimistic, saying 'all the trump cards were in our hand'.[1]

On 4 April Beck and Halifax talked in the morning at the Foreign Office. Beck said any pact with Russia would provoke the Germans and possibly 'accelerate the conflict'; Polish survival depended on preserving her independence from both Russia and Germany, and if Britain and Russia signed any agreement Poland would have to disassociate herself publicly. Chamberlain saw Beck after lunch and the latter reiterated that he could not accept any agreement which linked Poland with Russia for fear of provoking Germany. Chamberlain was stymied, having given a rash

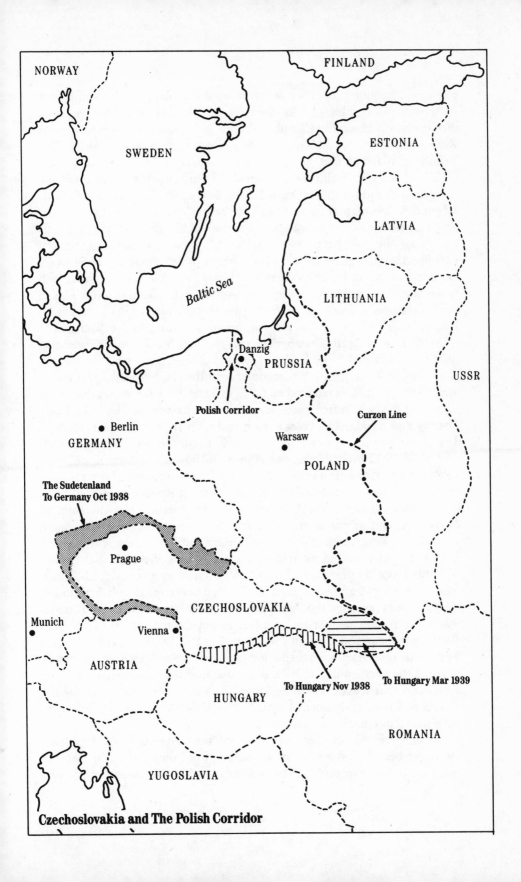

NORWAY

SWEDEN

FINLAND

ESTONIA

LATVIA

Baltic Sea

LITHUANIA

Danzig

PRUSSIA

USSR

Polish Corridor

Curzon Line

Berlin

GERMANY

Warsaw

POLAND

The Sudetenland
To Germany Oct 1938

Prague

Munich

Vienna

CZECHOSLOVAKIA

To Hungary Nov 1938

To Hungary Mar 1939

AUSTRIA

HUNGARY

ROMANIA

YUGOSLAVIA

Czechoslovakia and The Polish Corridor

guarantee, he found that his new ally refused any co-operation with Russia – the only power which could make the British guarantee effective. Beck disingenuously denied to Chamberlain that in his recent conversations with Ribbentrop in Berlin the Germans had issued threats about Danzig. The British soon found that he was lying, because on 22 April Lipski gave Ogilvie-Forbes in Berlin the full details of Ribbentrop's threats, and the German demand for the return of Danzig and an autobahn to East Prussia. When this information was sent to London Halifax minuted: 'Is it not the case that Beck gave us to understand there had been no definite proposals . . . If so, he has been less than frank.' This was discouraging, but Chamberlain had given Beck a blank cheque which made the Poles over-confident in face of Hitler's demands. They ignored the fact that the British Government wanted them to negotiate a settlement of Danzig with Hitler so as to avoid the need of a deal with the Russians. Beck, much to Chamberlain's surprise, also refused to join in a guarantee to Romania.[2]

Nettled, on 4 April Chamberlain told the Polish Foreign Minister that public opinion had been led to expect an arrangement whereby various States would 'band themselves around Great Britain, France and Poland as a nucleus'. Beck then relented so far as to agree to sign a secret document which left the British free to continue negotiations with Romania, the Little Entente and Russia. The Poles already had a Treaty with Romania made in 1931, but it only applied to an attack from the east. On 15 April Chamberlain announced that the British and French had given unilateral guarantees to Romania and Greece. The main motivation had been reports that Germany could not undertake a war without Romanian oil.[3]

Chamberlain had changed his umbrella into a sword. His guarantee to Poland was out of character, and contradicted the policy of appeasement which he had been reiterating to the country and Parliament only ten days before. It was intended as a frank warning to the dictators, but neither Mussolini nor Hitler paid any attention. They were convinced Britain would never fight, and six days later Albania was occupied by Italian troops. The dictators regarded the Polish guarantee as bluff on the grounds that it was accompanied neither by an effort to get military co-operation from Russia nor the introduction of conscription in Britain. So unconcerned was Hitler that on 3 April he issued a military directive to Keitel for Operation White – the overrunning of Poland. If Chamberlain had announced to the Commons that Russia would be included in the Polish guarantee (as the dissident Cabinet Ministers wanted), it is improbable that Hitler would have dared to embark on this plan.

Chamberlain told the Cabinet on 5 April 'the conversations with Colonel Beck had been by no means unsatisfactory, [but] they had not turned out quite as we had expected . . . he had very considerable distrust of Russia, and had no confidence that we should obtain active and constant support from that country.' Herein lay the seeds of the disaster that was to come. Chamberlain began negotiations for a pact with Russia, but because of legal quibbles these talks lasted until August and were never completed. Not unnaturally the Russians in the end took this as meaning that Britain did not really want an alliance.[5]

A significant comment made by Maisky to a small, informal group of Tory MPs was that Russia was 'quite firm they were going to have a black and white Alliance or nothing'. Leo Amery knew Chamberlain intimately, and he has summed up the Prime Minister's attitude, writing in his diary: 'The trouble with Neville is that he is being pushed into a policy which he does not like and hates abandoning the last bridges which might still enable him to renew his former policy.' Amery was right; as will be seen, Chamberlain wanted to run with the hare and hunt with the hounds by pursuing ostensibly an alliance with Russia while at the same time seeking to appease Hitler afresh.

Cadogan commented in his diary in May: 'In his present mood P.M. says he will resign rather than sign alliance with Soviet. So I have to go warily. I am, on balance, in favour of it. So, I think, is H. [Halifax]' Chamberlain would never even have entered into negotiations with Russia if it had not been for this pressure from Halifax and Cadogan.[6]

By the Polish refusal to have anything to do with Russia Chamberlain had found a good excuse for not proceeding to seek a pact with Russia. This was partially removed when on 14 April the French took the initiative out of his hands by telling the Russians they would sign a bilateral mutual assistance agreement supplemented by concrete military arrangements. On 18 April Russia put the cat among the pigeons by proposing an agreement containing eight clauses by which France, Russia and Britain should sign a mutual assistance agreement in case of a direct attack and promise to assist against aggression to *all* east European countries bordering on the USSR from the Baltic to the Black Sea. This was to be accompanied by a military convention and promises not to enter into a separate peace once hostilities started. The French were delighted; here at last was the chance to undo the damage to Anglo-French-Soviet relations caused by Munich. It turned out to be the last effective opportunity of stopping the outbreak of the Second World War. But the Russians wanted a quick and enthusiastic response, which the British would not give.

Another fateful FPC meeting was held on 19 April to consider these dramatic proposals. Cadogan circulated his comments beforehand. Halifax was not present, and the Committee were told that 'owing to pressure of other business' the Foreign Secretary had not had time to give any detailed study to the matter, 'and still less to formulate a line of policy'. The failure of Halifax to concentrate immediately and form an opinion upon the most important post-war Russian offer calls into question his fitness to be Foreign Secretary. However, as Chamberlain was acting virtually as his own Foreign Secretary, perhaps Halifax's supineness on this occasion has not much historical importance.*[7]

Cadogan's memorandum contained twenty negative points against the Russian proposals; it was 'extremely inconvenient', and we would have to balance the advantage of a paper commitment by Russia to join in a war on our side against the disadvantage of associating ourselves with that country. It implied that if Germany attacked Poland, Russia would send troops over Polish territory; 'That is exactly what frightens Poland . . . we should be extending our own guarantee to Latvia, Estonia and Finland.' Cadogan summed up 'there was every argument against accepting the Russian proposal . . . it would arouse the suspicions of our friends and aggravate the hostility of our enemies.'

Ominously Cadogan ended by writing: 'There is great difficulty in refusing the Soviet offer . . . the Left in this country may be counted on to make the most of this. There is further the risk – though I should have thought it a very remote one – that if we turn down this proposal the Soviets might make some non-intervention agreement with the German Government'. This briefing accorded with Chamberlain's views (and perhaps this was why Cadogan so phrased his arguments).

Chamberlain told the FPC on 19 April all the information went to bear that out the view that the Russian fighting services were at present of little military value for offensive purposes: 'Several foreign Prime Ministers had spoken to him in this sense and their opinion had been corroborated by Mr. R. S. Hudson and Sir Percy Loraine.' What Hudson and Loraine knew about it is obscure; the Chiefs of Staff had only given their view as 'U.S.S.R. are an uncertain military quantity, and they were unable to form any considered opinion as to the extent of her military intervention in the allied cause'. Chamberlain was also flouting two memoranda in March by the British Chiefs of Staff that Poland could not withstand a German invasion without Soviet military aid.

Chamberlain's remarks prompted Hoare to say it was essential the Chiefs of Staff should produce a report on Russia's military value, and that without her Poland would be able to offer little military resistance. Inskip thought the approach was 'a mere attempt to entangle us, but if Russia meant business she would be of some considerable value'. Morrison took the

---

*Sir Ivo Mallet (then Halifax's principal private secretary) told the author that as far as policy to Germany was concerned Chamberlain to all intents and purposes acted as his own Foreign Secretary and Halifax was extremely weak, nearly always condoning this conduct.

Chamberlain line as usual telling the Committee the Russian approach did not imply any sincere desire to help 'since Mr. Litvinov must be as aware as we are of the effect of their proposal on our potential friends'. Inskip said the general view of the Committee appeared to be that the political arguments against a military alliance between this country, France and Russia were irresistible, and such as to outweigh any military advantage.

Chamberlain summed up: 'while therefore not turning down the Russian proposal we should endeavour to convey the impression that the time for a military alliance was not yet ripe'. After further support for the Prime Minister from Morrison, the Committee decided not to accept the Soviet proposal and to make efforts to keep it secret on the grounds that 'it would give little additional security; it would arouse the suspicions of our friends and aggravate the hostility of our enemies'. Fear of aggravating Hitler was a potent factor with the Prime Minister.[8]

On 26 April the Cabinet endorsed the decision of the FPC to reject Russia's proposed alliance. Halifax said it would be 'desirable for Russia to remain neutral or then join the Allied side', and 'the value of Russia was by no means as high as seemed to be believed by some members of the Labour Party'.[9]

Rejection of the Soviet proposal was a disaster. Stalin was genuinely trying to build a front to contain Hitler, and this rebuff coming on top of the snub to Russia at Munich made him doubtful if Britain would ever go to war to stop Hitler in the east. Undoubtedly rejection triggered off Stalin's machinations for a possible alternative common front with Hitler, although the Russians built up a façade of desire for alignment with France and Britain by prolonged negotiations.

Meanwhile the British tried to kill French enthusiasm for the Triple Alliance and Maisky reported to Stalin that while Chamberlain was Prime Minister Britain would never sign a treaty with Russia. He was not far wrong.[10]

The first indication of a likely change in Soviet policy was the dismissal of Litvinov on 3 May. Litvinov was pro-Western, and he was replaced by Molotov, who was much less friendly to France and Britain.

The negotiations with Russia became shadow boxing, with Chamberlain and most of his Cabinet opposed to a meaningful deal, and the Russians gradually veering towards a rapprochement with Germany unless there was a sudden change in British policy.

Two days after Litvinov's dismissal François-Poncet, French Ambassador in Rome, told Loraine the sinister story that Stalin had sacked Litvinov in order to make an arrangement with Germany which would enable Hitler to attack Poland and retake the Corridor with impunity. Loraine wrote that he found this 'very difficult to swallow', and on the next day a message was received in the Foreign Office from an emissary of Goerdeler that German generals had received a 'new and unexpected offer from the Soviet Union which might entirely change the situation'. Three days later Henderson reported that the French Ambassador in Berlin told him he had had several indications that Hitler might come to an understanding with Stalin which might take the form of a Non-Aggression Pact, while the German press had been 'far from unfriendly about Molotov's appointment'. A Foreign Office minute stated 'This story is very persistent but is not supported by the telegrams from Moscow, and is inherently improbable.'[11]

However, François-Poncet had genuine evidence upon which to base his story; it turned out to be correct that Stalin was keeping his options open in case Britain dragged her feet over the Russian alliance.

In Cabinet Chamberlain and Halifax expressed their lukewarmness towards an alliance with Russia; this had a baneful effect on negotiations. On 17 May Halifax said 'the procedure adopted by the Soviet Government in the last month did not fill him with any confidence . . . generally the Russian proposal represented a wide departure from our own previous plans . . . He also thought that the conclusion of an Alliance with Russia might be held to make war more likely.' He reminded his colleagues of the statement by Mr Gafencu (Romanian Foreign Minister) that 'while, if war was certain, he would favour a close alliance with Russia, so long as there was a five per cent chance of peace he would avoid such an alliance'.[12]

On 19 May Chamberlain told the FPC 'many influential persons in Germany were trying to persuade Herr Hitler that the time to strike was when the Three Power Pact was concluded, and that the conclusion of such a Pact would unite Germany as nothing else could do.' Hoare took an opposite view, saying 'if we failed to come to an arrangement with Russia the whole of Germany would proclaim that the peace front had been broken'. Morrison had 'no doubt that if we entered the war with Germany because of German aggression against Poland or Romania the whole empire would stand by us, but he doubted if this would be the case if we got involved in a war of aggression by Germany against Russia in which the other Eastern European countries were not involved'.[13]

In the middle of May, much to Chamberlain's annoyance, the Chiefs of Staff swung round – in Cadogan's words to support for 'whole hog' alliance with Russia. Cadogan had also come round in favour of a Russian alliance, as had Stanley, Hoare, Malcolm MacDonald, Chatfield, Inskip and Burgin in the Cabinet. On 24 May Chamberlain told the Cabinet 'he viewed anything in the nature of an alliance with Russia with considerable misgiving . . . an alliance . . . would arouse considerable opposition and objection in many quarters . . . However he did not wish to envisage breakdown especially so soon after the conclusion of the German-Italian

Pact.' Halifax echoed the Prime Minister with 'he had never disguised from his colleagues his own views on the subject of a close association with the Russian Government . . . however it was not possible to contemplate a breakdown of the negotiations.'

Reluctantly Chamberlain gave way, and on 24 May the Cabinet agreed a formula with the French. However, at Chamberlain's insistence the written British proposals were so wrapped up with references to the League of Nations that they were ill received by Stalin.[14]

The Cabinet and the Foreign Office felt that now they had at last taken the plunge after weeks of agonizing deliberations constructive work on resisting Hitler could begin. To their astonishment Molotov rejected the Anglo-French proposals out of hand. Sir William Seeds, the British Ambassador, and the French Chargé d'Affaires Jean Payart, went to the Kremlin to see Molotov, who astounded them by saying the proposals were unacceptable because they were 'calculated to ensure the maximum of talk and the minimum of results', while the British and French were prepared to visualize Moscow being bombed while 'Bolivia' blocked all action at Geneva; also he complained that nothing definite was said on the military side and too much regard was paid to the susceptibilities of other powers. Seeds feared Molotov wanted to break off the negotiations, and advised Halifax to negotiate a military treaty simultaneously. He discovered that the Russians would insist on a guarantee of the Baltic states. On 31 May in a speech to the Supreme Soviet Molotov hinted that the current negotiations with Britain and France did not preclude commercial negotiations with Germany. Seeds took the hint and telegraphed on 1 June that a German–Soviet political agreement was 'just a possibility'.[15]

Chamberlain was annoyed. He had counted on a quick conclusion of a treaty, and felt he had been generous in suggesting Britain would guarantee Communist Russia against attack. If only Chamberlain had made a 'generous gesture' in April immediately he received the Russian 8–point proposal the course of history would have been different. Now Anglo-French-Soviet negotiations began to founder and enter the realm of farce. On 2 June Molotov handed the British and French Ambassadors a draft treaty which specified that aggression against Belgium, France, Greece, Turkey, Romania, Poland, Latvia, Estonia and Finland would automatically produce war. Holland and Switzerland were excluded, and no 'separate peace' was stipulated. Sharp controversy between Moscow and London centred on the definition of indirect aggression, no separate peace, and guarantees to Holland and Switzerland.

Chamberlain had the false impression that 'Russia could not afford to break off negotiations' and wanted to drive 'a hard bargain'. On 9 June he decided to send Strang to Moscow to help Seeds. It had been suggested that a Cabinet Minister ought to go. Halifax toyed with the idea that he might go himself but quickly rejected it, and Chamberlain thought it 'unnecessary'. If the Foreign Secretary had gone himself the situation might have been redeemed, but Halifax was in the wrong frame of mind.[16]

Strang and Seeds were told by Molotov (on 16 June) the British and French Governments were treating the Russians as 'simpletons and fools' and a way must be found to guarantee the Baltic states.

Chamberlain then agreed that all reference to the League of Nations could be dropped, and Halifax instructed Strang that military staff talks should begin as soon as political agreement was reached, and that speed in the negotiations was essential. On 20 June the FPC reluctantly agreed to the 'no separate peace' clause, but Chamberlain insisted that Holland and Switzerland must be added to the secret protocol of states. Molotov refused out of hand because they did not have diplomatic relations with the USSR; he also insisted that aggression should be defined as including an internal *coup d'état*. This had not been mentioned in the original draft treaty, but was not unreasonable in view of what had occurred in Czechoslovakia and Memel.

On 4 July another crucial FPC meeting took place to discuss the proposed Russian Treaty. By now secret German negotiations were under way, but it is probable that a complete acceptance by Britain of all the Soviet demands could have saved the Treaty even at this late hour. Over Switzerland and the Netherlands Cadogan had minuted: 'we must dig our toes in; if that leads to a breakdown I doubt whether we should really be worse off, as Soviet insistence on this point would mean that they really do not intend to have an agreement anyway.'[17]

Halifax told the FPC that if Britain guaranteed countries in Eastern Europe without receiving from Russia equivalent guarantees for Holland and Switzerland the arrangement would be difficult to defend, and he had inside information that the TUC and other responsible authorities in the Labour movement would approve the Government's rejection of such a proposition. Hoare and Stanley did not attach the same importance to Holland and Switzerland; Stanley insisting realistically that it was all-important to secure Russia's guarantee for Poland, 'which was the one country that really mattered at the moment'. Halifax showed a hint of clairvoyance, saying that if war arose out of the Polish situation and the Soviet Government thought the moment opportune for the partition of Poland they would share it with Germany without a qualm.

Morrison emphasized that the definition of indirect aggression was 'most objectionable – a real stumbling block, and its object was to ensure that we would come to the assistance of Russia in crushing Nazi or right wing movements in countries now under more liberal regimes [the Baltic

States]'. Chamberlain then said it would be 'quite impossible' to justify or defend in public this definition, which he regarded with the utmost apprehension. Simon suggested 'we' should give in over guarantees for Holland and Switzerland in exchange for Molotov dropping his unwelcome definition of indirect aggression. However, Chamberlain insisted that unless Molotov fell in with Simon's suggested compromise there should be no tripartite military alliance, but instead they would fall back on a milder tripartite pact with provisions for consultation.

During another FPC meeting on 19 July, after a disagreement between Hoare and Chamberlain with the latter wanting to call 'the Soviet bluff by laying down once and for all our final conditions', instructions were sent to Moscow that the British definition of indirect aggression must be fully accepted. Bonnet was horrified, as he considered this would mean the breakdown of negotiations, and told the British Chargé d'Affaires in Paris that even the most humiliating concession was preferable to a disastrous rupture in the negotiations.

Without consulting the FPC, Chamberlain and Halifax decided to climb down, with Halifax writing to Seeds on 22 July: 'I do not like this, but it would avoid a definite break.'[18]

On 23 July all went well between Seeds, Strang and Molotov. Molotov asked 'why it was thought necessary to waste time upon points of detail and delay consideration of the essential problem; i.e. the military conversations without which the Treaty would have no substance.' The British Government agreed to start military talks although the political pact was still in the air, and there was no assurance Russia would become an ally.

Halifax told the Cabinet on 26 July the Russians looked on these talks 'as a test of good faith'. The Cabinet gave instructions that they should proceed very slowly until a political pact had been concluded and the Russians must not be allowed to discover Allied secrets, although they should be probed about their own intentions. Unfortunately, the procedure adopted by the British left the Russians in no doubt about these secret instructions.[19]

Admiral Sir Reginald Drax was appointed mission leader. He was a bluff naval man, and a strong opponent of Munich and advocate of conscription. (Churchill wrote he was only appointed because he was out of a job.) Maisky reported to Moscow that because of their subordinate posts the delegation would stay in Moscow indefinitely, and the Russian military attaché in Paris said their intention would be 'to find out above all else the condition of our army'. Drax was instructed to treat the Russians with reserve until the political agreement was concluded, and that there was a danger of leakage to the Germans 'since there may be contacts between the Russians and German General Staffs'. However, the Chiefs of Staff recommended 'there must be no delay in the initiation of the Staff conversations if the political atmosphere was to be cleared to allow a treaty to be concluded'.

It was suggested in Cabinet that to impress world opinion the mission should travel with an escort of cruisers and destroyers. Halifax thought it might be 'provocative to send a cruiser into the Baltic', and turned it down. Aeroplanes carrying the mission could not overfly Germany, nor could they cross Germany by train. Instead an old ship, the *City of Exeter*, was chartered (although they could have travelled by air via Oslo). Her engines were in such a bad state that she could only travel at thirteen knots instead of the twenty-eight knots of a cruiser. The mission did not arrive in Moscow until seventeen days after the decision to open military talks.

Chamberlain made the disastrous mistake of leaving out any well-known diplomatic or military figure from the mission to Moscow. On 2 August Seeds noticed a nasty change in Molotov. He telegraphed to London that Molotov was different, and 'I feel our negotiations have received severe setback.'[20]

The Anglo-Soviet military conversations in Moscow, at first cordial, soon ran into heavy weather, and foundered altogether on 14 August. Marshal Voroshilov quite reasonably insisted on a clear answer as to whether Russian troops would be allowed to cross Poland to fight the Germans in East Prussia. Drax and General Heywood then had a lengthy conference and Drax replied that the answer could only be given by Poland. Voroshilov then said it was useless continuing the talks without knowing if Russian troops would be admitted to Poland and Romania in case of war. The meeting was adjourned, and Drax told his colleagues 'Our mission is finished.' He was right. This news was telegraphed to London, where it produced alarm, and in Warsaw Beck was pressed to agree to Russian troops entering Poland, both by Kennard and by the French Ambassador. Beck remained 'absolutely obdurate', and warned that if Poland agreed to Russian troops entering 'Hitler would see red,' and precipitate a war.

The British and French had been pursuing a will o'the wisp. There had never been any chance of a Pact with Russia unless the Poles agreed to transit rights for Russian troops. This had been clear since the beginning of the negotiations in March, but Chamberlain and Halifax would not face up to it; they and their Cabinet colleagues either lived in a dream world or did not care whether the negotiations were successful or not.

Retribution was quick to follow. On 23 August Beck agreed to a small concession which would sanction Polish–Soviet military collaboration under certain conditions, but not enough to satisfy Voroshilov. On the same day two plane-loads carrying Ribbentrop and 30 German officials landed at Moscow. In direct conversations with Stalin, Ribbentrop achieved in forty-eight hours the German–Soviet Non-Aggression Pact and a secret protocol by which Poland was to be divided between Germany and Russia.[21]

Chamberlain's foreign policy was in ruins. France and Britain faced the stark situation that they must abandon Poland or fight Germany without Russian aid. Yet Chamberlain never considered resignation. Nor was it demanded by the Cabinet or his Party.

★　　★　　★

Reports had been continually reaching the Foreign Office during 1939 of a possible German-Soviet rapprochement. Unfortunately, they were not given the attention they deserved, and Chamberlain was never conscious of the danger that, failing a quick accord with Russia, Stalin and Hitler would come together.

In January the *Sunday Pictorial* carried a sensational front-page story that Hitler was planning a secret alliance with Russia, and the British Embassy in Paris reported similar rumours. Simultaneously Sir P. Ramsay, head of the British delegation in Copenhagen, reported that the Associated Press correspondent there had been asked from London to verify rumours that negotiations for a German–Soviet non-aggression pact had been opened. Lascelles, in the Russian Department, minuted that this report was on the same lines as 'the sensational and improbable article' in the *Sunday Pictorial* on 22 January. Collier thought the rumour was connected with some German trade delegation shortly to go to Moscow.

At a New Year reception in Berlin Hitler surprised everybody by talking in a very friendly fashion with the Russian Ambassador, and in January 1939 at a reception for the diplomatic corps at the Kremlin Stalin caused astonishment by drawing the German military attaché aside for a conversation. At the same time Germany ceased its anti-Soviet radio and newspaper propaganda.

On 23 January the British Embassy in Berlin reported that Countess von Platen had overheard Ribbentrop saying that conversations between Berlin and Moscow were either contemplated or in progress, and on the same day *The Times* carried a story that a German trade delegation would arrive in Russia the next week.[22] Fitzroy Maclean, of the British Moscow Embassy, talked to a German colleague who told him of fresh rumours of a rapprochement. Laurence Collier, head of the Northern Department in the Foreign Office, minuted that this was 'too vague and secret' to write about, and no minutes were sent to the Foreign Secretary. Collier also dismissed as 'unfounded' a report from the Moscow Embassy that Litvinov had been asked to arrange a German interview with Beria, the Commercial Commissar.

Vernon Bartlett wrote an article in the *News Chronicle* on 30 January on 'the danger of Soviet-German rapprochement'. The Tass Agency in Moscow repeated the substance of the article, and it appeared in the newspapers. Seeds cabled 'The fact that such an article has been allowed to appear is regarded here as indicating at least that the Soviet Government are not averse from encouraging rumours of a Russo-German flirtation.' Seeds's telegram was ignored by Collier's department.[23]

An ominous letter came from Phipps in Paris on 26 May stating Cambon had shown him a long dispatch from the French Ambassador in Berlin reporting that even Ribbentrop in his desire to destroy France was pressing for an understanding with Russia:

> According to Coulondre Herr Hitler has not yet agreed, but von Ribbentrop with his usual obstinacy had not given up hope.
> M Cambon asked what I thought of this report. I said we had received information from two different sources recently to the effect that Ribbentrop claimed to be about to inflict a signal diplomatic defeat on England. It had been suggested that he had been referring to some agreement with Russia and this possibility had always to be borne in mind. Nevertheless it would be a mistake to imagine that a Russo-German agreement could be so easily concluded as some people in Germany thought. It did not necessarily follow that when the Germans were ready for an agreement the Russians would at once fall in with their wishes.[24]

This time Collier passed on the letter to his superiors. Sargent, Cadogan, Oliphant and Halifax initialled it without comment.

The British Embassy in Washington at the end of May reported that General Krivitski, a Soviet dissident who had defected to America, was obtaining much press publicity for revelations that Stalin had for long been working for an understanding with Hitler. Krivitski, high in the Soviet secret service, had defected to France at the end of 1937; after twice escaping assassination by Russian agents in France, he emigrated with his family to the USA. He was found dead in a hotel bedroom in 1941, presumably murdered by Soviet secret agents.

The Krivitski articles claimed that Stalin was playing the Rome–Berlin Axis against the London–Paris Axis, and 'Stalin's predilection has always been for Germany. His respect is for power. His distrust of the western democracies is greater than of the totalitarian states.' Krivitski wrote that Litvinov personified the Soviet policy of support for the League of Nations and collaboration with the democratic powers. 'That policy has collapsed, and the dismissal of Litvinov was the parting of the ways for Stalin. Stalin's secret diplomacy was always set upon a course of an intimate understanding with Hitler's Germany and Fascist Italy.'

According to Krivitski, Stalin's speech early in March* was an open bid for Hitler's friendship and it had been followed by the seizure of Prague. He recalled the sending of Stalin's personal emissary Kandelski in secret to Hitler, which he claimed led to a secret accord between Stalin and Hitler in the spring of 1937, and 'With the dropping of Litvinov, Stalin's policy is likely to follow a zig-zag course and he will camouflage his conciliation of Hitler by advances towards Paris and London.[25] With hindsight this was a remarkably accurate forecast, but how far Krivitski was correct about Stalin's secret wooing of Hitler prior to Munich remains a grey area.

Seeds told the Foreign Office that the Krivitski articles had

> excited considerable interest amongst our diplomatic colleagues and the general consensus of opinion is that they may well be genuine and may well represent the truth . . . it seems almost certain that Stalin has always kept and still wishes to keep open the possibility of rapprochement with Germany. The State Department in Washington advised 'the articles are not to be ignored, but not to be taken literally either'.

Seeds's view that the articles might be 'genuine' and 'represent the truth' did not appeal to the Northern Department in the Foreign Office despite Seeds having more knowledge of Russia than any other British diplomat. Krivitski's allegation that Stalin was hankering after an agreement with Hitler was also rejected out of hand.

Lascelles minuted: 'I do not think we need any more of this which seems to be mostly twaddle.' Another of his minutes was: 'this paper confirms my view that the General's revelations are not worth taking seriously and I do not think we need ask the Washington Chancery to let us have any more of them'. Collier minuted: 'I agree most of this is so directly contrary to all our information that I cannot believe the "General" to have had any important post.' On Seeds' message Lascelles commented: 'I still think he is talking nonsense,' and his final comment was 'Krivitski appears to have a bee in his bonnet.'

Collier decided not to draw the attention of his superiors to the dangers ahead if Krivitski was correct, and upon him lies a grave responsibility for not forewarning the Foreign Secretary of the likelihood of a German–Soviet

---

*On 10 March Stalin at the Eighteenth Congress of the Communist Party of the Soviet Union for the first time in years did not attack the Germans and Italians. Instead he claimed the appeasement policy of the western countries would divert the main thrust of the aggressors (Germany and Italy) towards the USSR, and he warned the democracies were playing a dangerous game which might very well backfire on them.[26]

understanding to forestall the Russian Alliance which was being so slowly and painfully negotiated. (Though all Cabinet Ministers would have had the Washington telegrams about Krivitski circulated to them.)[27]

On 17 May Mason Macfarlane wrote from Berlin that he had heard rumours of negotiations between Germany and Russia and 'I gather from many quarters that the German Army is vigorously renewing its efforts of a few years ago to arrive at a military alliance with Russia' and 'Oberst Nicolai, one of the Führer's most intimate military advisers, is also doing all he can to urge a rapprochement with Russia.' Forwarding this comment Henderson added: 'One never hears anything against the USSR in the Soviet press', and on the same day Vansittart told Halifax he had secret information that 'Hitler has been negotiating with Stalin through General Sirovy [a Czech general]'.[28]

On 2 June British naval intelligence reported that Ribbentrop had sent three of his best assistants to Moscow to prepare the ground, and direct contact between Moscow and Berlin had been restored.

In Moscow Seeds noted extra activity at the German Embassy, and Georgi Astrahakob, the Russian Commerical Attaché, confirmed to the British that 'commercial conversations between Moscow and Berlin had started'.

Vansittart heard again from his anti-Nazi contacts that the Germans and Russians were in contact and the German aim appeared to be to neutralize Russia. Erich Kordt, a senior official in Ribbentrop's office and an anti-Nazi, sent a message to Vansittart that 'if you want an agreement with Russia you had better be quick about it'.[29]

The next episode in the saga was a memorandum by Stafford Cripps, then prominent as the leader of the extreme left group of the Labour Party. Cripps on 9 June wrote for Halifax's information a memorandum which he said was based on confidential sources of information emanating from the best governmental sources in Berlin:

> Not only have negotiations between Russia and Germany been resumed lately – though at the moment they are again suspended – but this has become common knowledge even to the extent of people asking jokingly "When will Comrade Stalin be paying his visit to the Führer?" This is regarded as significant of the possibility – in the event of no alliance being concluded between the western democracies and Russia – of an arrangement being come to between Russia and Germany on which a new eastern frontier for Germany will be agreed, and Germany's power released for an attack on the west; this is hypothesis but my informant emphasized the very important fact that 'bankers, civil servants, office workers, everyone' were speaking quite openly about the possibility which even a few weeks ago would have meant internment risk from the Gestapo . . . I have known my informant for very many years most intimately and I believe him to have very exceptional opportunities of observation.[30] [David Astor tells the author that Adam von Trott was the informant.]

On 16 June Erich Kordt on a private visit to London sent a message to Ridsdale in the News Department of the Foreign Office that the Germans and Russians were 'definitely in contact' as a result of an approach by Ribbentrop to the Soviet Ambassador in Berlin, and the Germans were encouraged by his reception of their approach.[31]

On 23 June there were sensational reports in Spanish newspapers of a Hitler-Stalin accord. They were discounted by Collier, who again did not pass the file on to his superiors although Malleson had minuted that 'it confirmed reports from more reliable sources that the Germans are making a special effort to come to an understanding with the Russians. We still having nothing positive to show the Russian reaction to these advances, but I fear M Molotov's recent reaction to these advances is symptomatic.'[32]

On 26 June Colonel Dennis Daly, the assistant British military attaché in Berlin, talked to Colonel Dannfeldt, the Swedish military attaché, who said he felt the conversations between the French and British and Russians would not be successful, and from the information he now had 'an agreement between Germany and Soviet Russia might possibly soon be negotiated'. Roberts minuted: 'I think the Swedish military attaché is too gloomy.'

Halifax's attention was not drawn to this prophetic memorandum from Berlin.[33]

Similar rumours followed the next day from more weighty sources (27 June). Iveagh MacDonald, the diplomatic correspondent of *The Times* who was trusted by Halifax and the Foreign Office, told Charles Peake that he had received from two sources – one of which he regarded as 'completely reliable' – an alarming tale. This was to the effect that Attolico, the Italian Ambassador in Berlin, had recently suggested to the Soviet Ambassador in Berlin a German–Soviet agreement under which both countries would undertake not to interfere in each other's internal affairs; that there should be closer trade relations between the two countries; and much more importantly, 'Germany is prepared to guarantee all States lying between Germany and Russia, including Poland, once the Danzig question has been settled if Russia will do the same.' Peake sent a memorandum to Cadogan, who passed it on to Vansittart and Halifax, but neither commented.[34]

However, probably as a result of a talk to the Foreign Secretary about this report Cadogan asked the War Office for their views on the possibilities of a Soviet–German rapprochement based on their MI 2 secret service reports. The War Office produced a long report on 4 July. This stated that in the pre-Hitler period relations between Germany and Russia were 'comparatively close' and there was active contact between the two General Staffs, with Germany gaining experience of equipment forbidden to her by Versailles. After Hitler appeared on the scene in 1933 the German attitude changed to one of abuse, and most competent observers believed Hitler was 'violently anti-Soviet'.

The War Office stated that during the first three months of 1939 there had been several rumours of a rapprochement

> though it seemed more likely that they really referred to the possibilities of a commercial agreement. At the same time there were suggestions that the reports might have been spread in order to bring pressure on the western powers (to conclude an agreement with Russia). In May there was a sudden crop of rumours traceable almost entirely to prominent German or Italian officials which suggested that if a rapprochement had not actually been arranged, at any rate it would be concluded very shortly. At the same time the absence of attacks on either party in the other party's press was most noticeable. Early in June there were still further reports, mainly from German sources, of efforts towards an agreement in which the head of the secret service (Canaris) was reported to have said that negotiations were in progress that the U.S.S.R. would not support Poland in war and that they should supply Germany with raw materials. On the other hand Hitler is reported to have consulted his leading Generals as to the prospect of success in a war in which Soviet Russia was aligned against Germany, a fear which he need hardly have entertained if, in fact, Germany and the Soviet were about to conclude an agreement.

The War Office concluded:

> There seems to be no real circumstantial evidence of negotiations being in progress although a commercial agreement was likely, but the danger of such a rapprochement cannot be discounted and it is still wise to watch the situation very carefully. Nevertheless there is no conclusive evidence of it at present, and the conclusion of an Anglo–French–Soviet alliance would make a rapprochement more difficult.

Collier minuted on the MI 2 report: 'I do not believe therefore there is any danger of an actual Russo–German political rapprochement as long as Hitler is in power.'

Chamberlain and Halifax were thus not adequately warned by their advisers of the deadly danger lying ahead. When the Ribbentrop–Molotov Pact was signed they were taken completely by surprise.[35]

In Cabinet on 1 July Halifax said it seemed that discussions of some kind were proceeding between the German and Soviet Governments; it was impossible to assess their real value, but it seemed likely that they related to industrial matters; whereupon Chamberlain said he could not believe a real alliance between Germany and Russia was possible. Eleven days later Chamberlain said that 'on the whole he was disposed to take the view that the Soviet Government intended to make an agreement with us, but were probably in no hurry to do so'. The Soviet Government had in March been ready for an alliance, but only if it was done quickly and spontaneously, while the delay was due to Britain dragging her feet.[36]

Rab Butler, Under-Secretary for Foreign Affairs and answerable for them to the Commons, returned from holiday in the South of France on 24 August when the German–Soviet Pact was announced and Cadogan sent him urgently the War Office paper of 4 July. Butler minuted to Cadogan plaintively the next day:

> Thank you for the attached paper on secret intelligence on Russo–German intrigues . . . Should not our intelligence reports have come more into the picture at an earlier stage, e.g. when the FPC was considering sending the mission to Russia should not the meeting have started with an intelligence report? In the Commons last night everyone was asking me what was our Intelligence up to?

The next day a long paper was prepared for him hurriedly by Collier, who realized he was to blame for failing to give the correct emphasis to Cripps and the other reports of Russo–German moves. Collier had a distinguished academic career, being Brackenbury Scholar at Balliol and taking a First in history, but was not considered by his colleagues to have a flair for diplomacy. He did his best with a bad brief:

> It is notoriously difficult to obtain reliable information direct from Soviet sources. We have had very little information from them on German–Soviet relations; and such information as we have had tended to show that a Soviet–German political rappochement was unlikely.
>
> Information from direct German sources was much more plentiful but was contradictory. On the one hand were reports that certain sections of German opinion favoured an understanding with the Soviet Government and even that attempts were being made to bring this about by various means such as Italian mediation, [the Ciano Diaries establish that this was a myth] which as my minutes show I thought worthy of attention, but on the other hand we had numerous indications from sources which we had no reason to think any less reliable that the Germans did not see how such a rapprochement could be brought about, that Hitler was opposed to it and that the policy favoured in the highest Nazi circles was one of disrupting the Soviet regime and removing Stalin personally, and our reports from Soviet sources suggested that these last named aims were known to Stalin and were a reason why he was never likely to make an agreement with the Germans . . . it was in the interests of both the Russians and the Germans – particularly the latter, to spread rumours of a Russo–German rapprochement for purposes of blackmail in their dealings with us . . . It appears indeed that only a very few Soviet personalities were in the secret at all. Maisky, for example, is reported to have been completely left in the dark . . . we did not, and still do not know what inducements could be offered to them (Russians) to make them reverse their previous avowed policy of hostility to German expansion.

Collier was naive if he did not realize 'the inducement' to Russia must be a slice of Poland. Sargent minuted: 'The fact remains that we were never told that the Germans and Russians had started negotiations with one another –

315

which was the only thing that mattered.'* The Foreign Office had let the Government down badly, even though their relevant file also contained the words '. . . we know from secret sources that certain elements in Germany have been contemplating a deal with the Soviet Union involving a fresh partition of Poland' Butler was unrancorous, accepting Collier's note courteously and writing:

> I am informed that the outline terms of the agreement which were ultimately signed were known to our Intelligence and reached this office. I do not know if they reached here in a confidential form. I am sorry to be persistent but I have suffered very much from Hon. Members who kept asking me until recently why we did not know. Meanwhile I am much obliged by Mr. Collier's valuable note.[37]

Jebb was immediately told to see Butler and assure him that the details of the Molotov–Ribbentrop Pact had not been known in advance. Seeds in Moscow was always aware that Stalin might make an agreement with Hitler, and nothing can excuse the Foreign Office (and particularly Collier) for its failure to brief Halifax and Butler about the evidence they were receiving of German–Russian conversations.[39]

German Foreign Office documents published after the war reveal the Soviet–German negotiations about which the Foreign Office received rumours. Attempts at trade negotiations broke down in February 1939; Mikoyan, the Soviet Commissar for Foreign Trade, then recorded that he had been placed in an awkward position vis-à-vis his own Government, and he needed convincing not only of the sincerity of Germany's intentions, but of the likelihood of positive results being achieved by the reopening of negotiations.[40]

The Germans then proposed that Julius Schnurre should pay a visit to Moscow. Mikoyan would only agree if his earlier proposals (which had been rejected in February) were accepted in substance. From the Moscow Embassy von Tippelskirch reported to Weizsäcker on 18 June that Mikoyan suspected 'a political game behind our offer of negotiation' and believed Germany 'expected some advantage from the resumption of economic negotiations just at the present time'.[41]

---

*He was ignoring a dire warning in a telegram from Henderson dated 16 August: 'I was impressed by . . . Weizsacker's calm . . . He seemed very confident and professed to believe that Russian assistance to the Poles would be not only entirely negligible, but that the U.S.S.R. would even in the end join in sharing the Polish spoils.'

Steinhard, the American Ambassador in Moscow, had since July continually warned Washington of an impending German–Russian Agreement. These were passed on to Lindsay, but a telegram imparting this information dated 18 August was not decyphered for four days. Thus the Government knew about the Pact just after it had been signed instead of before. Roberts minuted: 'It is a great pity that this telegram was not decyphered until four days after receipt with the result that we were taken by surprise.[38]

Despite this unfavourable reception Germany persisted, but Mikoyan remained obdurate, reiterating that he required clearer signs of resolving differences before he would agree to Schnurre coming to Moscow. On a telegram from Tippelskirch from Moscow on 25 June Weizsäcker noted: 'We must not lose patience.' But Hitler was annoyed and sent a petulant note that the Russians were to be informed he was not interested in a resumption of the economic discussions 'at present'.

However, the indications in July were that the British and French negotiations for a Russian alliance were likely to be successful, and in a Berlin restaurant on 26 July Asthakov and Barbarin, head of the Russian trade delegation, met Julius Schnurre and over good food and wine came almost to the heads of an agreement on a German–Russian understanding. Schulenberg (German Ambassador in Moscow) was told to approach Mikoyan and offer concessions with the rider that 'conversations with Mikoyan must incidentally not be conducted in such a way as to assume the character of pressure by Germany . . . we should on no account place ourselves in the position of suppliants'.[42]

In August the German Foreign Office received reports that France had proposed a new initiative in order to break the deadlock in the Anglo–French–Russian conversations; Hitler decided on 14 August on a dramatic intervention. Ribbentrop telegraphed to Schulenberg that he proposed coming himself to Moscow to see Molotov on the grounds that 'the crisis which has been produced in German–Polish relations by English policy as well as English agitation for war and the attempts at an alliance which are bound up with that policy made a speedy clarification of German–Russian relations necessary.[43]

On 16 August Schulenberg reported he 'had been received warmly by Molotov, who had been quite unusually compliant and candid' and flattered personally by the proposal of Ribbentrop's visit. He suggested that the ground should be prepared beforehand and that Ribbentrop should hold off his visit until then.

Ribbentrop on 18 August sent a most urgent telegram asking Schulenberg to impress on Molotov the need for a rapid consent to his visit and stating that 'in this connection you must keep in mind the decisive fact that an early outbreak of open German–Polish conflict is probable, and that we therefore have the greatest interest in my visit to Moscow taking place immediately'. Molotov's initial reaction was to re-emphasize that Ribbentrop should delay coming to Russia until the economic agreement had been signed and made public so that there would be time for it 'to achieve its effect abroad, and after that would come the turn of the non-aggression pact'. However, on the same day, 20 August, Schulenberg was summoned to the Kremlin, handed the draft of the non-aggression pact and told that

Ribbentrop would be welcomed in Moscow one week after publication of the economic agreement. Schulenberg wrote: 'I assume that Stalin intervened.'

Hitler's plans to invade Poland were now so far advanced that this timetable was too slow for him, and the same evening, 20 August, he sent a telegram to Stalin accepting the draft proposals and asking for Ribbentrop to be received in Moscow on Tuesday, 22 August (or at the latest 23 August) 'with the fullest powers to draw up and sign the non-aggression pact and the protocol'. Hitler's grounds for this request were that the tension between Germany and Poland had become 'intolerable'. Stalin agreed Ribbentrop should come on 23 August, and the Pact was signed on 25 August.

The delay in the arrival of the Anglo-French military mission and the British failure to nominate someone with sufficient prestige as its head had caused Molotov and Stalin to change their minds. In addition Hitler was able to offer the bait of a restoration to Russia of their pre-1914 territory in Poland. This sad tale demonstrates the folly of Chamberlain and the British Cabinet in not accepting the Russian proposals of April enthusiastically. The long-drawn-out bargaining, coupled with the simultaneous efforts by Britain to negotiate further appeasement with Hitler (which were well known to the Kremlin), convinced Russia that Britain was not serious about the alliance and really aimed at plunging Russia and Germany into an all-out war.[44]

Recklessly Chamberlain in the summer of 1939 accompanied his negotiations for an alliance with Russia by further efforts at appeasing Hitler. Although disillusioned with Hitler by the occupation of Prague, the Prime Minister was even more unhappy at the idea of collaboration with Russia. As a result he snatched at any opportunity of reopening negotiations with the Führer. All the British openings towards Germany were reported to Stalin.

Henderson's despatches from Berlin continually advocated appeasement of Germany and reiterated that Hitler did not want to go to war, and that his territorial ambitions could be easily satisfied. These despatches were immediately leaked to the Russians. There was a Russian spy in the communications department of the Foreign Office in London, Captain John King, who was arrested in October and sentenced to ten years imprisonment. The Foreign Office were aware of the leaks, and the final efforts at conciliating Hitler were done from Downing Street by Chamberlain with Halifax's knowledge, but bypassing the Foreign Office. On top, of course, the Germans passed on to the Russians information about British overtures to them.[45]

Russian suspicions of British intentions were aroused when Dr Wohltat came to London in the middle of July on the flimsy excuse that he was attending a whaling conference. He talked to Robert Hudson (Secretary, Department of Overseas Trade) on 20 July, and to Horace Wilson on 24 July. Wilson, with Chamberlain's approval, wrote on 10 Downing Street notepaper a memorandum proposing an Anglo–German Treaty of non-aggression, a disarmament agreement and trade co-operation.

The Wohltat conversations were leaked to the press, which reported a sensational story of an enormous British loan to Germany to prevent war.[46]

For some unexplained reason Hudson gave an exclusive interview to the *Daily Express* which came out with headlines 'I Planned the Peace Loan to Germany. Minister tells of his talk with Wohltat.'

The German Ambassador, Dirksen, in a memorandum for Hitler stated that 'Wilson affirmed that the conclusion of an Anglo–German entente would practically render Britain's guarantee policy nugatory . . . and would enable Britain to extricate herself from her predicament in regard to Poland.' The Ambassador wrote to Ribbentrop that Britain had not pledged herself a hundred per cent to support Poland in any conflict, and 'a programme of negotiations' could be expected.[47]

Harvey wrote in his diary 'The story (*Daily Express*) is calculated to do infinite harm to Soviet negotiations . . . I can hardly believe it to be true – it is a very silly proposal linked up with pre-election propaganda.' Vansittart commented 'It has been an unhappy and damaging affair.' But Chamberlain wrote to his sister a week later that he wanted to continue 'discreet conversations with Germany'. Jebb minuted to Cadogan '. . . the immediate effect of this piece of super-appeasement has been to arouse the suspicions of the Bolsheviks, discourage the Poles, and encourage the Germans into thinking we are prepared to buy peace. I doubt whether folly could be pushed to a further extreme.'[48]

Chamberlain then sent an unofficial emissary to Germany, E. D. W. Tennant – a rich Mincing Lane commodity broker sympathetic to the Nazis (though critical of their anti-semitism), who had been an intimate and useful friend to Ribbentrop while the latter was Ambassador in London. He stayed at Ribbentrop's country house near Salzburg on 22 July. Ribbentrop told Tennant 'the return of Danzig was now inevitable; it was only a question of time . . . Britain could do nothing to save Poland whose army would be wiped out; it does not compare with the Czech army which the Germans always recognised would be a serious problem . . . If Britain had not interfered a settlement would have been reached. The British support of Poland and negotiations with Russia had welded the German nation together.' Ribbentrop also said that in March Hitler had made a generous offer to Poland of a permanent and final settlement. No other German

Chancellor, not even Stresemann or Brüning, would have dared to make such an offer, and 'the Reichstag were astounded and at first displeased when Hitler told them he had offered to give up the Corridor in return for an autobahn and Danzig'. Tennant suggested to Ribbentrop a British loan of £1 billion. One interesting point was that Ribbentrop told Tennant Hitler had not forgiven Mussolini for treating him like a commercial traveller when they first met in Venice.[49]

Horace Wilson had a long discussion with Tennant at No. 10 when he returned to London and reported direct to Chamberlain. Notwithstanding the barren result of Tennant's trip, Chamberlain now enlisted the willing services of the two newspaper barons Lords Kemsley and Rothermere. Kemsley had a long talk to Hitler at Bayreuth on 27 July, and in the evening at the Opera met Unity Mitford, who he found had been told of the talk by Hitler. Hitler told Kemsley a few months before he had 90 per cent of the country behind him; now because of British opposition to his taking Danzig he had 100 per cent. He went on that every country, even small countries like Belgium and Holland, had their colonies and it was ludicrous that a great country like Germany with its eighty million people should be without. They must have colonies, and preferred those they had previously owned. Hitler mentioned the Wilson–Wohltat talks, and said these did not interest him because Germany was not after money. In addition he insisted that the Versailles Treaty must be cancelled.

Kemsley discussed his interview with Chamberlain and Wilson on 1 August. The Prime Minister asked Kemsley to draft a letter to Otto Dietrich requesting the Führer to put forward his proposals in writing. Kemsley was enjoined to strict secrecy, and the Foreign Office were not consulted or informed. Chamberlain and Wilson amended Kemsley's draft letter in their own handwriting and the letter was delivered by hand by Kemsley's secretary. It was a strange way to conduct diplomacy. Halifax was told what was going on, and raised no objection. Hitler's bleak reply was: 'Until confidence has been restored there is no object in preparing for conversations.' It was another abortive initiative.

Undeterred, Chamberlain encouraged Rothermere to try, this time with Ribbentrop, by an exchange of letters. Ribbentrop replied to Rothermere, referring courteously to their old friendship and co-operation for an understanding, but pointing out that apart from 'Rothermere's own newspapers' (*Mail, Mirror, Evening News*) Great Britain had since 30 January 1933 led a continuous and ferocious propaganda campaign against Germany, and 'the policy of trying to prevent the return of Danzig and a communication between East Prussia and Germany is taken by the German people as a sign that Great Britain always stands in the German way even if no vital British interests are at stake,' and this British campaign of hatred is producing a 'deep hatred' in the heart of every German against Britain. Thus the Rothermere effort was also unproductive.[50]

Chamberlain and Halifax became interested in a move by Charles Buxton MP, a prominent unofficial Labour spokesman on foreign policy. Buxton had numerous contacts in Germany through the Quakers. He had prepared a memorandum for the Labour Party National Executive arguing that the object should be to remove 'the legitimate grievances of the have-not powers' with the return of colonies to Germany and rescinding of the war guilt clauses of Versailles. Buxton saw Halifax on 13 July and Kordt on the 29th, when he went even further than in his written memorandum, arguing that Britain and Germany should define their spheres of influence. Kordt assumed that Buxton's approach and ideas had been approved by Chamberlain. This is probable, and Dirksen sent an account of the conversation on to Berlin, where Hitler took it as yet another indication that Britain was weakening on her guarantees in Central Europe.[51]

Rab Butler was unenthusiastic for the Russian Alliance. Chamberlain, in a letter to his sister, referred to Butler as 'the only supporter for my views'. Butler also disapproved of the Polish guarantee. When the Ribbentrop––Molotov pact was signed he sent a note to Chamberlain: 'It gave Russia just the excuse not to defend herself against Germany since we had gratuitously planted ourselves in East Europe. It thus led to Russia going in with Germany.'[52]

A memorandum from Butler to Halifax in Butler's handwriting on 17 July is striking evidence of how appeasement-minded both Butler and Halifax were, because Butler would not have written in this vein if it was contrary to his superior's opinion. Butler described the Buxton memorandum as 'attractive' (which makes it seem likely that Halifax and Chamberlain had approved it) and pointed out:

1) We have still a task to do to persuade Hitler we are not preparing for aggression or a preventive war.
2) We are so keen to fortify the Poles (and our other allies) that we tend to make them very rigid.

Butler continued that 'the Danzig problem should be solved simply by persuading Col. Beck to negotiate a settlement . . . We should merge the Danzig problem by getting Hitler to make an approach as Henderson suggests thus enabling him to make Nuremberg a Peace Rally.' This was appeasement in full swing, and Butler, who was an incorrigible gossip and notably indiscreet, would have talked to the same effect, and this would have been repeated to Maisky.

Moreover, Butler also made clear his antipathy to an alliance with Russia: 'The best hopes of obtaining an approach to Hitler lie in concluding something *ANODYNE* with Russia . . . and in preserving a *"SILENCE*

MENAÇANT" broken only by an indication that we refuse to join anyone intending to attack Germany.' This is further evidence, if it is required, that Chamberlain and some members of the Cabinet all through the Russian negotiations agreed with Butler and wanted something 'anodyne' with Stalin while they returned to their pre-Prague policy of caressing Hitler.[53]

Kordt knew Butler was cold over the Russian alliance and anxious for more negotiations with Hitler. Accordingly he called at Butler's house during the evening of 2 August to say 'goodbye' before the recess. Kordt asked 'would we recognise a German Lebensraum in Eastern Europe if they indicated quietitude by some concrete act', and in addition whether Wilson's and Hudson's conversation with Wohltat meant anything. Butler had not seen these records and would not comment. Then Kordt said he had been recalled to Berlin and wished to talk to some 'very authoritative person' before he went, so that he could take a message to Weizsäcker. Kordt told Butler that 'Danzig' was too nailed up to be solved as an individual problem, and in the east of Europe 'we should have eventually to arrange that our new friends undertook to embark on no aggressive economic or military attacks on Germany if we were to hope for a settlement'. Butler saw Chamberlain in the lobby the same evening and the Prime Minister agreed Horace Wilson should talk to either Kordt or Dirksen the next day.

The next day Dirksen, the Ambassador, not Kordt, came to see Wilson at 10 Downing Street. Dirksen told Wilson he wanted to find out what help he or Kordt might give towards furthering discussion. Wilson replied that the answer rested solely with the German Government, but there were three propositions which he and Kordt might keep in mind:

1) What instructions had the Führer given to the follow-up of Wohltat's report?
2) What will the German Chancellor do to prevent the position from becoming worse during the next few weeks? Will he so arrange the events during these weeks that they are non-provocative?
3) Assuming an agenda and programme to have been worked out, what will the German Chancellor do to show his determination to give the lead in creating a suitable atmosphere so that the agenda and programme may be discussed with due prospect of success?
   3.8.39   H. W.[54]

For once Wilson was firm and said it was useless to bother about an agenda while German troops 'were marching up and down the Polish frontier'. In his report to Berlin, Dirksen wrote that Chamberlain would probably be forced to resign if details of Anglo–German negotiations leaked out. This is not in Wilson's version, but Hitler believed it. Wilson also said Britain would regard 'patience' over Danzig, demobilization or a declaration that Bohemia and Moravia would eventually have home rule as the concrete gesture from Hitler which they were looking for.

Dirksen replied that Hitler wanted something 'concrete' from Britain and had 'no confidence in Britain', but he asked for an agenda to be framed on points which interested Hitler. Wilson discussed this talk with Chamberlain in the evening. Chamberlain said 'the wise course would be to keep the movement alive'. The next morning Wilson saw Halifax, who expressed 'satisfaction' and went so far as to discuss possible procedure and 'a hypothetical agenda'.

Hitler's object at this stage was not genuinely to seek talks, but to discourage the British from coming to a firm arrangement with the Russians; the message Kordt took to Berlin confirmed Hitler in his view that Britain wanted appeasement and would not fight. On 20 August Hitler sent a secret message to Wilson that the talks could not be continued, which shows how bogus this approach was, but it deceived Halifax and Chamberlain, and encouraged them to believe that Hitler could still be appeased and war prevented.[55]

The Prime Minister's and Foreign Secretary's hopes of starting negotiations with Hitler were raised when a message came that Goering would come to England in strict secrecy on 23 August. According to Halifax's account, he would come if he could 'be assured that he will be able to see the Prime Minister'. The British agreed to the Goering visit, and arrangements were made for him to land at 'some deserted aerodrome' and be taken by car direct to Chequers. The regular household were to be sent on leave and be replaced by secret service personnel, and the telephone disconnected. Halifax thought it would be 'a dramatic interlude', but instead word came on 24 August that Hitler would not allow it.

Unfortunately, there is nothing in the archives to explain how Goering's visit could be kept anonymous in view of his enormous bulk which would be impossible to camouflage. Then at the moment the Ribbentrop–Molotov talks came to fruition Goering's visit was definitively cancelled. Possibly Hitler had been keeping his options open in case his Russian talks failed; more probably he was not genuinely seeking an agreement with Britain but instead was dangling out hopes in order to deter Chamberlain from endorsing a firm arrangement with the Russians.

On Hitler's side the British reaction confirmed his belief that Chamberlain would never go to war for the sake of Danzig and the Corridor.[56]

To try to begin negotiations with Hitler while the military mission was slowly steaming towards Russia was duplicity. Halifax and Chamberlain were deceiving not only the Russians, but also their own military and diplomatic advisers and Parliament. Butler's phrase ANODYNE indicates only lip service was being paid to the Government's declared intention of negotiating an alliance with Russia. The unscrupulous and acquisitive Stalin was aware of this double-dealing, and it must have been a key factor in making him decide on a deal with Hitler, with the attraction of the return of a lump of Poland to Russia.

CHAPTER FIFTEEN

INTO THE ABYSS

Halifax to Ciano on 2 September 1939: 'Do your best with Berlin' – to persuade Hitler to come to a Conference after German troops had invaded Poland and bombed Polish towns. The Cabinet ignored Polish requests for urgent RAF action against Germany, although British bombers had already flown to French airfields.

WHEN THE Cabinet met in the afternoon of 22 August the atmosphere was gloomy. The news of the German–Soviet Agreement was a relief to some members (and also many Tory MPs) who were opposed to an alliance with Russia, and the general feeling was that Poland should appease Hitler by giving away Danzig and allowing a German autobahn through the Corridor. However, they overlooked the hostage to fortune Britain had given by a guarantee which could force her into war with Germany if Hitler attacked Poland.

The Cabinet still hoped to rescue the Moscow talks, and Halifax said that in the hope of doing so he had telegraphed 'four alternative formulae defining "indirect aggression" ' under the draft Treaty, and had authorized Seeds to resume political talks with Molotov 'in whatever way he thought best'. Ominously, Halifax told the Cabinet that the Poles considered the Russian objective was to occupy Polish territory permanently, but he expected this attitude to be modified if war broke out; while the French, according to Halifax, had exceeded their authority from the Poles by instructing Doumenc to tell Voroshilov that Russian armies would have transit rights once war broke out; Halifax disclosed he had 'a great deal of secret information' that Germany intended to attack Poland between 25 and 28 August.

Chamberlain in a rare moment of resolution declared it was 'unthinkable that we should not carry out these obligations [to Poland]' and a press statement to this effect was authorized. This attitude was in sharp contrast to his behaviour twelve months before over Czechoslovakia, but it did not last because he soon began to pressurize Poland to give in to Hitler's demands. He then obtained the consent of the Cabinet to sending a personal letter to Hitler; a draft was available, and after discussion it was approved by the whole Cabinet.

It was reported that Burckhardt had seen Hitler on 11 August and found the Führer irrational and ambivalent. Hitler had told him: 'If the slightest incident happens now I shall crush the Poles without warning in such a way that no trace of Poland can be found afterwards.' However, Hitler, with a rare touch of humanity, warned Burckhardt that his family would be safer in Switzerland than in Danzig. Hitler had produced his usual carrot for the British, saying 'I want to live in peace with England,' and that a chance to meet a German-speaking Englishman would be welcome. Burckhardt suggested General Sir Edmund Ironside to Henderson, but Chamberlain rejected the suggestion.[1]

Chamberlain's letter was strong in that it affirmed that any German–Soviet agreement would not alter Britain's obligations to Poland, and any German success on any one front would not bring an early end to hostilities, and went on: 'If only a situation of confidence could be restored to enable discussions to be carried on in an atmosphere different from that which prevails today'. Henderson took the letter personally to Hitler on 23 August. Hitler, with his Soviet non-aggression pact in the bag, was arrogant, saying Britain had poisoned the atmosphere by the guarantee to Poland, and that the question of Danzig and the Corridor would be settled one way or another. Henderson without instructions from the Government then gave an unauthorized indication of Britain's willingness for further appeasement by stating that he (the Ambassador) had never believed in an Anglo–French–Soviet Pact, and proof of Chamberlain's friendship lay in the exclusion of Churchill from the Cabinet, and astonishingly 'The hostile attitude to Germany did not represent the will of the British people. It was the work of Jews and enemies of the Nazis.' Nothing could be calculated to do more to indicate to Hitler that Britain would not fight for Poland.[2]

At the Cabinet on 29 August Halifax was optimistic, explaining that Molotov considered Russia would still be free to make arrangements with the French and British Governments directed against Germany in the event of the latter committing aggression, and that Lipski had now returned to Berlin and had accepted an invitation to shoot stags with Goering. Halifax was far adrift. It Stalin intended to help France and Britain in the event of a

German attack on Poland, he would not have agreed to the non-aggression pact.[3]

The only good news on 29 August was that Mussolini had decided not to fight. Mussolini was timid and worried about the prospect of war as his military forces were ill prepared. He had sent Ciano to see Hitler on 12 August, and the German dictator said he would definitely strike against Poland before the end of the month, and that France and Britain would not intervene. Neither would the USSR, which thoroughly detested Poland.[4]

When Ciano told Mussolini of Hitler's intention the Duce was horrified because on 22 May 1939 the Pact of Steel had been signed at Salzburg between Italy and Germany; this obliged Italy unconditionally to support Germany in any war with all her forces, even if it was an act of aggression by Hitler. During the negotiations Hitler had told Ciano he had no intention of attacking Poland. A few hours after he had signed the Treaty, the Führer gave orders to his generals to prepare for an attack on Poland, but to keep it secret from Germany's new ally Italy.[5] As a result almost in panic forty-eight hours after the news of the German Soviet Pact, Mussolini on 25 August reminded Hitler that when the Pact of Steel was signed Hitler had promised not to unleash a war until 1942 and then only after Italy had been provided with the necessary war material. Mussolini instructed the Italian Foreign Office to send a note to Berlin that the total material required by Italy before she could declare war amounted to 1½ million tons, which would have needed 17,000 trains of 50 wagons each and almost the sole use of the Italian railway system for a year with 50 trains a day. Loraine sent this news from Rome.[6]

Meanwhile shooting incidents on the Polish–German frontier increased; the Nazi press campaign against Poland became feverish, and the great number of German troops on the Polish frontier could not be disguised.

On 22 August Hitler had issued orders at a Conference to his generals to attack Poland on 28 August. (Lochar, an American journalist, had given Henderson a copy of the account of the meeting when Goering was alleged to have jumped on the table with joy. Goering denied this at Nuremberg.) Two events made him change this plan on 26 August (4 days later). The first was Mussolini's decision not to go to war; the second was the announcement from London that the Anglo–Polish Treaty had been signed. The signature meant nothing extra. The legal difficulties of putting the April agreement into the form of a Treaty had taken many weeks, and it was by a coincidence, not intention, that it was published on 25 August.

The German Foreign Office attributed far more importance to the signing of the Anglo–Polish Treaty than it deserved. Von Selim, Counsellor at the German Embassy in London, saw Strang on the morning of 26 August, and told him the signature of the Treaty was 'a bombshell in Berlin because they had doubted our resolution to do it; now they could no longer do so.' According to General Halder, the Führer was considerably shaken. Anyway, Hitler postponed his plans for war at the eleventh hour, summoning Keitel urgently on 26 August. Keitel was able (though with difficulty) to cancel the operations scheduled for 28 August, but one small unit advanced over the Polish frontier before it could be recalled. When Goering conferred with Keitel and Hitler, Keitel asked if the operation was postponed temporarily or permanently. Hitler replied that he could not give the answer until he knew whether he could eliminate British intervention.[7]

Hitler was on the horns of a dilemma. He knew that the Poles could not offer much resistance without Russian support, but he had been warned by his General Staff that the French would be able to break through the Siegfried Line if they launched a resolute attack, and Gamelin had promised the Poles to do so fourteen days after war started. In evidence at Nuremberg Jodl said that Germany had only twenty-three divisions on the West Wall, and it was only the inactivity of the Allies which saved Germany from defeat. Keitel said:

> A French attack during the Polish campaign would have encountered only a German military screen, not a real defence . . . We soldiers thought the Western powers had not serious intentions because they did not take advantage of the extremely favourable situation.[8]

In addition, Hitler knew there was opposition from his generals. Henderson was informed by a high-ranking anti-Nazi (probably Hassell) that they had objected to a war on two fronts because the German weakness on the West Wall made a French breakthrough likely. Brauchitsch was said to have stated that such a war was out of the question; the same informant also said Hitler had had a nervous breakdown on 26 August, and the General Staff had at first considered bringing about a military coup to depose him, but Hitler had quickly recovered. The informant confirmed that Hitler did not believe there would be a strong French attack on the West Wall. (The truth of this was confirmed by General Halder after the war.) Ribbentrop and Himmler were pushing Hitler into war while Goering wanted peace and astonishingly was able to use an unofficial Swedish emissary who acted as a shuttlecock between Hitler's Chancellery and 10 Downing Street. The emissary was Berger Dahlerus, a Swedish businessman with many contacts in British comercial circles; he was an intimate friend of Goering, and under financial obligations to him. He may have been Anglophile, but he was extremely bigoted against Poland. Chamberlain described Dahlerus to the Cabinet as someone who did not come quickly to the point and often spent time in discussing unimportant details. 'He was not a man who saw fundamental points quickly. Nevertheless he was a useful person since he had the confidence of Goering.' Dahlerus's role was not made known to the Poles. Sargent minuted 'we must be on our guard in dealing with Dahlerus', but Frank Roberts told the author he got to know him well then and thought him sincere and honest, but naive; in Roberts's view Goering was strongly opposed to war because he had too many of the good things of life. Sir Peter Tennant, who saw Dahlerus for six years in Stockholm during the war, formed a less favourable opinion.[9]

At the Nuremberg Trials the British prosecutor, David Maxwell Fyfe, sought to establish that in 1939 Goering was not sincere in trying to avoid war but wanted only to stop British intervention. Dahlerus was a fair-weather friend of Goering's because his evidence confirmed the impression desired by Maxwell Fyfe. The evidence points to Goering doing his best to prevent Hitler attacking Poland in August 1939; but Ribbentrop – who wanted war – prevailed with Hitler. This was Henderson's view but he died before the Nuremberg Trials.[10]

On 26 August Dahlerus arrived in London with a message from Goering, approved by Hitler, expressing the Führer's desire for an understanding with Britain; Goering promised he would do everything in his power to facilitate this. Halifax saw Dahlerus that evening, and the Swede said that he was sure official negotiations with Germany would lead to a settlement. The next morning, 27 August, Dahlerus told Halifax that Goering was very pleased with what Halifax termed some platitudinous message of his 'expressing a desire for peace'. Then Halifax took Dahlerus to see the Prime Minister at No. 10 where they had an abortive discussion in which Dahlerus insisted Goering was working hard for peace and 'the situation was not hopeless'. Chamberlain and Halifax began to hope the personal letter to Hitler would produce good results.

Henderson later that day arrived back in London and confirmed that Hitler had told him he did not want war provided he achieved his territorial claims on Poland which, according to Henderson, were not 'exorbitant'. Henderson brought a message from the Führer that he must 'solve' the problem of Danzig and the Corridor and then he would make a large comprehensive offer to England under which he would personally guarantee that the British Empire and Germany's western frontiers were fixed and final.[11]

Surprisingly Dahlerus, not Henderson, was instructed to take a reply to Berlin that Britain was willing to negotiate giving away Danzig and the Corridor, and once the crisis was solved Britain would discuss the return of Germany's former colonies. Goering communicated this to Hitler, who, Goering alleged, welcomed Britain's wish for a peaceful settlement and even asked whether Britain wanted a Treaty or a Pact.

On 26 August the Cabinet did not meet until 6.30 p.m. Halifax told them that Hitler had provided a German aeroplane to fly Henderson to London and this was not consistent with a plan for the immediate invasion of Poland; he also said Dahlerus had suggested he should postpone signing the Anglo–Polish Treaty. Henderson told the Cabinet he doubted whether there was any agreement to partition Poland (between Germany and Russia) but at the same time it seemed likely there was some *quid pro quo* which did not form part of the published German–Soviet agreement (this was strange reasoning). Henderson added that the situation was different from last year because Hitler had a hate for Beneš but was well disposed towards Beck and Lipski, although Lipski had seen no representative of the German Government for four months. Halifax told the Cabinet that it would be made clear that Dahlerus was not carrying our answer to Hitler, but rather preparing the ground for our main communication.[12]

Late on 26 August Goering took Dahlerus to see Hitler. From the Dahlerus account of the interview it is clear Hitler was vacillating after cancelling his battle orders for 28 August. After the Führer had launched into an excitable and irrational harangue Dahlerus asked Hitler to state his minimum demands on Poland. Hitler replied that Danzig and the Corridor must go back to Germany together with Gdynia.

Goering then tore a page out of an atlas and marked in red pencil the Polish areas which Hitler was demanding. These were the German-speaking parts of the Corridor. Dahlerus took this rough map with him to London, and the next morning (27 August) was back at 10 Downing Street explaining to Chamberlain and Halifax that Goering had persuaded Hitler not to go to war, and that Goering's map was a good basis for an amicable settlement.[13]

On 28 August Henderson went back to Berlin with the official British reply to Hitler. He was received with a guard of honour at the Chancellery and a roll of drums while Meisner, Minister of State, and Bruckener, Hitler's aide-de-camp, received him at the entrance to the Chancellery. Chamberlain and Halifax had worked on the document which Henderson was carrying for two days, and had persuaded Beck to agree to begin direct negotiations with Hitler over Danzig and the Corridor. The British urged that the German–Polish direct negotiations should be opened at once on a basis which would safeguard Poland's essential interests, and 'the settlement should be secured by international guarantee', after which Britain hoped 'the way would be open to a wider and more complete understanding between Britain and Germany.' Hitler was cordial when he saw Henderson and listened quietly to his explanation of the British viewpoint; the Führer promised an answer by the next evening. Henderson left the Chancellery optimistic. If the Poles would agree to come to Berlin another Munich was in sight.

Henderson reported that this was 'the sole chance of preventing war' and proof of his (Hitler's) sincerity in his desire for friendship with Britain. There was optimism in Whitehall; it looked as if war had been prevented although the price would be the cession of Danzig and much of the Corridor which would be an enormous boost to Hitler's popularity. The British Cabinet's chief worry now was whether the nation would endorse a fresh surrender to Hitler on the lines of Munich. Significantly, Halifax noted 'Everybody felt that if Hitler insists on invading Poland there is nothing to do but try and smash him.'[14]

On the same day (28 August) Hesse, the Press Councillor at the German London Embassy, saw Horace Wilson. Producing Ribbentrop's letter to Rothermere, Hesse said Hitler had been favourably impressed by the reports he had received from Wohltat and Dirksen, but any settlement must now be by direct talks between Poland and Germany.

Possibly Hitler was considering a peaceful settlement, and Goering was temporarily prevailing on Hitler.

The next day (29 August) Hitler changed his mind. Henderson (according to his autobiography) before he went to see Hitler at 7.15 p.m. was confident that Hitler 'was ready to open negotiations with the Poles'. To his consternation he found Hitler cold and uncompromising, stating that the German Foreign Office had drafted proposals for Danzig and the Corridor which Hitler insisted Poland must sign or reject immediately. Hitler declared a Polish emissary with full powers must arrive in Berlin the next day (30 August). Henderson said this 'sounded like an ultimatum' whereupon the interview became 'stormy'. Ribbentrop had persuaded Hitler to put into the document the demand for a Polish delegation to come to Berlin within twenty-four hours, knowing such a demand would make war almost inevitable because the proud Poles would never agree.

By 10 p.m. Halifax was receiving from Henderson the first instalment of a telegram recounting that evening's meeting with Hitler. He noted: 'At first it looked pretty bad, but the final text looked much better.' His first reaction was the correct one.[15]

Goering claimed he was horrified when he read an account of the Hitler–Henderson talk. He immediately told Dahlerus that he blamed Henderson for angering Hitler because the German proposals were reasonable and the excesses of the Poles against the German minority justified Hitler in demanding immediate cession; Hitler was preparing a generous offer to the Poles involving only the return of Danzig and a plebiscite in the Corridor. Goering drew rough lines on a map showing the areas where the plebiscite would be held; they were zones which probably had a majority of Germans. Goering insisted to Dahlerus that the principle of a plebiscite was a 'climb down' by Hitler.

On 30 August Dahlerus popped up again in 10 Downing Street with what he considered was 'hot' good news that Hitler would offer a plebiscite in the disputed territory in the Corridor. Dahlerus was told by Halifax to 'rub into Goering' that Hitler's proposals to the Poles 'must not be couched in the form of a Diktat'. Dahlerus claims that Chamberlain asked him to emphasize to Goering how anxious the British were for a solution involving the transfer immediately of Danzig and the Corridor to Germany.

The Prime Minister, who had been advised by Vansittart not to agree to Berlin as the venue for German–Polish negotiations, told Dahlerus he was very doubtful about Berlin as a meeting-place, and in any case the request should not be put in 'this peremptory form and it was only reasonable to give a little more time for consideration'. Chamberlain asked Dahlerus whether it was in the German view an essential condition that a Polish delegation presented itself in Berlin 'today'. Dahlerus replied he thought not, and then phoned to Goering from 10 Downing Street. This is Horace Wilson's record of the Dahlerus–Goering phone call on the morning of 30 August.[16]

> *Note of telephone conversation between Monsieur Dahlerus and General Göring, August 30th, 12.30 p.m.*
>
> General Göring will not guarantee that the Führer will suggest a plebiscite but he is nearly certain, because he is most anxious to secure the friendship of Great Britain and show the world that the Germans are not so black as they are painted. He therefore feels that the principle of a plebiscite will be accepted. Herr Hitler is now drafting his proposals, which General Göring thinks will include the idea of a plebiscite.
>
> Herr Hitler will suggest, as regards minorities, that they should have the right to be evacuated if they so desire. Those who remain should be released from military service and the Germans in Poland treated as Germans. Vice versa in Germany.
>
> Monsieur Dahlerus suggested drafting terms and communicating them through Monsieur Lipski. He thought this would be a better procedure than someone coming to Berlin.
>
> General Göring seemed to accept this idea.
>
> Monsieur Dahlerus said that he presumed that the terms might be ready tonight, to which General Göring replied 'the Führer's on it'. General Göring kept emphasising the need for urgency.
>
> Monsieur Dahlerus did *not* put the point about a neutral meeting-place because he thinks the suggestion for communicating the proposals through M. Lipski is a better one.

After reading this account Halifax stressed to the Swede that no doubt must be left in the mind of Goering and anyone else he saw in Berlin that 'we were prepared to do our best in negotiations only if it really was negotiation and not dictation on the Czechoslovakian model', and the Foreign Secretary asked Dahlerus to phone Goering again from Downing Street suggesting 'that much would depend on the *manner* in which the proposals were put forward i.e. they should not be put forward in the form of a Diktat'. This is the official record of Dahlerus's second and third conversations with Goering from 10 Downing Street:

> Monsieur Dahlerus got through again to General Göring, who said that the Führer was drafting his proposals in the form of a "Diskussionsgrundlage" (Basis for discussion). This, he said, was "fabelhaft" (Miraculous)!
> *But*, it was an absolute condition that someone should come from Poland to fetch the proposals.
> The Secretary of State asked Monsieur Dahlerus whether he could put it that this would create a bad impression: could not Herr Hitler send Monsieur Lipski to Warsaw in the same way as he had sent Sir N. Henderson to London. [e.g. by a German plane]
> At 3 p.m. Monsieur Dahlerus reported that he had spoken again to General Göring, who maintained that it was essential for a Polish representative to come from Warsaw.

On receiving these messages from Goering via Dahlerus Halifax and Chamberlain agreed that Poland must send emissaries to Berlin immediately. As over Czechoslovakia, Chamberlain was now prepared to force Poland to yield to Hitler's demands, and his only stipulation was that it must be done with the outward appearance of a reasonable diplomatic negotiation as at Munich, and not as an ignominious surrender to Hitler's ultimatum. Halifax sent telegrams to Henderson in Berlin and Kennard in Warsaw. To Henderson he gave British consent for direct German–Polish negotiations; to Kennard he sent instructions to urge the Polish Government to negotiate with Hitler and said he believed the German terms were not the minimum and they could be reassured of British support. Kennard was told to plead for the immediate despatch of Polish emissaries to Berlin. Beck refused out of hand to go personally to Berlin, saying he would not put himself in the same position as Hácha had done in March.[17]

On August 29 Ashton-Gwatkin sent the reassuring news from Stockholm that he had met Goerdeler who told him authoritatively that Hitler had stayed his hand on 26 August because his generals had objected strongly to the war, and that the way to prevent war would be to reject any ultimatum from Hitler in the strongest terms. According to Goerdeler, Ribbentrop kept on telling Hitler that England would not in the end support Poland, and it was vital to contradict this.[18]

At midnight on 30 August Henderson saw Ribbentrop, having previously on Halifax's instructions sent a message that it was unreasonable for the Germans to expect that 'we' can send a Polish representative to Berlin today. At this stage Ribbentrop knew that his war policy had triumphed over Goering's peace policy, and he was rude. He refused to give Henderson the typescript of Hitler's new 'generous' offer, only quoting extracts at speed which Henderson, with his imperfect knowledge of German, had difficulty in understanding. Dahlerus was with Goering, and the British Embassy immediately rang up to tell the Swede what had occurred. Goering said to Dahlerus 'Ribbentrop is sabotaging my efforts to preserve peace. For God's sake let the British Ambassador have a copy of Hitler's generous terms as soon as possible.' Goering gave Dahlerus a copy of the typescript, claiming mendaciously that he was doing it without permission from Hitler, and Dahlerus handed it to Henderson at 10 a.m. on the morning of 31 August. Henderson tried to contact Lipski by phone but found he had gone out for a walk, so he sent Ogilvie Forbes and Dahlerus round to the Polish Embassy to impress on the Poles the vital need to send a plenipotentiary urgently to Berlin. Lipski was unmoved. He could not believe Dahlerus was the trusted emissary of both the British and German Governments, and told Ogilvie Forbes he was already packing for departure, and that he was uninterested in the German proposals because if war came the Nazis would be overthrown and 'the Polish army would probably arrive in Berlin in triumph'.[19]

Dahlerus returned to the British Embassy, and from Henderson's desk in the presence of the Ambassador he telephoned to 10 Downing Street and spoke to Horace Wilson, telling him that he had spent most of the night with Goering, who declared Hitler's proposals were 'extremely liberal and had been formulated to show how extremely anxious the Führer was to reach an agreement with Great Britain'.

Dahlerus went on to explain that he and Ogilvie-Forbes had seen Lipski, who had said acceptance was out of the question; according to Dahlerus it was clear to 'us' that the Poles were obstructing negotiations and people around Hitler were doing their best to restrain him, but that 'if the Poles would not come to Berlin . . .' At that moment Wilson cut him off because he had heard German voices on the line and knew the call was being monitored in Berlin. Wilson sent an urgent coded message to Henderson; 'You really must be careful of telephone. D's conversation at midday from Embassy was most indiscreet and was certainly heard by Germans.' Dahlerus then went back to Goering, who told him the German Foreign Office had intercepted a telegram to Lipski instructing him not to start negotiations, and this had made Hitler decide on war.[20]

Urged by Henderson, Lipski asked to see Ribbentrop, but the interview was fruitless because Lipski stated firmly he had no authority to enter into negotiations, and could not say when a Polish plenipotentiary would arrive in Berlin. This was exactly what Ribbentrop wanted to report to Hitler.

During the morning of 31 August Ciano telephoned twice to Halifax to the effect that Mussolini would try to persuade Hitler to agree to a conference if Britain could 'get' the Poles to give up Danzig; the date suggested was 5 September, and the object would be to revise the Treaty of Versailles. Halifax said firmly that Britain could not advise the Poles to give up Danzig at this stage. Daladier, when consulted by phone by Halifax, was lukewarm about a Mussolini-inspired conference. However, Ciano in Rome confirmed to Loraine that Italy would not fight France and Britain.[21]

On paper the terms were reasonable. Danzig, but not Gdynia, was to return to Germany and both cities were to be demilitarized. A plebiscite would decide the future of the Corridor, and an international Commission of Enquiry would deal with complaints from minority Poles or Germans. However, Hitler was not being sincere. He had decided on war unless a Polish plenipotentiary came immediately in humiliation to Berlin to give him another glittering diplomatic triumph. Henderson made a final effort to get Hitler's terms accepted, telegraphing to London:

> I cannot reconcile it with my duty to you and HMG not still to do my utmost to avoid war. The German proposals certainly do not endanger Polish independence,

and he would be 'pessimistic' if Ribbentrop conducted the negotiations, but not if Goering did. Kennard telegraphed simultaneously from Warsaw he did not agree the terms were reasonable because *inter alia* they were 'peremptory and humiliating'; if Poland's allies accepted them as a negotiating basis Poland might resist single-handed, and the Polish Government would not accept a document containing a demand unless the methods of procedure had been agreed.[22]

At 4.30 on the morning of 1 September the German army advanced into Poland after a fabricated incident at a frontier station with German criminals in Polish uniforms shot by German soldiers to simulate a Polish attack. The town centres of Cracow and Katowice were bombed.

At 7.30 a.m. the Foreign Office learnt of the attack. Cadogan waited until 9 a.m. before informing Halifax, and there was little sense of urgency. The Cabinet met at 11.30 a.m. Meanwhile the Polish Ambassador in London, Raczynski, had seen Halifax at 10.30 and asked for immediate assistance from the RAF because of German bombing attacks on Poland. Dahlerus telephoned to the Foreign Office saying Hitler's intentions were peaceful, and Henderson telegraphed that Hitler's speech to the Reichstag that morning might lead to another peace effort.

The Cabinet were told of the message from Dahlerus that Hitler did not want to start a world war, and instead wanted direct negotiations with Great Britain. They decided to send a stiff reply stressing the only way in which a world war could be avoided would be if German troops left Polish territory, and held out no hope that Great Britain would act as mediator between Germany and Poland. Halifax said the French wanted to declare war before 'we' did since the French Government were anxious not to appear to be dragged into war by 'us'. The Cabinet agreed that the right course would be to declare war at the same time.

The Cabinet were more enthusiastic for another Mussolini-inspired conference like Munich than for immediate resource to force. They ignored the Polish request for urgent RAF action against Germany, and would not go further than sending a leisurely warning note to Hitler via Henderson without a time limit.[23]

On 29 August Mussolini, alarmed at the prospect of war, had sent an urgent personal telegram to Hitler appealing to him to open discussions and suggesting these should include talks on raw materials and colonies. At lunchtime on 31 August Ciano in Rome explained to Loraine the Duce's calculation was that if he put the suggestion to Hitler of a conference at San Remo at once, and could state that England and France had already accepted in principle, Hitler could hardly refuse – 'or if he does, the cat will be belled'.[24]

Halifax told the Cabinet of this Ciano–Loraine conversation of the previous day, but said it had been overtaken by events. At 6 p.m. Chamberlain told the Commons the 'note' had been sent to the German Government; when one MP called out 'Time limit!' the Prime Minister went on that if the German reply was unfavourable Henderson had been told to ask for his passport. This satisfied the House, and Harold Nicolson recorded: 'The general feeling of the House is one of deep sympathy for him.'[25]

During the morning of 1 September, as Poland was writhing under a fierce German land and air attack, Cadogan telephoned to Bonnet and said the British Government wanted the answer about the time limit and also the French reaction to a Mussolini-inspired international conference. Bonnet replied that France needed another forty-eight hours before declaring war for evacuation of children and to complete mobilization, and he favoured a Mussolini conference. Cadogan then asked if German withdrawal from Poland was a prerequisite. Bonnet said 'they would deliberate'. Cadogan, by even asking such a question, betrayed his Government's lack of resolution.

Daladier at first said he would rather resign than agree to a conference, but he was overruled by the French Cabinet. In the early hours of 2 September the French issued a press statement that they were giving a favourable response to the Duce's suggested conference. Ivo Mallet commented this was unfortunate but 'nothing can be done about it'. Loraine reported from Rome at midday that Hitler had sent a message to Ciano asking that the 'non-ultimatum' character of the British and French notes should be confirmed through Rome and whether he could have until noon on 3 September in order to work out the question of an armistice and the Duce's proposed conference. Ribbentrop told Attolico in Berlin the Führer was not against the suggestion of an armistice to be followed immediately by Mussolini's international conference. Ciano recorded in his diary 'Contrary to what I expected, Hitler does not reject the proposal absolutely.' Hitler only wanted to delay British and French intervention in Poland and had no intention of halting his troops in Poland.

At 2.35 p.m. Ciano rang Halifax, who at once confirmed the non-ultimatum character of the British note of the previous day. Meanwhile Beck had refused to attend the proposed conference, saying the only point of it could be to assess compensation payable by Germany to Poland for the damage done by the air and land attacks. Halifax then told Ciano that Britain could not agree to the conference unless Hitler withdrew his troops.

Ciano with "some emphasis" told Halifax that the Germans would not listen to a demand for withdrawal of their troops from Polish territory, and the maximum Mussolini could obtain would be a suspension of hostilities on 3 September and the convening of the conference on the following day.

At 4 p.m. Halifax talked to Bonnet and said the British Government were not yet in a position to state its view on the conference, but his personal opinion was the Cabinet at the meeting about to take place would insist on a withdrawal of German troops first. Bonnet said Hitler would probably not accept the condition of withdrawal but he thought a conference 'might be contemplated' provided that Poland was represented and Ciano's proposition of an immediate armistice accepted. Halifax put the conference proposal to the Cabinet when it met at 4.15 p.m. on 2 September, and stressed that the British note was not an ultimatum, and, although it would be very difficult to have any negotiations with Germany while German troops remained on Polish territory, he revealed his desire for the conference by saying he thought 'We might be prepared to consider an extension of the time limit from 12 noon tomorrow (2 September) until midnight on 3/4 September.' Chamberlain was also weak and asked 'should we give Germany more time to consider the Duce's proposal?' Obviously Chamberlain and Halifax hoped the conference would take place, and if Hitler had agreed to suspension of hostilities they would have pressurized their colleagues to allow it.

The said colleagues were more resolute. Hoare stated the 1 September note had been regarded in the nature of an ultimatum, and he thought there would be tremendous risks in accepting any delay which might have considerable reactions on public opinion. Stanley said in addition to withdrawal from Polish soil the status quo in Danzig must be restored. Belatedly Chamberlain said that this was what he and Halifax intended.

The Cabinet then overruled Chamberlain and Halifax and decided Germany should be allowed no longer than midnight that evening (2/3 September) to make up her mind to withdraw from Polish soil.

At 5.22 p.m. Loraine telephoned that Ciano had told him after learning the conference must depend on withdrawing troops that there was no chance of the Duce proceeding further. Chamberlain had been encouraged to hope that Hitler might agree to an armistice by a strange episode in 10 Downing Street.[26] Hesse called on Wilson with a message that Hitler would remove his troops from Poland provided he was given Danzig and the Corridor, and Britain should act as mediator in the German–Polish dispute. Wilson firmly told Hesse that negotiations could only proceed if German troops withdrew from Polish territory. Cadogan minuted: 'These indirect approaches rather reassure me. The Germans must be feeling the draught.' He could not have been more wrong. Every hour gained by Hitler to pursue his Polish campaign without Allied intervention was a bonus, and this message was an obvious delaying tactic, not a genuine effort at peace.

Immediately after the Cabinet meeting Halifax telephoned to Ciano (6.38 p.m. 2 September) and told him the Cabinet would not 'favour' a conference as long as German troops were on Polish soil. Ciano replied that Hitler would not accept this condition. Halifax then 'urged him to try his best – if he could accomplish this it would be possible to get back to the original basis of negotiations', but it was also essential that Danzig should revert to the status quo. Ciano repeated Hitler would not accept this. Halifax then emphasized that the note to Hitler was not an ultimatum, but Ciano repeated a third time that the whole scheme was 'impossible for Hitler'. When Halifax said Chamberlain was about to make a statement in Parliament about the proposed conference Ciano remarked that in his opinion it would be better not to mention it. Finally Halifax asked Ciano again 'to do his best with Berlin'.

Thus as Halifax put down the receiver at 6.45 p.m. (2 September) the conference proposal was dead. Ciano recorded in his diary that with this conversation 'The last note of hope has died'; during the night Bonnet asked Ciano if he could not attain 'a symbolic withdrawal of German forces from Poland'; Ciano recorded he threw this proposal into the waste paper basket. So as Chamberlain prepared his speech for the Commons on the evening of 2 September, Mussolini's conference proposal was stillborn and the British Cabinet had plumped for an immediate declaration of war. With characteristic obstinacy, Chamberlain refused to accept this.[27]

At 8 p.m. (2 September) Chamberlain rose in the Commons. Everyone, including his Cabinet colleagues, expected him to state that Britain would be at war the next day. Instead he disregarded the decision of the Cabinet and in 'limping sentences' explained that Britain and the French were considering what further time-limit to put on Hitler's answer. This, coming thirty-six hours after the invasion of Poland, was too much for the House; there was an ugly scene frequently described in political memoirs. Greenwood summed it up to the Commons the next day, 'Resentment, apprehension, anger, reigned over our proceedings last night, aroused by a fear that delays might end in national dishonour and sacrifice of the Polish people to German tyranny.'

Chamberlain had an acute political sense, and realised immediately his premiership was in danger. His offending phrases were:

> Delay may be caused by Italian proposal that hostilities should cease and there should be an immediate conference between five powers – Britain, France, Poland, Germany and Italy. If the German Government should agree to withdraw their forces then HMG would be willing to regard the position as being the same as it was before the German forces crossed the frontier. I am the last man to neglect any opportunity which I consider affords a serious chance of avoiding the great catastrophe of war at the last moment.

The Cabinet Ministers were appalled by the scene in the Commons, which put the future of the Government in doubt. Chamberlain's speech differed fundamentally from the Cabinet decision of a few hours before, and his colleagues felt their own reputations were in jeopardy. In a body they insisted on seeing Chamberlain in his room before he left the Commons. Simon, the arch-appeaser, was their spokesman, and collectively they advised Chamberlain he could not face the Commons again unless he could announce the time of the expiry of an ultimatum to Germany. Chamberlain summoned Halifax, Cadogan and Corbin to 10 Downing Street and did a quick U-turn. Almost in a panic Chamberlain telephoned Daladier and told him there had been an angry scene in the Commons and the situation had become grave after he had said he was consulting with the French on the time-limit to be allowed to Germany, and that his Cabinet colleagues were also disturbed because they had decided that afternoon the time-limit to Hitler was to expire at midnight (tonight) but in the absence of French concurrence he had been unable to say so in the House, and if the French were to insist on a time limit of forty-eight hours to run from midday tomorrow 'it would be impossible to hold the situation here'. Chamberlain proposed that the British and French Ambassadors should present an ultimatum 'at 8 a.m. tomorrow' (3 September), giving the Germans until midday to decide. It would have been better for Chamberlain's reputation if he had made this phone call before, and not after his nasty reception in the Commons. Daladier said that unless British bombers were ready to act at once it would be better for France to delay. RAF bombers were actually arriving on French aerodromes, but without orders to attack.

Half an hour later Halifax spoke to Bonnet and persuaded the hesitant French Foreign Secretary to agree to Chamberlain's proposal. Gamelin helped by confirming to the French Cabinet the French mobilization was sufficiently advanced to allow France to declare war.[28]

An emergency Cabinet was held on 2 September at 11.30 p.m. in the Prime Minister's room in the Commons. Simon repeated it was essential that when Chamberlain met the Commons on the next day (Sunday, 3 September) he could state that an ultimatum had been delivered. It was agreed that Henderson should see Ribbentrop at 9 a.m. the next morning (3 September) and inform the German Government that unless they suspended all aggressive action against Poland by 11 a.m. and were prepared to withdraw their forces from Polish territory a state of war existed as from that hour. Chamberlain said 'This means war.' He had been dragged into it against his will only because he realized that otherwise the Cabinet and the Conservative Parliamentary Party would no longer support him. The French fell into line; war was declared by Britain at 11 a.m. on 3 September, and by France at 5 p.m.

TABLES

Table 1   Reich Elections 1924 – 33 (excluding minor parties)

	May 1924	Dec 1924	May 1928	Sept 1930	July 1932	Nov 1932	March 1933
D.N.V.P. Nationalist (right wing)	19.5%	20.5%	14.2%	7%	2.959%	8.3%	8%
N.S.D.A.P. Nazis	6.5%	3%	2.6%	18.3%	37.3%	33.1%	43.9%
Centre	13.4%	13.6%	12.1%	11.8%	12.5%	11.9%	11.2%
S.P.D. Social Democrats	20.5%	26.0%	29.8%	24.5%	21.6%	20.4%	18.3%
K.P.D. Communists	12.6%	9.0%	10.6%	13.1%	14.1%	16.9%	12.3%
D.V.P. People's Party Liberals	9.2%	10.1%	8.7%	4.5%	1.2%	1.9%	1.1%

Note:

The Communist vote never rose above 16.9%.

Stresemann belonged to the D.V.P. (People's Party) which he founded in 1918, and whose vote dwindled to almost nothing after he died.

Brüning and von Papen belonged to the Centre Party, Müller to the Social Democrats.

The Nazi vote fell sharply between July 1932 and November 1932, and the rise in March 1933 was due to the Nazi Government stifling the opposition.

There was an astonishing rise in the Nazi vote after Stresemann died and the economic depression hit Germany, illustrated by the following table:

May 1928 (Reichstag)	2.6 per cent of votes cast
September 1930 (Reichstag)	18.3 per cent of votes cast
March 1932 (1st presidential election)	30 per cent of votes cast
April 1932 (2nd presidential election)	36.7 per cent of votes cast
April 1932 (Prussian Diet)	36.3 per cent of votes cast
July 1932 (Reichstag)	37.3 per cent of votes cast

Ebert, the Republic's first President, died unexpectedly in February 1924, aged only fifty-four. His term of office had only four months to run, and it was assumed by all parties he would be re-elected. Hindenburg was reluctantly persuaded to stand by the right wing and he narrowly defeated Marx by 14,655,000 votes to 13,751,000, with the Communist candidate getting 1,931,000. This was a misfortune for Germany.

In March 1932 when Hindenburg's term of office was up Hitler stood against him and secured 37% of the poll.

341

Sir Horace Rumbold made it crystal-clear to the British Government that the Weimar Republic was gravely threatened by the spectacular electoral successes of the Nazis. Thus the lack of generosity to the Brüning Government shown by the British is indefensible.

GREAT BRITAIN

Date of taking office	Prime Minister	Foreign Secretary	Chancellor of the Exchequer
1922	D. Lloyd George	Lord Curzon	Sir R. Horne
Oct. 1922	A. Bonar Law	Lord Curzon	S. Baldwin
May 1923	S. Baldwin		N. Chamberlain
Jan 1924	J. R. MacDonald	J. R. MacDonald	P. Snowden
Nov 1924	S. Baldwin	Sir A. Chamberlain	W. Churchill
June 1929	J. R. MacDonald	A. Henderson	P. Snowden
Aug 1931		Marquis of Reading	
Nov 1931		Sir J. Simon	N. Chamberlain
June 1935	S. Baldwin	Sir S. Hoare	
Dec 1935		A. Eden	
May 1937	N. Chamberlain		Sir J. Simon
Feb 1938		Viscount Halifax	

FRANCE

Date of taking office	Prime Minister	Foreign Minister	Finance Minister
1921	A. Briand	A. Briand	P. Doumer
Jan 1922	R. Poincaré	R. Poincaré	M. de Lasteyrie
June 1924	E. Herriot	E. Herriot	E. Clementel
May 1925	M. Painlevé		
Nov. 1925	A. Briand		
Aug 1926	R. Poincaré	A. Briand	R. Poincaré
Nov 1928			H. Cheron
July 1929	A. Briand		
Nov 1929	A. Tardieu	A. Briand	P. Reynaud
Dec 1930	M. Steeg		
Jan 1931	P. Laval		
Feb 1932	A. Tardieu	A. Briand	P-E Flandin
June 1932	E. Herriot	P. Laval	
Dec 1932	J. Paul-Boncour	A. Tardieu	
Jan 1933	E. Daladier	E. Herriot	M. Germain- Martin
Oct 1933	A. Sarraut	J.Paul-Boncour	H. Cheron
Nov 1933	C. Chautemps		G. Bonnet

Tables

FRANCE

Date of taking office	Prime Minister	Foreign Minister	Finance Minister
Jan 1934	E. Daladier		
Feb 1934	G. Doumergue	E. Daladier	F. Piétri
Oct 1934			P. Marchandeau
Nov 1934	P-E Flandin	Louis Barthou	M. Germain-Martin
June 1935	F. Bouisson	P. Laval	
June 1935	P. Laval		J. Caillaux
Jan 1936	A. Sarraut	P-E Flandin	
June 1936	L. Blum	Y. Delbos	V. Auriol
June 1937	C. Chautemps		G. Bonnet
Jan 1938			P. Marchandeau
Mar 1938	L. Blum	J. Paul-Boncour	L. Blum
Apr 1938	E. Daladier	G. Bonnet	P. Marchandeau
Nov 1938			P. Reynaud

GERMANY

Date of taking office	Prime Minister (Chancellor)	Foreign Minister	Finance Minister
1921	J. Wirth		A. Hermes
Jan 1922		W. Rathenau	
Nov 1922	W. Cuno	H. von Rosenberg	
Aug 1923	G. Stresemann	G. Stresemann	
Nov 1923	W. Marx		H. Luther
Jan 1925	H. Luther		O.von Schleiben
Jan 1926			H. Reinhold
May 1926	W. Marx		H. Kohler
June 1928	H. Müller		R. Hilferding
Oct 1929		Stresemann died aged 51 J. Curtius	P. Moldenhauer
Apr 1930	H. Brüning		H. R. Dietrich
Oct 1931		H. Brüning	
June 1932	F. von Papen	K. von Neurath	L. E. Schwerin von Krosigk
Nov 1932	K. von Schleicher		
Jan 1933	A. Hitler		
Feb 1938		J.von Ribbentrop	

SOURCE NOTES

Initials and numbers refer to classification in the Public Record Office:

DBFP are *Documents on British Foreign Policy*. DDI are *Documenti Diplomatici Italiani*. DDF are *Documents Diplomatiques Francaises*. DGFP are *Documents on German Diplomatic Policy*. LONJ are *League of Nations Journal*. FRUS are *Foreign Relations United States*.

Extracts from Chamberlain's letters and diaries come from the Chamberlain Archives, University of Birmingham, unless there is another reference.

CHAPTER ONE
Versailles and the Reparations Crisis (pp. 3–26)

1. DBFP Series 1, Vol XIX pages 1–7.
2. Ibid pages 8–11. D'Abernon *Ambassador of Peace*, Vol 1, page 244.
3. DBFP Series 1, Vol XIX pages 111; 135
4. Ibid pages 170–192. Lloyd George, *Truth About Reparations and War Debts*, page 69.
5. DBFP Series 1, Vol XIX pages 409–21; 487; 491; 846–58.
6. Ibid pages 422–31 Bar Le Duc speech DBFP Series 1 Vol XX page 236.
7. DBFP Series 1 Vol XIX page X (Preface)
8. T 172/1788.
9. Lloyd George op cit, pages 115–16; Middlemas, *Baldwin* page 133.
10. Lloyd George op cit, pages 71–3.
11. Tardieu *Truth About the Treaty*, page 33; Lloyd George op cit, page 74.
12. Blake, *Unknown Prime Minister*, page 487.
13. Cab 23/32. 29 December 1923.
14. Blake, op cit, page 489–90.
15. FO 371/8627; FO 371/8627; D'Abernon op cit, Vol II, page 150.
16. Cab 23/33. 11 January 1924; FO 371/8625; FO 371/8505.
17. Middlemas op cit, page 156; Lloyd George op cit, page 116.
18. FO 371/8503; Blake op cit, pages 490–2.
19. Cab 23/33. FO 371/8503; FO 371/8504.
20. Cab 23/33.
21. DBFP Series 1, Vol XXI page 21. Preface by Deakin pages V – XIII.
22. D'Abernon op cit, Vol III pages 19–20.
23. DBFP Series 1, Vol XXI pages 734–6.
24. FO 371/8818; Bullock, *Hitler*, pages 118–20.
25. D'Abernon op cit, Vol II page 262.
26. Ibid page 284.
27. Jacobson, *Locarno Diplomacy*, pages 84–98. FO 371/1133.
28. D'Abernon op cit, Vol III page 266; FO 371/1133.
29. Jacobson, op cit pages 143–83.
30. Cab 23/60. T 160/268/F111150/02/03.
31. Jacobson op cit, pages 279–349.

CHAPTER TWO
Italy, Abyssinia and the League of Nations 1922–4 (pp. 27–39)

1. FO 371/8410.
2. Ibid. For Duke of Portland Howarth, *Intelligence Chief Extraordinary* Page 73.
3. Cecil, *Great Experiment*, pages 145–6.
4. DBFP Series 1, Vol XXIV, pages 952–60; 972–3.
5. Ibid, pages 972–80; page 1002.
6. Ibid, pages 1046–7.
7. Robert Dell, *Geneva Racket*, page 53.
8. FO 371/8900.
9. DBFP Series 1, Vol XXIV page 1092.
10. FO 371/9952.
11. Ibid.
12. DBFP Series 1, Vol XXVI pages 29; 54–56; 121–2; 167.
13. FO 371/9951. FO 317/9952

CHAPTER THREE
Reparations and the Fall of Brüning (pp. 40–68)

1. DBFP Series 2, Vol 1 pages 491–3, 493–501.
2. Ibid, pages 535–542.
3. FO 371/15213.
4. Ibid.
5. FO 371/15215. FO 371/15226. FO 371/15217.
6. FO 371/15157; FO 371/14980; FO 371/14982; Cecil, *Great Experiment* page 203.
7. *Directionary of National Biography* 1930–50; Cab 27/624.
8. FO 371/149181.
9. DBFP Series 2 Vol I page 346; Carlton, *MacDonald v Henderson* page 27; Cab 27/624.
10. DBFP Series 2 Vol II pages 1–24. FO 371/15159; Cab 23/67; Cab 24/221; DBFP op cit page 46.
11. DBFP op cit page 46. FO 371/15178.
12. FO 371/15159. FO 371/15160.
13. DBFP op cit pages 41–55. Carlton op cit pages 190–1.
14. Cab 23/67.
15. LONJ Vol XII No 7 pages 1068–71. DBFP op cit pages 56–85. FO 371/15163.
16. FO 371/15214.
17. DBFP Series 2 Vol II pages 71–7. FO 371/15214.
18. FO 371/15226.
19. FRUS Vol 1, pages 11–14.
20. FO 800/283.
21. Prem 1/95. T 160/394/F11300/032/04.
22. Wheeler-Bennett, '*Wreck of Reparations*' pages 54; 124–71.
23. DBFP Series 2, Vol II page 251; 285–92.
24. FO 371/15216.
25. DBFP Series 2, Vol II page 350.
26. FO 800/286; FO 371/15216; FO 371/15217.
27. DBFP Series 2, Vol II pages 322–5.
28. Wheeler-Bennett, op cit pages 124–57; 172.
29. FO 800/286.
30. T 160/450 F 130501.
31. DBFP Series 2, Vol III page 795. T 160/436/F 12630/02.

32. FO 800/326.
33. Cab 23/71.
34. Leith Ross, *Money Talks* page 148.
35. Cab 23/72.
36. DBFP Series 2, Vol III page 239.
37. DBFP Series 2, Vol III pages 291–5.
38. DBFP Series 2, Vol III, pages 281–4.
39. Papen Memoirs, pages 178–81.
40. Cab 23/72.
41. DBFP Series 2, Vol III, pages 340–7.
42. Ibid, pages 408–9.
43. International Military Tribunal Vol XVI, page 249.
44. Papen op cit, page 186.
45. DBFP Series 2, Vol III, pages 442–6.

CHAPTER FOUR
The Disarmament Conference Fails (pp. 69–89)

1. Quoted in Dell, op cit page 90.
2. Petrie *Twenty Years Armistice* pages 121–3. Petrie quotes Wheeler-Bennett.
3. DBFP Series 2, Vol IV page 377.
4. Von Papen Memoirs, page 206.
5. FO 371/37348.
6. DBFP Series 2, Vol IV pages 433, 451, 465.
7. Cab 27/505.
8. DBFP Series 2, Vol IV pages 503–4.
9. Ibid page 520; Dell op cit p.10
10. DBFP Series 2, Vol V pages 226–8.
11. Cab 27/505.
12. DBFP Series 2, Vol V pages 214–17.
13. Ibid.
14. Ibid pages 227–8 and 237.
15. Cab 27/505.
16. DBFP Series 2, Vol V pages 600–6; 617–21.
17. FO 371/176367. DBFP Series 2, Vol V page 658.
18. Dell op cit, pages 102–103. Cab 27/505 7.11.33.
19. Avon, op cit page 128.
20. DBFP Series 2, Vol V, pages 711–14.
21. DBFP Series 2, Vol VI page 25; page 33.
22. Ibid page 50; 52.
23. Ibid page 164. Cab 27/505.
24. Ibid pages 137; 145; 149; 167; 179; 191; 229; 235; 245. FO 371/16711. FO 371/17375.
25. FO 371/18515.
26. Ibid.
27. DBFP Series 2, Vol VI page 371.
28. Rhodes James, *Anthony Eden* page 136; Avon op cit, page 75. FO 371/18519. DBFP Series 2 Vol VI pages 470–1.
29. FO 371/18519.
30. Ibid.
31. DBFP Series 2, Vol VI page 637. Cab 25/505.
32. DBFP Series 2, Vol VI pages 728–9.

CHAPTER FIVE
Mussolini Saves Austria (pp. 93–104)

1. Gilbert, *Winston Churchill* Vol V pages 142; 224–225; 457, Petrie Life and Letters of Austen Chamberlain pages, 295–6. DBFP Series 2, Vol V, pages 238–484.
2. FO 371/116638. FO 371/116639.
3. FO 371/16646. DBFP Series 2 Vol V, pages 534, 535.
4. Selby op cit, page 18. DBFP Series 2 Vol VI, page 404. Cab 27/506.
5. Ibid page 256.
6. Selby op cit, pages 16–17. Kindermann, *Hitler's Defeat in Austria* page 44.
7. DBFP Series 2 Vol VI, pages 762–3. Starhemberg *Between Hitler and Mussolini* page 150.
8. Kindermann op cit, page 100.
9. Kindermann op cit, pages 113–5. DGFP Series C Vol II page 281.

CHAPTER SIX
Hitler Rearms (pp. 105–124)

1. FO 371/17696.
2. Cook and Ramsden *By Elections in British Politics* pages 118–38.
3. Ibid page 127. Bartlett, *This is my Life* pages 188/92. Wheeler-Bennett, *The Disarmament Deadlock* page 181.
4. Macleod, *Neville Chamberlain* page 177; Middlemas and Barnes page 747.
5. FO 371/17697.
6. DBFP Series 2, Vol XII pages 279; 281.
7. FO 371/17696. Cab 27/508.
8. Cab. 27/508.
9. Cab 27/508. FO 371/17696.
10. DBFP Series 2 Vol XII, pages 279–82. FO 371/17696.
11. Cab 27/508.
12. Marquand *MacDonald*, page 770. DBFP Series 2 Vol XII, pages 279–82.
13. DBFP Series 2, Vol XII pages 419–20.
14. Roskill, *Hankey* pages 163–5. Cab 3/6 DBFP Series 2, Vol III, pages 155–64.
15. DBFP Series 2, Vol XII pages ??? FO 371/18824.
16. DBFP Series 2, Vol XII page 601.
17. Ibid page 660.
18. Ibid pages 703–46. FO 371/18832.
19. *Grand Strategy*, pages 155–69. Watt 'Anglo–German Naval Agreement', in *Journal of Modern History*, June 1956. FO 371/18845.
20. *Grand Strategy*, pages 165–6. FO 371/18734. Selby *Diplomatic Twilight*, p 49.
21. Churchill, *Second World War* Vol I page 111.
22. FO 371/18734.
23. Cab 23/82. FO 371/18734.
24. FO 371/17765. DBFP Second series VI pages 623–6.
25. FO 371/18734.
26. Rothermere, *My Fight to Rearm Britain* page 111. FO 371/17665.
27. DBFP Series 2, Vol VI page 302.
28. Charles H. Bogart. War Monthly No. 75. Various documents and evidence of Admiral Downitz and Admiral Raeder – See IMT Index Vol. XXIV. *Covert German Rearmament 1919–1939* Barton Whaley (University Publishers of America 1987) for a general survey.
29. T. B. Martin conversation with author, August 1988. Cross, *Hoare* pages 184–5. Thompson, *Anti Appeasers*, page 65.

30. Griffiths *Fellow Travellers of the Right*, page 169. Lord Home letters and conversation with author. Viscountess Simon conversation with author, October 1988. Barnes, *End of Empire*, pages 696. J. Amery, *Approach March*, page 78. Lees Milne, *Nicholson* page 92.
31. Selby op cit, page 47. Gladwyn op cit, page 40.

CHAPTER SEVEN
Stresa and the Abyssinian War (pp. 125–165)

1. Cab 23/81.
2. DBFP Series 2 Vol XII, pages 919; 921. FO 371/18560.
3. Ibid, pages 862–914.
4. Ibid, page 927.
5. McCallum, *Public Opinion and the Lost Peace* page 150.
6. DBFP Series 2 Vol XII, pages 918; 922.
7. FO 371/18836. DBFP Series 2 Vol XII, pages 928–9.
8. Dell op cit, page 227.
9. Adamthwaite, *Making of Second World War* pages 133–4.
10. Adamthwaite op cit, page 150. Largardelle, *Mission Rome Paris 1935* pages 275–7.
11. Times, 10 May 1933. Conversation Viscountess Simon with author, November 1988.
12. MacDonald Papers, P.R.O. 30/69/7.
13. DBFP Series 2 Vol IV, pages 110–11.
14. Ibid pages 176–177. FO 371/19105.
15. Cab 23/82. FO 371/19164.
16. Thompson *Front Line Diplomat* page 95. DBFP Series 2 Vol XIV pages 220–8. FO 401/35.
17. Dell op cit, page 111.
18. Roskill op cit, Vol III page 191. Gladwyn, *Memoirs* page 48.
19. DBFP Series 2 Vol XIV, page 281; pages 306–9; 311–12.
20. Guariglia *Ricordi* 1922–1946.
21. Cab 23/81. For Manchuria Dell op cit pages 65–90.
22. DBFP Series 2 Vol XIV, pages 318; 323–6; 329–34.
23. FO 371/19163.
24. DBFP Series 2 Vol XIV page 467.
25. Cab 23/81. Cab 21/411. FO 371/19123.
26. FO 401/35.
27. Aloisi *Mia attivita a servizio del pace*, pages 57–60. Committee of Five. FO 401/35.
28. Gladwyn op cit, page 47.
29. Cab 23/82; Cab 48/38; FO 371/19155; FO 371/19159.
30. Ibid.
31. FO 401/35; Cab 16/1361.
32. FO 371/19157. Cab 16/1361.
33. FO 371/19164; FO 317/19186.
34. FO 371/19160.
35. DBFP Series 2 Vol XV pages 264–8.
36. FO 371/19165; FO 371/19164; Jones, *Diary* with *Letters*, page 159.
37. Cab 16/130.
38. FO 371/19163.
39. FO 371/19164; PR0 30/69/7 (MacDonald Papers)
40. FO 371/19163.
41. Prem 1/177B
42. FO 371/19164.
43. Ibid.
44. FO 371/19164.
45. Cab 23/82; FO 371/19168;

46. Cab 23/82.
47. Avon op cit, page 286.
48. FO 371/19168; Cab 23/82.
49. Parker, 'English Historical Review' Vol 89, 1974. Avon op cit, pgs 298–9; Rhodes James op cit, page 154; FO 371/19168; Cab 23/882;
50. Cab 23/82. Cross op cit, page 249.
51. FO 371/19168; Cab 23/82. McClachan, *In the Chair: The Times 1927–1948*, pages 164–7.
52. Waley, *British Public Opinion and the Abyssinian War*, page 64.
53. DBFP Series 2 Vol XV pages 462–4.
54. Cab 23/82; Avon op cit, page 301.
55. Lamb, *The Failure of the Eden Government* page 258.
56. The Cabinet Minutes for 18 December 1935 are reproduced in the Appendix to DBFP Series 2 Vol XV. Also Cab 23/82.

CHAPTER EIGHT
Rhineland Disaster 1936 (pp. 166–192)

1. FO 371/20159.
2. Cab 23/83. FO 371/ 20159.
3. Cab 27/599. Cab 23/83.
4. DBFP Series 2 Vol XV, pages 624/96.
5. Cab 27/622.
6. DBFP Series 2 Vol XV pages 610–13. Avon op cit page 332. DGFP Series C, Vol IV page 1112.
7. DBFP Series 2 Vol XV, pages 675–704. DGFP Series C, Vol IV page 1207.
8. DBFP Series 2 XV page 22. Cab 23-92.
9. Ibid page 39. DGFP Series C Vol IV page 24.
10. DBFP Series C Vol IV page 36 (7 March); page 123 (10 March).
11. Jones op cit, page 239.
12. DDF Series 2 Vol 1, pages 15–19. Parker *Europe*, pages 293–4. Churchill, *Gathering Storm* page 1.
13. IMT Vol XV Pages 347–52.
14. DGFP Series C Vol XV page 41. DBFP Series 2 Vol XVI pages 46; 80.
15. DBFP Series 2 Vol VXI pages 66–8. Cab 23/63.
16. DDF Series 2 Vol I pgs 444–8. DGFP Series 2 Vol V pages 254–6.
17. DDF Series 2 Vol 1 pgs 504–5. Schweppenberg, *Critical Years London* pages 62–3. DGFP Series C Vol V page 134.
18. DGFP Series C Vol V pages 75; 106; 134.
19. DDF Series Vol 1 No 392.
20. Cab 23/83. DBFP Series 2 C Vol V, page 111, Vol XVI page 96. Cab 23/83.
21. DBFP Series 2 Vol XVI page 96; Cab 23/83.
22. Flandin *Politique Francais* pages 201–821. DBFP Series.
23. Cab 23/83. DBFP Series 2 Vol XVI page 66.
24. DBFP Series 2 Vol XVI page 192; page 152; page 190; page 187.
25. Cab 23/83.
26. DBFP Series 2 Vol XVI pages 300–4.
27. Avon op cit, pages 366, 362, 376.
28. FO 371/19902.
29. Cab 23/84; FO 371/20181.
30. FO 371/20363.
31. DBFP Series 2 Vol XVI page 457; 461. FO 371/20181; Cab 27/622; Cab 23/84.
32. Avon op cit, pages 384–6. Cab 23/84. DBFP Series 2 Vol XVI page 486.
33. DBFP Series 2 Vol XVI pages 757–74.

34. Prem 1/194.
35. Ibid.
36. *Hansard* Commons 26 March 1936. *Hansard* Lords 6 April 1936.
37. *Hansard* Commons 9 April 1936.
38. Griffiths op cit, pages 192–244.
39. DBFP Series 2 Vol XVI page IX
40. DDF Series 11 Vol 11 No 214. Adamthwaite *France and the Coming of the Second World War* page 43. Avon op cit, page 374.
41. Prem 1/193.

CHAPTER NINE
Eden quits as Foreign Secretary 1938 (pp. 193–220)

1. DGFP Series C Vol IV pages 974; 1041–5.
2. Suvich, *Memorie 1932–36*, page 281. Burgwyn, '*Italy, the Heimwehr and the Austro German Agreement*' – Meitteilunger des Osterreichschen Staatsarchivs 38 1985 (Article).
3. Starhemberg op cit, page 221.
4. Schuschnigg, *Brutal Take Over* page 140; Ciano Diplomatic Papers, page 45.
5. Selby op cit, page 65. Times, 1 April 1936. Selby letter to *The Times*, 26 August 1956.
6. FO 371/19911. DBFP Series 2 Vol XVII page 30. Jones Diary with letters Vol 111 page 231.
7. DBFP Series 2 Vol XVII page 135; pages 90–1. FO 371/20534.
8. DBFP Series 2 Vol XVII pages 446–68 and 410.
9. Ibid pages 514–17.
10. Ibid pages 613–24.
11. Quoted in Gilbert, *Churchill* Vol V page 850.
12. Prem 1/261. Cab 27/622.
13. DBFP Series 2 Vol XVII page 513.
14. Harvey, *Diplomatic Diaries* page 65.
15. DBFP Series 2 Vol XVII page 752.
16. DBFP Series 2 Vol XVL pages 813; 513–16; 904–7.
17. Lamb *The Ghosts of Peace* pages 52–3.
18. Macmillan op cit, pages 469–70.
19. Prem 1/276.
20. Grandi, *25 Luglio Quarant anni dopo* page 170.
21. Prem 1/276.
22. Avon op cit, pages 454–5.
23. Prem 1/276. FO 800/309 Halifax Papers.
24. FO 800/309.
25. Cab 23/89.
26. DGFP Series D Vol I, pages 62–3.
27. Cab 23/90.
28. Ibid.
29. *Cadogan Diaries*, page 33.
30. Prem 1/276. FO 954/13. Eden Papers.
31. Cadogan op cit, pages 34–5. FO 954/13.
32. Prem 1/276. DBFP Series 2 Vol XIV pages 677–80 and 863–5; 1140–1.
33. Prem 1/263. Avon op cit, page 573.
34. Prem 1/276. Cadogan op cit, pages 40–6. FO 954/13. Cab 27/623 (FPC).
35. Cadogan op cit, pages 47; 69.
36. Prem 1/276.
37. Harvey op cit, page 83.
38. Prem 1/276. FO 954/13.
39. FO 954/13. Grandi op cit, pages 170–1. Amery op cit, page 501.

40. Harvey op cit, pages 422–3.
41. DBFP Series 2 Vol XIV pages 1143; 1150–1. Cab 23/90.
42. Harvey op cit, page 96. Carlton, *Anthony Eden* pages 129–30.
43. Macmillan, *Winds of Change* page 538.

CHAPTER TEN
Anschluss and British Overtures to Mussolini (pp. 221–238)

1. Cab 27/623.
2. Ibid.
3. Brooke Shepherd, *Anschluss* pages 21–76.
4. Ibid. DGFP Series D Vol I pages 515–17, page 563. DDF 2nd Series Vol IX pages 4–7, 21–23.
5. Wiskeman, *Rome Berlin Axis* page 100.
6. Cab 23/92. *Cadogan Diaries* page 63.
7. Cab 27/623.
8. Barnes op cit, page 499.
9. Gilbert *Winds of Change* page 543. Wheeler-Bennett *Munich*, page 36. Cab 23/93.
10. DBFP Series 3, Vol 1 pages 1–196.
11. Seton-Watson – 'Italian Gentleman's Agreement of January 1937 and its aftermath.' In *Fascist Challenge*, ed Monsom and Kettenacher.
12. Barnes op cit, page 503.
13. Wiskeman op cit, page 107.
14. Bullock 'Hitler' pages 444–5.
15. DBFP Series 3 Vol 1, pages 151–214; 97.
16. Ibid pages 631–3. L. Noel, *L'Aggression Allemande contre la Pologne* pages 198ff.
17. DGFP Series D Vol II pages 422; 350. DBFP Series 3 Vol 1, page 355.
18. FO 800/309.
19. DGFP Series D Vol II pages 356; 411.
20. Ibid pages 329–332.
21. Ibid pages 332, 385, 336, 341. Henderson's letter Prem 1/266A.
22. Ibid page 347.

CHAPTER ELEVEN
Munich – Hitler's Big Bluff (pp. 239–279)

1. FO 371/21717. DBFP Series 3, Vol 11
2. DBFP Series 3 Vol 11 pages 657, 659, 665.
3. Ibid pages 61–63. Hoffman, *History of the German Resistance* pages 59–63.
4. DBFP Series 3 Vol 11 pages 684–89. Hoffman op cit pages 59–63.
5. Cadogan op cit, pages 94–5. DBFP Series 3 Vol 11 pages 689–92.
6. DBFP Series 3 Vol 11 pages 257; 282.
7. Hoffman op cit pages 92–3.
8. Ibid page 329. Cab 12.9.38. Cab 23/95.
9. Kordt's message 12.9.38. DGFP Series D Vol II pages 754–755. DBFP Series 3. Vol 11 Page 329.
10. Prem 1/266A.
11. Cab 23/95. Prem 1/266A. Duff Cooper, *Old Men Forget* page 229.
12. Cab 23/95. *Dalton Diaries* pages 173–85.
13. FO 371/21741.
14. Prem 1/266A.

15. Ibid
16. Ibid *Daily Telegraph*, 24 September 1938.
17. Cab 23/95; Prem 1/266A; Cadogan op cit pages 103–104. Cab 27/624.
18. DBFP Series 3 Vol 11 page 453. FO 371/21669.
19. Cadogan op cit page 107. Cab 23/95.
20. Cab 23/95.
21. DBFP Series 3 Vol 11, page 519. Prem 1/331 A.
22. Slessor, *Blue Circle* page 151.
23. Prem 1/331A. Churchill, *The Gathering Storm* page 242. Telford Taylor, *Munich* page 863. Cab 23/
24. Prem 1/266A. DBFP Series 3 Vol 11, pages 510; 513; 535; 558. FO 371/21741 for Mallet. Harvey op cit page 59.
25. Prem 1/266A. DBFP Series 3 Vol 11, page 552.
26. Prem 1/266A. DBFP Series 3 Vol 11, pages 552–8; 576; 578.
27. Prem 1/266/A. *The Times*, August 1965. Taylor op cit page 889. Cadogan op cit page 110.
28. Prem 1/266A. Cab 27/646. Cab 23/95. DBFP Series 3 Vol 11 pages 587 et seq.
29. Conversation Godfrey Nicolson with author, August 1988.
30. Prem 1/266A
31. Ibid, Lamb, *Ghosts of Peace* page 87.
32. Prem 1/266A. Letter to author 1988 from Lord Home.
33. Cab 23/95. Duff Cooper, *Hansard* Commons 3 October 1938 Col 373.
34. Keitel International Military Tribunal Vol X, page 56 et seq. Jodl International Military Tribunal Vol X, page 361 et seq. Adam's unpublished memoirs are in Institut für Zeitgeschictle, Munich. Telford Taylor op cit, page 609.
35. Prem 1/266A. Harvey op cit, page 194.
36. Gilbert op cit, page 1033. DBFP Series 3 Vol 11, pages 86–8. Harvey op cit page 194.
37. DGFP Series D Vol 11 249 et seq.
38. DBFP Series 3 Vol 11 pages 354–5. Butler, *Art of the Possible* pages 69–72. Taylor op cit page 842. BDFP Series 3 VR VIII page 612.
39. Cab 27/646. Middlemas, *Price of Peace* page 381.
40. FO 800/301.
41. Cab 27/624. DBFP Series 3 Vol IV page 535.
42. Churchill, *The Gathering Storm* op cit pages 263–5. See also Neil Acherson *Observer*, 2 October 1988.
43. FO 371/46970.
44. Ibid
45. P. Meehan, *Foreign Office and the Opposition* Paper at Anglo–German Historical Conference, Leeds. May 1986. DBFP Series 3 Vol 11 pages 683–691. Keitel and Jodl's evidence at Nuremberg op cit. FO 371/46970. Lamb op cit, pages 93–1; 121.
46. A. J. P. Taylor, *Origins of the Second World War* page 189.
47. Cmd 5847. Cmd 5848.
48. FO 371/21742. Harvey op cit page 187.
49. Brueghel, *Czechoslovakia Before Munich* page 276. FO 371/21742. FO 371/21745.
50. C. Seton-Watson, *R. W. Seton-Watson and the Czechoslovaks 1935–1939*, paper presented to the November 1988 Conference of the Collegium Carolinum on 'Great Britain, the United States of America and the Bohemian Lands (1848–1938)' FO 371/21789. The author is grateful for information given by Professor Seton-Watson's son, Christopher Seton-Watson, who was an undergraduate at New College at the same time and helped his father. Profesor Seton-Watson had kept in close touch with Masaryk at the Czech London Embassy throughout the crisis. He was appalled by the Government's attitude and particularly by Halifax summoning Masaryk on 21 September and telling him that Czechoslovakia should agree to Hitler's Berchtesgaden demands and 'if Hitler got the Sudetenland we would ask no more but proceed to discuss a general European settlement'. On 27 September Seton-Watson sent a memorandum to all MPs and a selected list of peers with a summary from the key documents which he had obtained from the Czech Embassy and pointing out that Hitler's demands were

so humiliating and contrary to the spirit of Britain that MPs should be in possession of the full facts 'pending publication of the full texts.'

Seton-Watson spent 1½ hours with Eden before the Commons debate on 2 October which accounts for the cogency of Eden's argument. In the debate on 3 October Dalton challenged Hoare to say whether Seton-Watson's 'paper' was totally accurate or not; Hoare replied it was 'substantially, I might say totally, inaccurate.' However, Seton-Watson was totally vindicated.

51. DBFP Series 3 Vol 11 pages 398–9. 380–381. Cab 23/96.
52. DBFP Series 3 Vol 11 page 379–81. Cab 23/96.
53. Petrie, *Twenty Years Armistice* op cit page 217.
54. Lord Hailsham, conversation with author November 1988.
55. Cook and Ramsden op cit pages 140–165.
56. Barnes, *Empire at Bay* pages 528–9.
57. FO 371/21697. FO 371/21671. R. Land in *Independent* 9.11.88.

CHAPTER TWELVE
False Hopes of Peace (pp. 280–290)

1. Gladwyn op cit, pages 83–88. *Daily Telegraph*, 13 January 1939. Ciano *Diaro*, Vol 1 Rome 1946, pages 11–21. For attitude of British to Italian claims against France BDFP Series 3 Vol 1 Pages 291–359. On 11 March 1939 Corbin told Halifax it ought not to be too difficult to settle Djibuti and the Canal but Tunis was 'the real problem' (Page 344) For British journalists in Rome, January 1939, see E. Serra in *Rivista di Storia Contemporanea* Number 3 1986.
2. Cab 27/624. FRUS 1939 Vol 1 pages 2–6. Gladwyn op cit, page 87.
3. Cab 23/97.
4. DBFP Series 3 Vol IV pages 118–22; 162–5; 195–215.
5. FO 371/23896.
6. *Times*, 18 March 1939.
7. Cab 23/98. DGFP Series D Vol IV No 26.
8. DBFP Series 3 Vol III, page 67.
9. FO 371/23677. FO 371/23061. DBFP Series 3 Vol IV pages 202–8. Tilea page 283.
10. Rothschild, *'Peace for our Time'* London 1988, page 291.
11. Adamthwaite, op cit page 84.
12. DBFP Series 3 Vol IV pages 402; 573.
13. Cab 23/98. DBFP Series 3 Vol IV pages 422–8.
14. Cadogan op cit, pages 164–5. Colvin, *Vansittart in office* pages 298–311.
15. Cab 27/624.
16. Maisky, *Who Helped Hitler?* pages 107–8. Aster; *The Making of the Second World War* pages 112–13.
17. Cab 27/624.

CHAPTER THIRTEEN
Britain's Sluggish Rearmament 1936–9 (pp. 291–297)

1. Cab 53/29. Cab 23/86.
2. Cab 53/30. Cab 23/88.
3. Cab 24/273.
4. Cab 24/273. Cab 21/524.
5. Cab 3/7. Bond *British Military Policy between the two World Wars* page 363 for Ironside.
6. DBFP Series 3 Vol 11 pages 282; 317. Bond pages 291–2. Cab 23/96.
7. Cab 2/8 15 December. Bond op cit page 294 for Pownall.
8. Cab 23/99. DBFP Series 3 Vol 111 pages 284–311.

9. Cab 23/97. Bond op cit page 300. Gibbs op cit pages 509–11. Cab 53/8.
10. Cab 23/98. Prem 1/296.
11. Bond op cit page 328. Montgomery, *Memoirs* pages 49–50.
12. Collier, *Defence of U.K.* Appendix XXX. Howard, *Continental Commitment*, page 111.

CHAPTER FOURTEEN
Polish Guarantee and Soviet–German Pact 1939 (pp. 298–324)

1. Aster op cit, page 90.
2. DBFP Series 3 Vol V, page 286.
3. DBFP Series 3 Vol V, pages 1–9.
4. DGFP Series D Vol VI pages 186–187; 223–228. Schirer *Rise and Fall of Third Reich*, pages 467–9.
5. Cab 23/98.
6. Cab 23/98. Barnes op cit, page 553. Cadogan op cit page 182.
7. Cab 27/624.
8. Ibid
9. Cab 23/99
10. FO 371/23064. Maisky op. cit., pages 110–11.
11. DBFP Series 3 Vol V, pages 429–33; 463.
12. Cab 23/99.
13. Cab 27/625.
14. Cadogan op cit page 180. Cab 23/99.
15. DBFP Series 3 Vol V, page 736.
16. FPC 9 June. Cab 27/625.
17. DBFP Series 3 Vol V1 Nos 60, 69, 73, 103 Cab 27/625. FO 371/23069. FO 371/23072.
18. DBFP Series 3 Vol VI pages 383–4. Cab 27/625.
19. Cab 23/100. DBFP Series 3 Vol V1 page 458.
20. Aster op cit, pages 290–296. Cab 23/100. DBFP Series 3 Vol V1 pages 570–576. CAb 55/18. FO 371/23072.
21. FO 371/23072. DBFP Series 3 Vol V11 pages 558–614. Appendix 11. (Further material on Anglo–Soviet military conversations in Moscow, August 1939.) Aster op cit pp 303–14.
22. FO 371/23686.
23. FO 371/27286.
24. FO 371/22973. DDF 2nd Series Vol XVI pages 498 – 504.
25. FO 371/23697.
26. *Pravda* 11 March 1936.
27. FO 371/23697.
28. FO 371/23020. DBFP Series 3 Vol V pages 594–5.
29. FO 371/23000. FO 371/22869. FO 371/23687.
30. FO 371/22973. Astor letter to author.
31. DBFP Series 3 Vol V1 page 705.
32. FO 371/23686.
33. FO 371/23069.
34. FO 371/23069.
35. FO 371/27686.
36. Cab 23/100.
37. FO 371/22980. Collier conversation author with Lord Sherfield 1988.
38. FO 371/22976.
39. FO 371/22980.
40. DGFP Series D Vol V1 pages 608, 610, 620.
41. Ibid pages 687, 746.
42. DGFP Series D Vol V1 pages 731–60; 788; 810; 871.

43. DGFP Series D Vol V11 page 64.
44. Ibid pages 99; 122; 123; 149; 150; 157.
45. FO 366/1062.
46. Dirksen, op. cit., pages 237–242. DBFP Series 3 Vol V1 pages 385–91. Prem 1/330 A FO 371/22990.
47. FO 371/22990. Dirksen op. cit., pages 237–52.
48. Harvey op cit page 303. Gladwyn op cit page 93.
49. Prem 1/332.
50. Ibid. FO 800/316.
51. Ibid.
52. Howard, *Rab*, page 85.
53. FO 800/316.
54. Prem 1/330 A.
55. Prem 1/331 FO 371/23687. FO 371/23009. FO 371/22975. Aster op cit, pages 256–8.
56. FO 800/317. Prem 1/331. Cadogan op cit, page 199.

CHAPTER FIFTEEN
Into the Abyss (pp. 325–340)

1. Cab 23/100. DBFP Series 3 Vol V1 pages 691–6.
2. Ibid pages 170–172; 197–199; 351–354. Harvey, op. cit., page 309.
3. Cab 23/100.
4. Ciano page 125. DGFP Series D Vol V11 pages 39–47.
5. Mack Smith, *Mussolini's Roman Empire* page 164. DGFP Series D Vol VII pages 39–49.
6. Santoni *L'operative del Alleanza Italiana Tedesca* (Unpublished paper Montpelier Conference 1981).
7. Prem 1/330A DGFP Series D Vol V11 pages 237–42. DGFP Series D Vol VII pgs 309, 310, 313. For full text of Hitler's address to his generals Lamb *The Ghosts of Peace* pages 108–109. Shirer op cit page 519.
8. IMT Vol X page 422. IMT Vol IX page 465. DGFP Series D Vol VII pages 564–66.
9. FO 371/22979. Author's conversations with Sir Frank Roberts and Sir Peter Tennant.
10. Dahlerus cross examination, IMT Vol 1X Pages 476–489 Henderson, '*Failures of a Mission*' page 274.
11. DBFP Series 3 Vol VII pages 227–229. FO 371/22979.
12. Cab 23/100.
13. Dahlerus, *Last Attempt* pages 72–96. FO 800/317. FO 371/37918.
14. FO 800/317. Henderson op cit pages 264, 265.
15. DBFP Series 3 Vol VII pages 374–377. FO 800/317.
16. FO 800/317. FO 371/22982. Dahlerus, op. cit.
17. FO 371/22982. FO 800/317.
18. FO 371/22981. DBFP Series 3 Vol VI pages 385–98. This does not make it clear Dahlerus phoned to Goering twice from Downing Street.
19. DBFP Series 3 Vol VII pages 432–3; 440–2.
20. FO 371/22982. DBFP Series 3 Vol VII pages 440–2; FO 371/22982.
21. DBFP Series 3 Vol VII pages 442–3.
22. Ibid pages 446–7.
23. Cab 23/100. Prem 1/331.
24. FO 371/22980.
25. Cab 23/100. Nicolson op cit page 417.
26. Cab 23/100. FO 371/22981. *Ciano Diary* page 143.
27. DBFP Series 3 Vol VII pages 518–519. Ciano op cit page 143. FO 371/22981. DGFP Series D Vol VII pages 509–513. Hesse and Wilson. Ibid pages 527–528.
28. FO 371/22982. DBFP Series 3 Vol VII pages 524–526. Cab 23/100. Dahlerus op cit pages 116–20. N.B. The Cabinet minutes have been bound in the wrong order in the P.R.O.

BIOGRAPHICAL NOTES

A

ADAM, Wilhelm General *b.* 1877. Commander German armies on Siegfried Line 1938.
ALFONSO XIII 1886–1941. King of Spain 1902–31.
AMERY, Leopold 1873–1955. Conservative M.P. 1911–45. Sec of State for India 1940–5.
ANDERSON, Sir John, 1st Viscount Waverley, 1882–1958. Lord Privy Seal 1938–9.
ASHTON-GWATKIN, Frank 1889–1976. First Secretary Foreign Office 1938.
ASTOR, Nancy Langhorne, Viscountess 1879–1964. 1st woman MP for Plymouth (Sutton) 1919–45.
ATTLEE, Clement Richard 1st Earl 1883–1962. Labour MP Limestone Div. of Stepney 1922–50. Prime Minister 1945–51.

B

BALDWIN, Stanley, 1st Earl of Bewdley 1867–1947. Prime Minister 1923–4; 1924–9; 1935–7.
BALFOUR, Arthur James, 1st Earl of Balfour 1848–1930. Prime Minister 1902–5.
BALL, Sir Joseph 1885–1961. Director Conservative Research Dept. 1930–9. Editor of *Truth*.
BARTHOU, Jean Louis 1862–1934. Foreign Minister, France 1934. (Assassinated).
BECK, Joseph 1894–1944. Chef de Cabinet to Pilsudski 1926–29; Foreign Minister Poland 1932–9. Died in German captivity.
BECK, Gen. Ludwig, Cmmdr. German Armed Forces 1938. Leader of plot to kill Hitler in 1944.
BERTHELOT, Philippe 1866–1934. Secretary, French Foreign Office 1924–31.
BISMARCK, Prince Otto Christian Archibald von 1897–1976. At German Embassy London 1926–39. German Minister in Rome 1940–3.
BLOMBERG, Werner von 1878–1946. German Field Marshal, Minister for War 1935–8.
BLUM, Léon 1872–1950. Prime Minister France 1936–7; 1938; 1946–7. Socialist.
BOOTHBY, Robert 1st Baron 1900–1986. Cons. M.P. 1924–58. Parl. Sec. to Ministry of Food 1940–41.
BRIAND, Aristide 1862–1932. Prime Minister France 1909–11; 1913; 1915–17; 1921–2; 1925–6; 1929.
BRÜNING, Dr Heinrich 1885–1970. Chancellor of Germany 1930–2.
BURCKHARDT, Prof. Carl Jakob *b.* 1891. Swiss Diplomat.
BURNHAM, Harry Lawson 1st Viscount 1862–1933. Proprietor *Daily Telegraph* 1916–33.
BUTLER, Richard Austin (RAB) 1902–82. 1st Baron. Leading Conservative politician.

C

CADOGAN, Sir Alexander, 1884–1968. Perm Under Sec. of State Foreign Affairs 1938–46.
CAMPBELL, Sir Ronald N. 1885–1953. Minister, Paris 1929–35; Ambassador to France 1939–40; Ambassador to Portugal 1940–5.
CANARIS, Wilhelm 1887–1945. German Admiral. Chief of Abwehr 1935–4. Executed by Hitler.
CECIL, Edgar Algernon Robert, 1st Viscount of Chalwood 1864–1958. Member of Cabinet for League of Nations Affairs 1923–4; 1924–37.
CHAMBERLAIN, Sir Joseph Austen 1863–1937. Foreign Sec. 1924–9.
CHAMBERLAIN, (Arthur) Neville 1869–1940. Chancellor of Exchequer 1923; Prime Minister 1931–7; 1937–40.
CHAUTEMPS, Camille 1885–1963. Prime Min. France 1930 (for 3 days); Nov 1933 – Jan. 1934; June 1937 – Nov. 1938.
CHILSTON, Aretas Akers-Douglas, Viscount, 1876–1947. Ambassador to Moscow 1933–8.
CHURCHILL, Winston Leonard Spencer, Sir 1874–1965. Chan. of Exchequer 1924–9; Prime Minister 1940–5; 1951–3.

Biographical Notes

CIANO, Count Galeazzo 1903–44. (Son-in-law of Mussolini) Minister of Propaganda 1935; Min. Foreign Affairs 1936–43; Executed by Mussolini, Verona 1944.

CLEMENCEAU, Georges 1841–1929. Prime Minister France 1906–9, 1917–20.

CLERK, George Russell, Sir 1874–1951. Ambassador to Paris 1934–7.

CLIVE, Sir Robert, 1877–1948. Ambassador to Belgium; Minister to Luxembourg 1937–9.

COLLIER, Sir Laurence 1890–1976. Counsellor in charge of Russian desk at F.O. 1939.

COOK, Sir Joseph 1860–1947. Prime Minister, Australia 1913–14.

COOPER, Alfred Duff, 1st Viscount Norwich 1890–1952. Sec. State for War 1935–7; 1st Lord of Admiralty 1937–8; Ambassador to France 1944–7.

CORBIN, (Andre) Charles 1881–1970. French Ambassador to Gt. Britain 1933–40.

CRANBORNE, Robert Arthur James Gascoyne-Cecil, 5th Marquess of Salisbury 1893–1972. Parl. U. Sec. Foreign Affairs 1935–8; Lord Pres. of Council 1952–7.

CRESWELL, Michael Justin *b.* 1909. Minister to Cairo 1951–54; Ambassador to Finland 1954–58; Amb. to Yugoslavia 1960–64; Amb. to Argentine 1964–9.

CREWE, Robert Offley Ashburton Crewe-Milnes, 1st Viscount 1958–1945. Ambassador to Paris 1922–8; Liberal Cab. Minister under Asquith.

CRIPPS, Sir Stafford 1889–1951. Solicitor Gen., 1930–31; friend of Adam von Trott, leader of German Resistance to Hitler.

CROSSLEY, Anthony 1903–39. Parl. Sec. to Minister of Transport 1935–8.

CROWE, Sir Eyre 1864–1925. Perm. Under Secretary Foreign Office 1920–5.

CUNLIFFE-LISTER, Philip 1st Earl of Swinton 1884–1972. Pres. Board of Trade 1922–3; 1924–9; and 1931; Colonial Sec. 1931–5; Sec. State for Air 1935–8.

CUNO, Wilhelm 1876–1933. Chancellor Germany 1922.

CURTIUS, Julius 1877–1948. Foreign Minister, Germany 1929–31.

CURZON, George Nathaniel 1st Marquess of Kedleston, 1859–1925. For. Sec. 1919–24.

D

D'ABERNON, Edgar Vincent 1st Viscount, 1857–1941. Ambassador to Berlin 1920–6.

DALADIER, Eduard, 1884–1870. Prime Minister, France 1933–4; 1936; 1938–40.

DALTON, Hugh 1st Baron 1887–1962. Under Secretary Foreign Office 1929–31; Chancellor of Exchequer 1945–7.

DAWES, Brig. Gen. Charles Gates 1865–1951. Vice President U.S.A. 1925–9; Ambassador to Gt. Britain 1929–32.

DAWSON, George Geoffrey 1874–1949. Editor, *The Times*.

DE BONO, General Emilio, Fascist Chief Police Commander in Ethiopia; executed by Mussolini after Verona Trials.

DE LA WARR, Edward (Buck) 9th Earl 1900–1976. Minister for Education 1938–40.

DELBOS, Yvon *b.* 1885. French Foreign Minister in Blum Cabinet 1936, and under Chautemps 1937 and 1938.

DELL, Robert. *Manchester Guardian* Diplomatic Correspondent 1920–40.

DIRKSEN, Herbert von *b.* 1889. German Ambassador to London 1938–9.

DOENITZ, Karl 1891–1980. Grand Admiral and C-in-C German Navy 1943–45.

DOLLFUSS, Engelbert, Dr 1892–1934. Chancellor of Austria 1932–4.

DONOVAN, Richard Col. (Maj.-Gen. USA) 1885–1949.

DONNER, Sir Patrick William 1904–1988. Conservative MP.

DOUMENC, General. Head of French Military Mission in Moscow 1939.

DOUMERGUE, Gaston 1683–1937. Pres. French Republic 1924–31; Prime Minister France 1934.

DRAX, Admiral Hon. Sir Reginald Plunket Ernle Erle 1880–1967. Head of British. Military Mission in Moscow 1939.

DRUMMOND, James Eric 16th Earl of Perth 1876–1951. Sec. Gen. to League of Nations 1919–33; Ambassador to Italy 1937–40.

DUNCANNON, Viscount later Earl of Bessborough *b.* 1913. Cons. candidate 1935.

E

EBERT, Friedrich 1871–1925. President of the Republic, Germany 1922–5.

357

EDEN, Robert Anthony, 1st Earl of Avon, 1897–1977. Foreign Secretary 1935–8; 1940–45; 1951–5; Prime Minister 1955–57.

ELLIOT, Walter 1888–1958. Scottish Sec. 1936–38; Minister of Health 1938–40.

EYRES-MONSELL, Bolton Meredith, 1st Vis. Monsell 1887–1969. First Lord of Admiralty 1931–6.

F

FEY, Emil, Major 1886–1938. Austrian Vice Chanceller 1933–4.

FITZROY MACLEAN, Brig. *b*. 1911. Joined Diplomatic Service 1933. Cons. MP 1941–74.

FLANDIN, Pierre Etienne 1889–1958. Prime Minister France 1934–5.

FRANCO Y BAHAMONDE, General Francisco, 1892–1975. Head of Spanish State and Generalissimo of Spanish Armies from 1936.

FRANCOIS-PONCET, André 1887–1978. French Ambassador to Germany 1931–8; Ambassador to Italy 1938–40.

FRASER, Brig. Hon. William 1908–1964. Chief of UNNRA after war.

G

GAMELIN, Maurice G. 1872–1958. French Chief of Staff 1935; C-in-C Franco-British Forces 1939–40.

GARIBALDI, Gen. Giuseppe 1879–1950. Friend of Mussolini; grandson of liberator of Italy.

GARVIN, James 1868–1947. Editor *Observer*.

GLADWYN, Hubert Miles Gladwyn Jebb, *b*. 1900. 1st Baron. U.K. rep. to U.N. 1950–4; Ambassador to France 1954–60.

GOEBBELS, Dr. Josef 1897–1945. Director *Der Angriff* 1927–33; Head of Nazi Propaganda Movement from 1928.

GOERING, Hermann 1893–1946. Field Marshal. C-in-C German Air Force 1933–45.

GOMBOS, Gynla, 1886–1936. Hungarian Prime Minister 1932–6.

GORT, General, later F.M. 6th Viscount 1886–1946. C-in-C B.E.F. 1939–40.

GRAHAM, Sir Ronald William, 1870–1949. Ambassador to Italy 1921–33.

GRAHAM, William 1887–1932. Labour M.P. 1918–31. Pres. Board of Trade 1929–31.

GRANDI, Dino 1895–1988. Italian Foreign Minister 1929–32; Italian Ambassador to Gt. Britain 1932–9.

GUARIGLIA, Dr. Raffaele *b*. 1889. Italian Ambassador to Paris 1936–9.

H

HACHA, Emil 1872–1945. President of Czechoslovakia 1938–9.

HAILE SELASSIE, 1891–1975. Emperor of Ethiopia.

HAILSHAM, Douglas McGarel Hogg, 1st Viscount 1872–1950. Sec. State for War 1931–5; Lord Chancellor 1935–8.

HAILSHAM, Quintin 2nd Viscount *b*. 1907. Won a by election October 1938.

HALDER, Gen. Franz von. Survived the war and was one of the few witnesses of the plots against Hitler.

HALIFAX, Edward Frederick Lindley Wood, 1st Earl 1881–1959. Foreign Secretary 1938–40. Ambassador at Washington 1941–46.

HANKEY, Maurice Pascal Alers, 1st Baron 1877–1963. Sec. to Cabinet 1919–38; Min. Without Portfolio 1939–40; Chan. Duchy Lancaster 1940–1; Paymaster General 1941–2.

HABSBURG, Karl, 1887–1992. Emperor of Austria 1917.

HARVEY, Oliver 1st Baron 1893–1968. PPS to Eden and Halifax 1936–9; Minister Plenipotentiary to Paris 1940.

HARVEY, George 1864–1924. U.S. Ambassador to London 1921–3.

HASSELL, Ulrich von German Ambassador in Rome. Hassell was executed for his part in the July 1944 plot. To his credit, Mussolini made efforts to persuade Hitler to spare him.

HELLDORF, Wolf Herman von, President of Police in Berlin; executed for his part in 20 July bomb plot.

HENDERSON, Arthur 1863–1935. Labour Foreign Secretary 1929–31. President League of Nations Disarmament Conference.

HENDERSON Nevile, Sir, 1882–1942. Ambassador in Berlin 1937–9.

HERRIOT, Edouard 1872–1951. Prime Minister, France 1924; 1926 (one day); 1932.

HEYWOOD, Thomas George, Col. (later Maj–Gen) 1886–1943. Military Attaché in Paris 1932–6.

HINDENBURG, Paul von Beneckendorff und, 1847–1934. F.M. Pres. of Germany 1925–34.

HITLER, Adolf 1889–1945. Chancellor of Germany 1933–45.

HOARE, Sir Samuel 1st Viscount 1880–1959. Foreign Secretary 1935; Home Secretary 1937–9.

HOESCH, Leopold Gustav Alexander von, 1881–1936. German Ambassador to London 1932–6.

HOME of the Hirsel, Alexander Frederick Douglas-Home, Life Peer, *b.* 1903. Prime Min. 1963–4. PPS to Neville Chamberlain 1937–9.

HOOVER, Herbert C. 1874–1964. President of USA 1928–32.

HORE-BELISHA, Leslie 1st Baron 1898–1957. Sec. of State for War 1937–40.

HORNE, Sir Robert 1871–1940. Chancellor of the Exchequer 1921–2.

HORTHY, Admiral Nicholas, 1868–1957. Regent of Hungary from 1920; survived the war.

HUDSON, Sir Robert, 1st Viscount 1886–1957. Parl. Sec. Board of Trade 1933–40.

HUGENBERG, Alfred 1865–1951. Newspaper magnate and Nazi supporter.

I

INSKIP, Thomas 1st Viscount Caldecote 1896–1947. Minister for Co-ordination of Defence 1936–9; Sec. of State for Dominions 1939; Lord Chancellor 1939–40.

IRONSIDE, F.M. Sir Edmund 1st Baron 1880–1959. CIGS 1939–40.

J

JÈZE, Gaston 1869–1935. French lawyer; adviser to Haile Selassie.

JODL, General Alfred 1890–1946. Chief of Military Operations 1939–45.

JONES, Thomas 1870–1955. Deputy Secretary to Cabinet 1916–30.

K

KAHR, Gustav Ritter von 1862–1934. Premier of Bavaria 1920–3.

KALERGI, Coudenove, Count Richard 1894–1972. President Pan European Union which he founded in 1923; Founded European Parlimentary Union 1947. Awarded first Charlemagne prize 1950.

KEITEL, Field Marshal Wilhelm, 1887–1946. HItler's Army Commander.

KEMSLEY, James Gomer Berry 1st Viscount 1883–1968. Owner Kemsley Newspapers.

KENNARD, Sir Howard William, 1878–1955. Ambassador to Poland 1935–41.

KEYNES, John Maynard 1st Baron, 1883–1946. Principal representative of the Treasury at Paris Peace Conference 1919.

KOERBER, Victor von. Retired cavalry officer and a Monarchist.

KORDT, Dr Erich. Foreign Office official, Berlin.

KORDT, Dr Theodor. German chargé d'affaires in London 1938–9.

L

LANSBURY, George 1859–1940. Leader of Labour Party 1931–5.

LAVAL, Pierre, 1883–1945. French Prime Minister 1931–2; 1935–6; 1942.

LAW, Andrew Bonar 1858–1923. Prime Minister 1922–3.

LEEPER, Sir Reginald 1889–1968. Ambassador to Greece 1943–6.

LEGER, Alexis Saint-Léger 1887–1975. Chef de Cabinet at French Foreign Ministry 1925–32; (Left France for America in 1940).

LEITH-ROSS, Sir Frederick, 1889–1968. Chief Econ. Advisor to Govt. 1932–46.

LIDDELL-HART, Sir Basil 1895–1970. Military Corres. '*Daily Telegraph*' 1925–33, Military Corres. '*The Times*' 1935–9.

LINDSAY, Sir Ronald 1877–1945. Ambassador at Washington 1930–39.

LITVINOV, Maxim de Meet Wallach, 1876–1951. Soviet Foreign Minister 1930–9. Ambassador to USA 1941–3.

LLOYD, Geoffrey Life Peer *b.* 1902. Conservative MP 1931–45.

LLOYD, George Ambrose 1st Baron 1879–1941. Secretary of State for Colonies 1940.

LLOYD GEORGE, David 1st Earl of Dwyfor 1863–1945. Prime Minister 1916–22.

LONDONDERRY, Charles Stewart Henry Vane-Tempest-Stewart 1878–1949. Secretary of State for Air 1931–5; Lord Privy Seal 1935.

LORAINE, Sir Percy 1880–1961. Ambassador in Rome 1939–40.

LOTHIAN, Philip Henry Kerr, 11th Marquess 1882–1940. Sec. to Lloyd George 1916–21; Ambassador to Washington 1939–40.

LUDENDORFF, Erich 1865–1937. General. Political collaborator of Hitler.

LYTTON, Victor 2nd Earl 1876–1947. Head League of Nations Mission to Manchuria 1931.

M

MACDONALD, James Ramsay 1866–1937. Prime Minister 1924; 1929–35.

MACDONALD, Malcolm 1901–81. Sec. of State for Dominions 1935–9; Minister of Health 1940–1; Gov. Gen. Kenya 1963–4; High Commissioner Kenya 1964–5.

MACKENNA, Reginald 1863–1943. Chancellor of the Exchequer 1915–16.

MACMILLAN, Harold, 1st Earl of Stockton 1894–1987. Prime Minister 1957–64.

MAFFEY, John Loader, 1st Baron Rugby 1877–1969. Governor of Sudan 1926–33;

MALLET, Sir (William) Ivo 1900–88. Ambassador to Spain 1954–60.

MANDEL, Georges (born Jeroboam Rothschild) 1885–1944. French Minister of Colonies 1938–40; Minister of Interior 1940. Assassinated by Vichy militia 1944.

MANDER, Sir Geoffrey 1882–1962. Liberal MP. 1929–45.

MARTIN, T. B. *b.* 1901. Conservative MP for Blaydon 1931–38.

MASARYK, Jan 1886–1948. Czechoslovakian Minister in London 1925–38.

MATTEOTTI, Giacomo. Popular Italian MP murdered by Fascists shortly after Mussolini came to power.

MAUGHAM, Frederick 1st Viscount 1886–1958 (Brother of Somerset Maugham) Lord Chancellor 1938.

MAURIN, Louis 1869–1956. French General. Minister for War 1934–6.

MELLON, Andrew William 1855–1937. American Ambassador to Gt. Britain 1932–3.

MIKLAS, Dr Wilhelm. 1872–1956. Austrian President 1928–38.

MONTGOMERY, FM. 1st Earl 1887–1976.

MOORE, Thomas Cecil Russell 1886–1971. MP for Ayr Burgh 1925–50.

MORRISON, William Shepherd 1893–1961. 1st Viscount Dunrossil. Chan. Duchy of Lancaster 1939. Later Speaker, House of Commons.

MOUNSEY, Sir George Augustus 1879–1966. Sec. Ministry of Economic Warfare 1939–40.

MÜLLER, Hermann 1876–1931. Chancellor of Germany 1928–30.

MUSSOLINI, Benito 1883–1945. Italian Head of State 1922–43.

N

NEURATH, Constantin Freiherr von 1873–1956. German Foreign Minister 1932–8.

NEWTON, Sir Basil Cochrane 1889–1965. Counsellor, Berlin 1930–5; Minister in Prague 1935–8; Ambassador to Iraq 1939–41.

NOEL, Léon. Sec. General to French Cabinet.

NOEL-BAKER, Philip 1889–1983 (Baron Life Peer) PPS to Foreign Secretary 1929–31; Minister Fuel & Power 1950–1; Labour MP.

NICHOLS, Sir Philip 1894–1962. Ambassador to Holland 1948–51.

NICHOLSON, Sir Godfrey *b.* 1901. Conservative M.P. 1931–5; 1937–59.

NICOLSON, Sir Harold 1886–1968. H.M. Embassy Berlin 1927–9; Nat. Labour M.P. 1935–45.

NIEMEYER, Sir Otto 1883–1971. Treasury official.

NORMAN, Montagu 1st Baron 1871–1950. Governor, Bank of England 1920–44.

O

OGILVIE-FORBES, Sir George 1891–1954. Counsellor British Embassy, Berlin 1938.

OLIPHANT, Sir Lancelot 1881–1963. Expert on Middle East; Asst. Under Sec. at F.O. 1935; Ambassador to Belgium; Min. in Luxembourg 1939; POW 1940–1.

O'MALLEY, Sir Owen St. Clair, 1887–1974. Ambassador to Portugal 1945–7.

O'NEILL, The Hon. Sir Con 1912–88. Entered Foreign Office 1936.

ORLANDO, Vittorio Emanuele 1860–1952. Italian Prime Minister 1917–19.

ORMSBY-GORE, William George Arthur, 4th Lord Harlech 1885–1964. Colonial Sec. 1936–8.

P

PAPEN, Franz von 1879–1969. German Chancellor 1932. Ambassador in Vienna and Ankara.

PAUL-BONCOUR, Joseph 1873–1972. French Prime Minister 1932–3 (1 month); Foreign Minister 1932–34; & 1938.

PETERSON, Maurice Drummond, Sir 1889–1952. Ambassador to Spain 1939–40; Ambassador to Moscow 1946–9.

PETHICK-LAWRENCE, Frederick *b.* 1871. Labour M.P. 1935–43, Financial Sec. to Treasury 1929–31.

PHIPPS, Eric, Sir 1875–1945. Ambassador to Berlin 1933–37; to Paris 1937–9.

PLYMOUTH, Ivor. 2nd Earl 1889–1945. Under Sec. at Foreign Office 1936–9.

POINCARE, Raymond 1860–1934. French Prime Minister 1922–4; 1926–9.

POWNALL, Lt. Gen. Sir Henry 1877–1961. Dep. Sec. CID 1936; Director Military Operations 1938–9.

R

RAEDER, Erich 1876–1960. German Naval C-in-C (Grand Admiral from 1939) 1935–43.

RATHENAU, Walther 1867–1922. German Foreign Minister Feb.–June 1922.

READING, Rufus Daniel Isaacs, 1st Marquess 1860–1935. Viceroy of India 1924–6; Foreign Secretary 1931.

RIBBENTROP, Joachim von 1893–1946. German Ambassador to London 1936–8; German Foreign Minister 1938–45.

ROOSEVELT, Franklin Delano 1882–1945. 32nd President of USA.

ROSENBERG, Alfred 1893–1946. Head of Nazi Foreign Affairs Dept. 3rd Reich.

ROTHERMERE, Harold Harmsworth, 1st Viscount 1866–1940. Head of Associated Newspapers.

RUMBOLD, Sir Horace 1869–1941. Ambassador to Berlin 1928–33.

RUNCIMAN, Walter 1st Viscount 1870–1949. Liberal MP 1899–1900; 1902–18; 1924–37; Pres. Board of Trade 1914–16; 1931–7; Lord Pres. of the Council 1938–9.

S

SACKETT, Frederic Moseley Jnr. 1868–1941. US Ambassador to Germany 1930–3.

SARGENT, Orme Sir, 1884–1962. Permament Under Secretary Foreign Office 1946–9.

SARRAUT, Albert 1872–1962. French Prime Minister 1933; 1936.

SCHACHT, Dr Hjalmar, 1877–1970. Pres. of Reichsbank 1923–30; Hitler's Finance Minister.

SCHANZER, Carlo 1865–1953. Italian Foreign Minister 1923.

SCHLEICHER, Kurt von 1882–1934. Last Weimar Chancellor, Germany 1932.

SCHULENBERG, Frederick von, German Ambassador to Moscow 1939 and a prominent member of the Resistance to Hitler. Executed 1944.

SCHUSCHNIGG, Kurt von 1897–1986. Austrian Chancellor 1934–8; Imprisoned at Dachau until 1945.

SCHWERIN von Krosigk, Count Lutz 1887–1952. German Finance Minister 1932–45.

SCRIVENER, Sir Patrick Strafford, 1897–1966. Ambassador at Berne 1953–4.

SEEDS, Sir William 1882–1973. British Ambassador to Soviet Union 1939–40.

SELBY, Walford Harmwood Montague, Sir 1881–1965. Minister in Vienna 1933–7; Ambassador in Lisbon 1937–40.

SELDTE, Franz 1882–1947. German Minister of Labour 1933–45.

SETON-WATSON, R. W. Professor 1879–1951. Pres. Royal Historical Society; Professor of Czechoslovakian Studies, Oxford.

SEYSS-INQUART, Arthur 1892–1946. Austrian Nazi politician.

SHERFIELD, Roger Mellor Makins, 1st Baron *b.* 1904. Ambassador to USA 1953–56; Joint Perm. Sec. to Treasury 1956–9.

SIMON, John Allsebrook, 1st Viscount 1873–1954. Foreign Secretary 1931–5; Home Secretary 1935–37; Chancellor of Exchequer 1937–40.

SIMON, Viscountess *d.* 1955.

SINCLAIR, Archibald Henry MacDonald, 1st Viscount Thurso 1890–1970. Leader Liberal Parliamentary Party 1935–45; Secretary of State for Air 1940–5.

SLESSOR, Air Marshal Sir John, 1897–1979 Director of Plans, Air Ministry.

SNOWDEN, Philip 1st Viscount, 1864–1937. Chancellor of the Exchequer 1924; 1929–32.

ST QUENTIN, Count René de *b.* 1883. French Ambassador to Rome 1936. Ambassador to Washington 1938; Ambassador to Rio de Janeiro 1941–3.

STALIN, Joseph 1879–1953. Russian leader from death of Lenin in 1924.

STANHOPE, James Richard 7th Earl 1880–1967. Under Sec. for Foreign Affairs 1934–36; President Board of Education 1937–8; 1st Lord of Admiralty 1938–38; Lord President of the Council 1939–40.

STANLEY, Oliver Frederick George 1896–1950. Pres. Board of Education 1935–37; Board of Trade 1937–40.

STARHEMBERG, Prina Ernst Rüdiger von 1899–1956. Austrian Vice Chancellor 1934–6.

STIMSON, Henry L. 1867–1950. Secretary of State, America 1929–33; Secretary for War 1940–5.

STRANG, William, 1st Baron 1893–1978. Permanent Under Sec. Foreign Office 1949–53.

STRESEMANN, Dr Gustav 1878–1929. German Chancellor 1923; Foreign Minister 1923–9.

STULPNAGEL, Gen. Karl Heinrich von. Involved in 1944 bomb plot when as commander in Paris he arrested on 20 July all Gestapo SS leaders. Committed suicide 1944.

SUVICH, Fulvio Mussolini's Deputy Foreign Secretary.

T

TARDIEU, Andre Pierre Gabriel Amédée 1876–1945. French Prime Minister 1929–30; 1932.

TEMPERLEY, Arthur Cecil, Brig. (later Maj-Gen) 1877–1940. Military Representative at League of Nations 1925–35; *Daily Telegraph* military corresp. 1935–9.

THEUNIS, George 1873–1966. Prime Minister Belgium 1921–5; 1934–5.

THOMAS, James Henry, 1874–1949. Colonial Secretary 1930–5; became National Labour.

THOMPSON, Sir Geoffrey Harrington, 1898–1967. Ambassador to Bangkok 1947–50.

TILEA, Virgil 1896–1972. Romanian Minister in London 1938–40.

TITELESCU, Nicholas 1883–1941. Hungarian Foreign Minister 1932–6.

TORETTA, Marchese Della (Pietro Tomasi) Italian Ambassador in London 1922–27. Uncle of novelist Giuseppe Lampedusa.

TRYON, George 1st Baron 1871–1940. Postmaster General 1935–40.

TYRRELL, William 1st Baron, 1866–1947. Permanent Under-Secretary to Foreign Office 1925–28; Ambassador to Paris 1928–34.

V

VAN ZEELAND, Vicomte Paul 1893–1973. Belgian Prime Minister 1935–7.

VANSITTART, Robert 1st Baron, 1881–1957. Perm. Under Sec. to F.O. 1930–8. Chief Diplomatic Advisor 1938–41.

VOROSHILOV, Marshal Kliment 1881–1969. Soviet Military Commander.

VYVYAN, Michael *b.* 1906. Fellow Trinity College, Cambridge; served in Foreign Office.

W

WARNER, Sir Christopher Frederick Ashton, 1895–1957. Ambassador to Belgium 1951–5.

WEIZSAECKER, Baron Ernst von, 1882–1951. Head of German Foreign Office 1938–43.

WERTH, Alexander 1901–1969. Paris correspondent *Manchester Guardian* 1931–40; *Sunday Times* diplomatic corresp. 1940–1.

WEYGAND, General Maxime, 1867–1965. C-in-C French Army 1931–5 and 1940; French Minister of National Defence 1940.

WIGRAM, Ralph F. 1890–1936. First Secretary in Paris 1924–33.

WILMOT, John 1st Baron Wilmot of Silmeston, 1895–1964. Labour MP. Won East Fulham by-election 1933. Minister of Supply 1944.

WILSON, Sir Arnold, 1884–1940. Conservative MP 1933–40.

WILSON, Sir Horace 1882–1972. Adviser to 10 Downing Street 1937–40.

WILSON, Woodrow 1856–1924. President USA 1913–20.

WINTERTON, Edward Turnour 6th Earl, 1883–1969. MP Chancellor Duchy of Lancaster 1937–9; Paymaster General 1939.

WOOD, Kingsley Sir, 1881–1943. Minister of Health 1935–8; Secretary of State for Air 1938–40.

WITZLEBEN, F. M. E. von Field Marshal. Fervent anti-Nazi, plotted the overthrow of Hitler. Executed after the 1944 bomb plot.

Y

YOUNG, Owen 1874–1962. USA Lawyer. Chairman Committee of Experts on Reparations.

Z

ZETLAND, Lawrence John Lumley Dundas, 2nd Marquess 1876–1961. Secretary of State for India 1935–40.

BIBLIOGRAPHY

ADAMTHWAITE, Anthony: *France and the coming of the Second World War* (London, 1977).
ALOISI, Pompeo: *Mia attivita a servizio della pace* (Rome, 1946).
AMERY, Leo: *Diaries*, Vol 1 1896–1929 Ed. John Barnes and David Nicholson (London, 1980).
_____ *Diaries 1929–1945 The Empire at Bay* Ed. as above (London, 1988).
ASTER, Sidney: *1939 The Making of the Second World War* (London, 1973).
AVON, Earl of: *Memoirs – Facing the Dictators* (London, 1962).

BARTLETT, Vernon: *This is my Life* (London, 1938).
BLAKE, Robert: *The Unknown Prime Minister – Bonar Law* (London, 1955).
_____ *The Decline of Power 1915–64* (London, 1985).
BOGART, Charles H.: 'U Boat Development Between the Wars' *War Monthly* No. 75 1980.
BOND, B. J.: *British Military Policy Between the Two World Wars* (London, 1980).
BRUEGEL, J. W.: *Czechoslovakia before Munich* (London, 1973).
BULLOCK, Alan: *Hitler – A Study in Tyranny* (London, 1952).
BURGWYN, J.: 'Italy, the Heimwehr and the Austro-German Agreement' *Meitteilunger des Osterreichischen Staatsarchives* 38. (Vienna, 1985).
BUTLER, R. A.: *Art of the Possible* (London, 1971).

CAMPBELL, John: *Lloyd George – A Goat in the Wilderness 1922–1931* (London, 1977).
CARLTON, David: *MacDonald versus Henderson* (London, 1970).
_____ *Anthony Eden* (London, 1981).
CECIL, Viscount: *A Great Experiment* (London, 1941).
CHURCHILL, Winston S.: *Second World War – The Gathering Storm* (London, 1948).
_____ *Second World War – The Grand Alliance* (London, 1950).
CIANO, Count: 'Diario' Vol I (Rome, 1950).
_____ Diaries (ed. Malcolm Muggeridge) 1937–38. (London, 1952).
_____ 'Diplomatic Papers' (London, 1948).
COCKETT, Richard: *Twilight of Truth* (London, 1989).
COLLIER, Basil: *Defence of U.K.* HMSO (London, 1957).
COLVILLE, Sir John: *The Fringes of Power* (London, 1985).
COOK, Chris and RAMSDEN, John: *By Elections in British Politics* (London, 1973).
COOPER, Duff: *Old Men Forget* (London, 1953).
CROSS, J.A.: *Sir Samuel Hoare* (London, 1977).

D'ABERNON, Viscount: *Diary – An Ambassador of Peace* Vol. I. (London, 1929).
_____ *Diary – The Years of Crisis* Vol II. (London, 1929).
_____ *Diary – The Years of Recovery* Vol III. (London, 1930).
DAHLERUS, Berger: *The Last Attempt* (London, 1947).
DALTON, Hugh: *Call Back Yesterday* (London, 1953).
_____ *The Fateful Years 1931–45* (London, 1957).
_____ *Political Diary 1918–40; 1945–60* Ed. Ben Pimlott. (London, 1986).
DELL, Robert: *Germany Unmasked* (London, 1934).
_____ *The Geneva Racket* (London, 1940).
Dictionary of National Biography 1931–40 (Oxford, 1949).
Dictionary of National Biography 1940–50 (Oxford, 1959).
Dictionary of National Biography 1951–60 (Oxford, 1971).
Dictionary of National Biography 1961–1970 (Oxford, 1981).

DILKS, David: (Ed.) *Diaries of Sir Alexander Cadogan* (London, 1971).
DIRKSEN, Herbert: *Moscow Tokyo London* (London, 1951).
Documents on British Foreign Policy 1919–1939. Series 2 Vol I 1946.
Documents on British Foreign Policy 1919–1939. Series 2 Vol II 1947.
Documents on British Foreign Policy 1919–1939. Series 2 Vol III 1948.
Documents on British Foreign Policy 1919–1939. Series 3 Vol V 1952.
Documents on British Foreign Policy 1919–1939. Series 3 Vol VII 1954.
Documents on British Foreign Policy 1919–1939. Series 1A Vol I 1966.
Documents on British Foreign Policy 1919–1939. Series 1A Vol II 1968.
Documents on British Foreign Policy 1919–1939. Series 1A Vol IV 1971.
Documents on British Foreign Policy 1919–1939. Series 1A Vol V 1973.
Documents on British Foreign Policy 1919–1939. Series 1 Vol XIX 1974.
Documents on British Foreign Policy 1919–1939. Series 1A Vol VI 1975.
Documents on British Foreign Policy 1919–1939. Series 1 Vol XXI 1978.
Documents on British Foreign Policy 1919–1939. Series 1 Vol XXVI 1985.
Documenti Diplomatici Italiani. 1920–39 (Rome, 1954 *et seq*).
Documents Diplomatiques Français, 1932–39 (Paris 1968–70).
Documents on German Foreign Policy (HMSO London, Series C and D).
DORPALEN, Andreas: *Hindenburg and the Weimar Republic* (Princeton, 1964).

EINZIG, Paul: *In the Centre of Things* (London, 1960).

FINK, Carole: *The Genoa Conference* (Chapel Hill and London, 1984).
FLANDIN, ?.: *Politique Français* (Paris, 1947).
FUCHSER, Larry William *Neville Chamberlain and Appeasement* (Toronto, 1982).

GIBBS, Norman: *Grand Strategy* Vol I 'Rearament Policy' HMSO (London, 1976).
GILBERT, M. and GOTT, R.: *The Appeasers* (London, 1963).
GILBERT, Martin: *The Roots of Appeasement* (London, 1966).
———— *Winston S. Churchill* Vol V 1922–39 (London, 1976).
———— *Road to Victory* (London, 1986).
GLADWYN, Lord: *Memoirs* (London, 1972).
GRANDI, Dino: *25 Luglio Quaranta, Anni Dopo* (Bologna, 1983).
GRIFFITHS, Richard: *Fellow Travellers of the Right* (Oxford, 1983).
GUARIGLIA, Raffaele: *Ricordi 1922–46* (Naples, 1949).

HASSELL, Ulrich von: *Hassell Diaries* (London, 1945).
HARVEY, John: *Diplomatic Diaries of Oliver Harvey 1937–40* (London, 1970).
HENDERSON, Sir Nevile: *Failure of a Mission* (London, 1940).
HOFFMAN, Peter: *The History of the German Resistance 1933–45* (London, 1977).
HOLLIS, Christopher: *Italy in Africa* (London, 1941).
HOWARD, Anthony: *RAB – Life of R.A. Butler* (London, 1987).
HOWARD, Michael: *The Continental Commitment* (London, 1972).
HOWARTH, Patrick *Intelligence Chief Extraordinary* (London, 1986).

International Military Tribunal (Nuremberg, 1948).
IRVING, David: *Hitler's War* (London, 1977).

JACOBSON, Jon: *Locarno Diplomacy* (Princeton, 1972).
JONES, Thomas: *Whitehall Diary* Vol I 1916–1925 (London, 1969).
———— *Whitehall Diary* Vol. II 1926–1939 (London, 1969).

KEYNES, John Maynard: *The Economic Consequences of the Peace* (London, 1919).

365

KINDERMAN, Gottfried Karl: *Hitler's Defeat in Austria 1933–34* (London, 1988).
KOLB, Eberhard: *The Weimar Republic* Trans. P. S. Falla (London, 1988).

LAMB, Richard: *The Ghosts of Peace* (Salisbury, 1987).
_____ *The Failure of the Eden Government* (London, 1987).
LEES MILNE, James: *Harold Nicholson* Vol. II (London, 1981).
LEITH ROSS, Sir Frederick: *Money Talks* (London, 1968).
LLOYD GEORGE, Earl: *The Truth About Reparations and War Debts* (London, 1932).

MACLEOD, Iain: *Neville Chamberlain* (London, 1961).
MACMILLAN, Harold: *Winds of Change 1914–39* (London, 1966).
MAISKY, Ivan: *Who Helped Hitler?* (London, 1964).
MARQUAND, David: *Ramsay MacDonald* (London, 1977).
McCALLUM, R. B.: *Public Opinion and the Lost Peace* (London, 1944).
McLACHLAN, Donald: *In the Chair* (London, 1971).
MIDDLEMAS, K. and BARNES, J.: *Baldwin* (London, 1969).
MIDDLEMAS, K.: *Diplomacy of Illusion* (London, 1972).
MOCKLER, Anthony: *Haile Selassie's War* (London, 1984).
MONTGOMERY, Bernard: *Memoirs* (London, 1958).

NERE, Jacques: *The Foreign Policy of France 1914–45* (London, 1975).
NICOLSON, Nigel (Ed.) *Harold Nicolson Diaries* Vol II and *Letters* (London, 1957).
NOEL, L.: *L'Aggression Allemande contre la Pologne* (Paris, 1946).
NORTHEDGE, F. S.: *The Troubled Giant 1916–39* (London, 1966).

PAPEN, Franz von: *Memoirs* (London, 1952).
PARKER, R. A. C.: *Europe 1919–45* (London, 1969).
_____ Hoare-Laval Pact English Historical Review Vol. 89 (1974).
PEDEN, G. C.: *British Rearmament and the Treasury 1932–39* (London, 1979).
PETRIE, Sir Charles: *Twenty Years' Armistice* (London, 1940).
_____ *Life and Letters of Austen Chamberlain* Vol I (London, 1939).
_____ *Life and Letters of Austen Chamberlain* Vol 2 (London, 1940).

RHODES JAMES, Robert: *Memoirs of a Conservative* (London, 1969).
_____ *Anthony Eden* (London, 1986).
RICH, Norman: *Hitler's War Aims* (New York, 1973).
ROBERTSON, E. M.: *The Origins of the Second World War* (London, 1971).
ROSKILL, Stephen: *Hankey, Man of Secrets* Vol. 3 (London, 1974).
ROTHERMERE, Lord: *My Fight to Rearm Britain* (London, 1939).
ROTHSCHILD, Robert: *Peace for our Time* (London, 1988).

SCHLABRENDORFF, Fabian von: *Secret War Against Hitler* (London, 1956).
SCHMIDT, Paul: *Hitler's Interpreter* (London, 1951).
SCHUSCHNIGG, Kurt von: *Brutal Take Over* (London, 1971).
SCHWEPPENBERG, Geyr von: *Critical Years London* (London, 1952).
SELBY, Sir Walford: *Diplomatic Twilight 1930–40* (London, 1953).
SETON-WATSON, Christoper: *Italian Gentleman's Agreement of Jan. 1937 and its Aftermath* in Monsom and Kettenacher (Eds) *Fascist Challenge.* (London, 1983).
SHEPHERD, Robert: *A Class Divided* (London, 1988).
SHEPHERD, Gordon Brooke: *Anschluss* (London, 1977).
SHIRER, William *The Rise and Fall of the Third Reich* (London, 1973).
SLESSOR, John: *Blue Circle* (London 1946).

SMITH, Denis Mack: *Mussolini* (London, 1981).
—————— *Mussolini's Roman Empire* (London, 1976).
SNOWDEN, Philip: *An Autobiography* Vol. 2 (London, 1934).
STARHEMBERG, Prince Ernst Rudiger *Between Hitler and Mussolini* (London, 1942).
STRONG, Maj. Gen. Sir Kenneth: *Intelligence at the Top* (London, 1968).
SUVICH, F.: *Memorie 1932–36* (Milan, 1984).

TARDIEU, A.: *Truth about the Treaty* (London, 1921).
TAYLOR, A. J. P.: *The Origins of the Second World War* (London, 1961).
TAYLOR, TELFORD: *Munich* (London, 1979).
TEMPLEWOOD, Lord: *Nine Troubled Years* (London, 1954).
THOMPSON, Geoffrey: *Front Line Diplomat* (London, 1959).

TURNER, Henry A.: *Stresemann and the Politics of the Weimar Republic* (Princeton, 1963).

VALLENTIN, Antonina: *Stresemann* (London, 1931).

WALEY, Daniel: *British Public Opinion in the Abyssinian War.* (London, 1975).
WATT, D. C.: 'Anglo-German Naval Agreement', *Journal of Modern History* (June, 1956).
WHALEY, Barton: *Covert German Rearmament* (New York, 1987).
WHEELER-BENNETT, J. & LATIMER, O.: *Information on the Reparation Settlement* (London, 1930).
WHEELER-BENNETT, J.: *The Wreck of Reparations* (London, 1933).
—————— *Munich* (London, 1948).
—————— *The Disarmament Deadlock* (London, 1934).
WHITE, Stephen: *The Origins of Detente* (Cambridge, 1985).
WISKEMAN: E.: *Rome Berlin Axis* (London, 1966).

Unpublished Papers

DILKS, David: *Britain and Germany 1937–39* Paper At Anglo-German Conference – '*German Resistance to Hitler and British Attitudes Towards It, 1937–44*' Held at Leeds (May 1986).
MALONE, Henry: *Adam von Trott – The Road to Conspiracy Against Hitler.* D.Phil thesis, University of Texas, 1980.
MEEHAN, Patricia *Foreign Office and the Opposition* Paper at Leeds Conference, op. cit.
NAVARI, Cornelia: *Briand Plan 1930.* Lothian Conference Royal Holloway College. (April, 1989).
SANTONI, A.: *L'Operative del Alleanza Italiana Tedesca* (Montpelier Conference 1981).
SETON-WATSON, Christopher: *R. W. Seton-Watson and the Czechoslovaks 1935–39.* Paper at Conference at Munich Collegium Carolinum (November, 1988).
TAYLOR, Ralph: *British response to French proposal for European Federal Union 1930.* Lothian Conference op. cit.

INDEX